FANTASTIC FOUR

Empyre

FANTASTIC FOUR VOL. 6: EMPYRE. Contains material originally published in magazine form as EMPYRE #0 FANTASTIC FOUR (2020), FANTASTIC FOUR (2018) #21-24 and EMPYRE FALLOUT: FANTASTIC FOUR (2020) #1. First printing 2020. ISBN 978-1-302-92047-0. Published by MARVEL WORLDWIDE, INC., a subsidiary of MARVEL ENTERTAINMENT, LLC. OFFICE OF PUBLICATION: 1290 Avenue of the Americas, New York, NY 10104. © 2020 MARVEL. No similarity between any of the names, characters, persons, and/or institutions in this magazine with those of any living or dead person or institution is intended, and any such similarity which may exist is purely coincidental. **Printed in Canada.** KEVIN FEIGE, Chief Creative Officer; DAN BUCKLEY, President, Marvel Entertainment; JOHN NEE, Publisher; JOE QUESADA, EVP & Creative Director; TOM BREVOORT, SVP of Publishing; DAVID BOGART, Associate Publisher & SVP of Talent Affairs; Publishing & Partnership; DAVID GABRIEL, VP of Print & Digital Publishing; JEFF YOUNGQUIST, VP of Production & Special Projects; DAN CARR, Executive Director of Publishing Technology; ALEX MORALES, Director of Publishing Operations; DAN EDING-TON, Managing Editor; RICKEY PURDIN, Director of Talent Relations; SUSAN CRESPI, Production Manager; STAN LEE, Chairman Emeritus. For information regarding advertising in Marvel Comics or on Marvel.com, please contact Vit DeBellis, Custom Solutions & Integrated Advertising Manager, at vdebellis@marvel.com. For Marvel subscription inquiries, please call 888-511-5480. **Manufactured between 10/2/2020 and 11/3/2020 by SOLISCO PRINTERS, SCOTT, QC, CANADA.**

10 9 8 7 6 5 4 3 2 1

A brilliant scientist — his best friend — the woman he loved — and her fiery-tempered kid brother! Together, they braved the unknown terrors of outer space and were changed by cosmic rays into something more than merely human! They became the...

FANTASTIC FOUR

Empyre

Dan Slott
WRITER

Empyre #0: Fantastic Four

R.B. Silva & Sean Izaakse
ARTISTS

Marte Gracia & Marcio Menyz
COLOR ARTISTS

Jim Cheung & Guru-eFX
COVER ART

Fantastic Four #23-24

Paco Medina
ARTIST

Jesus Aburtov
COLOR ARTIST

Nick Bradshaw & John Rauch
COVER ART

Fantastic Four #21-22

Paco Medina & Sean Izaakse
ARTISTS

Marcio Menyz with
Erick Arciniega (#21) &
Jesus Aburtov (#22)
COLOR ARTISTS

Nick Bradshaw & John Rauch
COVER ART

Empyre: Fallout — Fantastic Four

Sean Izaakse
ARTIST

Marcio Menyz
COLOR ARTISTS

R.B. Silva & David Curiel
COVER ART

VC's Joe Caramagna
LETTERER

Martin Biro
ASSISTANT EDITOR

Alanna Smith
ASSOCIATE EDITOR

Tom Brevoort
EDITOR

The Fantastic Four created by Stan Lee & Jack Kirby

COLLECTION EDITOR Jennifer Grünwald
ASSISTANT MANAGING EDITOR Maia Loy
ASSISTANT MANAGING EDITOR Lisa Montalbano
EDITOR, SPECIAL PROJECTS Mark D. Beazley

VP PRODUCTION & SPECIAL PROJECTS Jeff Youngquist
BOOK DESIGNERS Stacie Zucker with Adam Del Re
SVP PRINT, SALES & MARKETING David Gabriel
EDITOR IN CHIEF C.B. Cebulski

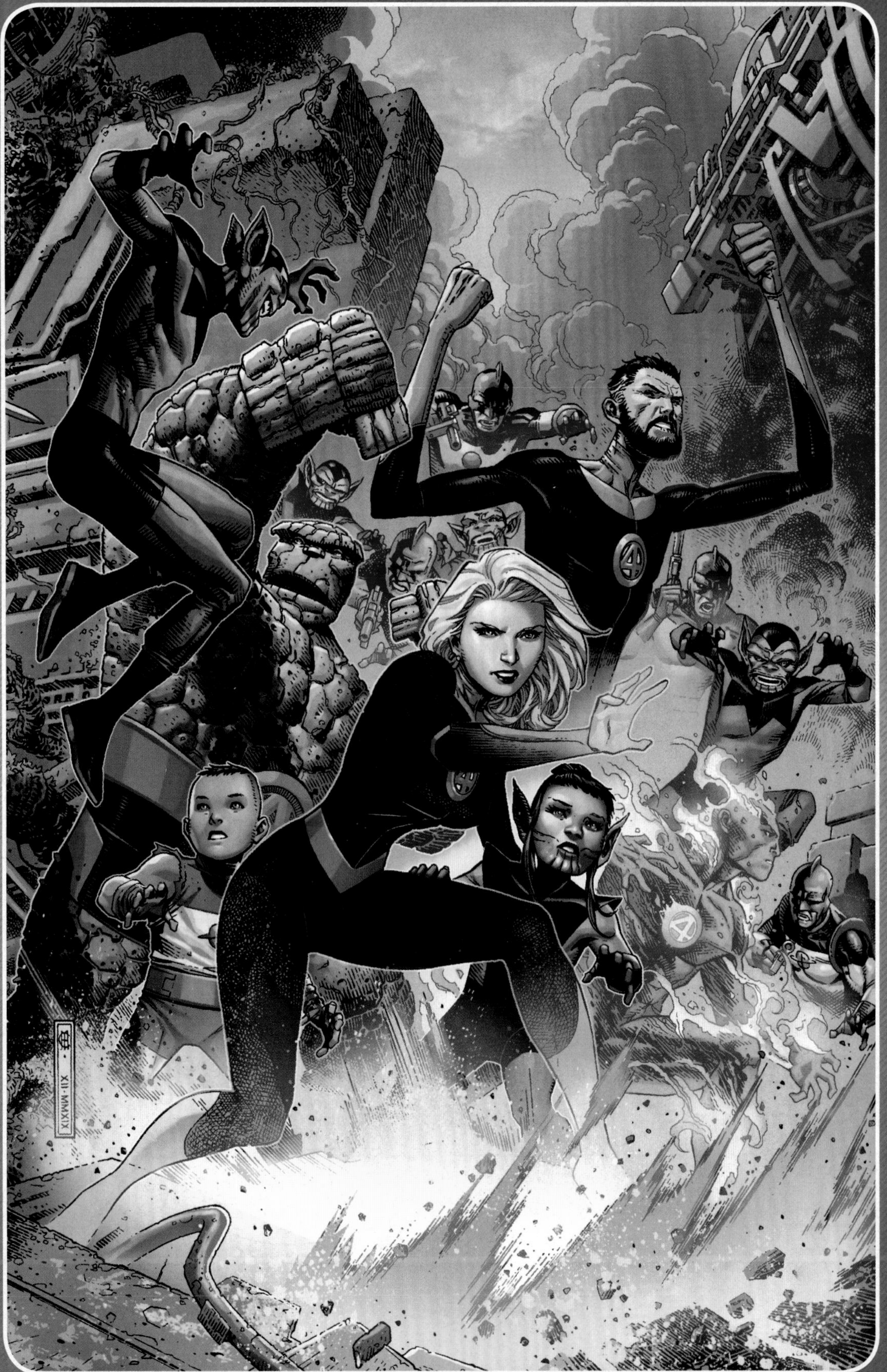

Empyre #0: Fantastic Four

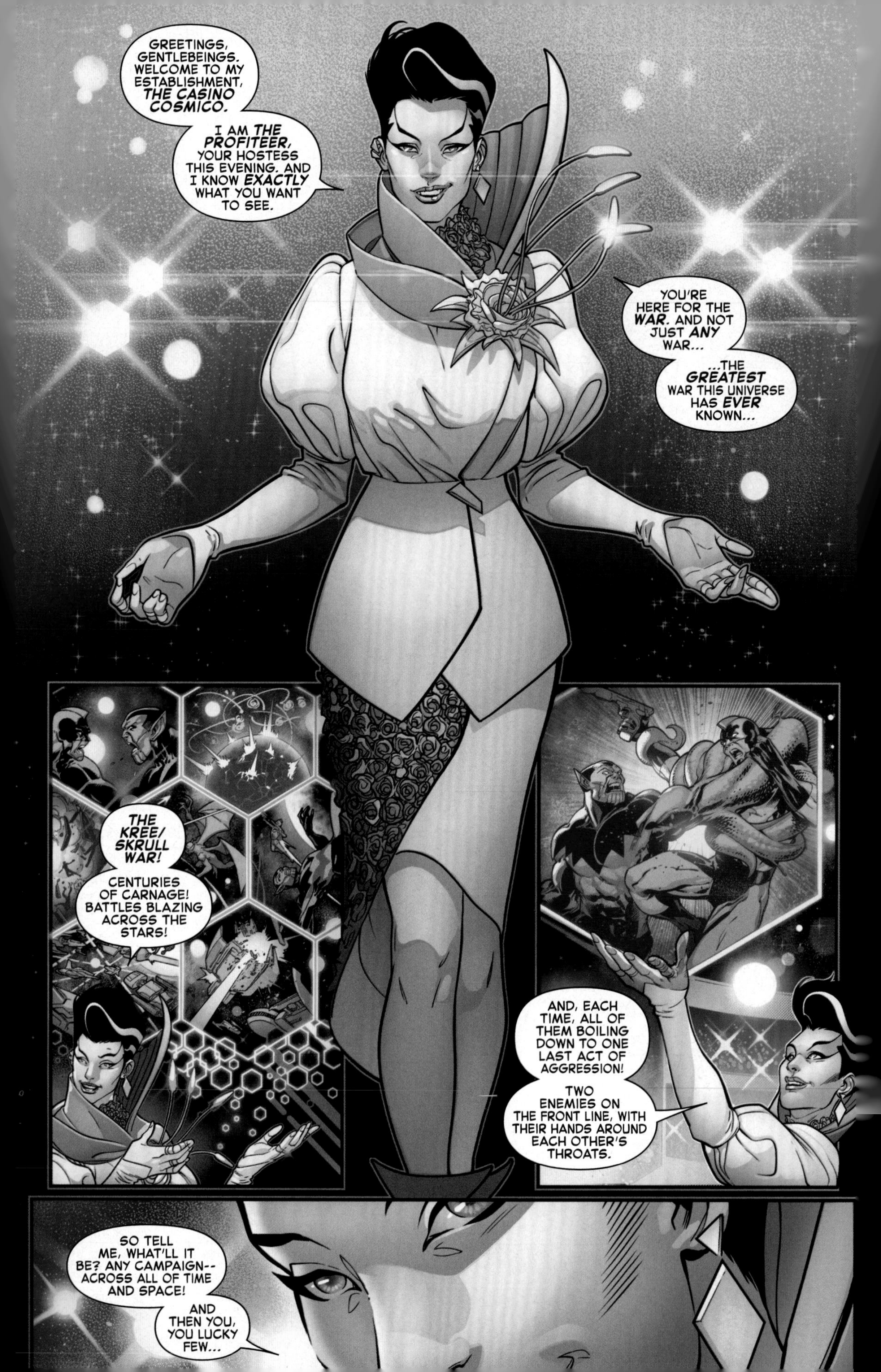
GREETINGS, GENTLEBEINGS. WELCOME TO MY ESTABLISHMENT, THE CASINO COSMICO.
I AM THE PROFITEER, YOUR HOSTESS THIS EVENING. AND I KNOW EXACTLY WHAT YOU WANT TO SEE.
YOU'RE HERE FOR THE WAR. AND NOT JUST ANY WAR...
...THE GREATEST WAR THIS UNIVERSE HAS EVER KNOWN...
THE KREE/ SKRULL WAR!
CENTURIES OF CARNAGE! BATTLES BLAZING ACROSS THE STARS!
AND, EACH TIME, ALL OF THEM BOILING DOWN TO ONE LAST ACT OF AGGRESSION!
TWO ENEMIES ON THE FRONT LINE, WITH THEIR HANDS AROUND EACH OTHER'S THROATS.
SO TELL ME, WHAT'LL IT BE? ANY CAMPAIGN-- ACROSS ALL OF TIME AND SPACE!
AND THEN YOU, YOU LUCKY FEW...

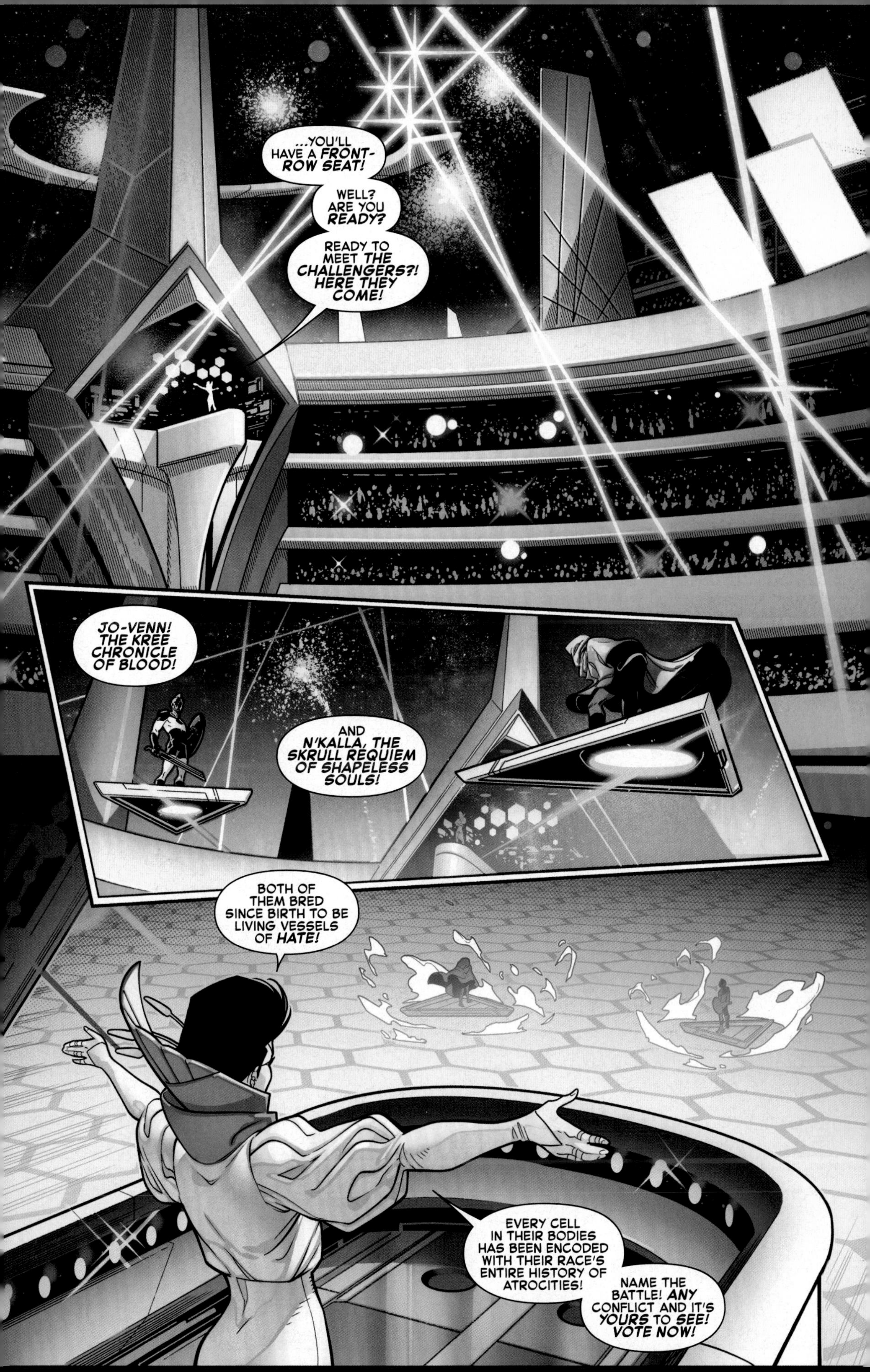
...YOU'LL HAVE A FRONT-ROW SEAT!
WELL? ARE YOU READY?
READY TO MEET THE CHALLENGERS?! HERE THEY COME!
JO-VENN! THE KREE CHRONICLE OF BLOOD!
AND N'KALLA, THE SKRULL REQUIEM OF SHAPELESS SOULS!
BOTH OF THEM BRED SINCE BIRTH TO BE LIVING VESSELS OF HATE!
EVERY CELL IN THEIR BODIES HAS BEEN ENCODED WITH THEIR RACE'S ENTIRE HISTORY OF ATROCITIES!
NAME THE BATTLE! ANY CONFLICT AND IT'S YOURS TO SEE! VOTE NOW!

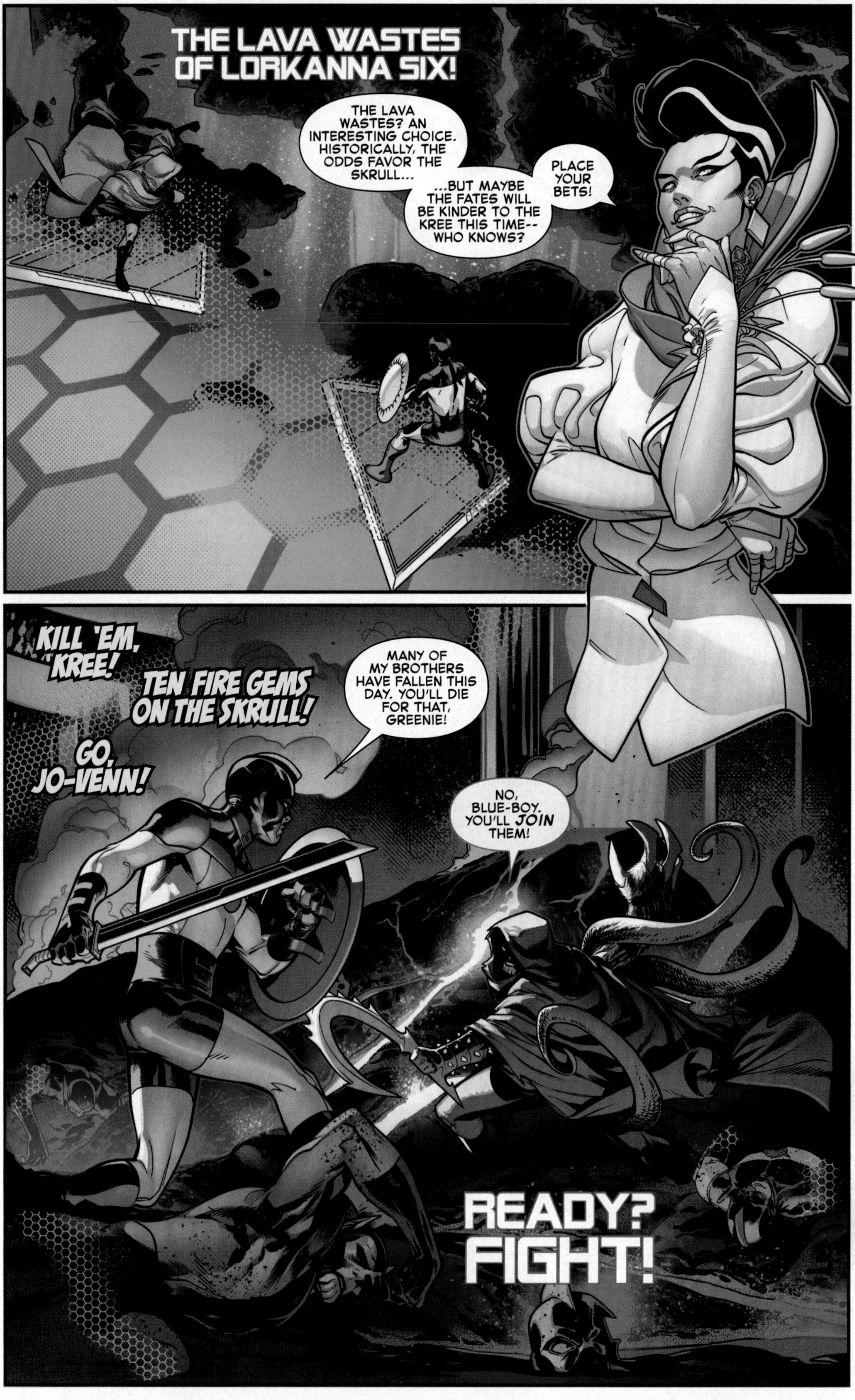

THE LAVA WASTES OF LORKANNA SIX!
THE LAVA WASTES? AN INTERESTING CHOICE. HISTORICALLY, THE ODDS FAVOR THE SKRULL...
...BUT MAYBE THE FATES WILL BE KINDER TO THE KREE THIS TIME-- WHO KNOWS?
PLACE YOUR BETS!
KILL 'EM, KREE!
TEN FIRE GEMS ON THE SKRULL!
GO, JO-VENN!
MANY OF MY BROTHERS HAVE FALLEN THIS DAY. YOU'LL DIE FOR THAT, GREENIE!
NO, BLUE-BOY. YOU'LL JOIN THEM!
READY? FIGHT!

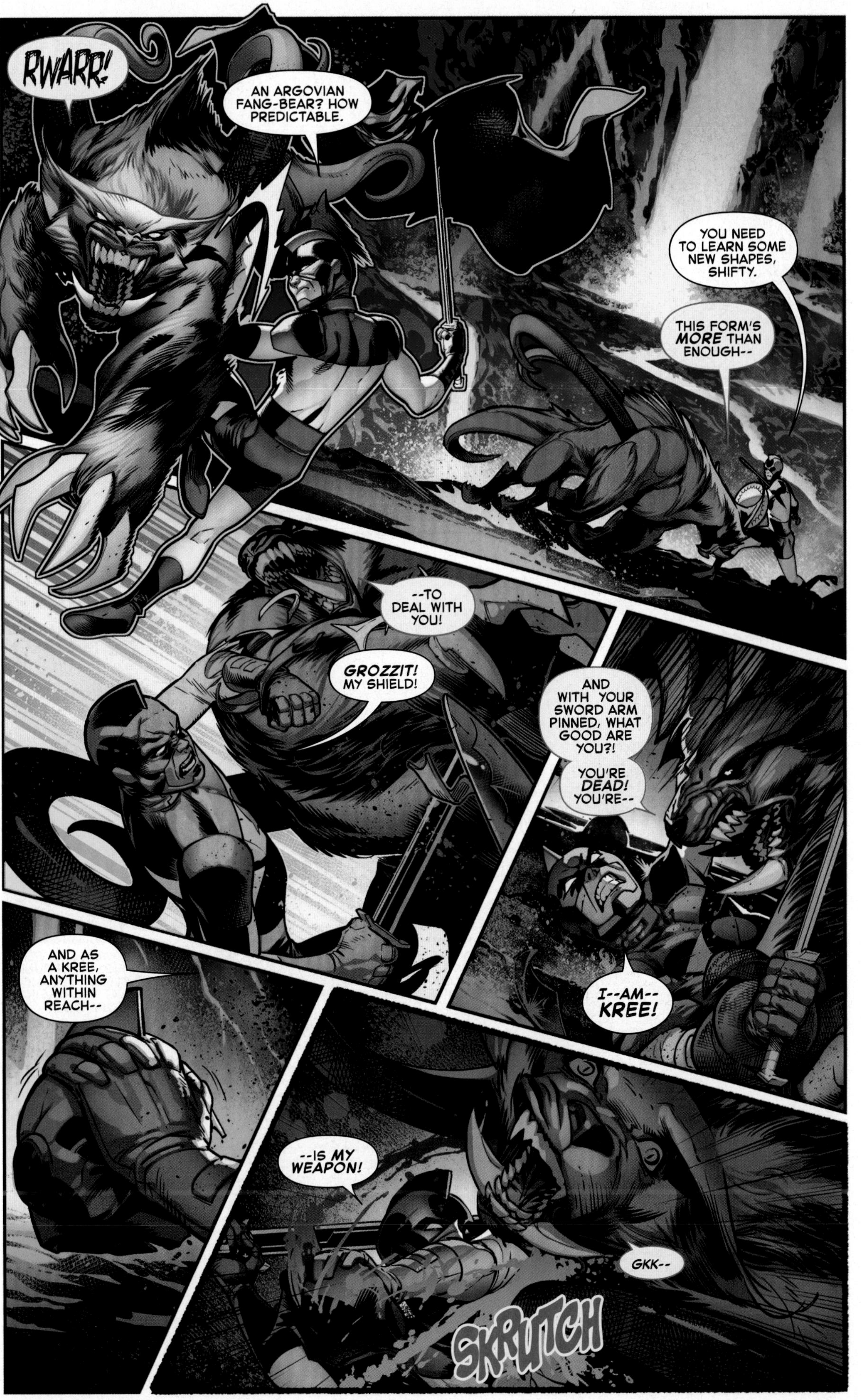
RWARR!
AN ARGOVIAN FANG-BEAR? HOW PREDICTABLE.
YOU NEED TO LEARN SOME NEW SHAPES, SHIFTY.
THIS FORM'S MORE THAN ENOUGH--
--TO DEAL WITH YOU!
GROZZIT! MY SHIELD!
AND WITH YOUR SWORD ARM PINNED, WHAT GOOD ARE YOU?!
YOU'RE DEAD! YOU'RE--
I--AM--KREE!
AND AS A KREE, ANYTHING WITHIN REACH--
--IS MY WEAPON!
GKK--
SKRUTCH

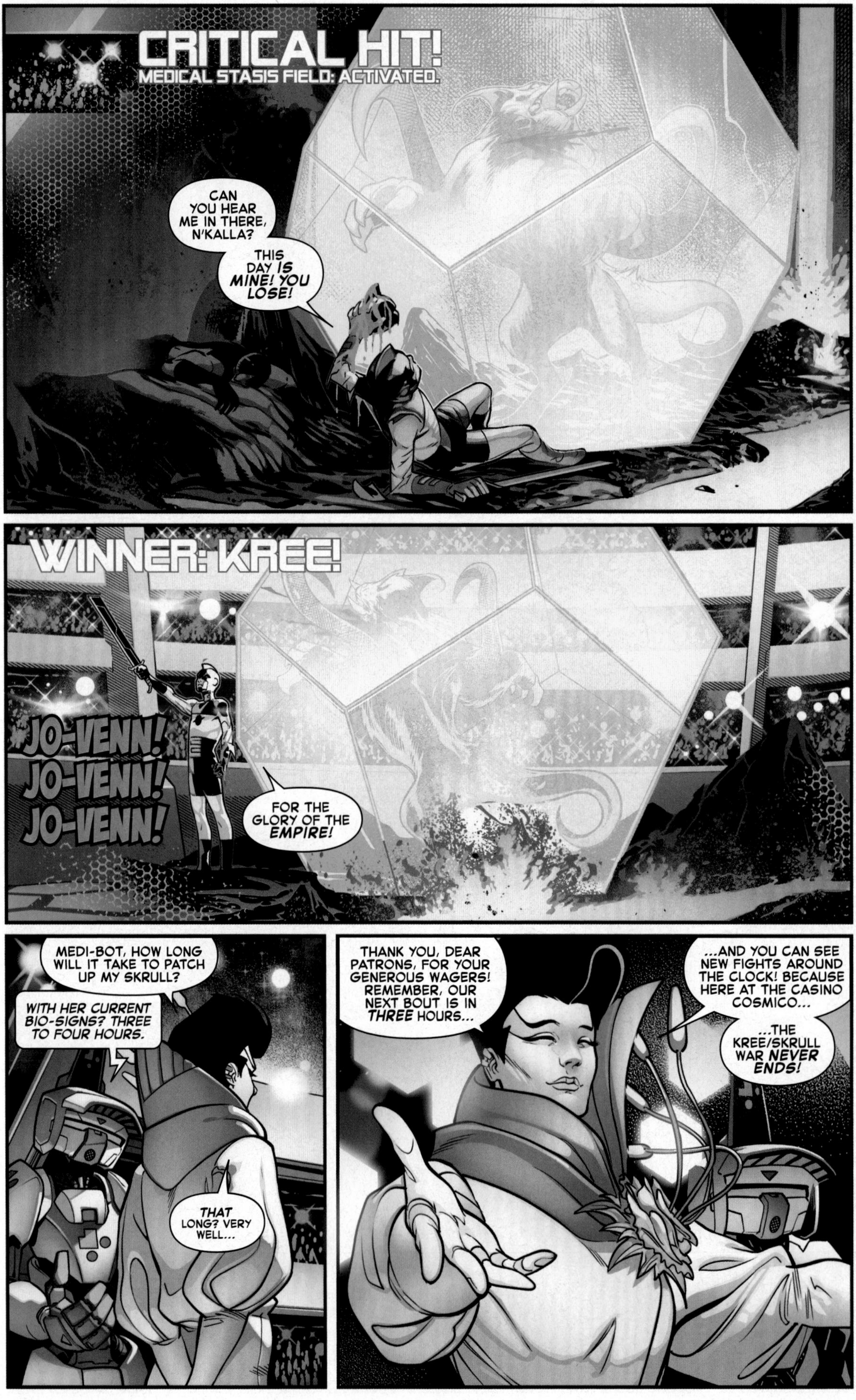
CRITICAL HIT!
MEDICAL STASIS FIELD: ACTIVATED.
CAN YOU HEAR ME IN THERE, N'KALLA?
THIS DAY IS MINE! YOU LOSE!
WINNER: KREE!
JO-VENN! JO-VENN! JO-VENN!
FOR THE GLORY OF THE EMPIRE!
MEDI-BOT, HOW LONG WILL IT TAKE TO PATCH UP MY SKRULL?
WITH HER CURRENT BIO-SIGNS? THREE TO FOUR HOURS.
THAT LONG? VERY WELL...
THANK YOU, DEAR PATRONS, FOR YOUR GENEROUS WAGERS! REMEMBER, OUR NEXT BOUT IS IN THREE HOURS...
...AND YOU CAN SEE NEW FIGHTS AROUND THE CLOCK! BECAUSE HERE AT THE CASINO COSMICO...
...THE KREE/SKRULL WAR NEVER ENDS!

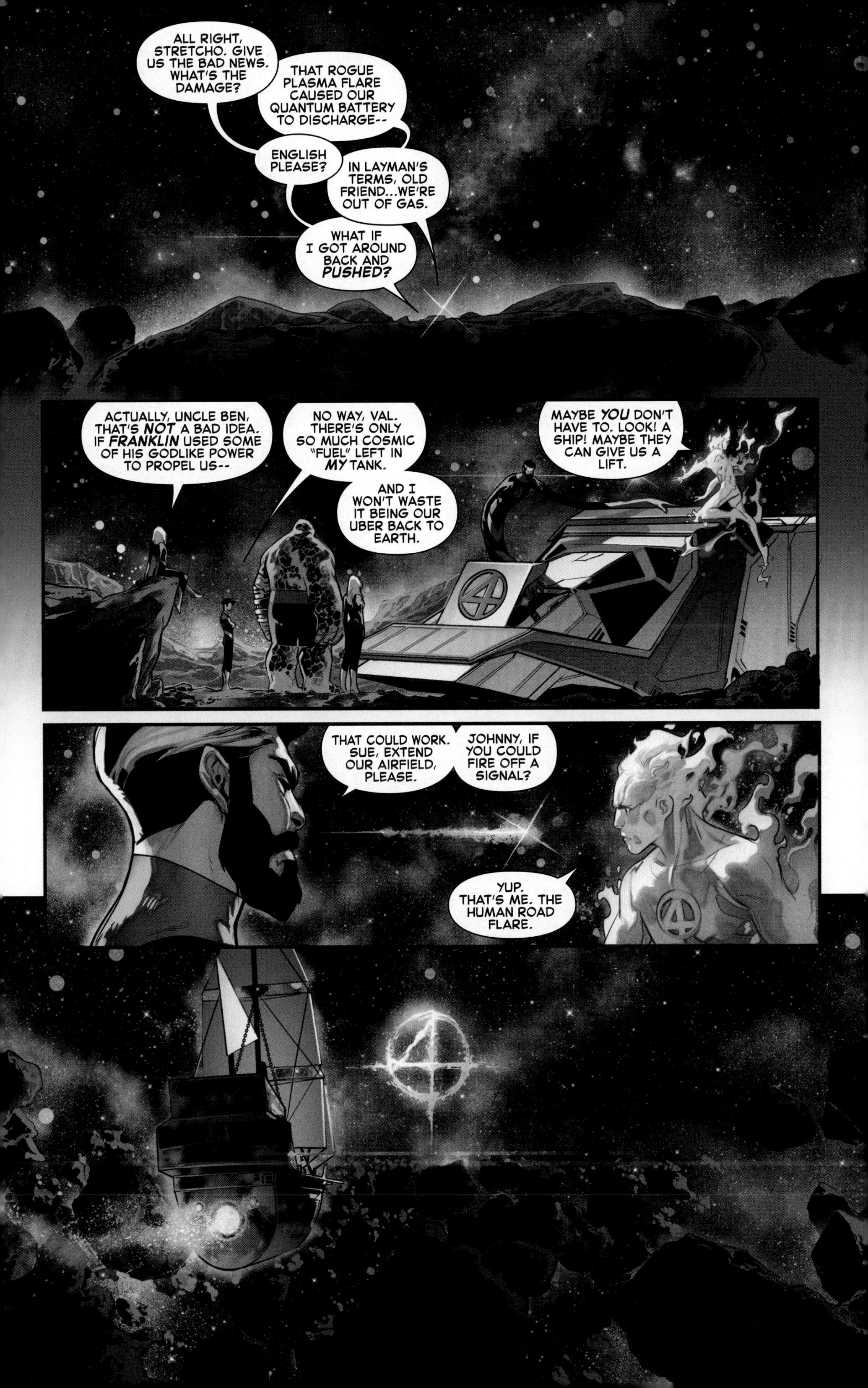
ALL RIGHT, STRETCHO. GIVE US THE BAD NEWS. WHAT'S THE DAMAGE?
THAT ROGUE PLASMA FLARE CAUSED OUR QUANTUM BATTERY TO DISCHARGE--
ENGLISH PLEASE?
IN LAYMAN'S TERMS, OLD FRIEND...WE'RE OUT OF GAS.
WHAT IF I GOT AROUND BACK AND *PUSHED?*
ACTUALLY, UNCLE BEN, THAT'S *NOT* A BAD IDEA. IF *FRANKLIN* USED SOME OF HIS GODLIKE POWER TO PROPEL US--
NO WAY, VAL. THERE'S ONLY SO MUCH COSMIC "FUEL" LEFT IN *MY* TANK.
AND I WON'T WASTE IT BEING OUR UBER BACK TO EARTH.
MAYBE *YOU* DON'T HAVE TO. LOOK! A SHIP! MAYBE THEY CAN GIVE US A LIFT.
THAT COULD WORK. SUE, EXTEND OUR AIRFIELD, PLEASE.
JOHNNY, IF YOU COULD FIRE OFF A SIGNAL?
YUP. THAT'S ME. THE HUMAN ROAD FLARE.

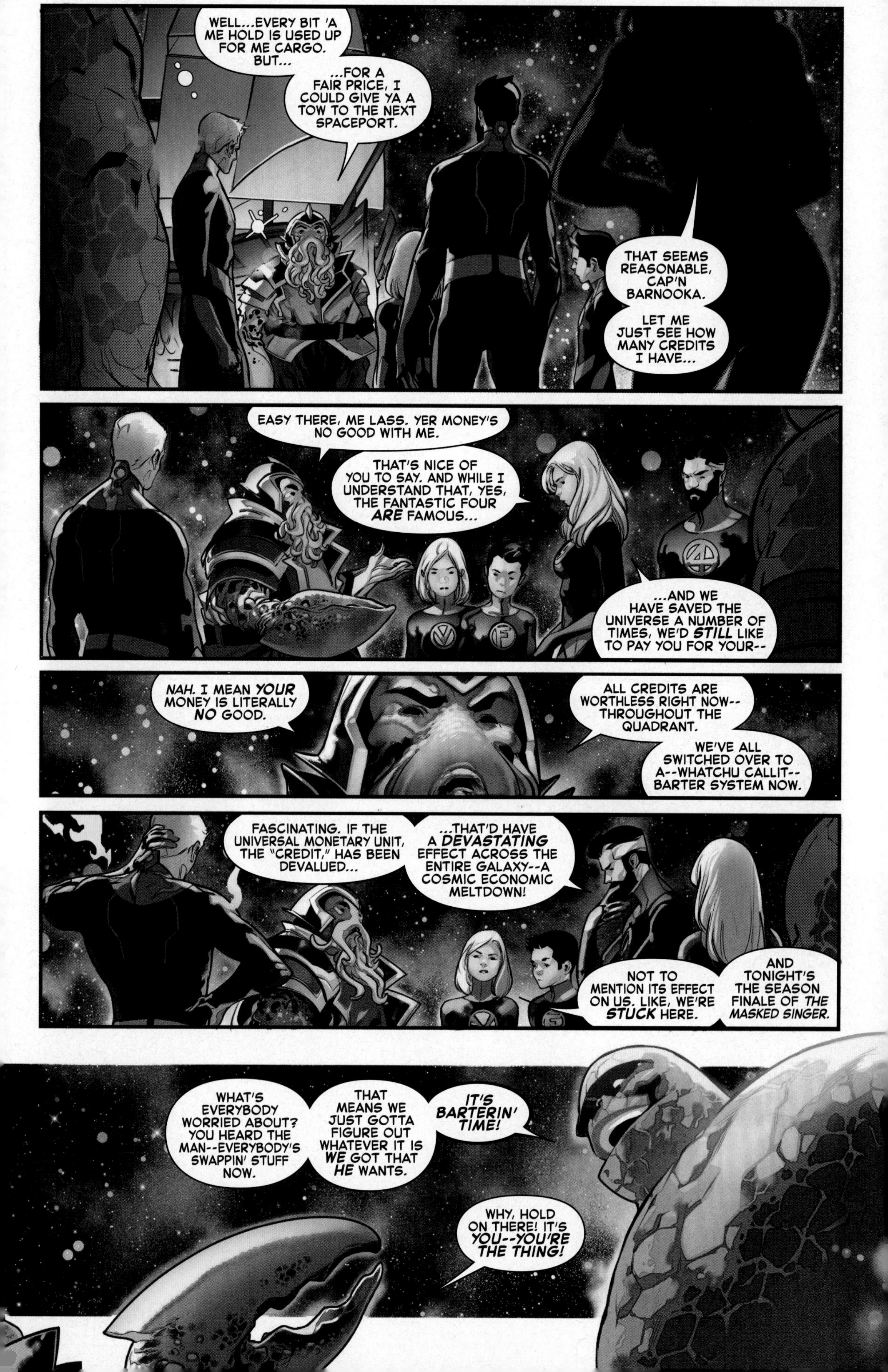
WELL...EVERY BIT 'A ME HOLD IS USED UP FOR ME CARGO. BUT...
...FOR A FAIR PRICE, I COULD GIVE YA A TOW TO THE NEXT SPACEPORT.
THAT SEEMS REASONABLE, CAP'N BARNOOKA.
LET ME JUST SEE HOW MANY CREDITS I HAVE...
EASY THERE, ME LASS. YER MONEY'S NO GOOD WITH ME.
THAT'S NICE OF YOU TO SAY. AND WHILE I UNDERSTAND THAT, YES, THE FANTASTIC FOUR *ARE* FAMOUS...
...AND WE HAVE SAVED THE UNIVERSE A NUMBER OF TIMES, WE'D *STILL* LIKE TO PAY YOU FOR YOUR--
NAH. I MEAN *YOUR* MONEY IS LITERALLY *NO* GOOD.
ALL CREDITS ARE WORTHLESS RIGHT NOW-- THROUGHOUT THE QUADRANT.
WE'VE ALL SWITCHED OVER TO A--WHATCHU CALLIT-- BARTER SYSTEM NOW.
FASCINATING. IF THE UNIVERSAL MONETARY UNIT, THE "CREDIT," HAS BEEN DEVALUED...
...THAT'D HAVE A *DEVASTATING* EFFECT ACROSS THE ENTIRE GALAXY--A COSMIC ECONOMIC MELTDOWN!
NOT TO MENTION ITS EFFECT ON US. LIKE, WE'RE *STUCK* HERE.
AND TONIGHT'S THE SEASON FINALE OF *THE MASKED SINGER.*
WHAT'S EVERYBODY WORRIED ABOUT? YOU HEARD THE MAN--EVERYBODY'S SWAPPIN' STUFF NOW.
THAT MEANS WE JUST GOTTA FIGURE OUT WHATEVER IT IS *WE* GOT THAT *HE* WANTS.
IT'S BARTERIN' TIME!
WHY, HOLD ON THERE! IT'S *YOU--YOU'RE THE THING!*

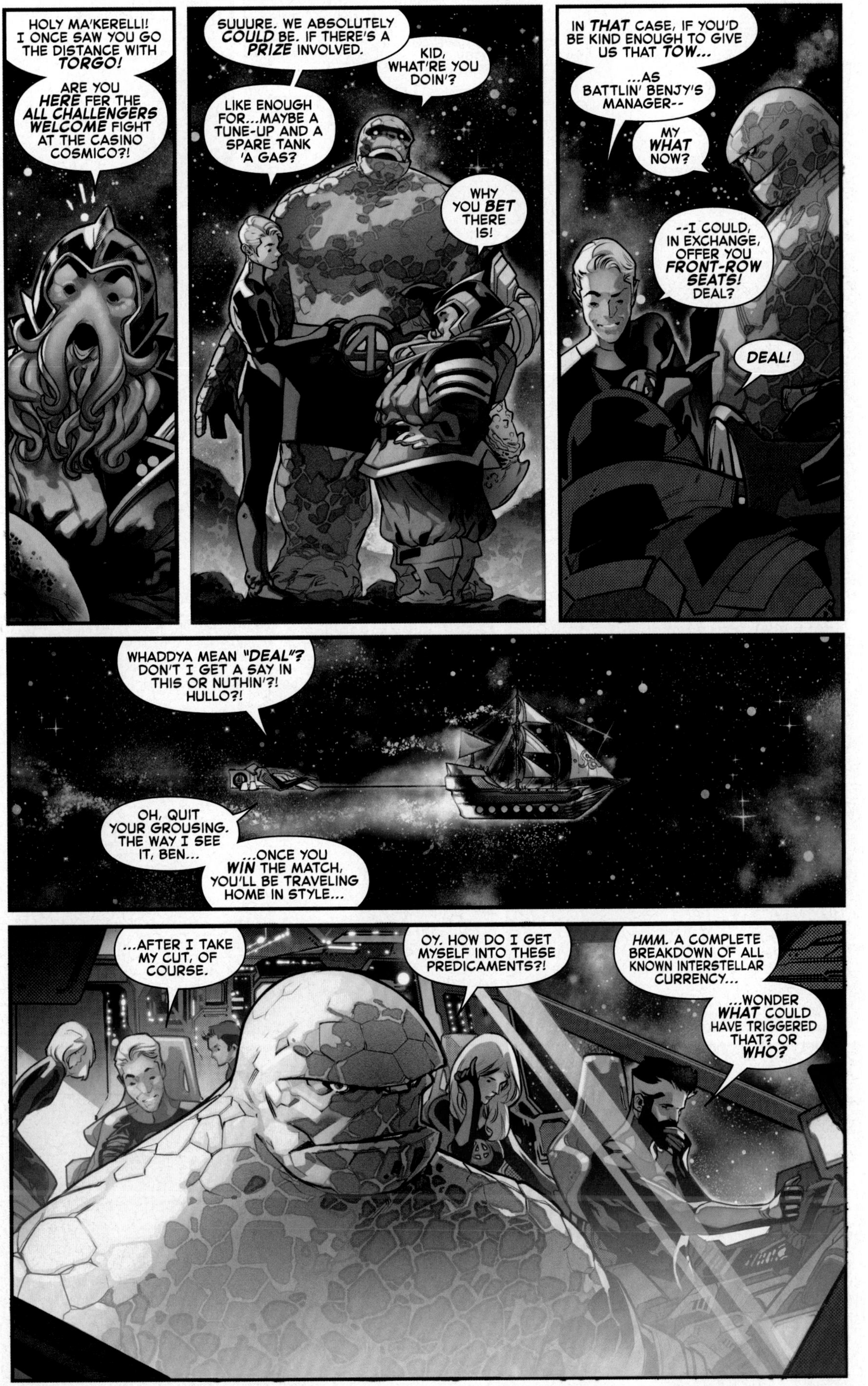
HOLY MA'KERELLI! I ONCE SAW YOU GO THE DISTANCE WITH TORGO!
ARE YOU HERE FER THE ALL CHALLENGERS WELCOME FIGHT AT THE CASINO COSMICO?!
SUUURE. WE ABSOLUTELY COULD BE. IF THERE'S A PRIZE INVOLVED.
KID, WHAT'RE YOU DOIN'?
LIKE ENOUGH FOR...MAYBE A TUNE-UP AND A SPARE TANK 'A GAS?
WHY YOU BET THERE IS!
IN THAT CASE, IF YOU'D BE KIND ENOUGH TO GIVE US THAT TOW...
...AS BATTLIN' BENJY'S MANAGER--
MY WHAT NOW?
--I COULD, IN EXCHANGE, OFFER YOU FRONT-ROW SEATS! DEAL?
DEAL!
WHADDYA MEAN "DEAL"? DON'T I GET A SAY IN THIS OR NUTHIN'?! HULLO?!
OH, QUIT YOUR GROUSING. THE WAY I SEE IT, BEN...
...ONCE YOU WIN THE MATCH, YOU'LL BE TRAVELING HOME IN STYLE...
...AFTER I TAKE MY CUT, OF COURSE.
OY. HOW DO I GET MYSELF INTO THESE PREDICAMENTS?!
HMM. A COMPLETE BREAKDOWN OF ALL KNOWN INTERSTELLAR CURRENCY...
...WONDER WHAT COULD HAVE TRIGGERED THAT? OR WHO?

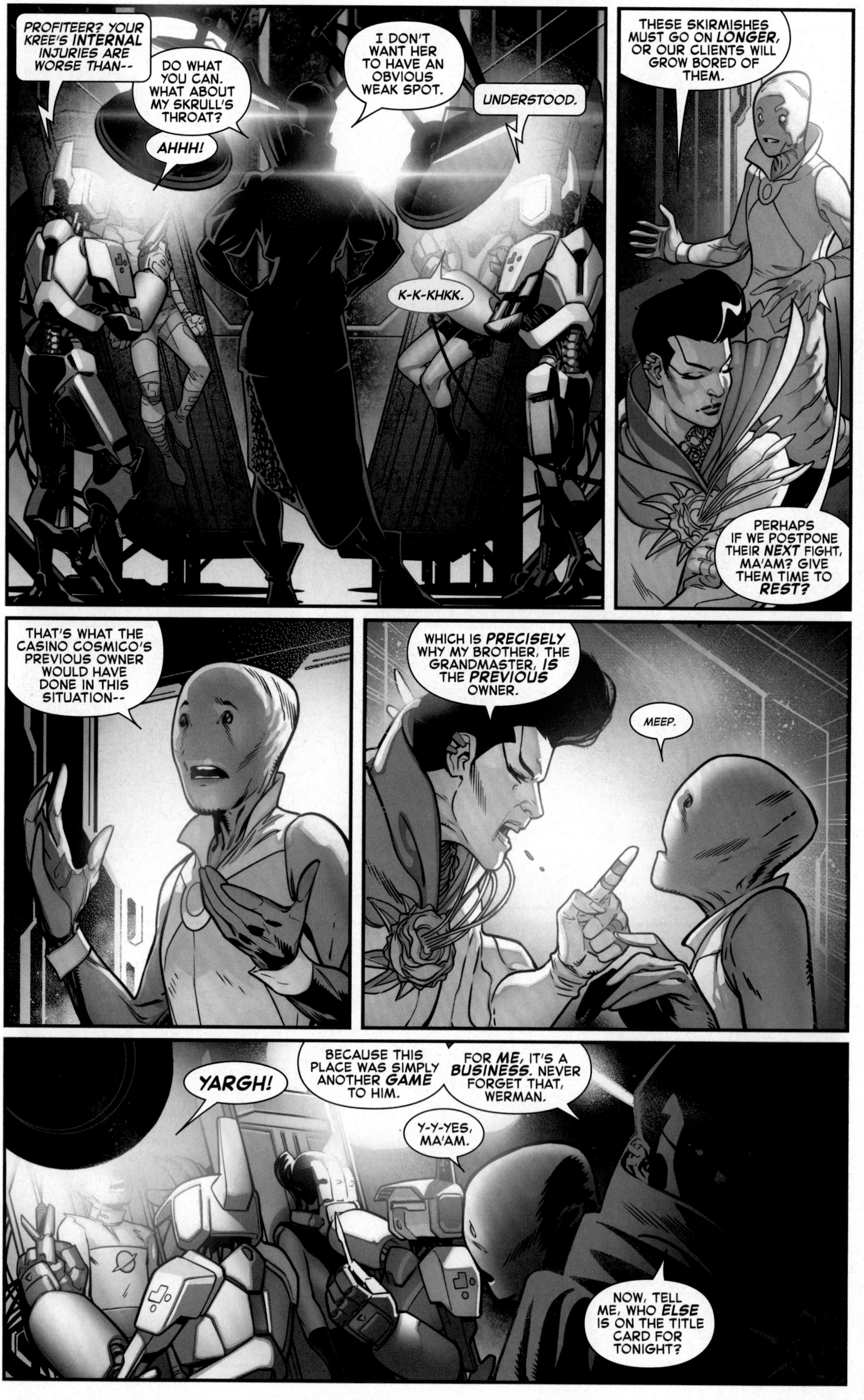
PROFITEER? YOUR KREE'S INTERNAL INJURIES ARE WORSE THAN--
DO WHAT YOU CAN. WHAT ABOUT MY SKRULL'S THROAT?
AHHH!
I DON'T WANT HER TO HAVE AN OBVIOUS WEAK SPOT.
UNDERSTOOD.
K-K-KHKK.
THESE SKIRMISHES MUST GO ON LONGER, OR OUR CLIENTS WILL GROW BORED OF THEM.
PERHAPS IF WE POSTPONE THEIR NEXT FIGHT, MA'AM? GIVE THEM TIME TO REST?
THAT'S WHAT THE CASINO COSMICO'S PREVIOUS OWNER WOULD HAVE DONE IN THIS SITUATION--
WHICH IS PRECISELY WHY MY BROTHER, THE GRANDMASTER, IS THE PREVIOUS OWNER.
MEEP.
YARGH!
BECAUSE THIS PLACE WAS SIMPLY ANOTHER GAME TO HIM.
FOR ME, IT'S A BUSINESS. NEVER FORGET THAT, WERMAN.
Y-Y-YES, MA'AM.
NOW, TELL ME, WHO ELSE IS ON THE TITLE CARD FOR TONIGHT?

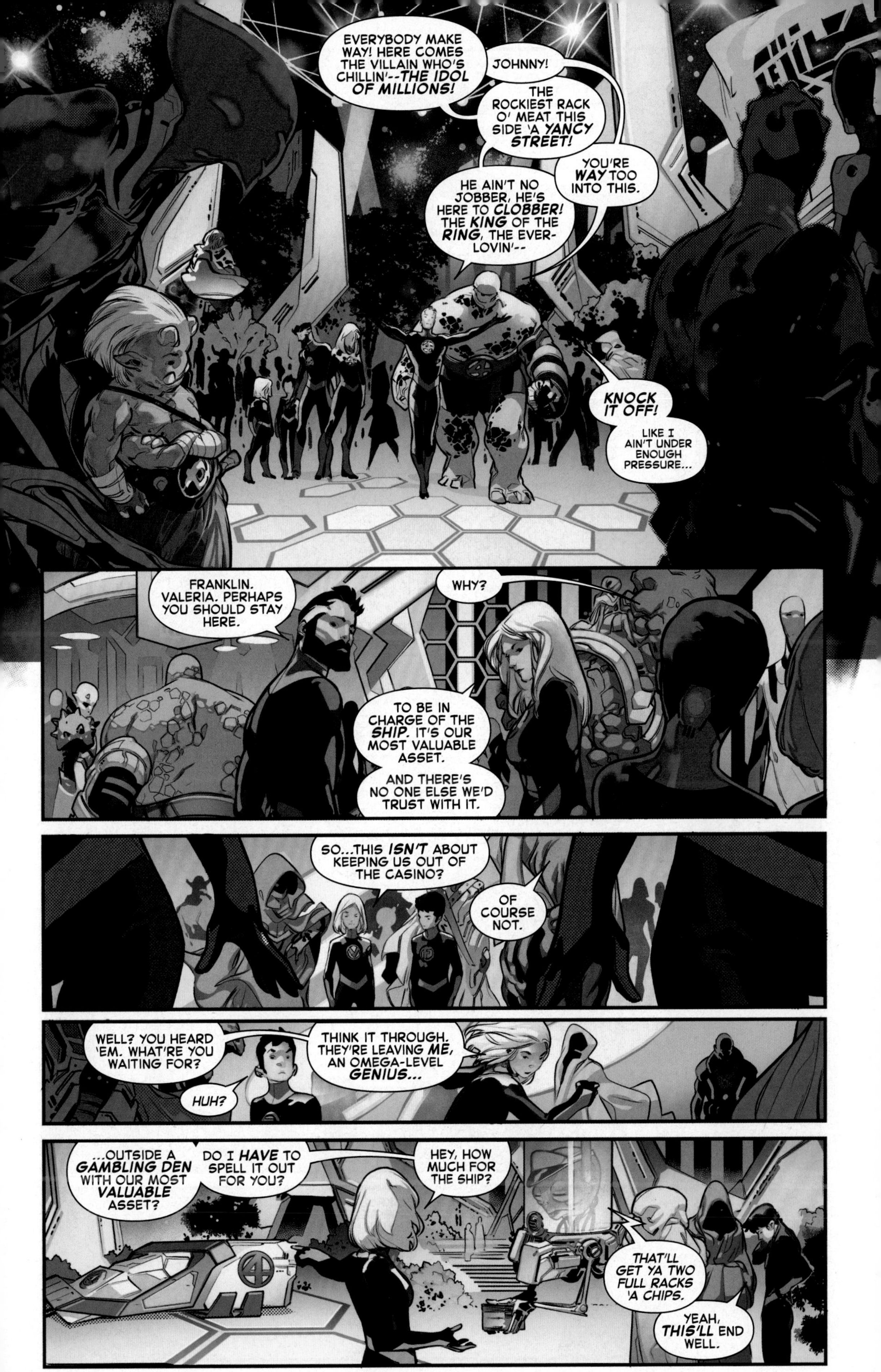
EVERYBODY MAKE WAY! HERE COMES THE VILLAIN WHO'S CHILLIN'--THE IDOL OF MILLIONS!
JOHNNY!
THE ROCKIEST RACK O' MEAT THIS SIDE 'A YANCY STREET!
YOU'RE WAY TOO INTO THIS.
HE AIN'T NO JOBBER, HE'S HERE TO CLOBBER! THE KING OF THE RING, THE EVER-LOVIN'--
KNOCK IT OFF!
LIKE I AIN'T UNDER ENOUGH PRESSURE...
FRANKLIN. VALERIA. PERHAPS YOU SHOULD STAY HERE.
WHY?
TO BE IN CHARGE OF THE SHIP. IT'S OUR MOST VALUABLE ASSET.
AND THERE'S NO ONE ELSE WE'D TRUST WITH IT.
SO...THIS ISN'T ABOUT KEEPING US OUT OF THE CASINO?
OF COURSE NOT.
WELL? YOU HEARD 'EM. WHAT'RE YOU WAITING FOR?
HUH?
THINK IT THROUGH. THEY'RE LEAVING ME, AN OMEGA-LEVEL GENIUS...
...OUTSIDE A GAMBLING DEN WITH OUR MOST VALUABLE ASSET?
DO I HAVE TO SPELL IT OUT FOR YOU?
HEY, HOW MUCH FOR THE SHIP?
THAT'LL GET YA TWO FULL RACKS 'A CHIPS.
YEAH, THIS'LL END WELL.

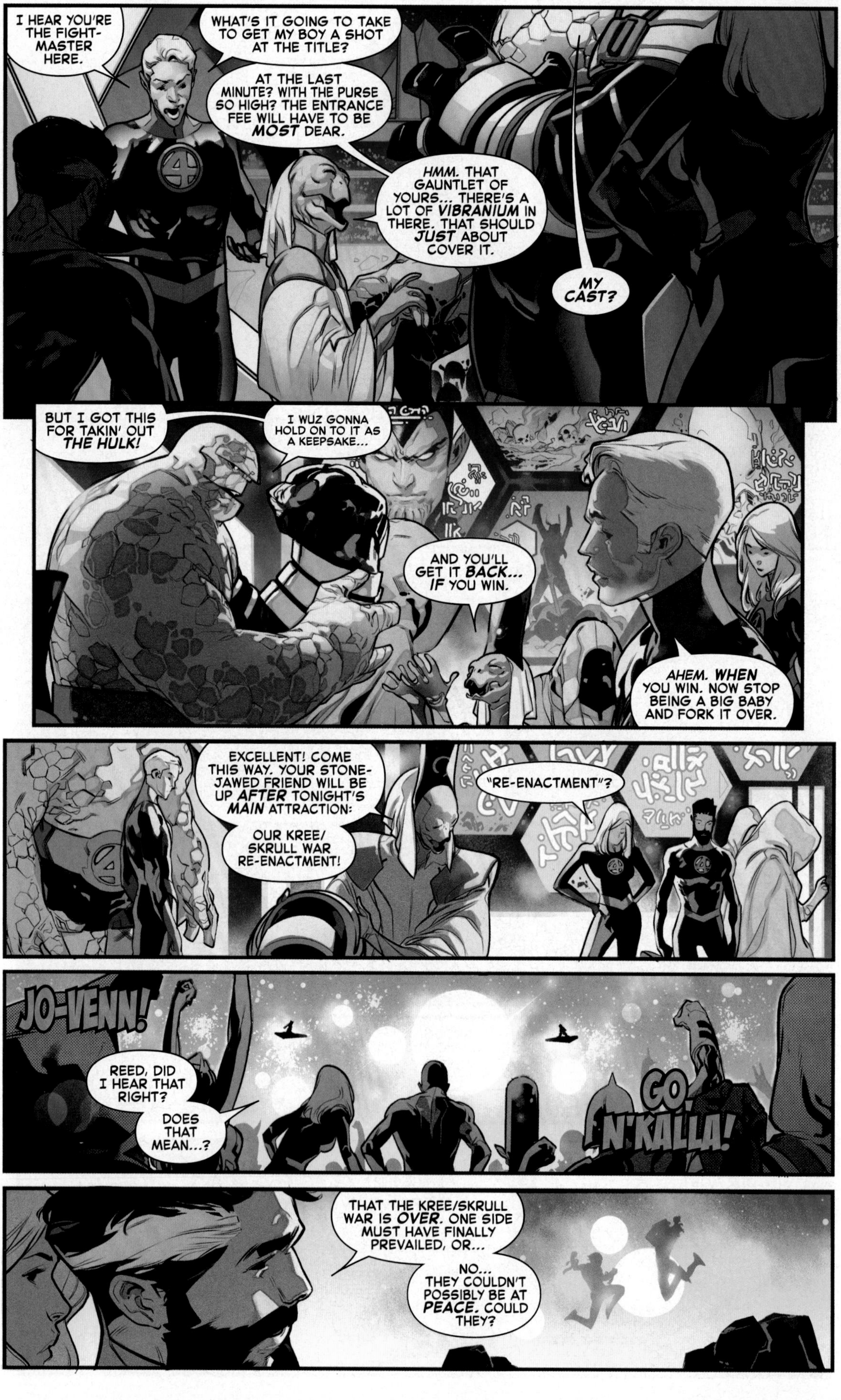
I HEAR YOU'RE THE FIGHT-MASTER HERE.
WHAT'S IT GOING TO TAKE TO GET MY BOY A SHOT AT THE TITLE?
AT THE LAST MINUTE? WITH THE PURSE SO HIGH? THE ENTRANCE FEE WILL HAVE TO BE MOST DEAR.
HMM. THAT GAUNTLET OF YOURS... THERE'S A LOT OF VIBRANIUM IN THERE. THAT SHOULD JUST ABOUT COVER IT.
MY CAST?
BUT I GOT THIS FOR TAKIN' OUT THE HULK!
I WUZ GONNA HOLD ON TO IT AS A KEEPSAKE...
AND YOU'LL GET IT BACK... IF YOU WIN.
AHEM. WHEN YOU WIN. NOW STOP BEING A BIG BABY AND FORK IT OVER.
EXCELLENT! COME THIS WAY. YOUR STONE-JAWED FRIEND WILL BE UP AFTER TONIGHT'S MAIN ATTRACTION:
OUR KREE/SKRULL WAR RE-ENACTMENT!
"RE-ENACTMENT"?
JO-VENN!
REED, DID I HEAR THAT RIGHT?
DOES THAT MEAN...?
GO N'KALLA!
THAT THE KREE/SKRULL WAR IS OVER. ONE SIDE MUST HAVE FINALLY PREVAILED, OR...
NO... THEY COULDN'T POSSIBLY BE AT PEACE. COULD THEY?

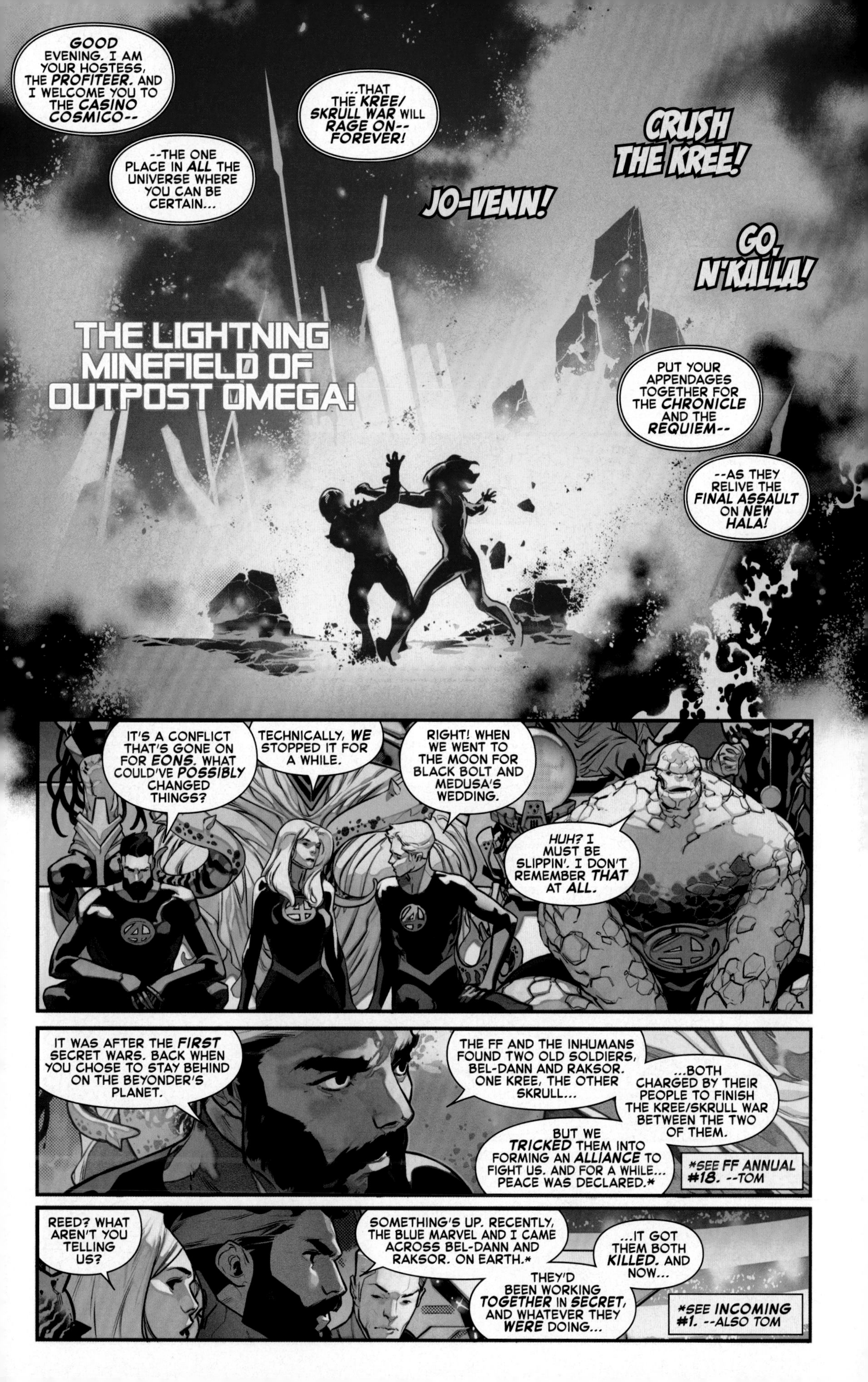
GOOD EVENING. I AM YOUR HOSTESS, THE PROFITEER. AND I WELCOME YOU TO THE CASINO COSMICO--
--THE ONE PLACE IN ALL THE UNIVERSE WHERE YOU CAN BE CERTAIN...
...THAT THE KREE/SKRULL WAR WILL RAGE ON--FOREVER!
CRUSH THE KREE!
JO-VENN!
GO, N'KALLA!
THE LIGHTNING MINEFIELD OF OUTPOST OMEGA!
PUT YOUR APPENDAGES TOGETHER FOR THE CHRONICLE AND THE REQUIEM--
--AS THEY RELIVE THE FINAL ASSAULT ON NEW HALA!
IT'S A CONFLICT THAT'S GONE ON FOR EONS. WHAT COULD'VE POSSIBLY CHANGED THINGS?
TECHNICALLY, WE STOPPED IT FOR A WHILE.
RIGHT! WHEN WE WENT TO THE MOON FOR BLACK BOLT AND MEDUSA'S WEDDING.
HUH? I MUST BE SLIPPIN'. I DON'T REMEMBER THAT AT ALL.
IT WAS AFTER THE FIRST SECRET WARS. BACK WHEN YOU CHOSE TO STAY BEHIND ON THE BEYONDER'S PLANET.
THE FF AND THE INHUMANS FOUND TWO OLD SOLDIERS, BEL-DANN AND RAKSOR. ONE KREE, THE OTHER SKRULL...
...BOTH CHARGED BY THEIR PEOPLE TO FINISH THE KREE/SKRULL WAR BETWEEN THE TWO OF THEM.
BUT WE TRICKED THEM INTO FORMING AN ALLIANCE TO FIGHT US. AND FOR A WHILE... PEACE WAS DECLARED.*
*SEE FF ANNUAL #18. --TOM
REED? WHAT AREN'T YOU TELLING US?
SOMETHING'S UP. RECENTLY, THE BLUE MARVEL AND I CAME ACROSS BEL-DANN AND RAKSOR. ON EARTH.*
THEY'D BEEN WORKING TOGETHER IN SECRET, AND WHATEVER THEY WERE DOING...
...IT GOT THEM BOTH KILLED. AND NOW...
*SEE INCOMING #1. --ALSO TOM

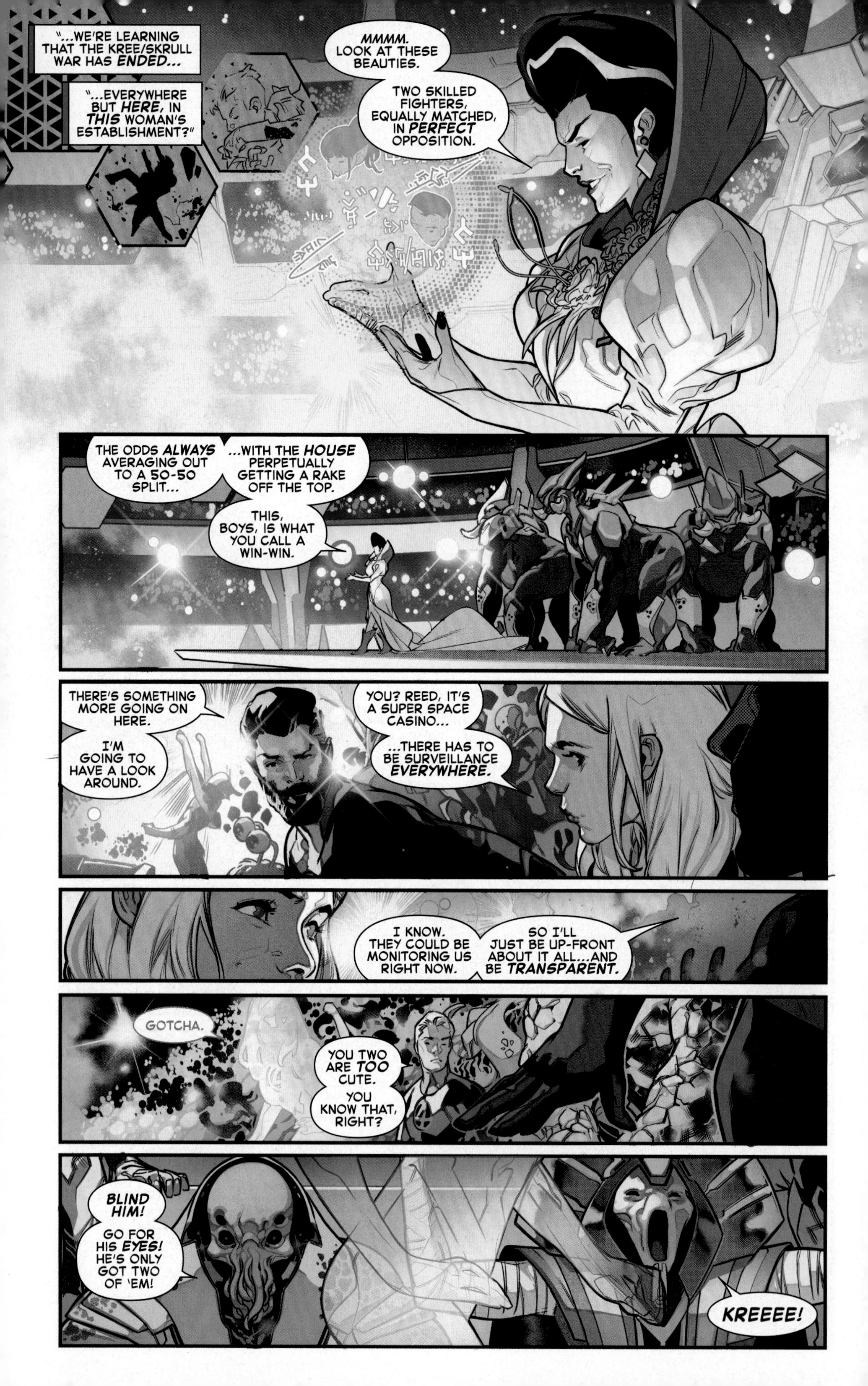
"...WE'RE LEARNING THAT THE KREE/SKRULL WAR HAS ENDED...
"...EVERYWHERE BUT HERE, IN THIS WOMAN'S ESTABLISHMENT?"
MMMM. LOOK AT THESE BEAUTIES.
TWO SKILLED FIGHTERS, EQUALLY MATCHED, IN PERFECT OPPOSITION.
THE ODDS ALWAYS AVERAGING OUT TO A 50-50 SPLIT...
...WITH THE HOUSE PERPETUALLY GETTING A RAKE OFF THE TOP.
THIS, BOYS, IS WHAT YOU CALL A WIN-WIN.
THERE'S SOMETHING MORE GOING ON HERE.
I'M GOING TO HAVE A LOOK AROUND.
YOU? REED, IT'S A SUPER SPACE CASINO...
...THERE HAS TO BE SURVEILLANCE EVERYWHERE.
I KNOW. THEY COULD BE MONITORING US RIGHT NOW.
SO I'LL JUST BE UP-FRONT ABOUT IT ALL...AND BE TRANSPARENT.
GOTCHA.
YOU TWO ARE TOO CUTE.
YOU KNOW THAT, RIGHT?
BLIND HIM!
GO FOR HIS EYES! HE'S ONLY GOT TWO OF 'EM!
KREEEE!

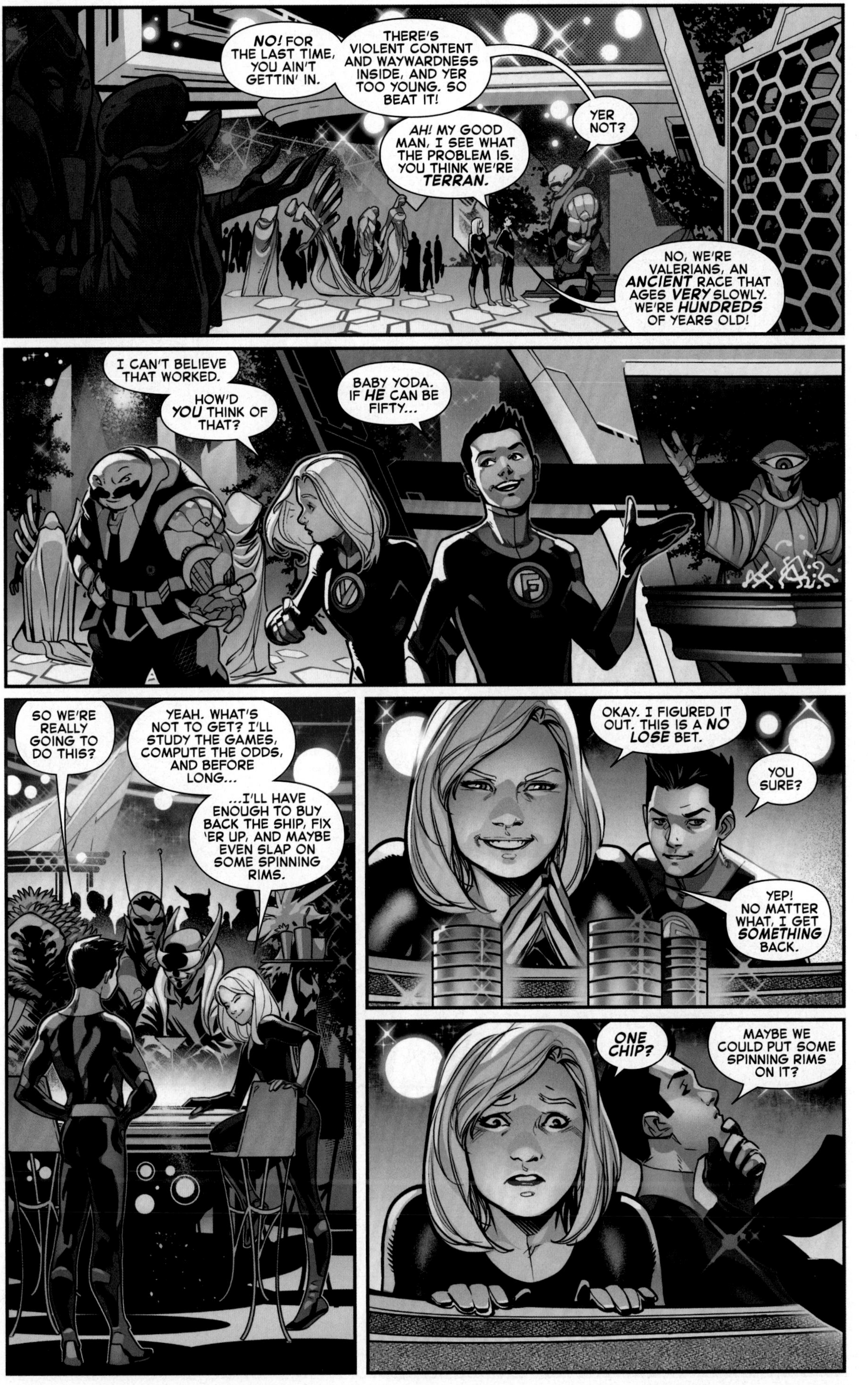
NO! FOR THE LAST TIME, YOU AIN'T GETTIN' IN.
THERE'S VIOLENT CONTENT AND WAYWARDNESS INSIDE, AND YER TOO YOUNG. SO BEAT IT!
AH! MY GOOD MAN, I SEE WHAT THE PROBLEM IS. YOU THINK WE'RE TERRAN.
YER NOT?
NO, WE'RE VALERIANS, AN ANCIENT RACE THAT AGES VERY SLOWLY. WE'RE HUNDREDS OF YEARS OLD!
I CAN'T BELIEVE THAT WORKED.
HOW'D YOU THINK OF THAT?
BABY YODA. IF HE CAN BE FIFTY...
SO WE'RE REALLY GOING TO DO THIS?
YEAH. WHAT'S NOT TO GET? I'LL STUDY THE GAMES, COMPUTE THE ODDS, AND BEFORE LONG...
...I'LL HAVE ENOUGH TO BUY BACK THE SHIP, FIX 'ER UP, AND MAYBE EVEN SLAP ON SOME SPINNING RIMS.
OKAY. I FIGURED IT OUT. THIS IS A NO LOSE BET.
YOU SURE?
YEP! NO MATTER WHAT, I GET SOMETHING BACK.
ONE CHIP?
MAYBE WE COULD PUT SOME SPINNING RIMS ON IT?

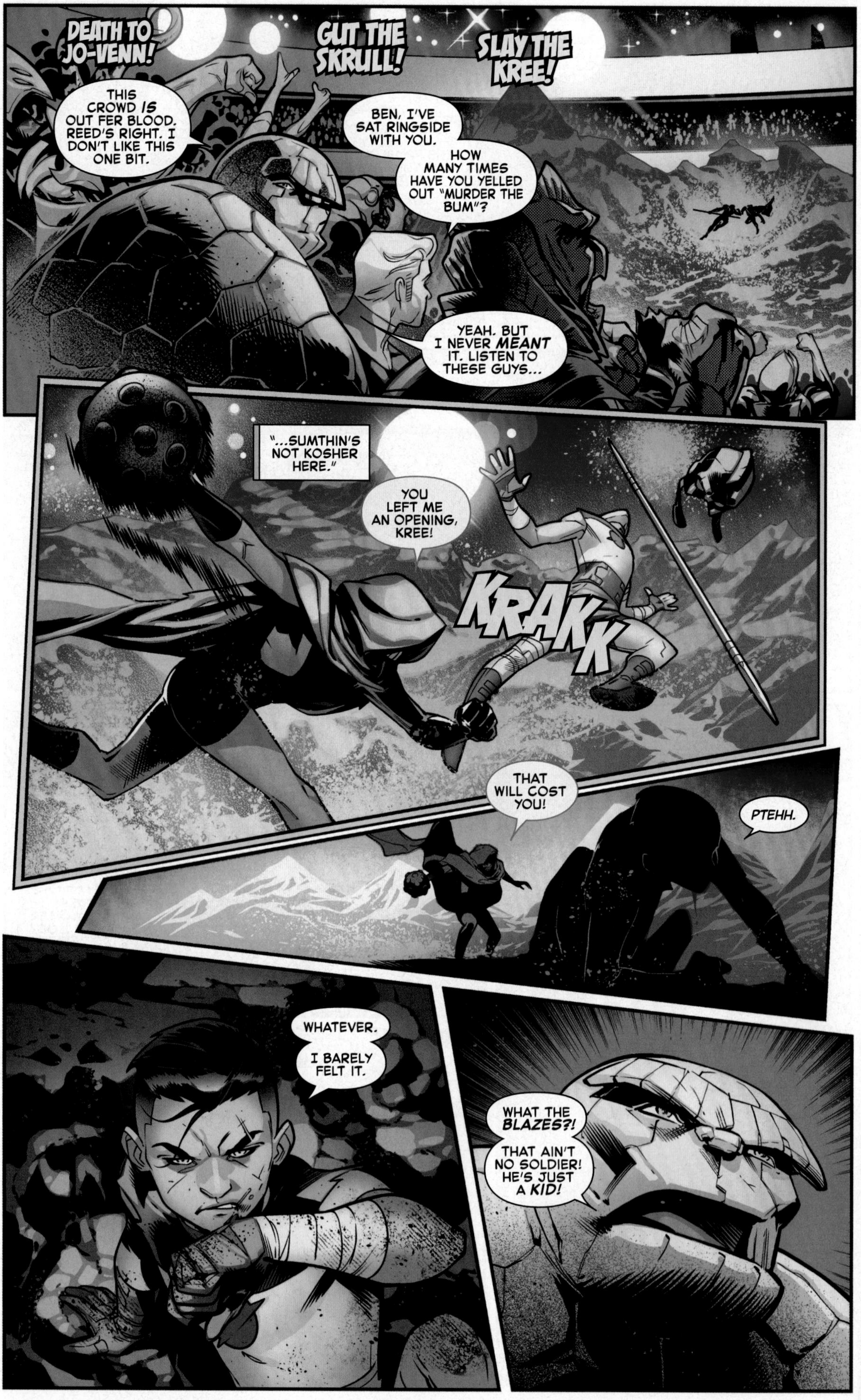
DEATH TO JO-VENN!
GUT THE SKRULL!
SLAY THE KREE!
THIS CROWD IS OUT FER BLOOD. REED'S RIGHT. I DON'T LIKE THIS ONE BIT.
BEN, I'VE SAT RINGSIDE WITH YOU.
HOW MANY TIMES HAVE YOU YELLED OUT "MURDER THE BUM"?
YEAH. BUT I NEVER MEANT IT. LISTEN TO THESE GUYS...
"...SUMTHIN'S NOT KOSHER HERE."
YOU LEFT ME AN OPENING, KREE!
KRAKK
THAT WILL COST YOU!
PTEHH.
WHATEVER.
I BARELY FELT IT.
WHAT THE BLAZES?!
THAT AIN'T NO SOLDIER! HE'S JUST A KID!

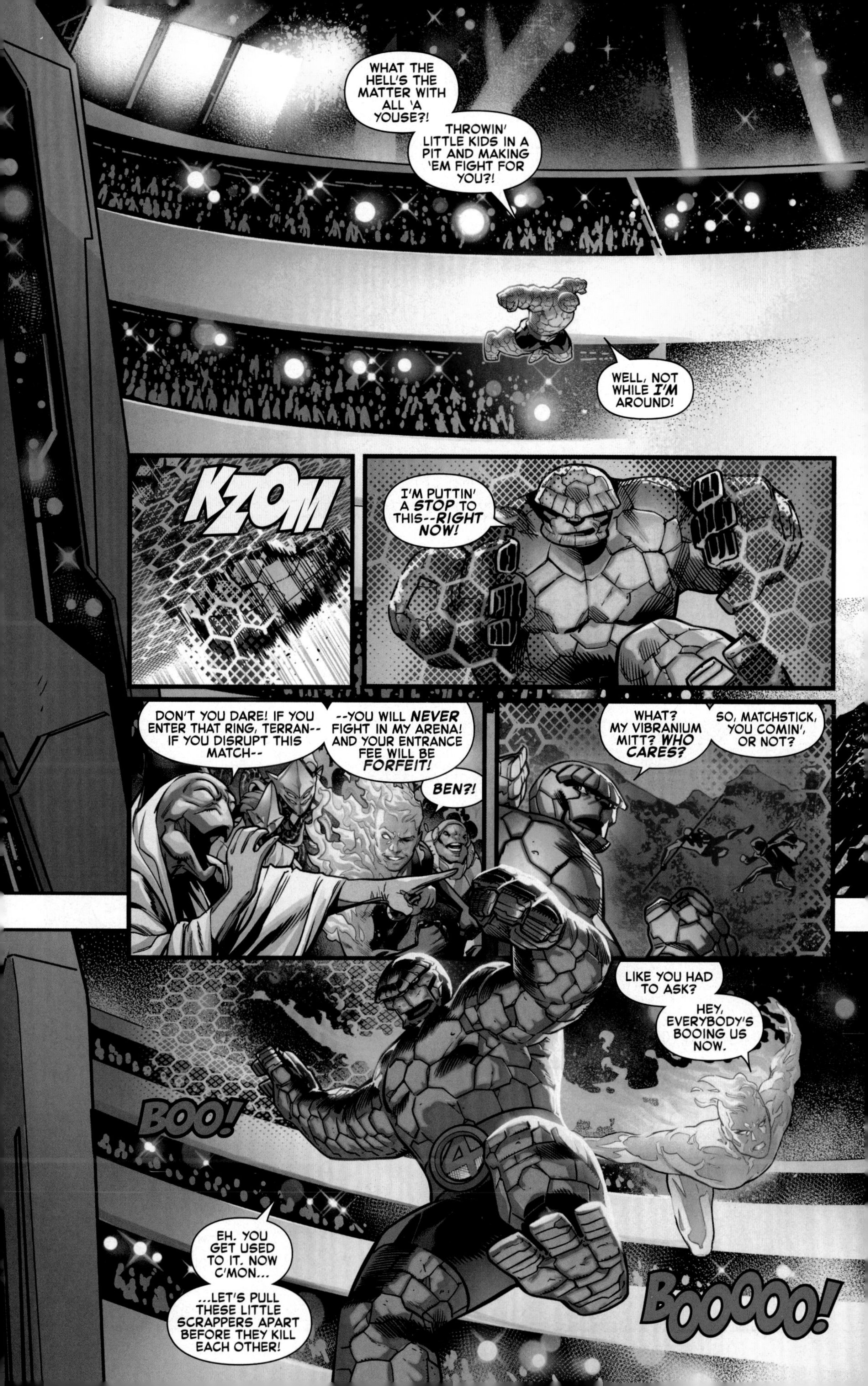
WHAT THE HELL'S THE MATTER WITH ALL 'A YOUSE?!
THROWIN' LITTLE KIDS IN A PIT AND MAKING 'EM FIGHT FOR YOU?!
WELL, NOT WHILE I'M AROUND!
KZOM
I'M PUTTIN' A STOP TO THIS--RIGHT NOW!
DON'T YOU DARE! IF YOU ENTER THAT RING, TERRAN-- IF YOU DISRUPT THIS MATCH--
--YOU WILL NEVER FIGHT IN MY ARENA! AND YOUR ENTRANCE FEE WILL BE FORFEIT!
BEN?!
WHAT? MY VIBRANIUM MITT? WHO CARES?
SO, MATCHSTICK, YOU COMIN', OR NOT?
LIKE YOU HAD TO ASK?
HEY, EVERYBODY'S BOOING US NOW.
BOO!
EH. YOU GET USED TO IT. NOW C'MON...
...LET'S PULL THESE LITTLE SCRAPPERS APART BEFORE THEY KILL EACH OTHER!
BOOOOO!

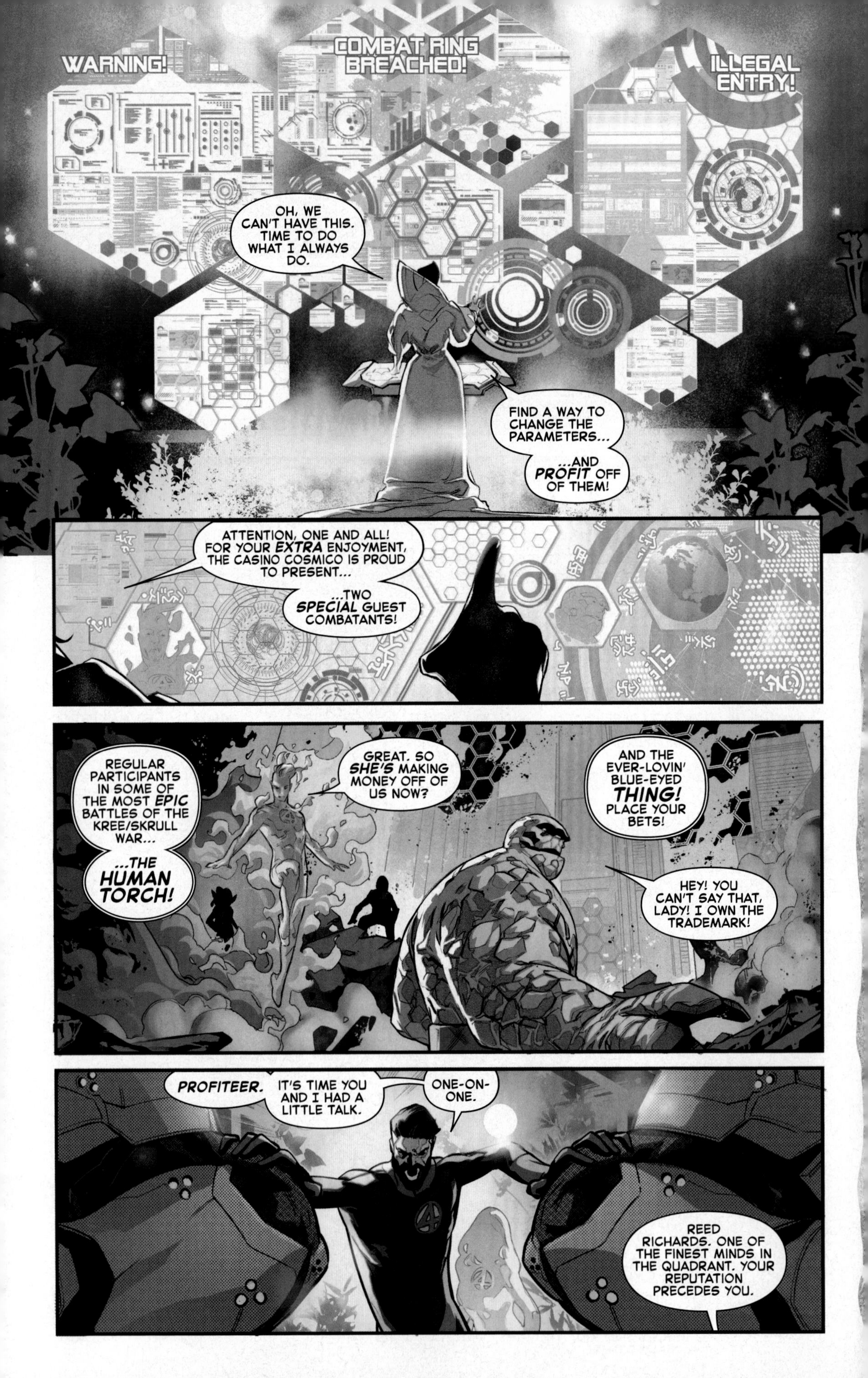
WARNING!
COMBAT RING BREACHED!
ILLEGAL ENTRY!
OH, WE CAN'T HAVE THIS. TIME TO DO WHAT I ALWAYS DO.
FIND A WAY TO CHANGE THE PARAMETERS...
...AND PROFIT OFF OF THEM!
ATTENTION, ONE AND ALL! FOR YOUR EXTRA ENJOYMENT, THE CASINO COSMICO IS PROUD TO PRESENT...
...TWO SPECIAL GUEST COMBATANTS!
REGULAR PARTICIPANTS IN SOME OF THE MOST EPIC BATTLES OF THE KREE/SKRULL WAR...
...THE HUMAN TORCH!
GREAT. SO SHE'S MAKING MONEY OFF OF US NOW?
AND THE EVER-LOVIN' BLUE-EYED THING! PLACE YOUR BETS!
HEY! YOU CAN'T SAY THAT, LADY! I OWN THE TRADEMARK!
PROFITEER.
IT'S TIME YOU AND I HAD A LITTLE TALK.
ONE-ON-ONE.
REED RICHARDS. ONE OF THE FINEST MINDS IN THE QUADRANT. YOUR REPUTATION PRECEDES YOU.

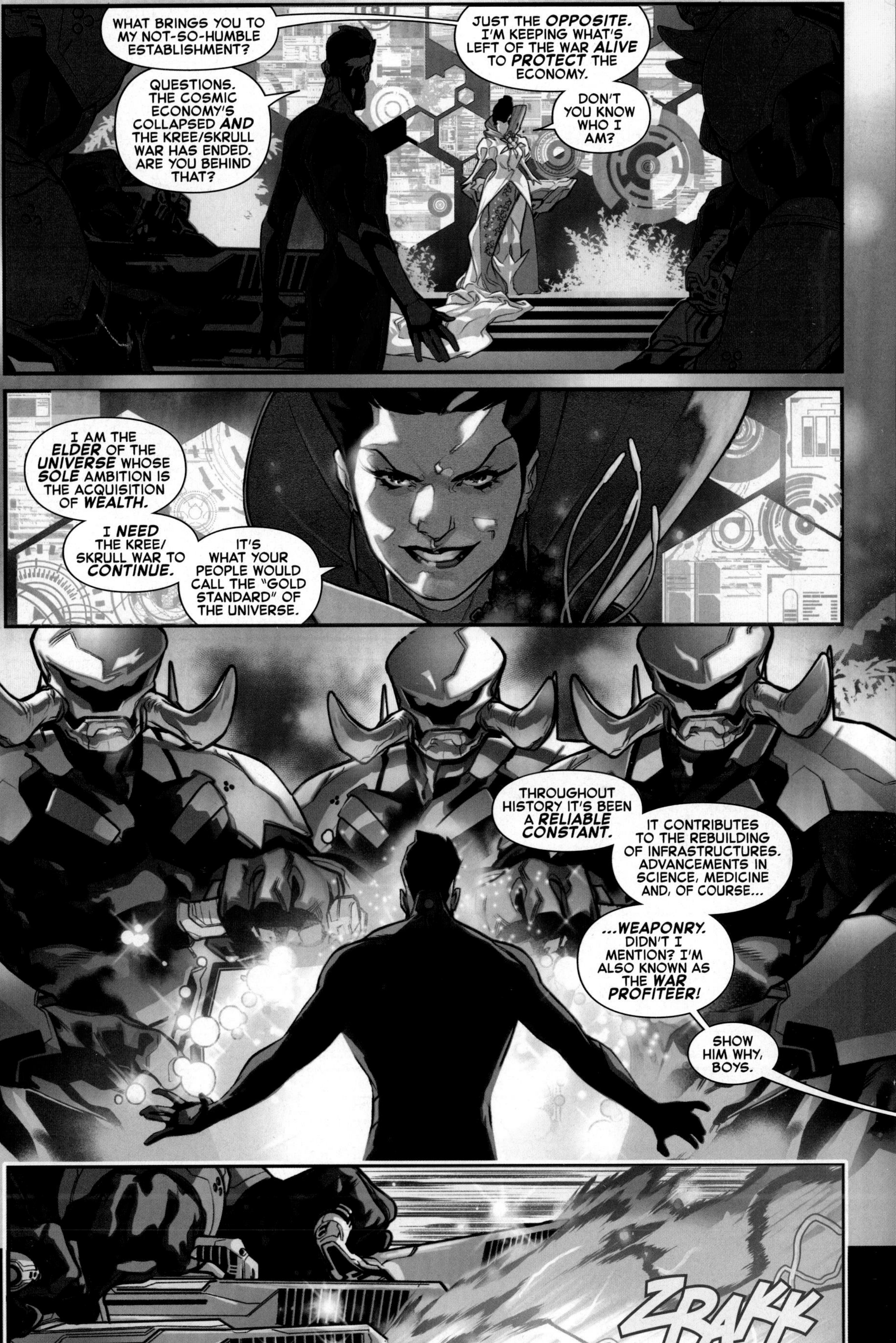
WHAT BRINGS YOU TO MY NOT-SO-HUMBLE ESTABLISHMENT?
QUESTIONS. THE COSMIC ECONOMY'S COLLAPSED AND THE KREE/SKRULL WAR HAS ENDED. ARE YOU BEHIND THAT?
JUST THE OPPOSITE. I'M KEEPING WHAT'S LEFT OF THE WAR ALIVE TO PROTECT THE ECONOMY.
DON'T YOU KNOW WHO I AM?
I AM THE ELDER OF THE UNIVERSE WHOSE SOLE AMBITION IS THE ACQUISITION OF WEALTH.
I NEED THE KREE/ SKRULL WAR TO CONTINUE.
IT'S WHAT YOUR PEOPLE WOULD CALL THE "GOLD STANDARD" OF THE UNIVERSE.
THROUGHOUT HISTORY IT'S BEEN A RELIABLE CONSTANT.
IT CONTRIBUTES TO THE REBUILDING OF INFRASTRUCTURES. ADVANCEMENTS IN SCIENCE, MEDICINE AND, OF COURSE...
...WEAPONRY. DIDN'T I MENTION? I'M ALSO KNOWN AS THE WAR PROFITEER!
SHOW HIM WHY, BOYS.
ZRAKK

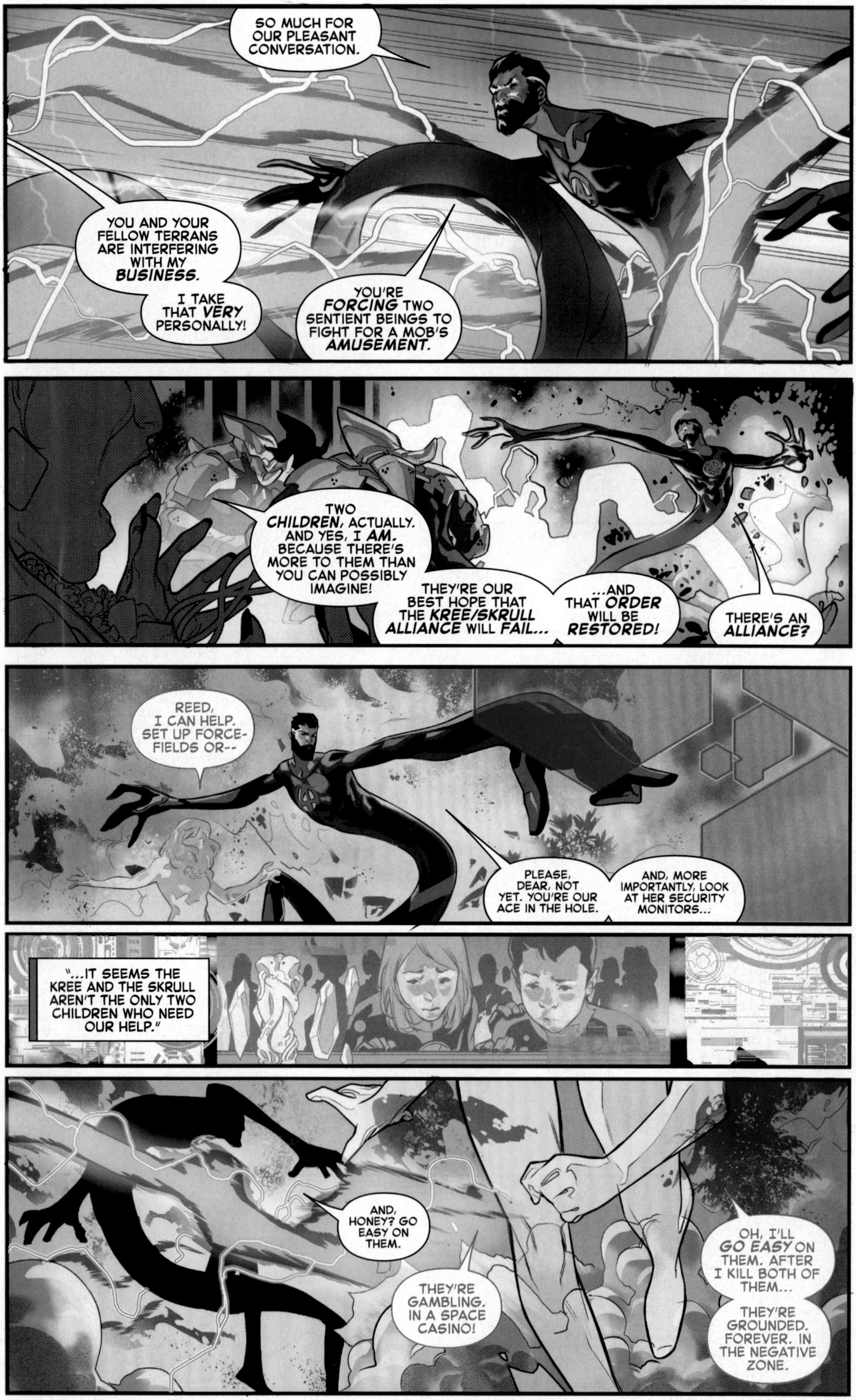
SO MUCH FOR OUR PLEASANT CONVERSATION.
YOU AND YOUR FELLOW TERRANS ARE INTERFERING WITH MY BUSINESS.
I TAKE THAT VERY PERSONALLY!
YOU'RE FORCING TWO SENTIENT BEINGS TO FIGHT FOR A MOB'S AMUSEMENT.
TWO CHILDREN, ACTUALLY. AND YES, I AM. BECAUSE THERE'S MORE TO THEM THAN YOU CAN POSSIBLY IMAGINE!
THEY'RE OUR BEST HOPE THAT THE KREE/SKRULL ALLIANCE WILL FAIL...
...AND THAT ORDER WILL BE RESTORED!
THERE'S AN ALLIANCE?
REED, I CAN HELP. SET UP FORCE-FIELDS OR--
PLEASE, DEAR, NOT YET. YOU'RE OUR ACE IN THE HOLE.
AND, MORE IMPORTANTLY, LOOK AT HER SECURITY MONITORS...
"...IT SEEMS THE KREE AND THE SKRULL AREN'T THE ONLY TWO CHILDREN WHO NEED OUR HELP."
AND, HONEY? GO EASY ON THEM.
THEY'RE GAMBLING. IN A SPACE CASINO!
OH, I'LL GO EASY ON THEM. AFTER I KILL BOTH OF THEM...
THEY'RE GROUNDED. FOREVER. IN THE NEGATIVE ZONE.

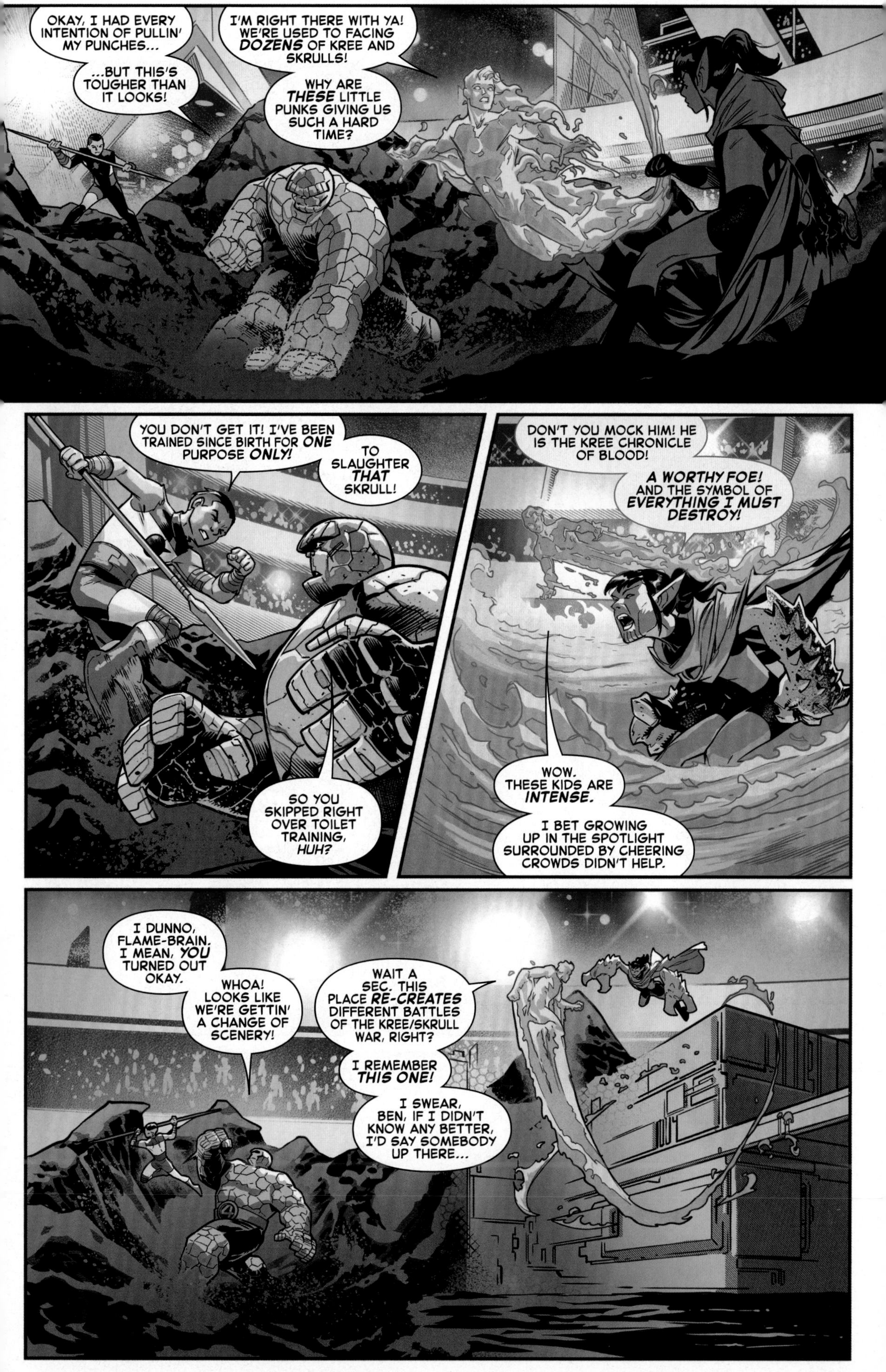
OKAY, I HAD EVERY INTENTION OF PULLIN' MY PUNCHES...
...BUT THIS'S TOUGHER THAN IT LOOKS!
I'M RIGHT THERE WITH YA! WE'RE USED TO FACING DOZENS OF KREE AND SKRULLS!
WHY ARE THESE LITTLE PUNKS GIVING US SUCH A HARD TIME?
YOU DON'T GET IT! I'VE BEEN TRAINED SINCE BIRTH FOR ONE PURPOSE ONLY!
TO SLAUGHTER THAT SKRULL!
SO YOU SKIPPED RIGHT OVER TOILET TRAINING, HUH?
DON'T YOU MOCK HIM! HE IS THE KREE CHRONICLE OF BLOOD!
A WORTHY FOE! AND THE SYMBOL OF EVERYTHING I MUST DESTROY!
WOW. THESE KIDS ARE INTENSE.
I BET GROWING UP IN THE SPOTLIGHT SURROUNDED BY CHEERING CROWDS DIDN'T HELP.
I DUNNO, FLAME-BRAIN. I MEAN, YOU TURNED OUT OKAY.
WHOA! LOOKS LIKE WE'RE GETTIN' A CHANGE OF SCENERY!
WAIT A SEC. THIS PLACE RE-CREATES DIFFERENT BATTLES OF THE KREE/SKRULL WAR, RIGHT?
I REMEMBER THIS ONE!
I SWEAR, BEN, IF I DIDN'T KNOW ANY BETTER, I'D SAY SOMEBODY UP THERE...

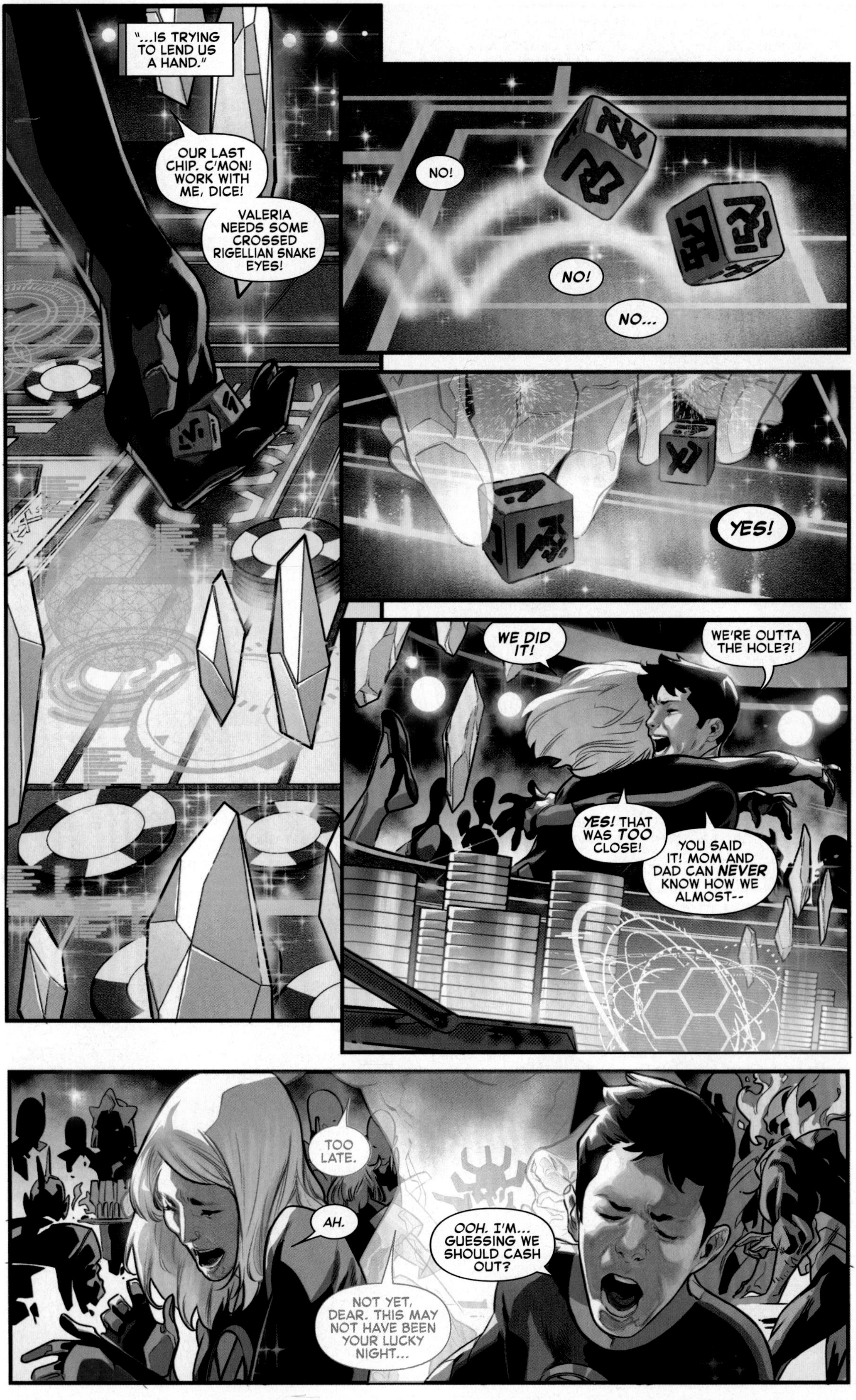
"...IS TRYING TO LEND US A HAND."
OUR LAST CHIP. C'MON! WORK WITH ME, DICE!
VALERIA NEEDS SOME CROSSED RIGELLIAN SNAKE EYES!
NO!
NO!
NO...
YES!
WE DID IT!
WE'RE OUTTA THE HOLE?!
YES! THAT WAS TOO CLOSE!
YOU SAID IT! MOM AND DAD CAN NEVER KNOW HOW WE ALMOST--
TOO LATE.
AH.
OOH. I'M... GUESSING WE SHOULD CASH OUT?
NOT YET, DEAR. THIS MAY NOT HAVE BEEN YOUR LUCKY NIGHT...

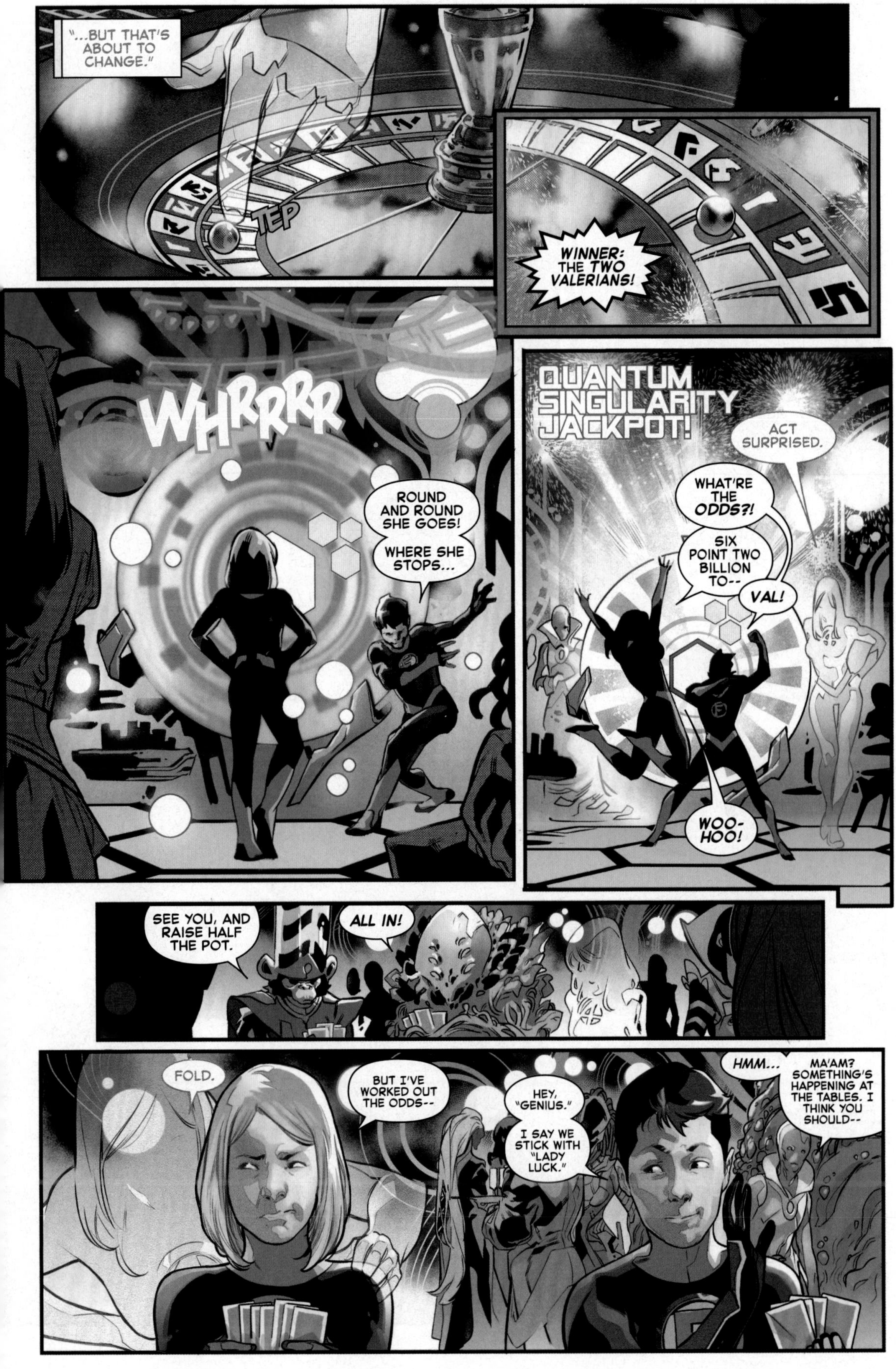
"...BUT THAT'S ABOUT TO CHANGE."
TEP
WINNER: THE TWO VALERIANS!
WHRRRR
ROUND AND ROUND SHE GOES!
WHERE SHE STOPS...
QUANTUM SINGULARITY JACKPOT!
ACT SURPRISED.
WHAT'RE THE ODDS?!
SIX POINT TWO BILLION TO--
VAL!
WOO-HOO!
SEE YOU, AND RAISE HALF THE POT.
ALL IN!
FOLD.
BUT I'VE WORKED OUT THE ODDS--
HEY, "GENIUS."
I SAY WE STICK WITH "LADY LUCK."
HMM...
MA'AM? SOMETHING'S HAPPENING AT THE TABLES. I THINK YOU SHOULD--

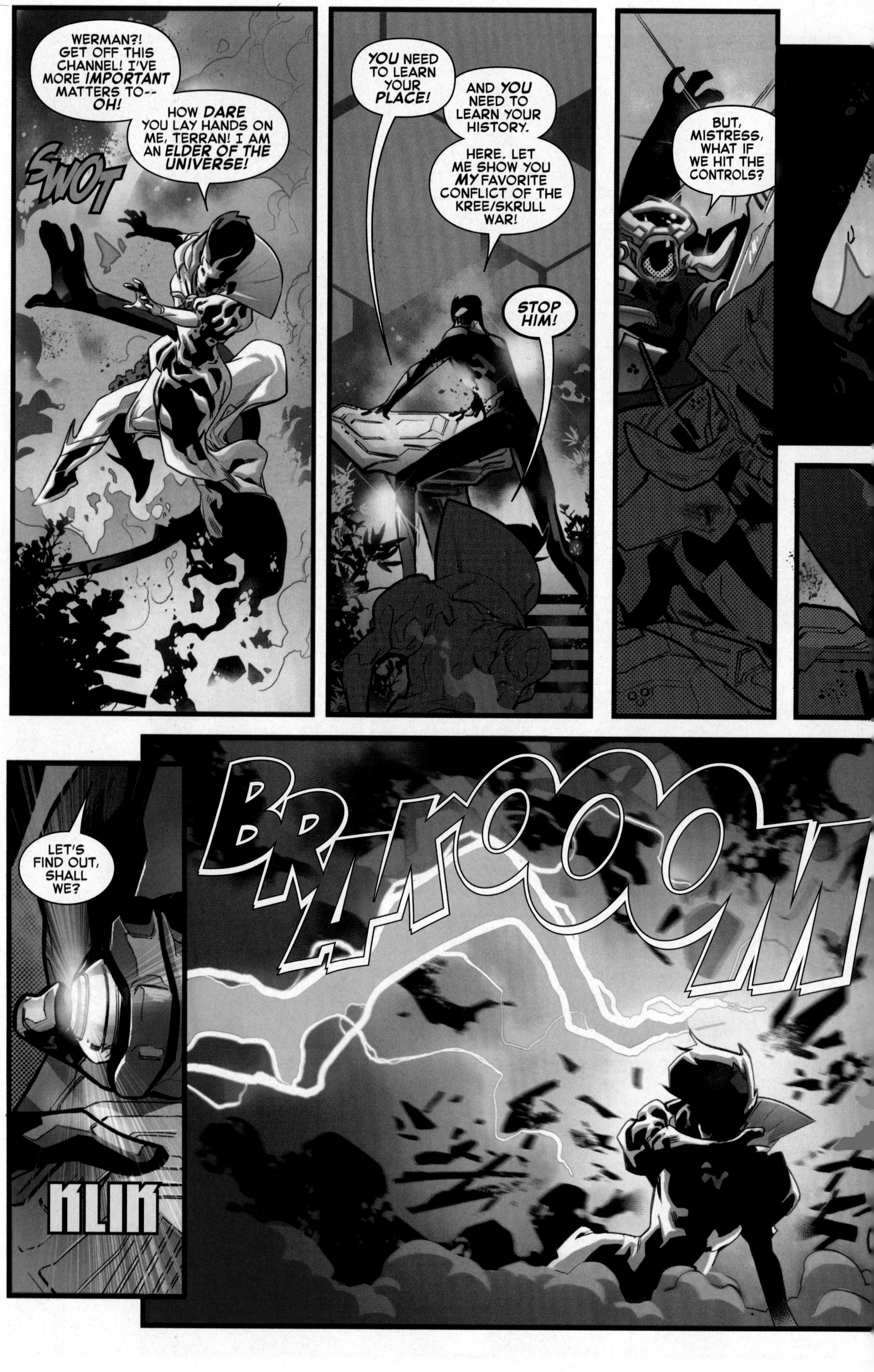
WERMAN?! GET OFF THIS CHANNEL! I'VE MORE IMPORTANT MATTERS TO-- OH!
HOW DARE YOU LAY HANDS ON ME, TERRAN! I AM AN ELDER OF THE UNIVERSE!
SWOT
YOU NEED TO LEARN YOUR PLACE!
AND YOU NEED TO LEARN YOUR HISTORY.
HERE. LET ME SHOW YOU MY FAVORITE CONFLICT OF THE KREE/SKRULL WAR!
STOP HIM!
BUT, MISTRESS, WHAT IF WE HIT THE CONTROLS?
LET'S FIND OUT, SHALL WE?
KLIK
BRZZOOOM

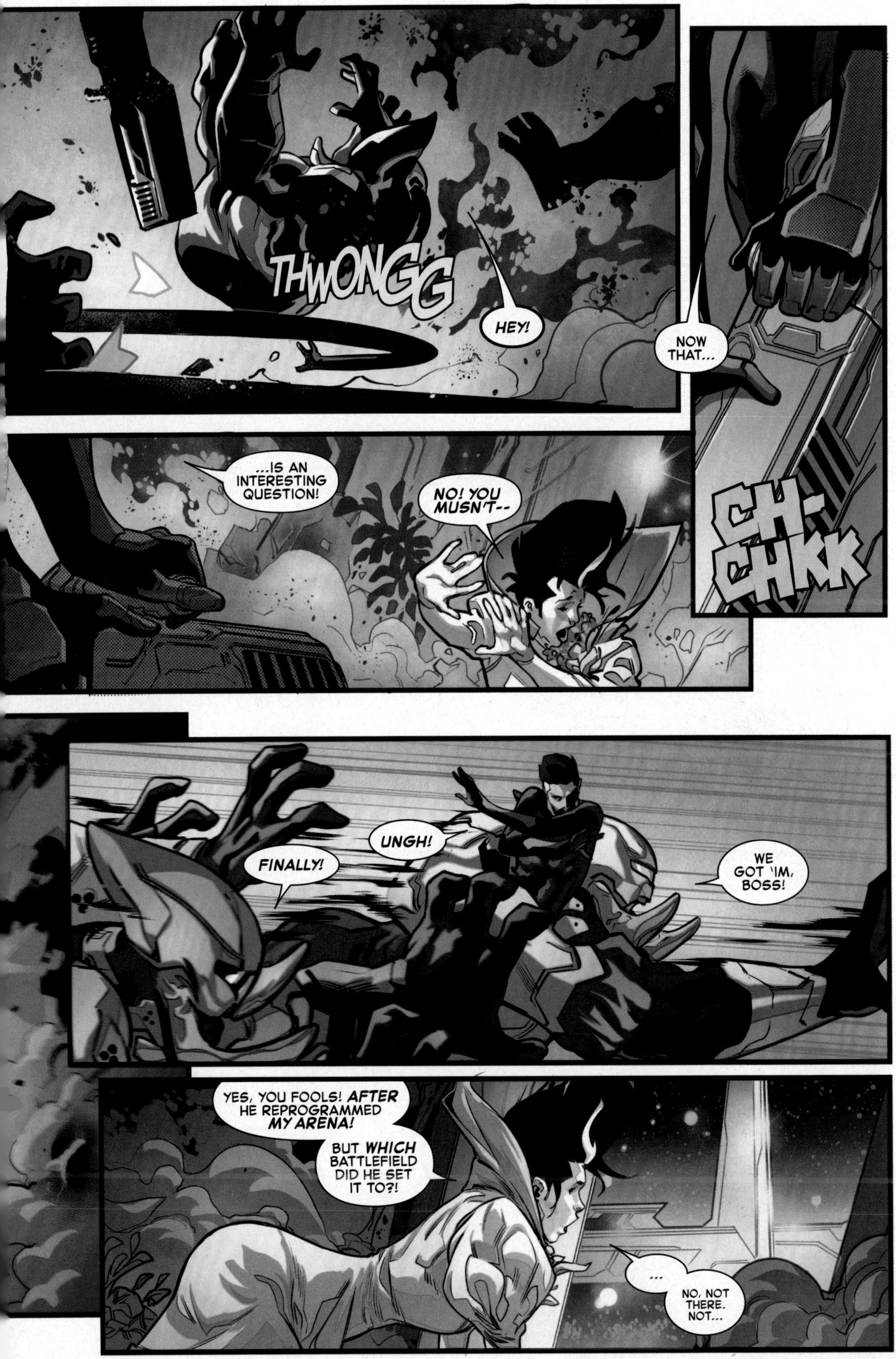
THWONGG
HEY!
NOW THAT...
CH-CHKK
...IS AN INTERESTING QUESTION!
NO! YOU MUSN'T--
FINALLY!
UNGH!
WE GOT 'IM, BOSS!
YES, YOU FOOLS! AFTER HE REPROGRAMMED MY ARENA!
BUT WHICH BATTLEFIELD DID HE SET IT TO?!
...
NO, NOT THERE. NOT...

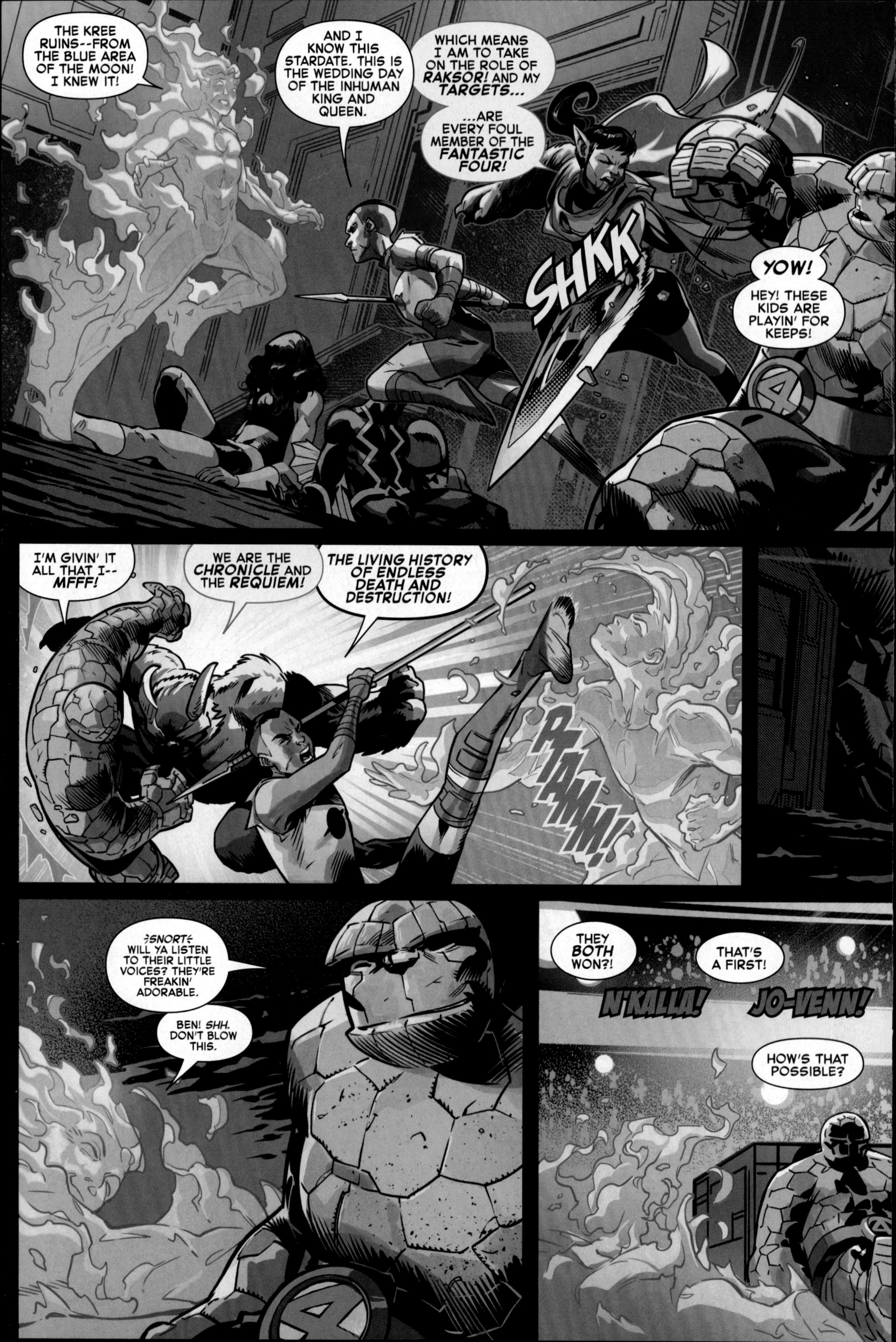
THE KREE RUINS--FROM THE BLUE AREA OF THE MOON! I KNEW IT!
AND I KNOW THIS STARDATE. THIS IS THE WEDDING DAY OF THE INHUMAN KING AND QUEEN.
WHICH MEANS I AM TO TAKE ON THE ROLE OF RAKSOR! AND MY TARGETS...
...ARE EVERY FOUL MEMBER OF THE FANTASTIC FOUR!
SHKK
YOW!
HEY! THESE KIDS ARE PLAYIN' FOR KEEPS!
I'M GIVIN' IT ALL THAT I-- MFFF!
WE ARE THE CHRONICLE AND THE REQUIEM!
THE LIVING HISTORY OF ENDLESS DEATH AND DESTRUCTION!
RRAMM!
SNORT
WILL YA LISTEN TO THEIR LITTLE VOICES? THEY'RE FREAKIN' ADORABLE.
BEN! SHH. DON'T BLOW THIS.
THEY BOTH WON?!
THAT'S A FIRST!
N'KALLA!
JO-VENN!
HOW'S THAT POSSIBLE?

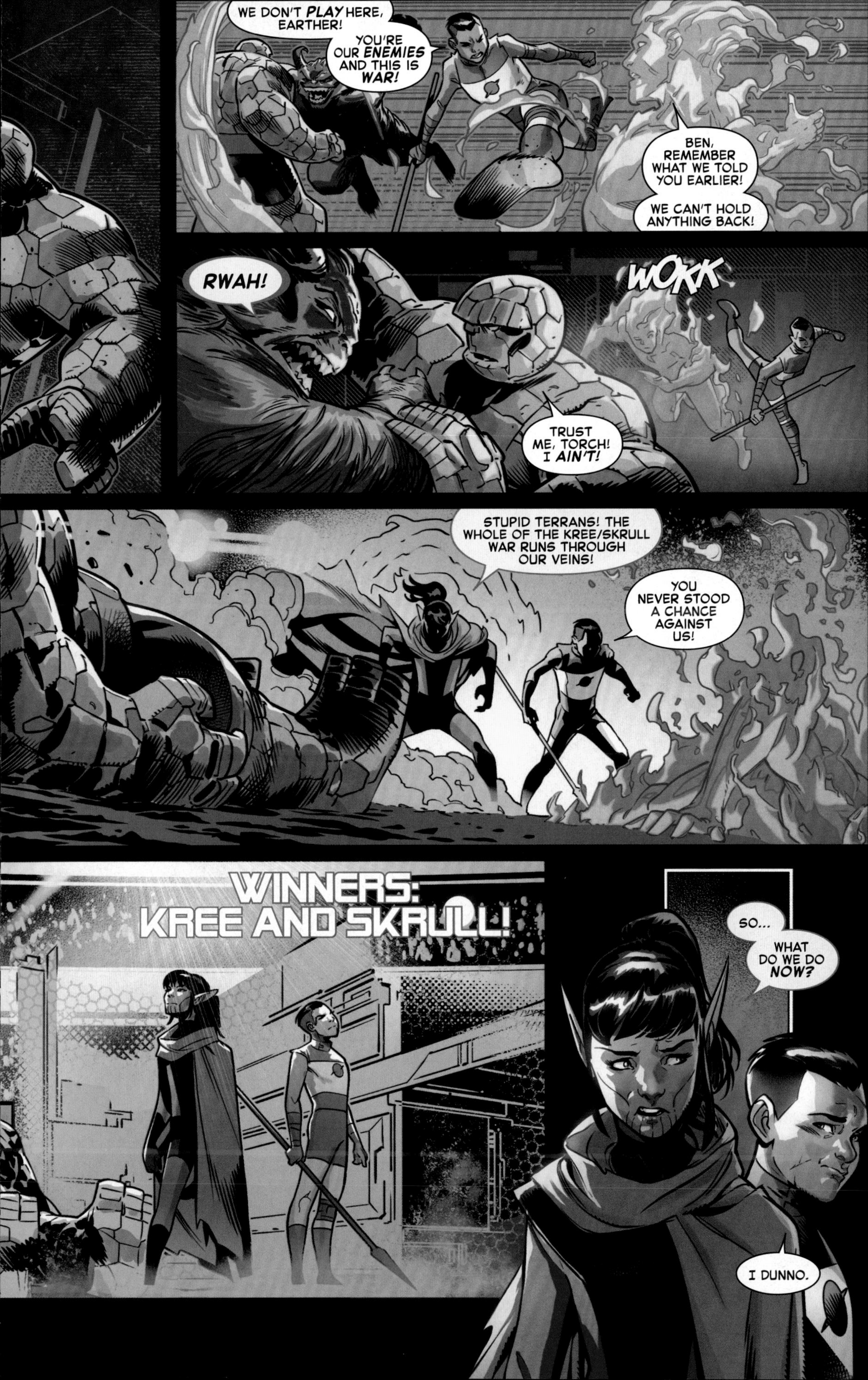
WE DON'T PLAY HERE, EARTHER!
YOU'RE OUR ENEMIES AND THIS IS WAR!
BEN, REMEMBER WHAT WE TOLD YOU EARLIER!
WE CAN'T HOLD ANYTHING BACK!
RWAH!
WOKK
TRUST ME, TORCH! I AIN'T!
STUPID TERRANS! THE WHOLE OF THE KREE/SKRULL WAR RUNS THROUGH OUR VEINS!
YOU NEVER STOOD A CHANCE AGAINST US!
WINNERS: KREE AND SKRULL!
SO...
WHAT DO WE DO NOW?
I DUNNO.

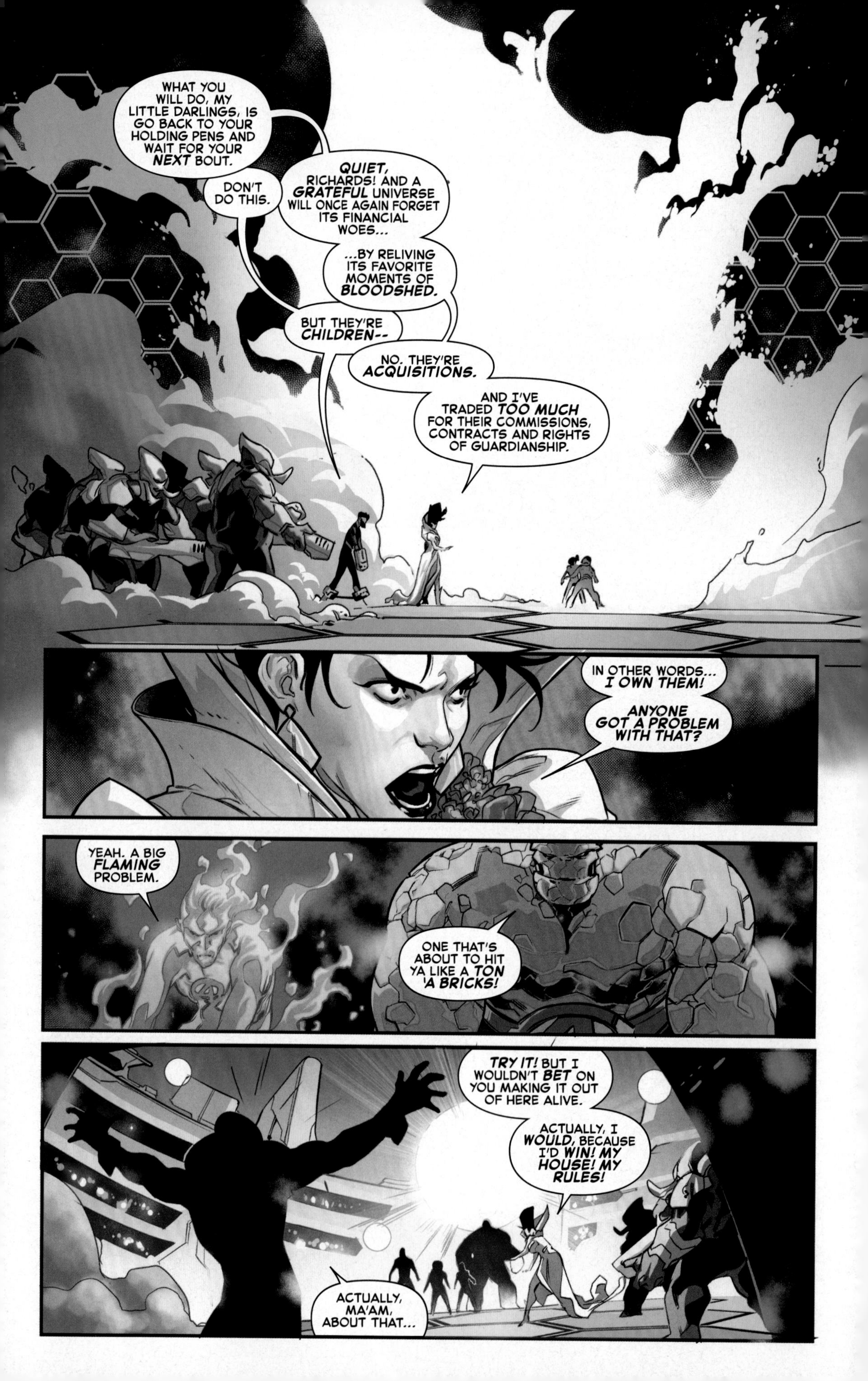

WHAT YOU WILL DO, MY LITTLE DARLINGS, IS GO BACK TO YOUR HOLDING PENS AND WAIT FOR YOUR NEXT BOUT.
DON'T DO THIS.
QUIET, RICHARDS! AND A GRATEFUL UNIVERSE WILL ONCE AGAIN FORGET ITS FINANCIAL WOES...
...BY RELIVING ITS FAVORITE MOMENTS OF BLOODSHED.
BUT THEY'RE CHILDREN--
NO. THEY'RE ACQUISITIONS.
AND I'VE TRADED TOO MUCH FOR THEIR COMMISSIONS, CONTRACTS AND RIGHTS OF GUARDIANSHIP.
IN OTHER WORDS... I OWN THEM!
ANYONE GOT A PROBLEM WITH THAT?
YEAH. A BIG FLAMING PROBLEM.
ONE THAT'S ABOUT TO HIT YA LIKE A TON 'A BRICKS!
TRY IT! BUT I WOULDN'T BET ON YOU MAKING IT OUT OF HERE ALIVE.
ACTUALLY, I WOULD, BECAUSE I'D WIN! MY HOUSE! MY RULES!
ACTUALLY, MA'AM, ABOUT THAT...

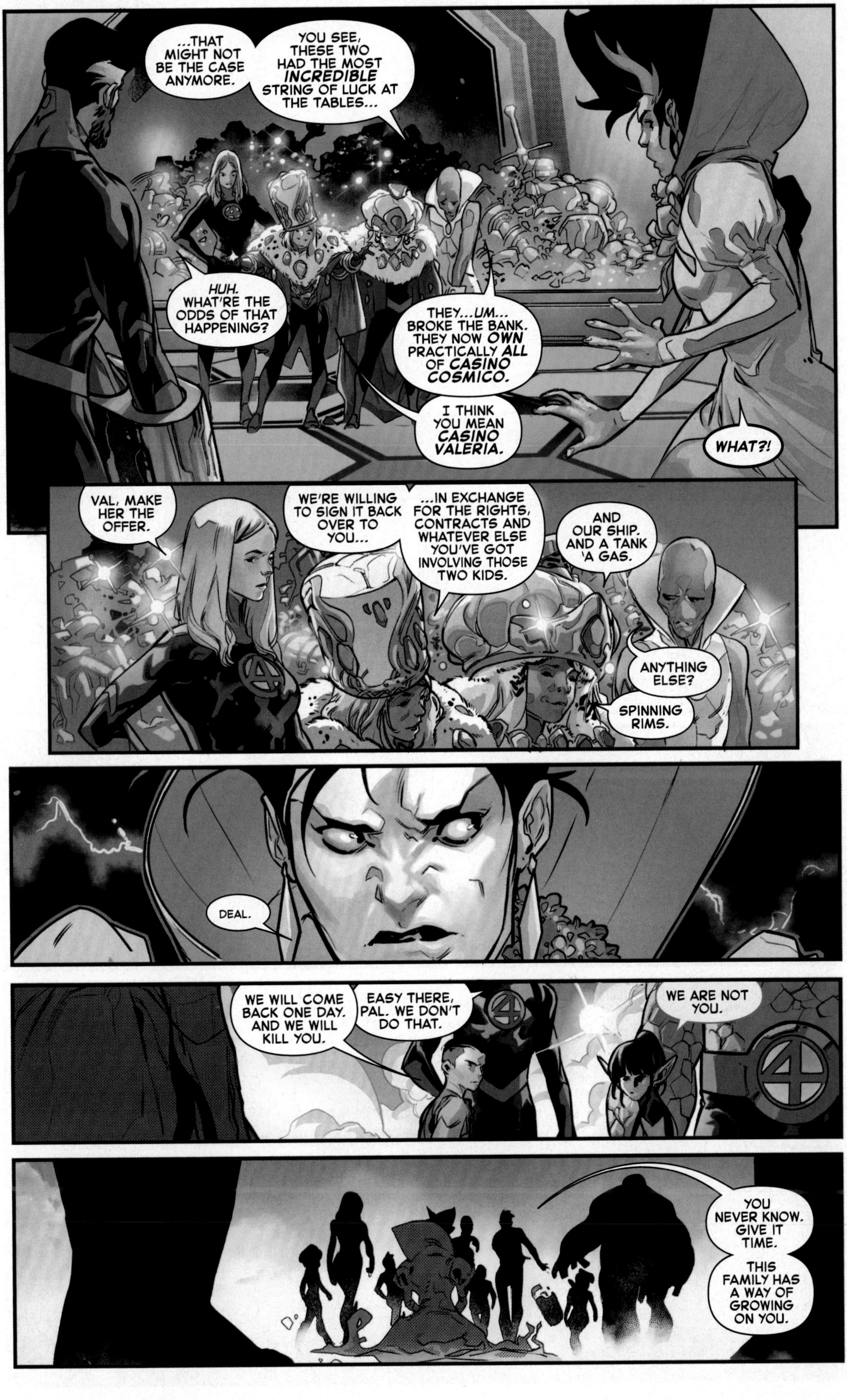
...THAT MIGHT NOT BE THE CASE ANYMORE.
YOU SEE, THESE TWO HAD THE MOST *INCREDIBLE* STRING OF LUCK AT THE TABLES...
HUH. WHAT'RE THE ODDS OF THAT HAPPENING?
THEY...UM... BROKE THE BANK. THEY NOW **OWN** PRACTICALLY **ALL** OF **CASINO COSMICO.**
I THINK YOU MEAN **CASINO VALERIA.**
WHAT?!
VAL, MAKE HER THE OFFER.
WE'RE WILLING TO SIGN IT BACK OVER TO YOU...
...IN EXCHANGE FOR THE RIGHTS, CONTRACTS AND WHATEVER ELSE YOU'VE GOT INVOLVING THOSE TWO KIDS.
AND OUR SHIP. AND A TANK 'A GAS.
ANYTHING ELSE?
SPINNING RIMS.
DEAL.
WE WILL COME BACK ONE DAY. AND WE WILL KILL YOU.
EASY THERE, PAL. WE DON'T DO THAT.
WE ARE NOT YOU.
YOU NEVER KNOW. GIVE IT TIME.
THIS FAMILY HAS A WAY OF GROWING ON YOU.

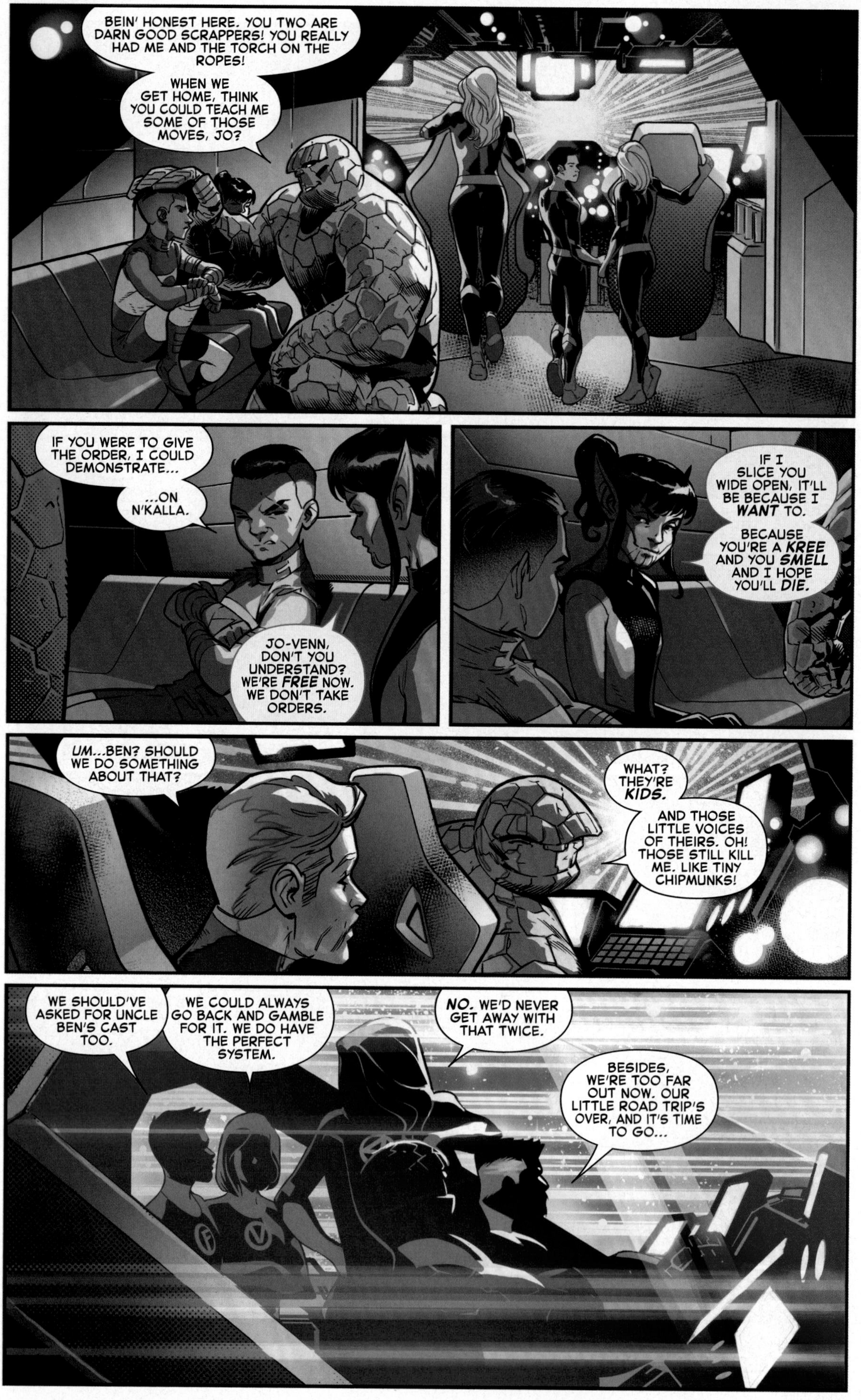
BEIN' HONEST HERE. YOU TWO ARE DARN GOOD SCRAPPERS! YOU REALLY HAD ME AND THE TORCH ON THE ROPES!
WHEN WE GET HOME, THINK YOU COULD TEACH ME SOME OF THOSE MOVES, JO?
IF YOU WERE TO GIVE THE ORDER, I COULD DEMONSTRATE...
...ON N'KALLA.
JO-VENN, DON'T YOU UNDERSTAND? WE'RE FREE NOW. WE DON'T TAKE ORDERS.
IF I SLICE YOU WIDE OPEN, IT'LL BE BECAUSE I WANT TO.
BECAUSE YOU'RE A KREE AND YOU SMELL AND I HOPE YOU'LL DIE.
UM...BEN? SHOULD WE DO SOMETHING ABOUT THAT?
WHAT? THEY'RE KIDS.
AND THOSE LITTLE VOICES OF THEIRS. OH! THOSE STILL KILL ME. LIKE TINY CHIPMUNKS!
WE SHOULD'VE ASKED FOR UNCLE BEN'S CAST TOO.
WE COULD ALWAYS GO BACK AND GAMBLE FOR IT. WE DO HAVE THE PERFECT SYSTEM.
NO. WE'D NEVER GET AWAY WITH THAT TWICE.
BESIDES, WE'RE TOO FAR OUT NOW. OUR LITTLE ROAD TRIP'S OVER, AND IT'S TIME TO GO...

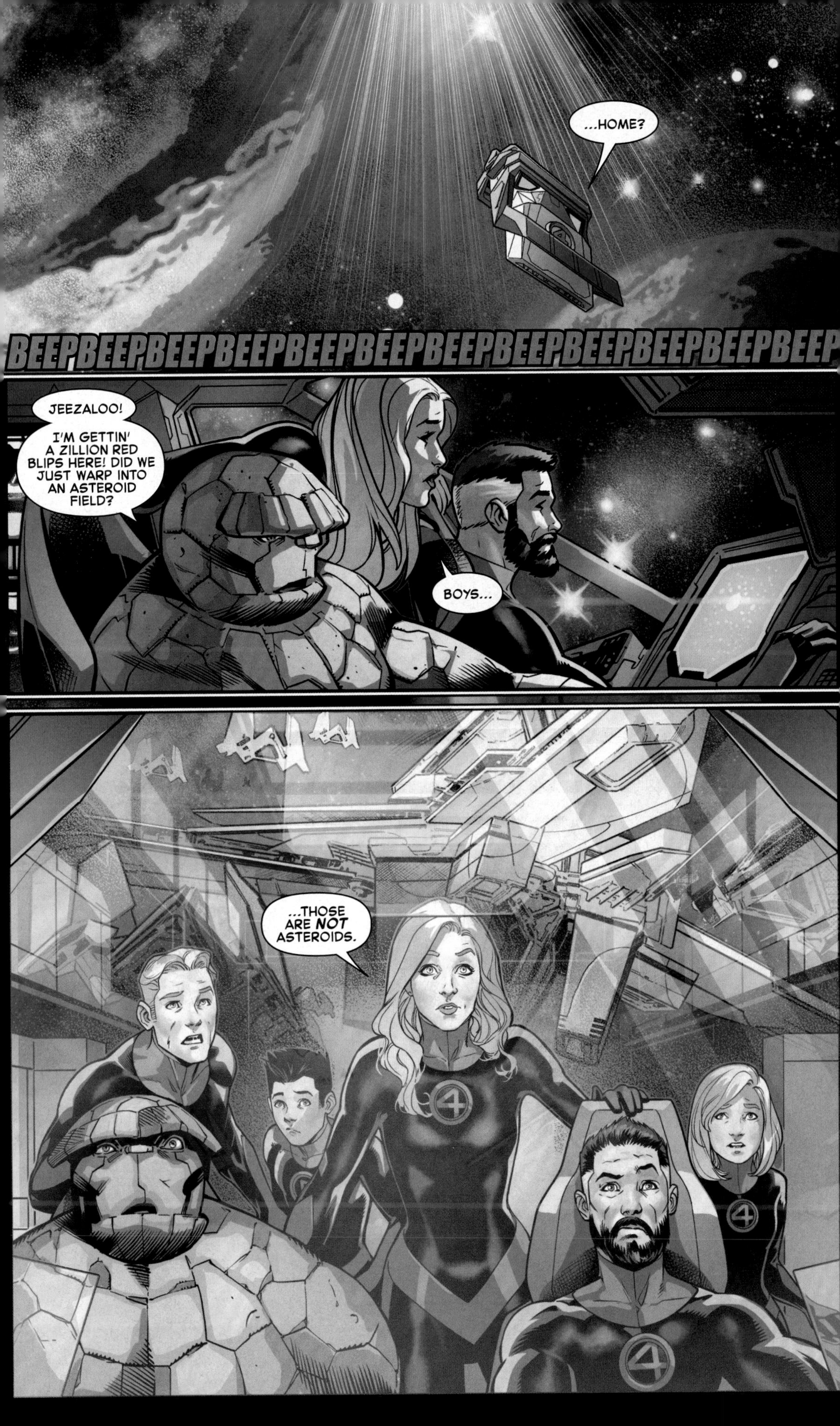
...HOME?
BEEPBEEPBEEPBEEPBEEPBEEPBEEPBEEPBEEPBEEPBEEPBEEPBEEP
JEEZALOO!
I'M GETTIN' A ZILLION RED BLIPS HERE! DID WE JUST WARP INTO AN ASTEROID FIELD?
BOYS...
...THOSE ARE NOT ASTEROIDS.

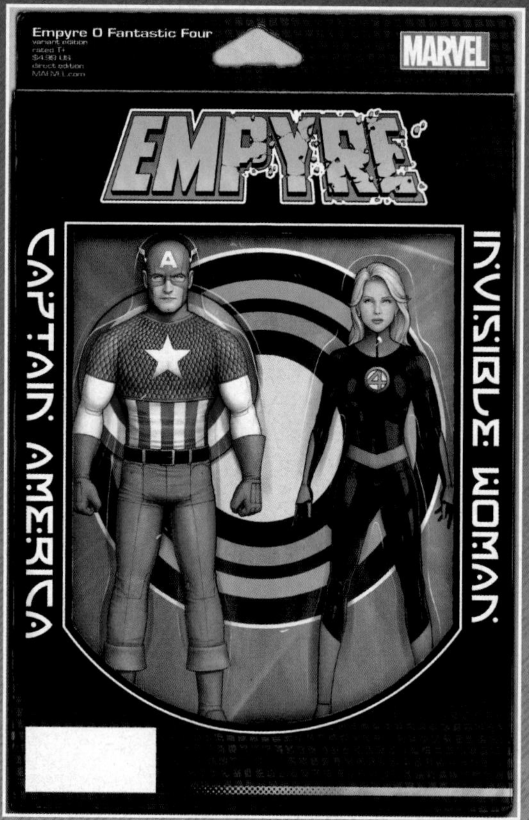
Empyre 0 Fantastic Four
MARVEL
EMPYRE
CAPTAIN AMERICA
INVISIBLE WOMAN

Empyre: Fantastic Four #0 Action Figure variant by
John Tyler Christopher

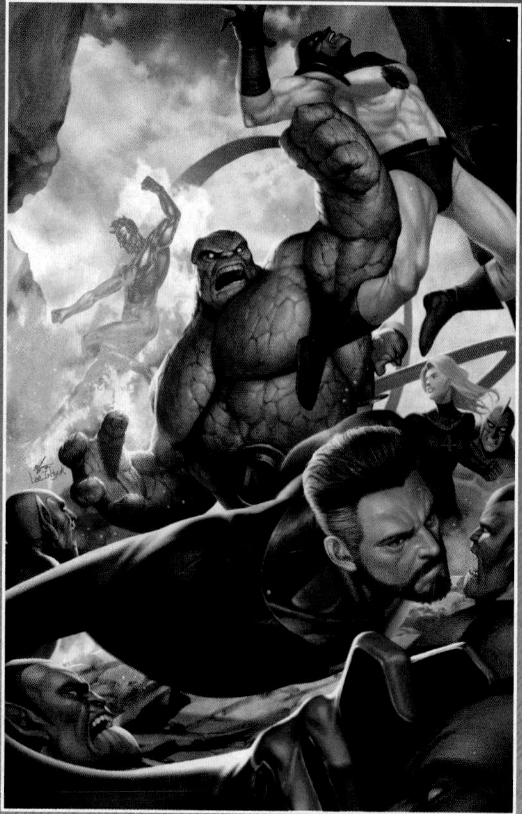

Empyre: Fantastic Four #0 variant by
InHyuk Lee

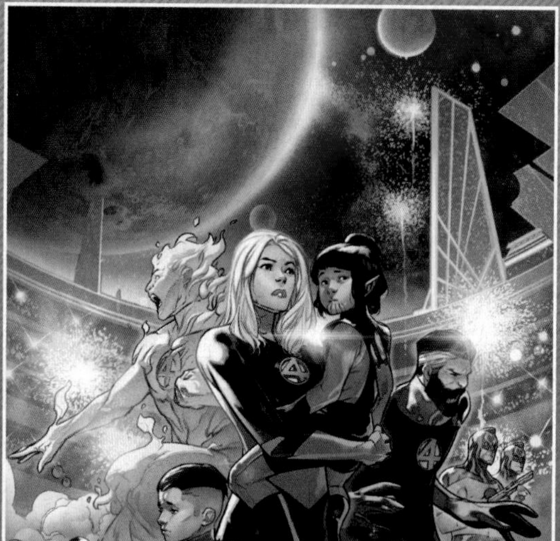

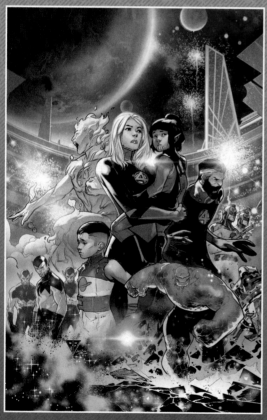

Empyre: Fantastic Four #0 variant by
R.B. Silva

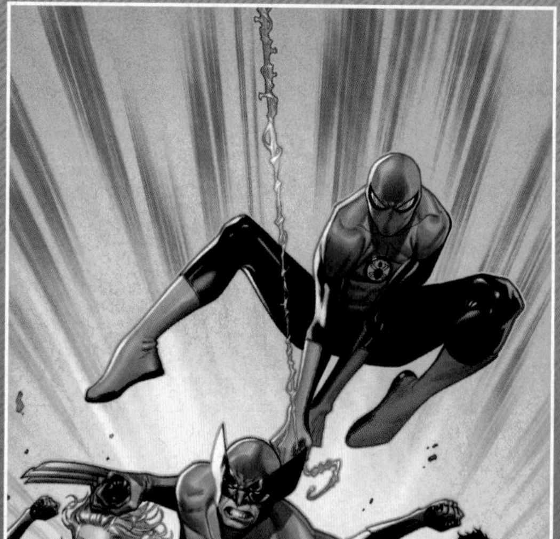

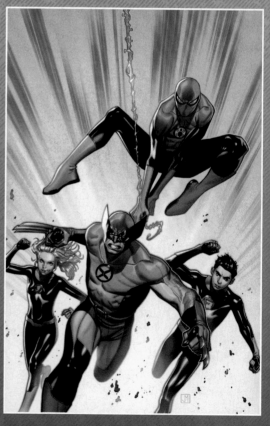

#21 variant by
Jorge Molina

21

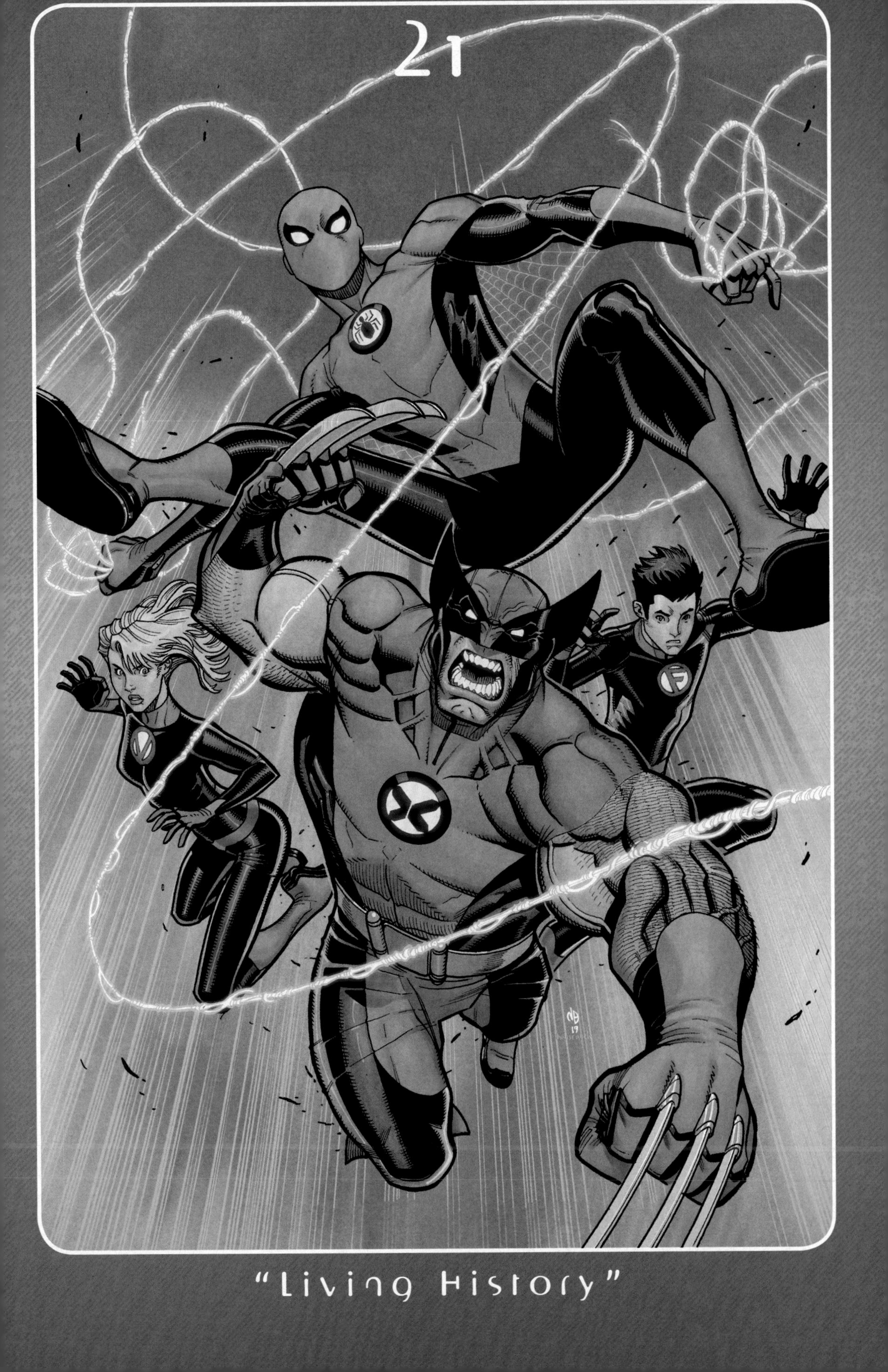

"Living History"

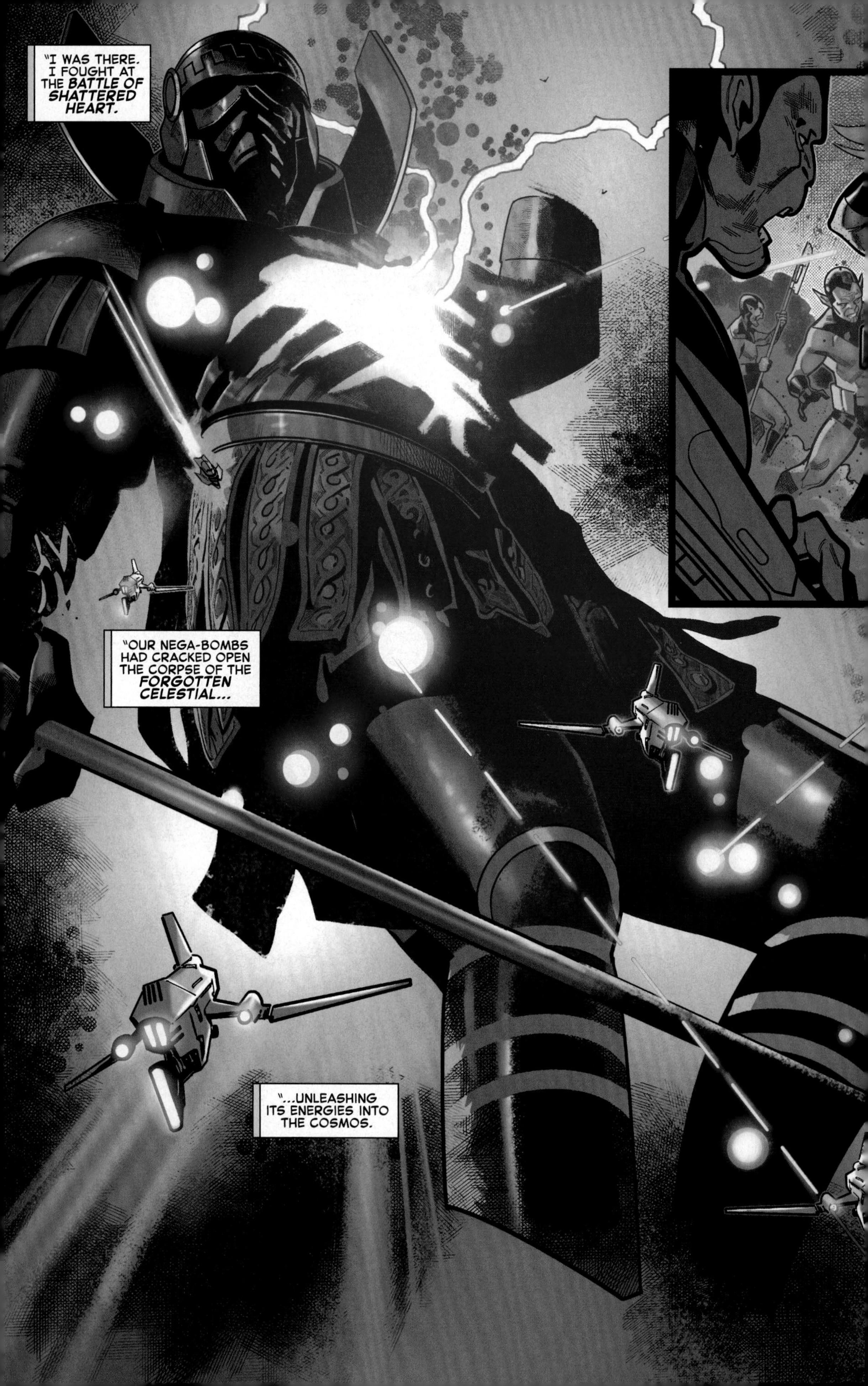
"I WAS THERE. I FOUGHT AT THE *BATTLE OF SHATTERED HEART.*
"OUR NEGA-BOMBS HAD CRACKED OPEN THE CORPSE OF THE *FORGOTTEN CELESTIAL...*
"...UNLEASHING ITS ENERGIES INTO THE COSMOS.

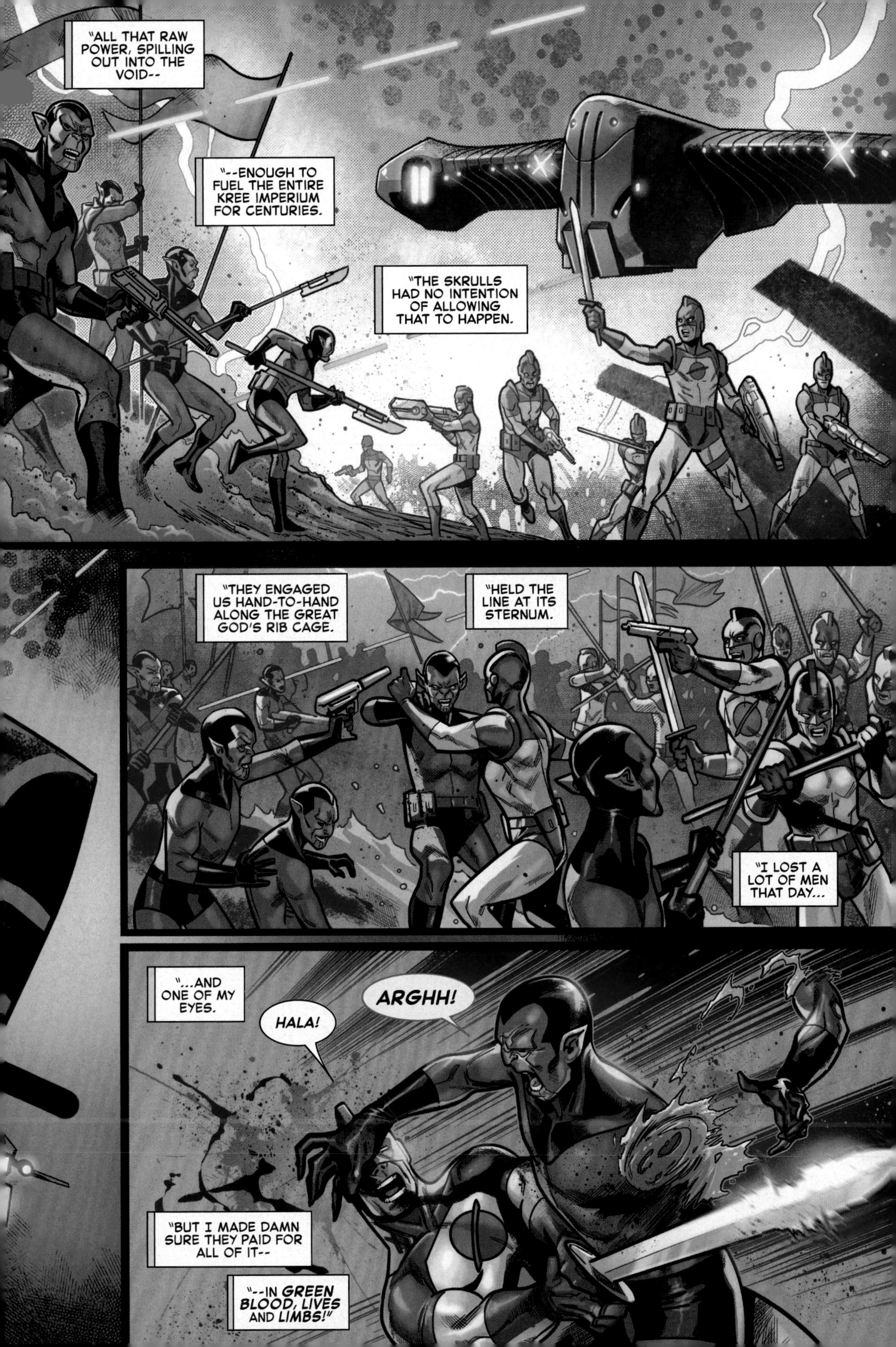
"ALL THAT RAW POWER, SPILLING OUT INTO THE VOID--
"--ENOUGH TO FUEL THE ENTIRE KREE IMPERIUM FOR CENTURIES.
"THE SKRULLS HAD NO INTENTION OF ALLOWING THAT TO HAPPEN.
"THEY ENGAGED US HAND-TO-HAND ALONG THE GREAT GOD'S RIB CAGE.
"HELD THE LINE AT ITS STERNUM.
"I LOST A LOT OF MEN THAT DAY...
"...AND ONE OF MY EYES.
HALA!
ARGHH!
"BUT I MADE DAMN SURE THEY PAID FOR ALL OF IT--
"--IN GREEN BLOOD, LIVES AND LIMBS!"

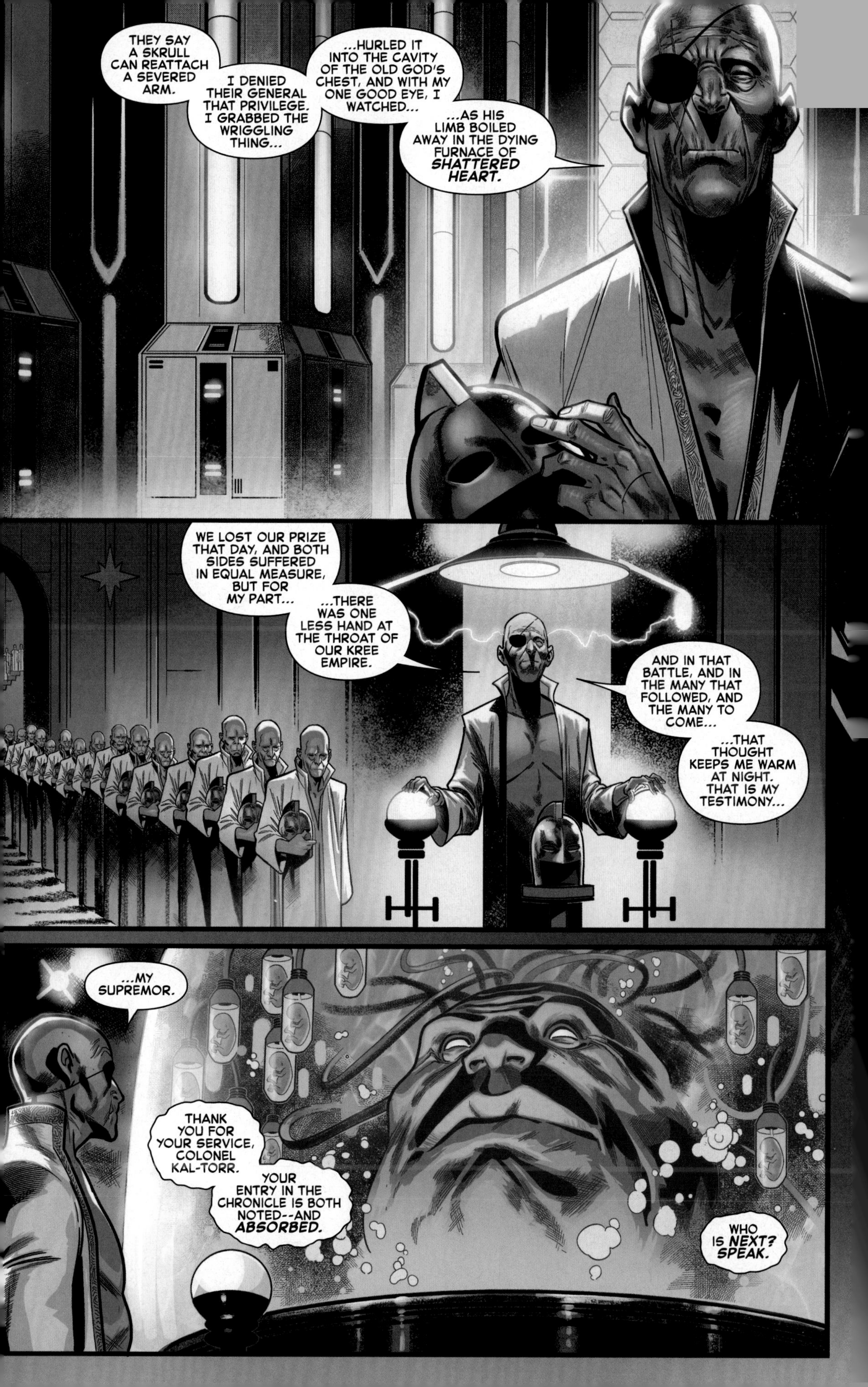
THEY SAY A SKRULL CAN REATTACH A SEVERED ARM.
I DENIED THEIR GENERAL THAT PRIVILEGE. I GRABBED THE WRIGGLING THING...
...HURLED IT INTO THE CAVITY OF THE OLD GOD'S CHEST, AND WITH MY ONE GOOD EYE, I WATCHED...
...AS HIS LIMB BOILED AWAY IN THE DYING FURNACE OF *SHATTERED HEART.*
WE LOST OUR PRIZE THAT DAY, AND BOTH SIDES SUFFERED IN EQUAL MEASURE, BUT FOR MY PART...
...THERE WAS ONE LESS HAND AT THE THROAT OF OUR KREE EMPIRE.
AND IN THAT BATTLE, AND IN THE MANY THAT FOLLOWED, AND THE MANY TO COME...
...THAT THOUGHT KEEPS ME WARM AT NIGHT. THAT IS MY TESTIMONY...
...MY SUPREMOR.
THANK YOU FOR YOUR SERVICE, COLONEL KAL-TORR.
YOUR ENTRY IN THE CHRONICLE IS BOTH NOTED--AND *ABSORBED.*
WHO IS *NEXT? SPEAK.*

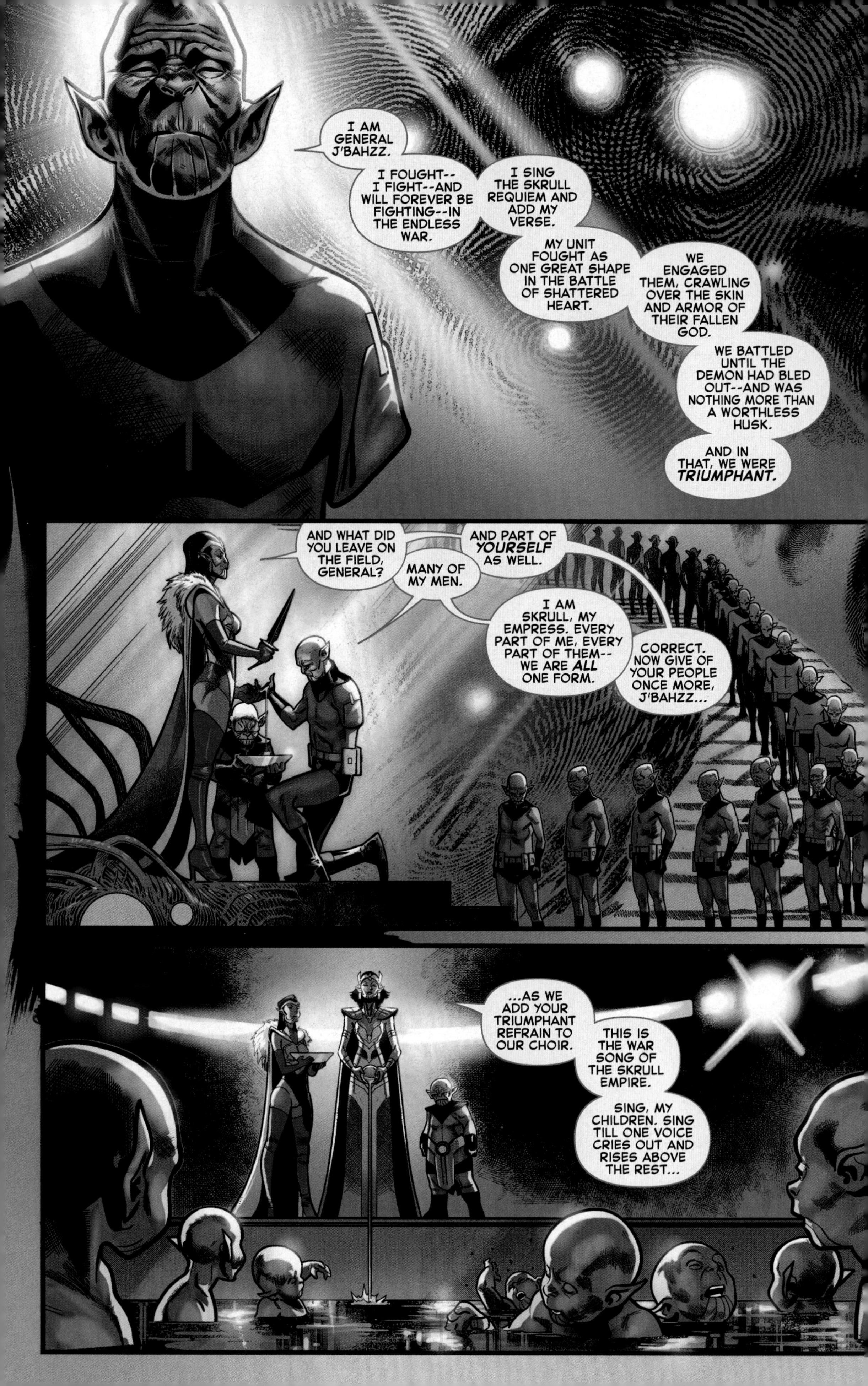
I AM GENERAL J'BAHZZ.
I FOUGHT--I FIGHT--AND WILL FOREVER BE FIGHTING--IN THE ENDLESS WAR.
I SING THE SKRULL REQUIEM AND ADD MY VERSE.
MY UNIT FOUGHT AS ONE GREAT SHAPE IN THE BATTLE OF SHATTERED HEART.
WE ENGAGED THEM, CRAWLING OVER THE SKIN AND ARMOR OF THEIR FALLEN GOD.
WE BATTLED UNTIL THE DEMON HAD BLED OUT--AND WAS NOTHING MORE THAN A WORTHLESS HUSK.
AND IN THAT, WE WERE *TRIUMPHANT.*
AND WHAT DID YOU LEAVE ON THE FIELD, GENERAL?
MANY OF MY MEN.
AND PART OF *YOURSELF* AS WELL.
I AM SKRULL, MY EMPRESS. EVERY PART OF ME, EVERY PART OF THEM--WE ARE *ALL* ONE FORM.
CORRECT. NOW GIVE OF YOUR PEOPLE ONCE MORE, J'BAHZZ...
...AS WE ADD YOUR TRIUMPHANT REFRAIN TO OUR CHOIR.
THIS IS THE WAR SONG OF THE SKRULL EMPIRE.
SING, MY CHILDREN. SING TILL ONE VOICE CRIES OUT AND RISES ABOVE THE REST...

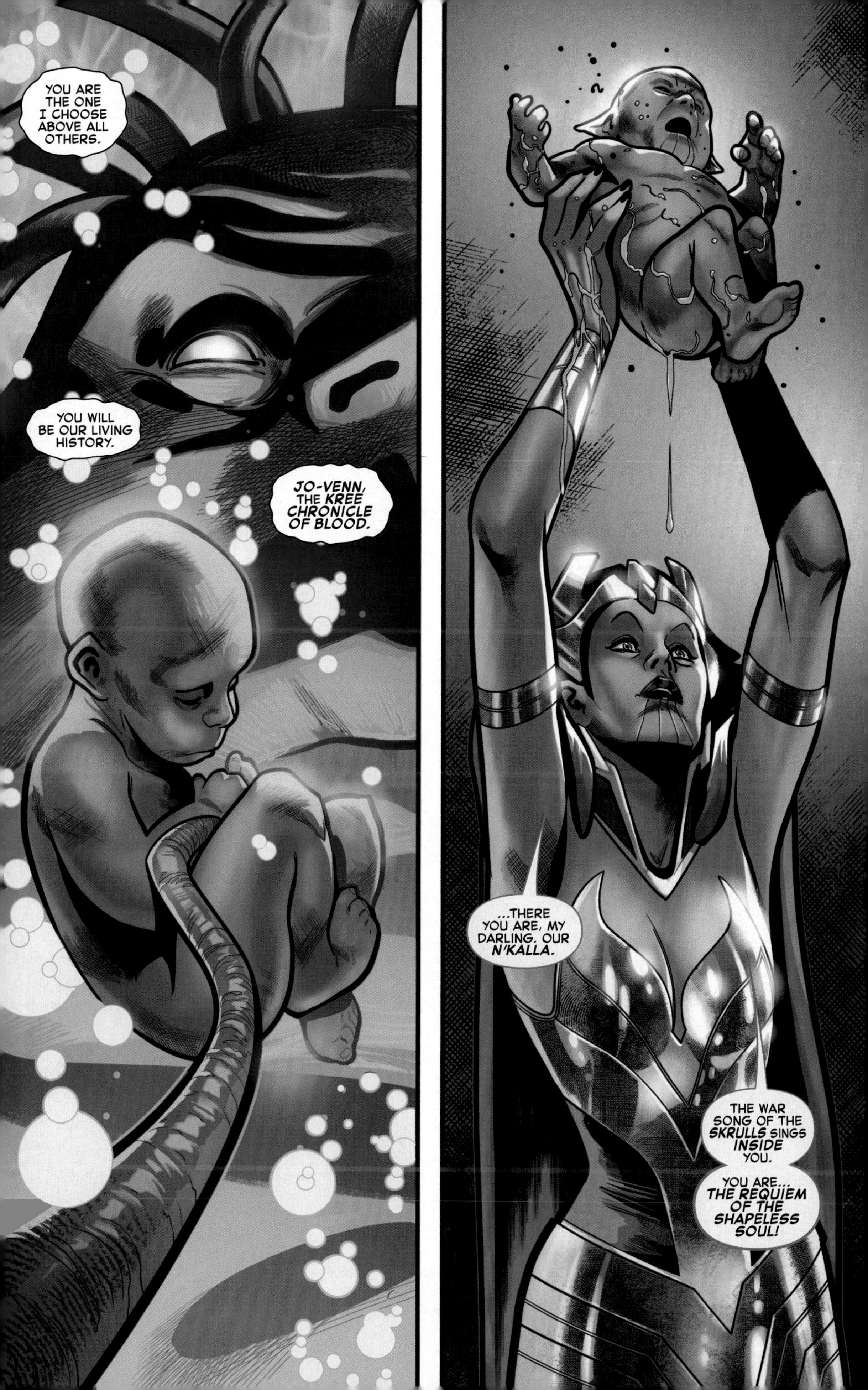
YOU ARE THE ONE I CHOOSE ABOVE ALL OTHERS.
YOU WILL BE OUR LIVING HISTORY.
JO-VENN, THE KREE CHRONICLE OF BLOOD.
...THERE YOU ARE, MY DARLING. OUR N'KALLA.
THE WAR SONG OF THE SKRULLS SINGS INSIDE YOU.
YOU ARE... THE REQUIEM OF THE SHAPELESS SOUL!

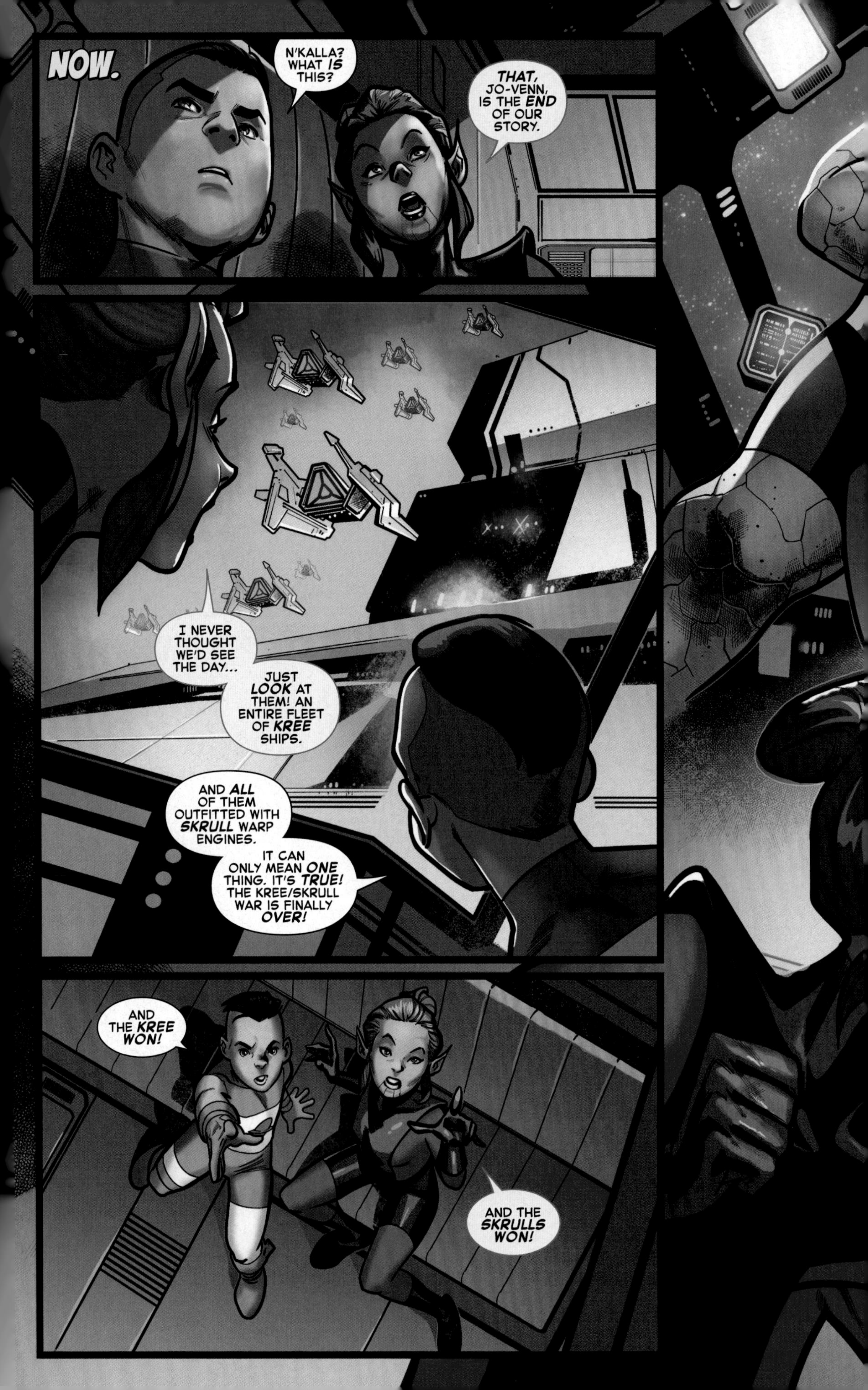
NOW.
N'KALLA? WHAT IS THIS?
THAT, JO-VENN, IS THE END OF OUR STORY.
I NEVER THOUGHT WE'D SEE THE DAY...
JUST LOOK AT THEM! AN ENTIRE FLEET OF KREE SHIPS.
AND ALL OF THEM OUTFITTED WITH SKRULL WARP ENGINES.
IT CAN ONLY MEAN ONE THING. IT'S TRUE! THE KREE/SKRULL WAR IS FINALLY OVER!
AND THE KREE WON!
AND THE SKRULLS WON!

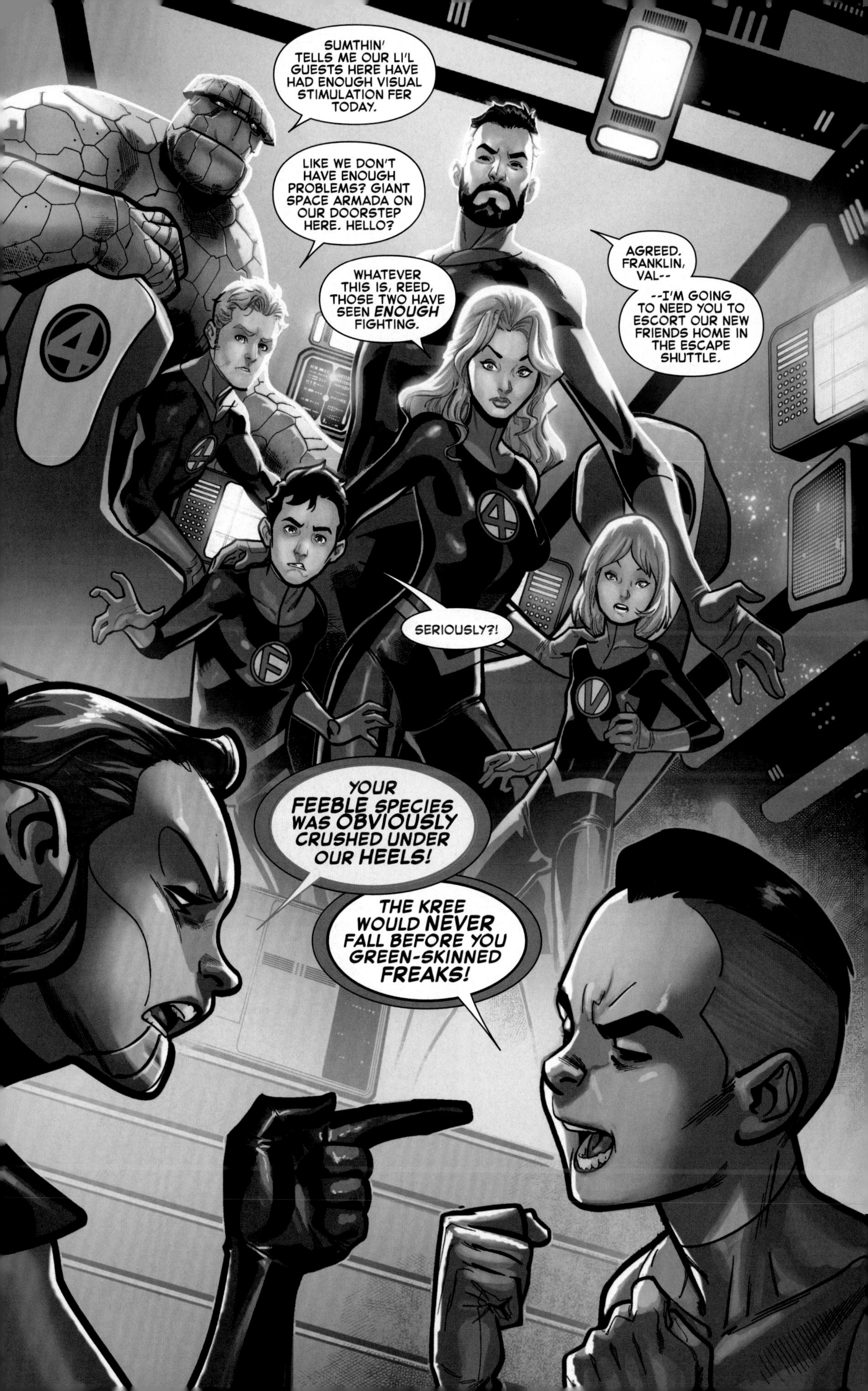
SUMTHIN' TELLS ME OUR LI'L GUESTS HERE HAVE HAD ENOUGH VISUAL STIMULATION FER TODAY.
LIKE WE DON'T HAVE ENOUGH PROBLEMS? GIANT SPACE ARMADA ON OUR DOORSTEP HERE. HELLO?
WHATEVER THIS IS, REED, THOSE TWO HAVE SEEN ENOUGH FIGHTING.
AGREED. FRANKLIN, VAL--
--I'M GOING TO NEED YOU TO ESCORT OUR NEW FRIENDS HOME IN THE ESCAPE SHUTTLE.
SERIOUSLY?!
YOUR FEEBLE SPECIES WAS OBVIOUSLY CRUSHED UNDER OUR HEELS!
THE KREE WOULD NEVER FALL BEFORE YOU GREEN-SKINNED FREAKS!

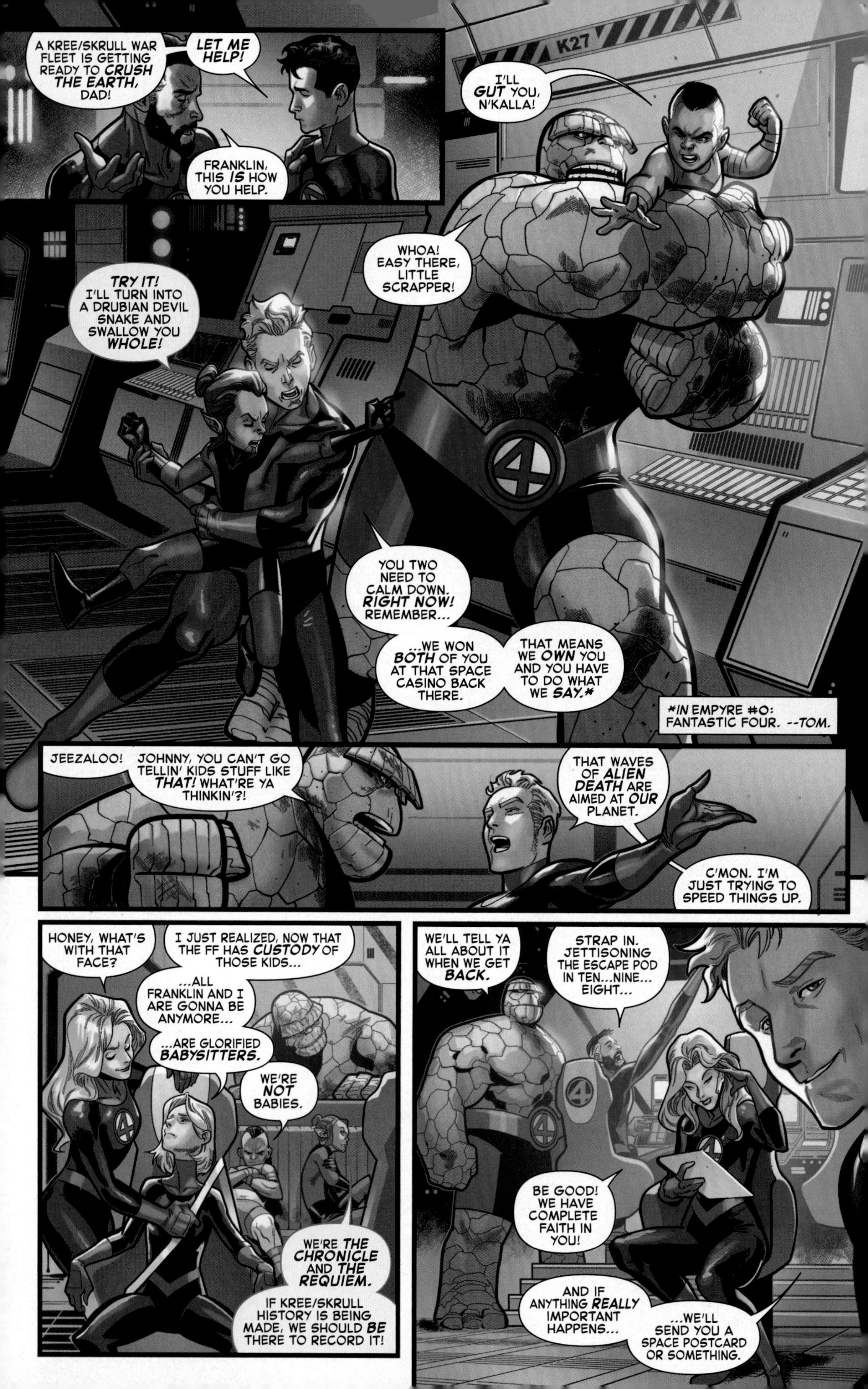

A KREE/SKRULL WAR FLEET IS GETTING READY TO CRUSH THE EARTH, DAD!
LET ME HELP!
FRANKLIN, THIS IS HOW YOU HELP.
I'LL GUT YOU, N'KALLA!
WHOA! EASY THERE, LITTLE SCRAPPER!
TRY IT! I'LL TURN INTO A DRUBIAN DEVIL SNAKE AND SWALLOW YOU WHOLE!
YOU TWO NEED TO CALM DOWN. RIGHT NOW! REMEMBER...
...WE WON BOTH OF YOU AT THAT SPACE CASINO BACK THERE.
THAT MEANS WE OWN YOU AND YOU HAVE TO DO WHAT WE SAY.*
*IN EMPYRE #0: FANTASTIC FOUR. --TOM.
JEEZALOO!
JOHNNY, YOU CAN'T GO TELLIN' KIDS STUFF LIKE THAT! WHAT'RE YA THINKIN'?!
THAT WAVES OF ALIEN DEATH ARE AIMED AT OUR PLANET.
C'MON. I'M JUST TRYING TO SPEED THINGS UP.
HONEY, WHAT'S WITH THAT FACE?
I JUST REALIZED, NOW THAT THE FF HAS CUSTODY OF THOSE KIDS...
...ALL FRANKLIN AND I ARE GONNA BE ANYMORE...
...ARE GLORIFIED BABYSITTERS.
WE'RE NOT BABIES.
WE'RE THE CHRONICLE AND THE REQUIEM.
IF KREE/SKRULL HISTORY IS BEING MADE, WE SHOULD BE THERE TO RECORD IT!
WE'LL TELL YA ALL ABOUT IT WHEN WE GET BACK.
STRAP IN. JETTISONING THE ESCAPE POD IN TEN...NINE... EIGHT...
BE GOOD! WE HAVE COMPLETE FAITH IN YOU!
AND IF ANYTHING REALLY IMPORTANT HAPPENS...
...WE'LL SEND YOU A SPACE POSTCARD OR SOMETHING.

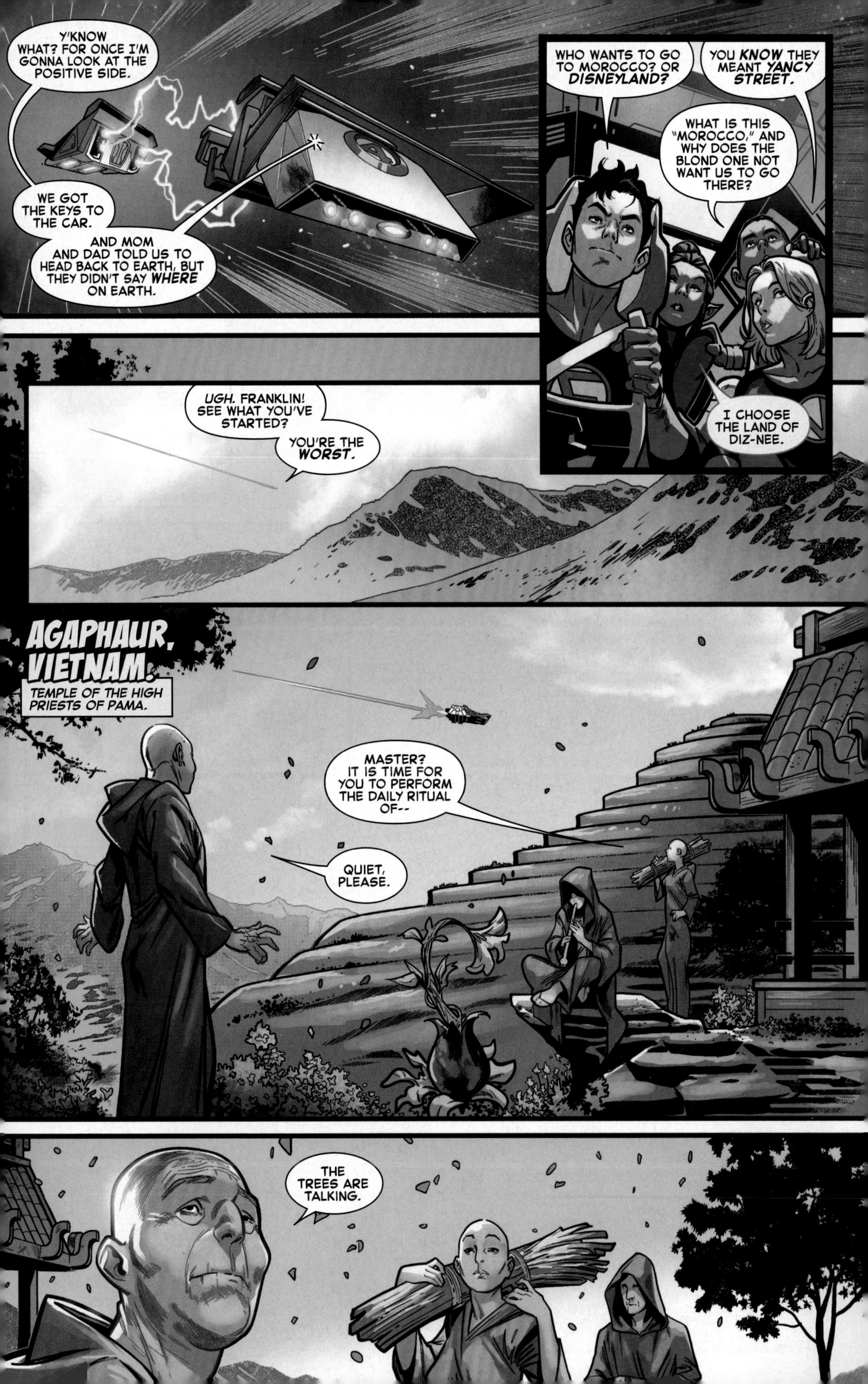
Y'KNOW WHAT? FOR ONCE I'M GONNA LOOK AT THE POSITIVE SIDE.
WE GOT THE KEYS TO THE CAR.
AND MOM AND DAD TOLD US TO HEAD BACK TO EARTH, BUT THEY DIDN'T SAY WHERE ON EARTH.
WHO WANTS TO GO TO MOROCCO? OR DISNEYLAND?
YOU KNOW THEY MEANT YANCY STREET.
WHAT IS THIS "MOROCCO," AND WHY DOES THE BLOND ONE NOT WANT US TO GO THERE?
I CHOOSE THE LAND OF DIZ-NEE.
UGH. FRANKLIN! SEE WHAT YOU'VE STARTED?
YOU'RE THE WORST.
AGAPHAUR, VIETNAM.
TEMPLE OF THE HIGH PRIESTS OF PAMA.
MASTER? IT IS TIME FOR YOU TO PERFORM THE DAILY RITUAL OF--
QUIET, PLEASE.
THE TREES ARE TALKING.

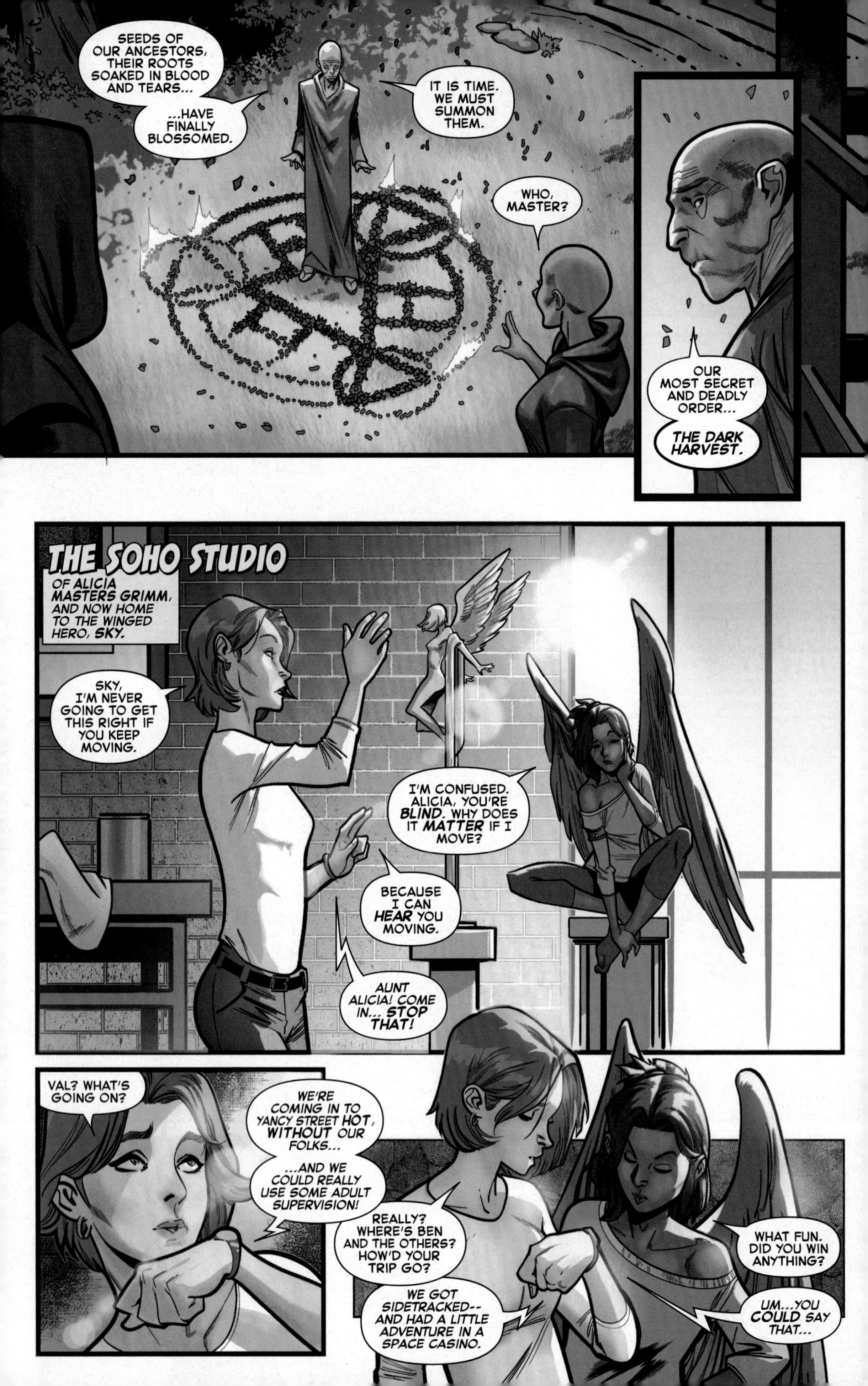
SEEDS OF OUR ANCESTORS, THEIR ROOTS SOAKED IN BLOOD AND TEARS...
...HAVE FINALLY BLOSSOMED.
IT IS TIME. WE MUST SUMMON THEM.
WHO, MASTER?
OUR MOST SECRET AND DEADLY ORDER...
THE DARK HARVEST.
THE SOHO STUDIO
OF ALICIA MASTERS GRIMM, AND NOW HOME TO THE WINGED HERO, SKY.
SKY, I'M NEVER GOING TO GET THIS RIGHT IF YOU KEEP MOVING.
I'M CONFUSED. ALICIA, YOU'RE BLIND. WHY DOES IT MATTER IF I MOVE?
BECAUSE I CAN HEAR YOU MOVING.
AUNT ALICIA! COME IN... STOP THAT!
VAL? WHAT'S GOING ON?
WE'RE COMING IN TO YANCY STREET HOT, WITHOUT OUR FOLKS...
...AND WE COULD REALLY USE SOME ADULT SUPERVISION!
REALLY? WHERE'S BEN AND THE OTHERS? HOW'D YOUR TRIP GO?
WE GOT SIDETRACKED-- AND HAD A LITTLE ADVENTURE IN A SPACE CASINO.
WHAT FUN. DID YOU WIN ANYTHING?
UM...YOU COULD SAY THAT...

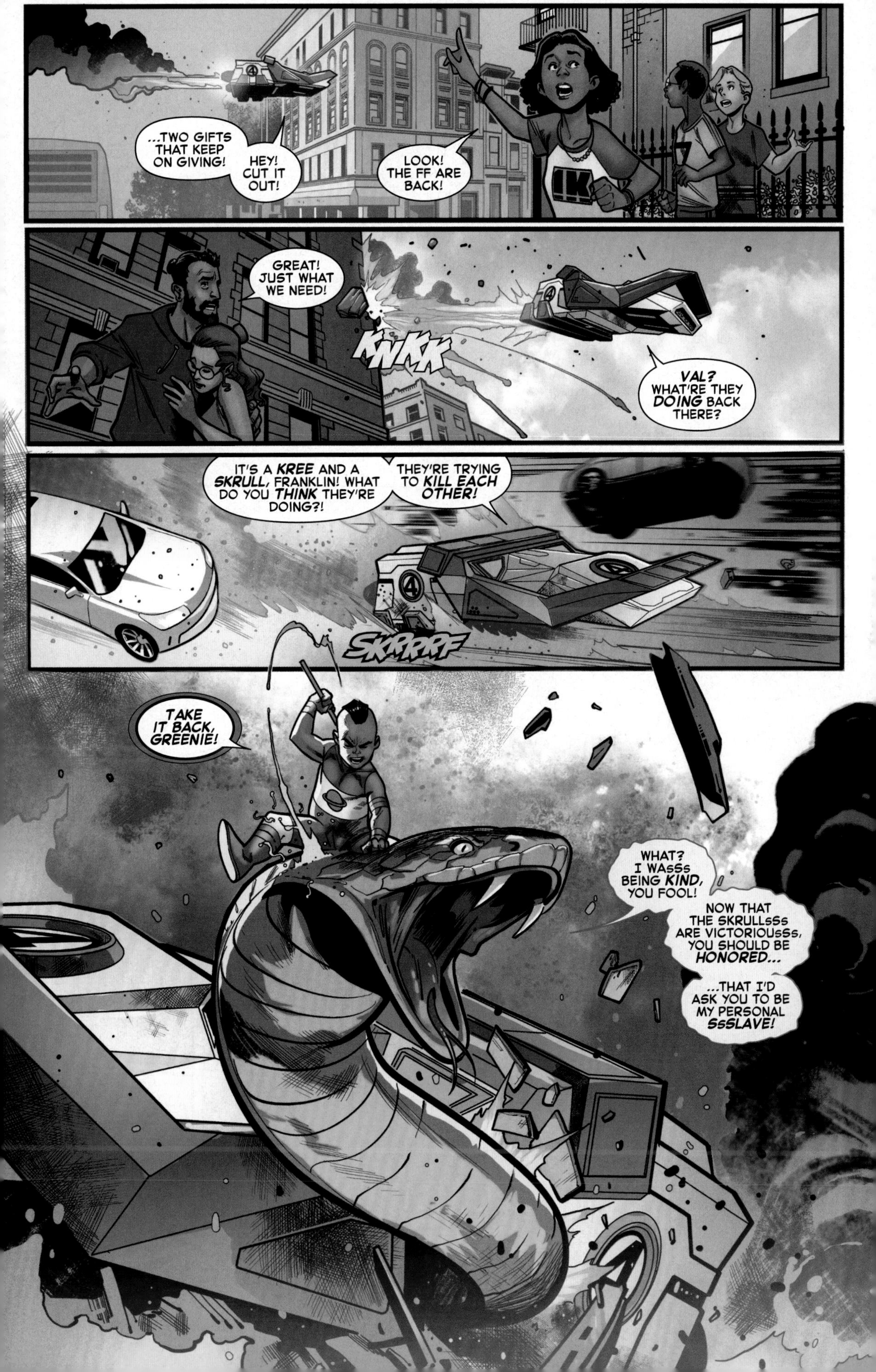
...TWO GIFTS THAT KEEP ON GIVING!
HEY! CUT IT OUT!
LOOK! THE FF ARE BACK!
GREAT! JUST WHAT WE NEED!
KNKK
VAL? WHAT'RE THEY DOING BACK THERE?
IT'S A KREE AND A SKRULL, FRANKLIN! WHAT DO YOU THINK THEY'RE DOING?!
THEY'RE TRYING TO KILL EACH OTHER!
SKRRRF
TAKE IT BACK, GREENIE!
WHAT? I WASsS BEING KIND, YOU FOOL!
NOW THAT THE SKRULLsSs ARE VICTORIOUsSs, YOU SHOULD BE HONORED...
...THAT I'D ASK YOU TO BE MY PERSONAL SsSLAVE!

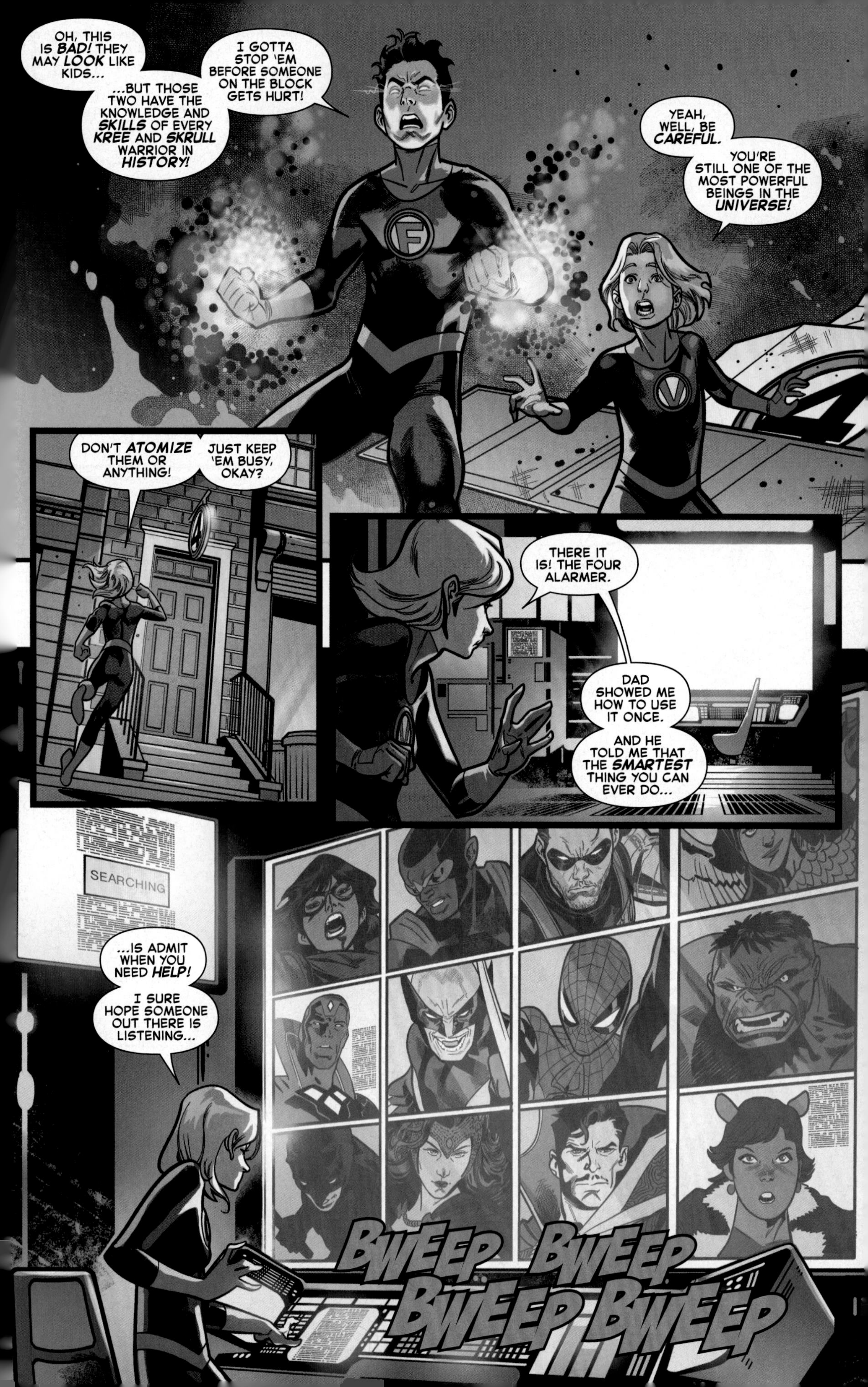
OH, THIS IS BAD! THEY MAY LOOK LIKE KIDS...
...BUT THOSE TWO HAVE THE KNOWLEDGE AND SKILLS OF EVERY KREE AND SKRULL WARRIOR IN HISTORY!
I GOTTA STOP 'EM BEFORE SOMEONE ON THE BLOCK GETS HURT!
YEAH, WELL, BE CAREFUL.
YOU'RE STILL ONE OF THE MOST POWERFUL BEINGS IN THE UNIVERSE!
DON'T ATOMIZE THEM OR ANYTHING!
JUST KEEP 'EM BUSY, OKAY?
THERE IT IS! THE FOUR ALARMER.
DAD SHOWED ME HOW TO USE IT ONCE.
AND HE TOLD ME THAT THE SMARTEST THING YOU CAN EVER DO...
SEARCHING
...IS ADMIT WHEN YOU NEED HELP!
I SURE HOPE SOMEONE OUT THERE IS LISTENING...
BWEEP BWEEP BWEEP BWEEP

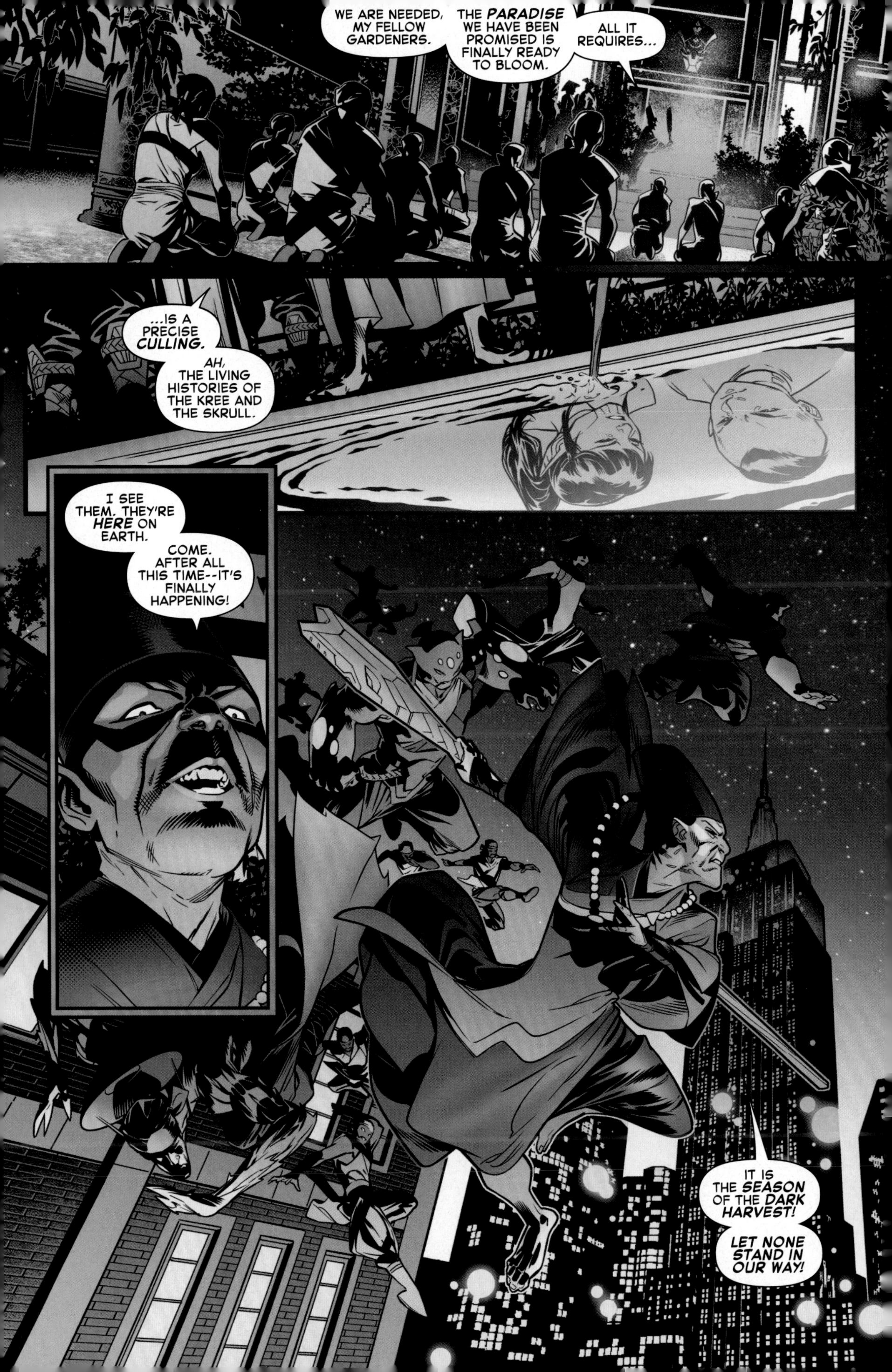
WE ARE NEEDED, MY FELLOW GARDENERS.
THE PARADISE WE HAVE BEEN PROMISED IS FINALLY READY TO BLOOM.
ALL IT REQUIRES...
...IS A PRECISE CULLING.
AH, THE LIVING HISTORIES OF THE KREE AND THE SKRULL.
I SEE THEM. THEY'RE HERE ON EARTH.
COME. AFTER ALL THIS TIME--IT'S FINALLY HAPPENING!
IT IS THE SEASON OF THE DARK HARVEST!
LET NONE STAND IN OUR WAY!

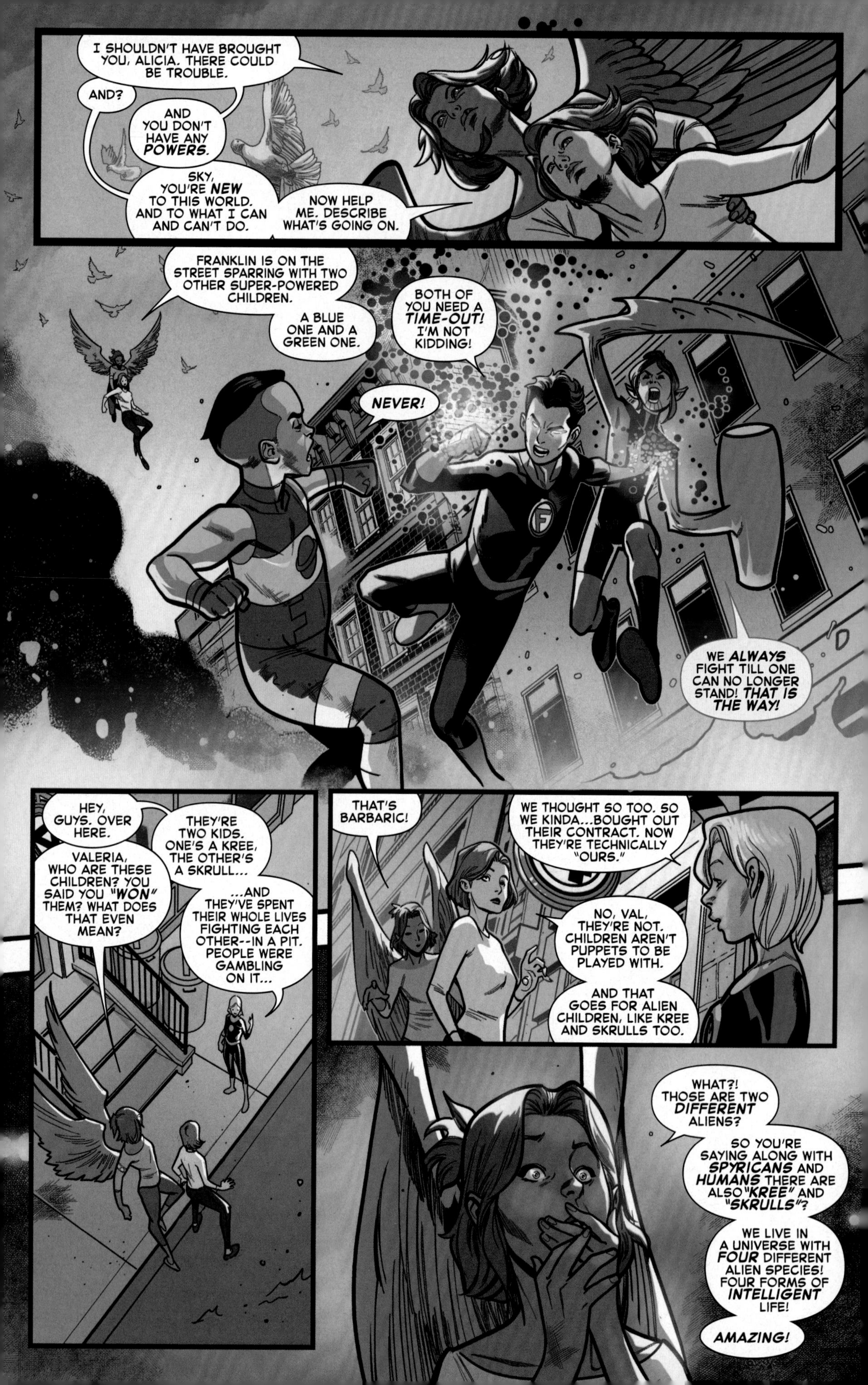

I SHOULDN'T HAVE BROUGHT YOU, ALICIA. THERE COULD BE TROUBLE.
AND?
AND YOU DON'T HAVE ANY POWERS.
SKY, YOU'RE NEW TO THIS WORLD. AND TO WHAT I CAN AND CAN'T DO.
NOW HELP ME. DESCRIBE WHAT'S GOING ON.
FRANKLIN IS ON THE STREET SPARRING WITH TWO OTHER SUPER-POWERED CHILDREN.
A BLUE ONE AND A GREEN ONE.
BOTH OF YOU NEED A TIME-OUT! I'M NOT KIDDING!
NEVER!
WE ALWAYS FIGHT TILL ONE CAN NO LONGER STAND! THAT IS THE WAY!
HEY, GUYS. OVER HERE.
VALERIA, WHO ARE THESE CHILDREN? YOU SAID YOU "WON" THEM? WHAT DOES THAT EVEN MEAN?
THEY'RE TWO KIDS. ONE'S A KREE, THE OTHER'S A SKRULL...
...AND THEY'VE SPENT THEIR WHOLE LIVES FIGHTING EACH OTHER--IN A PIT. PEOPLE WERE GAMBLING ON IT...
THAT'S BARBARIC!
WE THOUGHT SO TOO. SO WE KINDA...BOUGHT OUT THEIR CONTRACT. NOW THEY'RE TECHNICALLY "OURS."
NO, VAL, THEY'RE NOT. CHILDREN AREN'T PUPPETS TO BE PLAYED WITH.
AND THAT GOES FOR ALIEN CHILDREN, LIKE KREE AND SKRULLS TOO.
WHAT?! THOSE ARE TWO DIFFERENT ALIENS?
SO YOU'RE SAYING ALONG WITH SPYRICANS AND HUMANS THERE ARE ALSO "KREE" AND "SKRULLS"?
WE LIVE IN A UNIVERSE WITH FOUR DIFFERENT ALIEN SPECIES! FOUR FORMS OF INTELLIGENT LIFE!
AMAZING!

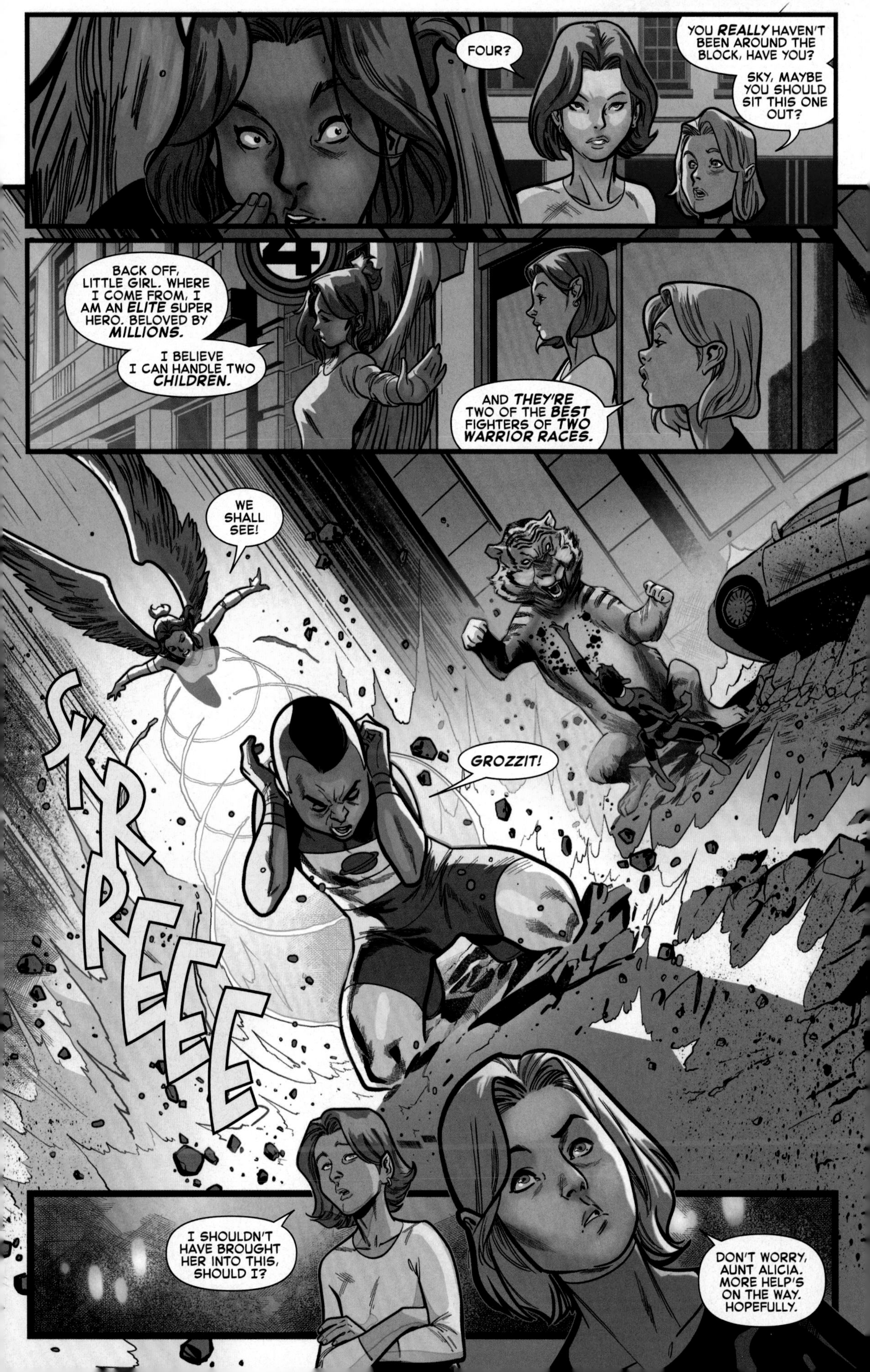
FOUR?
YOU REALLY HAVEN'T BEEN AROUND THE BLOCK, HAVE YOU?
SKY, MAYBE YOU SHOULD SIT THIS ONE OUT?
BACK OFF, LITTLE GIRL. WHERE I COME FROM, I AM AN ELITE SUPER HERO. BELOVED BY MILLIONS.
I BELIEVE I CAN HANDLE TWO CHILDREN.
AND THEY'RE TWO OF THE BEST FIGHTERS OF TWO WARRIOR RACES.
WE SHALL SEE!
SKREEEE
GROZZIT!
I SHOULDN'T HAVE BROUGHT HER INTO THIS, SHOULD I?
DON'T WORRY, AUNT ALICIA. MORE HELP'S ON THE WAY. HOPEFULLY.

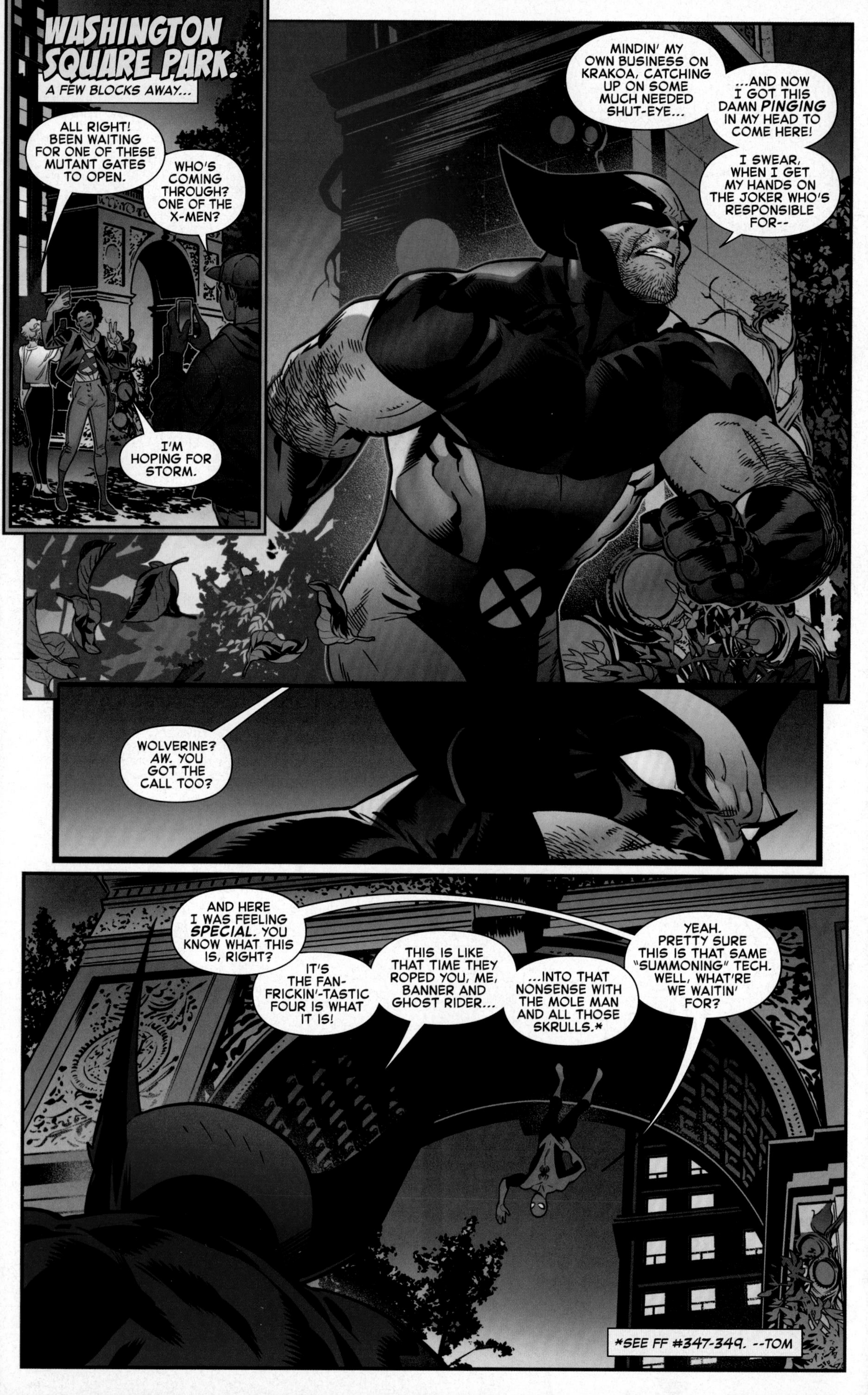
WASHINGTON SQUARE PARK.
A FEW BLOCKS AWAY...
ALL RIGHT! BEEN WAITING FOR ONE OF THESE MUTANT GATES TO OPEN.
WHO'S COMING THROUGH? ONE OF THE X-MEN?
I'M HOPING FOR STORM.
MINDIN' MY OWN BUSINESS ON KRAKOA, CATCHING UP ON SOME MUCH NEEDED SHUT-EYE...
...AND NOW I GOT THIS DAMN PINGING IN MY HEAD TO COME HERE!
I SWEAR, WHEN I GET MY HANDS ON THE JOKER WHO'S RESPONSIBLE FOR--
WOLVERINE? AW. YOU GOT THE CALL TOO?
AND HERE I WAS FEELING SPECIAL. YOU KNOW WHAT THIS IS, RIGHT?
IT'S THE FAN-FRICKIN'-TASTIC FOUR IS WHAT IT IS!
THIS IS LIKE THAT TIME THEY ROPED YOU, ME, BANNER AND GHOST RIDER...
...INTO THAT NONSENSE WITH THE MOLE MAN AND ALL THOSE SKRULLS.*
YEAH. PRETTY SURE THIS IS THAT SAME "SUMMONING" TECH. WELL, WHAT'RE WE WAITIN' FOR?
*SEE FF #347-349. --TOM

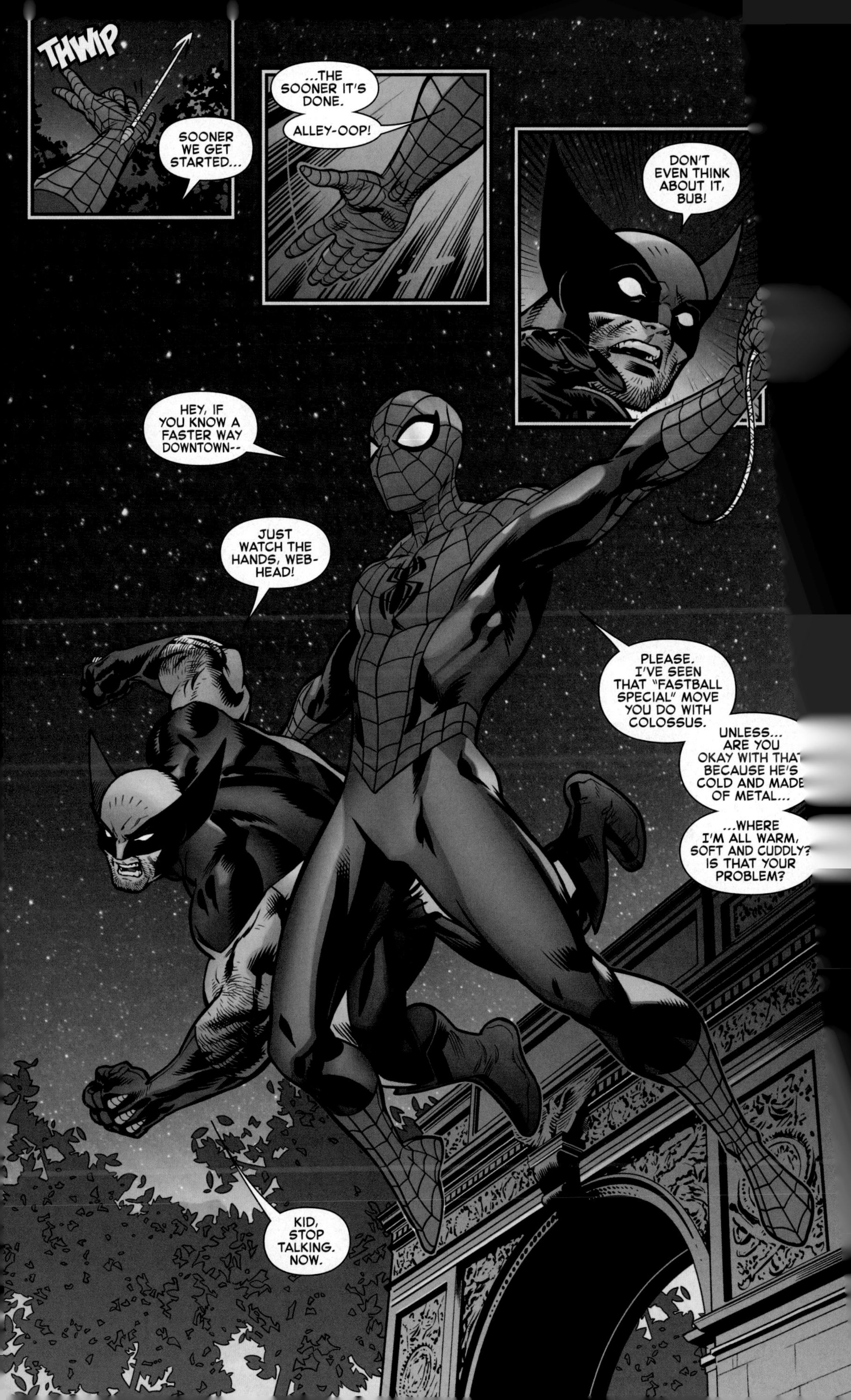
THWIP
SOONER WE GET STARTED...
...THE SOONER IT'S DONE.
ALLEY-OOP!
DON'T EVEN THINK ABOUT IT, BUB!
HEY, IF YOU KNOW A FASTER WAY DOWNTOWN--
JUST WATCH THE HANDS, WEB-HEAD!
PLEASE. I'VE SEEN THAT "FASTBALL SPECIAL" MOVE YOU DO WITH COLOSSUS.
UNLESS... ARE YOU OKAY WITH THAT BECAUSE HE'S COLD AND MADE OF METAL...
...WHERE I'M ALL WARM, SOFT AND CUDDLY? IS THAT YOUR PROBLEM?
KID, STOP TALKING. NOW.

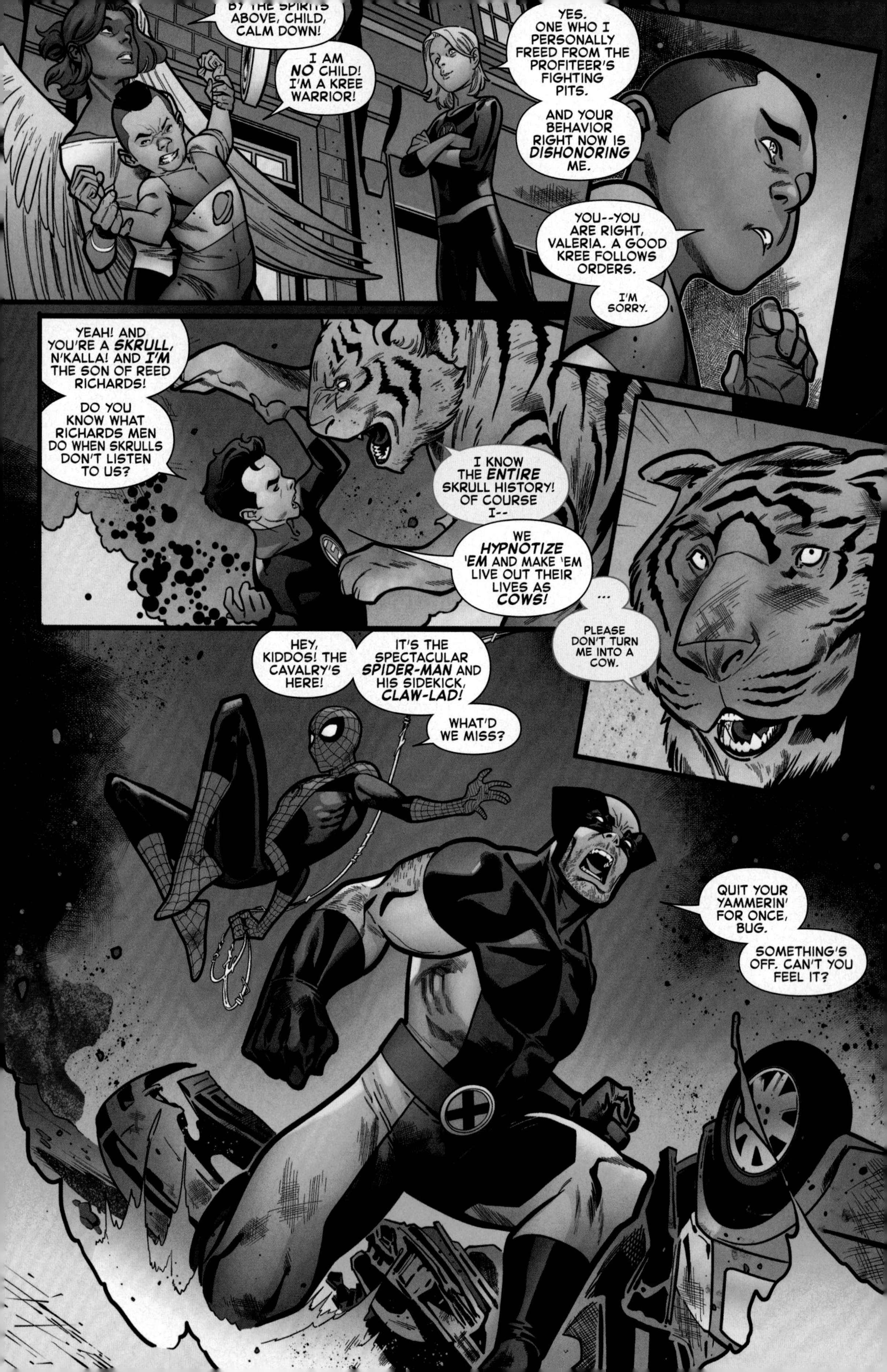
BY THE SPIRITS ABOVE, CHILD, CALM DOWN!
I AM NO CHILD! I'M A KREE WARRIOR!
YES. ONE WHO I PERSONALLY FREED FROM THE PROFITEER'S FIGHTING PITS.
AND YOUR BEHAVIOR RIGHT NOW IS DISHONORING ME.
YOU--YOU ARE RIGHT, VALERIA. A GOOD KREE FOLLOWS ORDERS.
I'M SORRY.
YEAH! AND YOU'RE A SKRULL, N'KALLA! AND I'M THE SON OF REED RICHARDS!
DO YOU KNOW WHAT RICHARDS MEN DO WHEN SKRULLS DON'T LISTEN TO US?
I KNOW THE ENTIRE SKRULL HISTORY! OF COURSE I--
WE HYPNOTIZE 'EM AND MAKE 'EM LIVE OUT THEIR LIVES AS COWS!
...
PLEASE DON'T TURN ME INTO A COW.
HEY, KIDDOS! THE CAVALRY'S HERE!
IT'S THE SPECTACULAR SPIDER-MAN AND HIS SIDEKICK, CLAW-LAD!
WHAT'D WE MISS?
QUIT YOUR YAMMERIN' FOR ONCE, BUG.
SOMETHING'S OFF. CAN'T YOU FEEL IT?

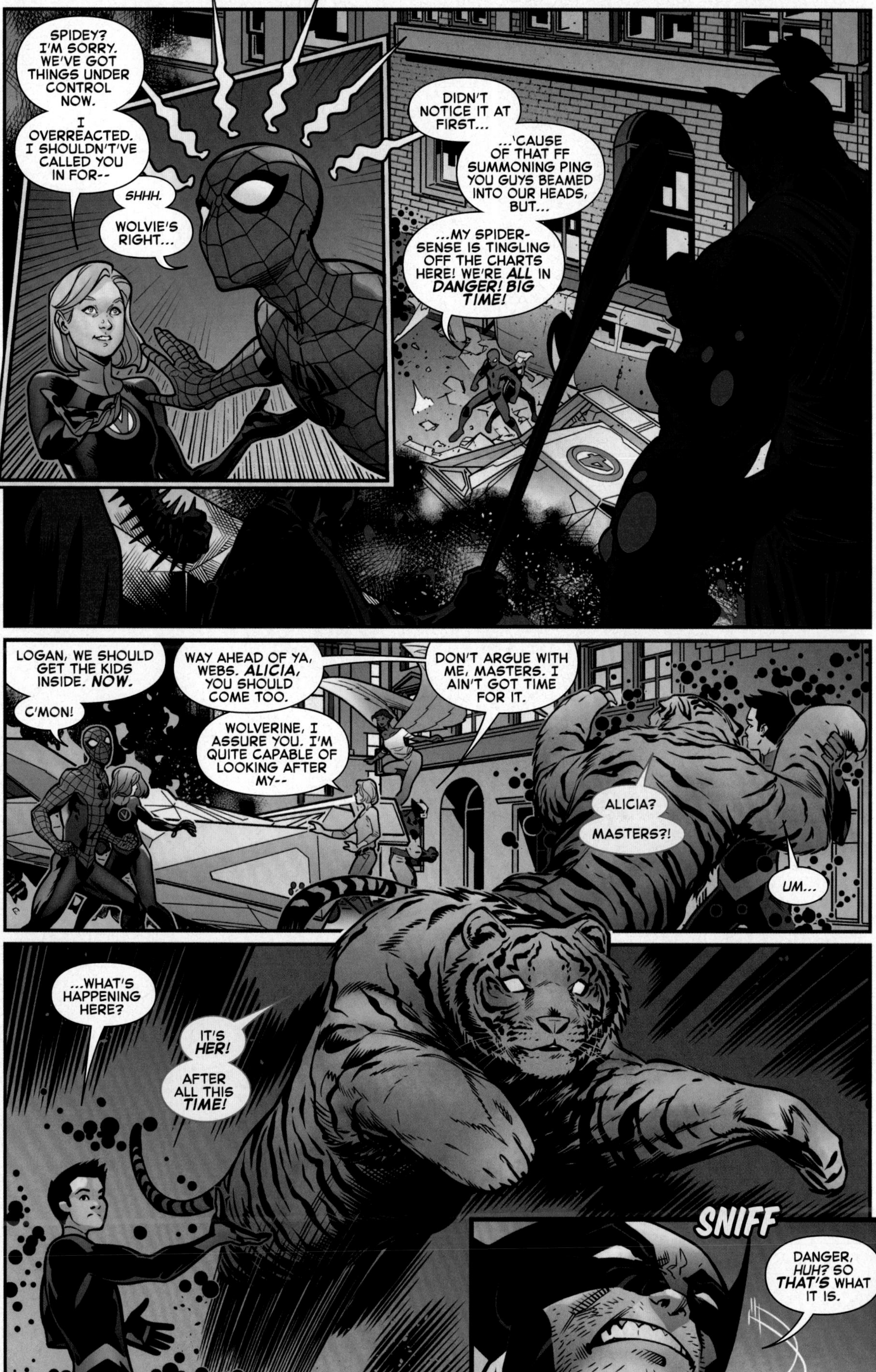

SPIDEY? I'M SORRY. WE'VE GOT THINGS UNDER CONTROL NOW.
I OVERREACTED. I SHOULDN'T'VE CALLED YOU IN FOR--
SHHH.
WOLVIE'S RIGHT...
DIDN'T NOTICE IT AT FIRST...
...'CAUSE OF THAT FF SUMMONING PING YOU GUYS BEAMED INTO OUR HEADS, BUT...
...MY SPIDER-SENSE IS TINGLING OFF THE CHARTS HERE! WE'RE ALL IN DANGER! BIG TIME!
LOGAN, WE SHOULD GET THE KIDS INSIDE. NOW.
C'MON!
WAY AHEAD OF YA, WEBS. ALICIA, YOU SHOULD COME TOO.
WOLVERINE, I ASSURE YOU. I'M QUITE CAPABLE OF LOOKING AFTER MY--
DON'T ARGUE WITH ME, MASTERS. I AIN'T GOT TIME FOR IT.
ALICIA?
MASTERS?!
UM...
...WHAT'S HAPPENING HERE?
IT'S HER!
AFTER ALL THIS TIME!
SNIFF
DANGER, HUH? SO THAT'S WHAT IT IS.

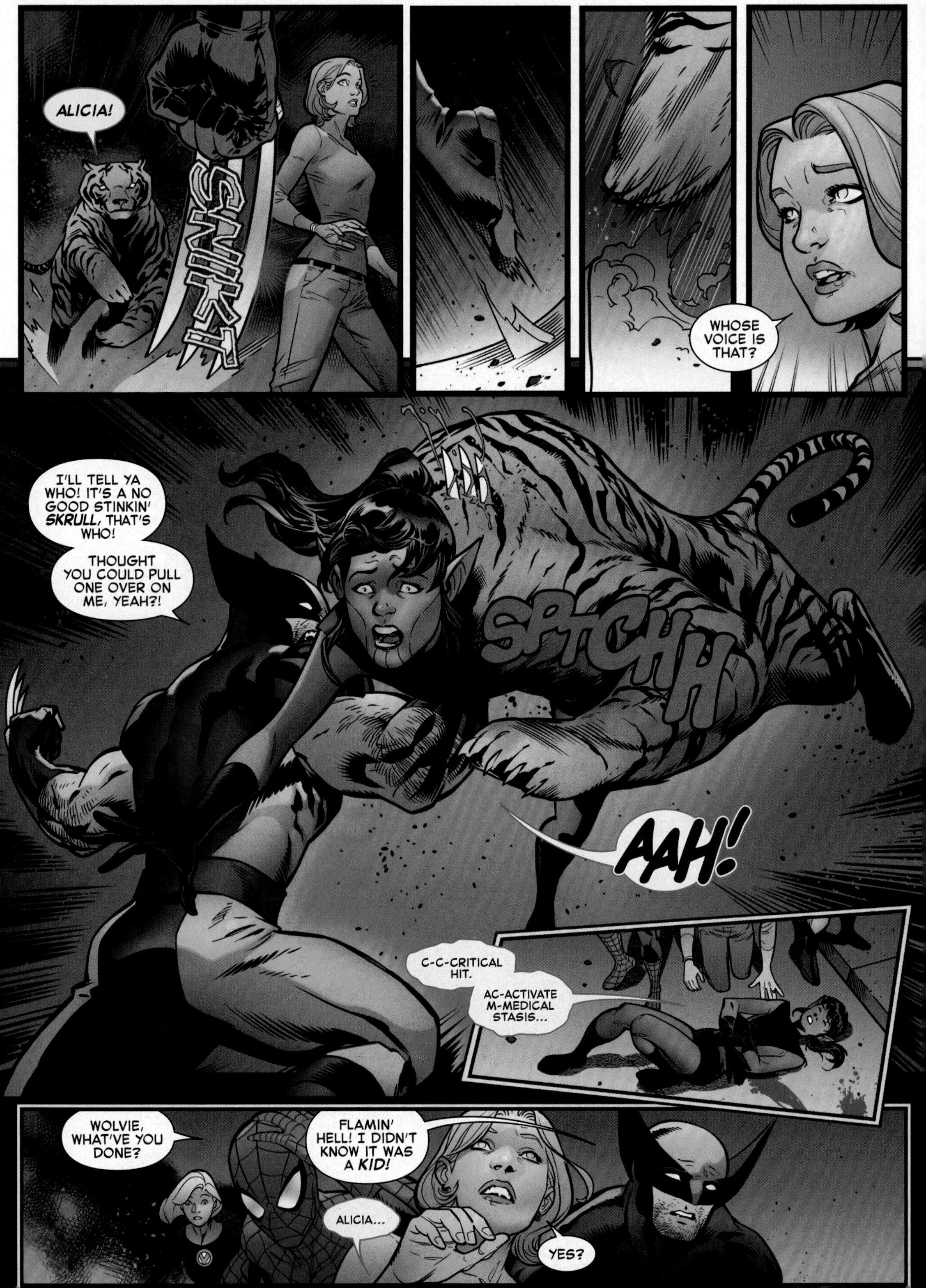
ALICIA!
SNIKT!
WHOSE VOICE IS THAT?
I'LL TELL YA WHO! IT'S A NO GOOD STINKIN' *SKRULL*, THAT'S WHO!
THOUGHT YOU COULD PULL ONE OVER ON ME, YEAH?!
SPTCHH
AAH!
C-C-CRITICAL HIT.
AC-ACTIVATE M-MEDICAL STASIS...
WOLVIE, WHAT'VE YOU DONE?
FLAMIN' HELL! I DIDN'T KNOW IT WAS A *KID!*
ALICIA...
YES?

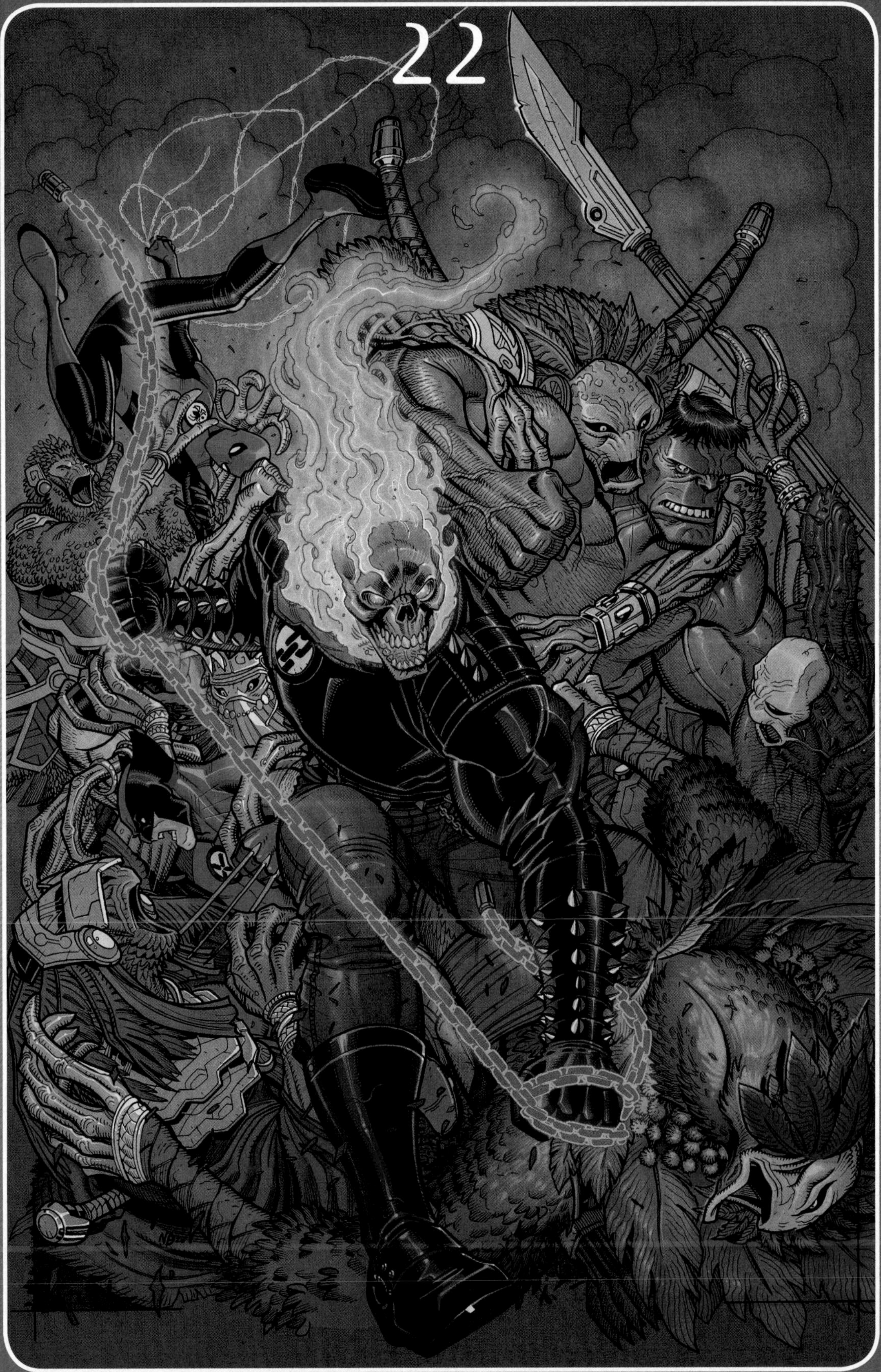
22

“You Had One Job”

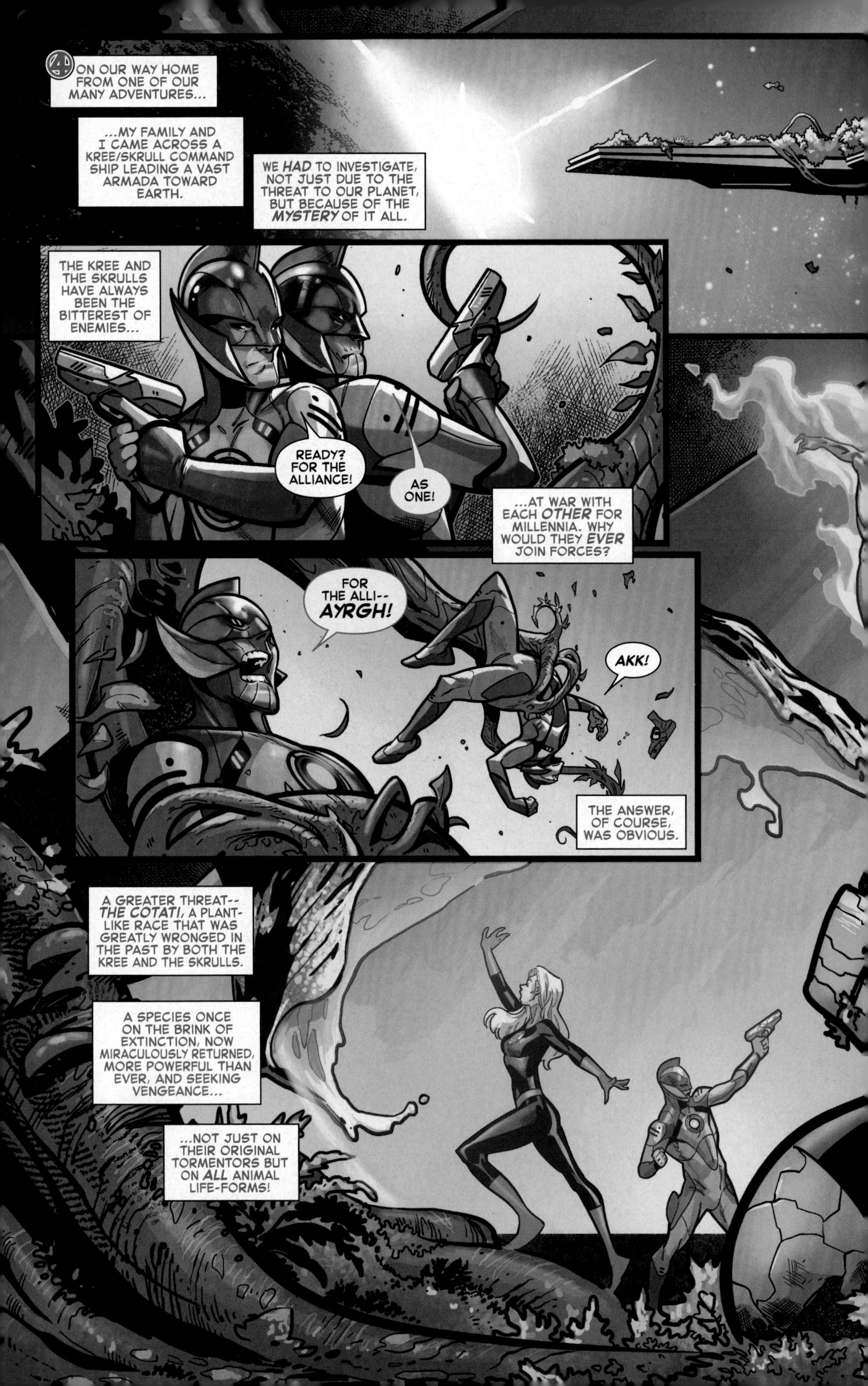

ON OUR WAY HOME FROM ONE OF OUR MANY ADVENTURES...
...MY FAMILY AND I CAME ACROSS A KREE/SKRULL COMMAND SHIP LEADING A VAST ARMADA TOWARD EARTH.
WE HAD TO INVESTIGATE, NOT JUST DUE TO THE THREAT TO OUR PLANET, BUT BECAUSE OF THE MYSTERY OF IT ALL.
THE KREE AND THE SKRULLS HAVE ALWAYS BEEN THE BITTEREST OF ENEMIES...
READY? FOR THE ALLIANCE!
AS ONE!
...AT WAR WITH EACH OTHER FOR MILLENNIA. WHY WOULD THEY EVER JOIN FORCES?
FOR THE ALLI-- AYRGH!
AKK!
THE ANSWER, OF COURSE, WAS OBVIOUS.
A GREATER THREAT-- THE COTATI, A PLANT-LIKE RACE THAT WAS GREATLY WRONGED IN THE PAST BY BOTH THE KREE AND THE SKRULLS.
A SPECIES ONCE ON THE BRINK OF EXTINCTION, NOW MIRACULOUSLY RETURNED, MORE POWERFUL THAN EVER, AND SEEKING VENGEANCE...
...NOT JUST ON THEIR ORIGINAL TORMENTORS BUT ON ALL ANIMAL LIFE-FORMS!

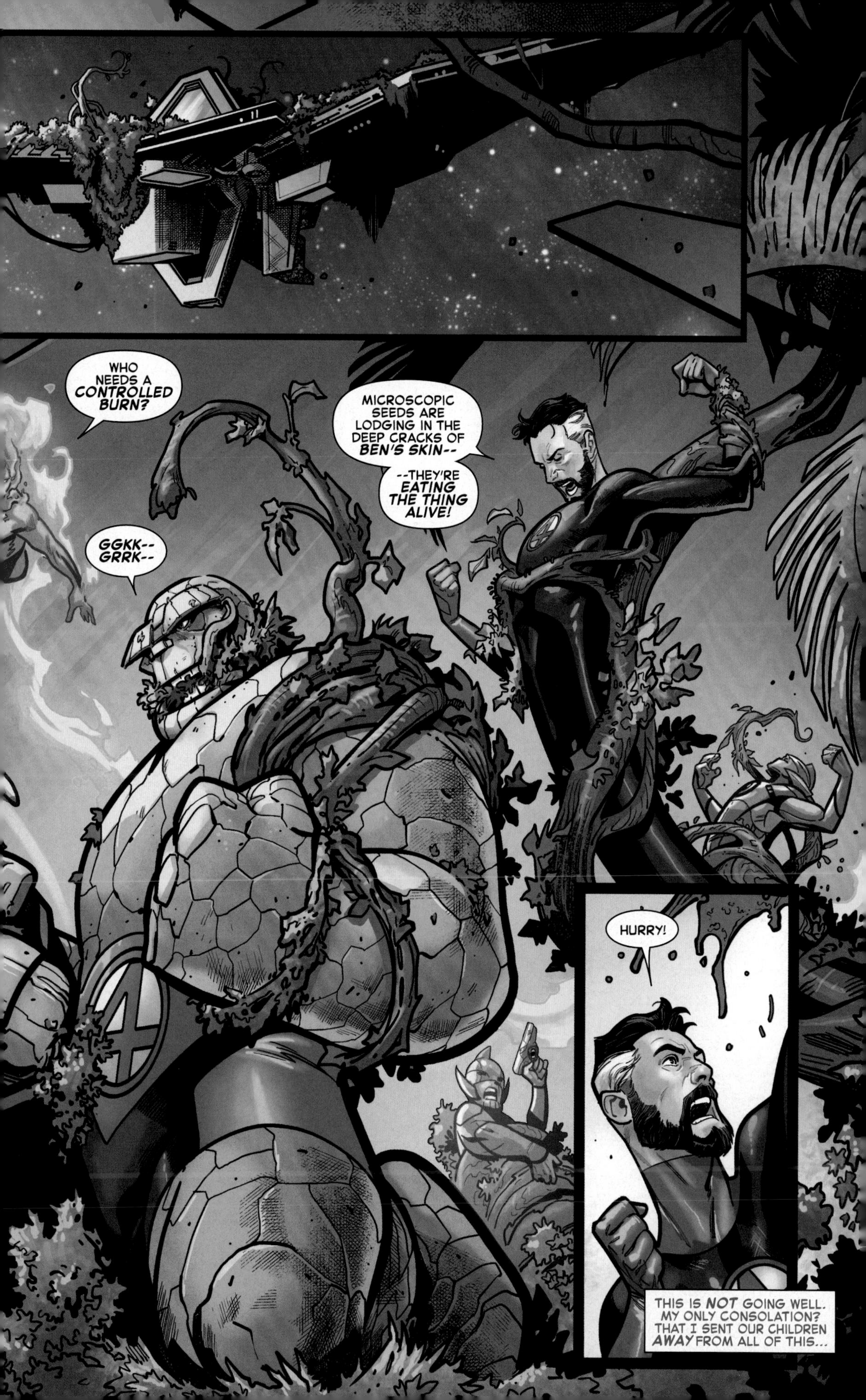
WHO NEEDS A CONTROLLED BURN?
MICROSCOPIC SEEDS ARE LODGING IN THE DEEP CRACKS OF BEN'S SKIN--
--THEY'RE EATING THE THING ALIVE!
GGKK-- GRRK--
HURRY!
THIS IS NOT GOING WELL. MY ONLY CONSOLATION? THAT I SENT OUR CHILDREN AWAY FROM ALL OF THIS...

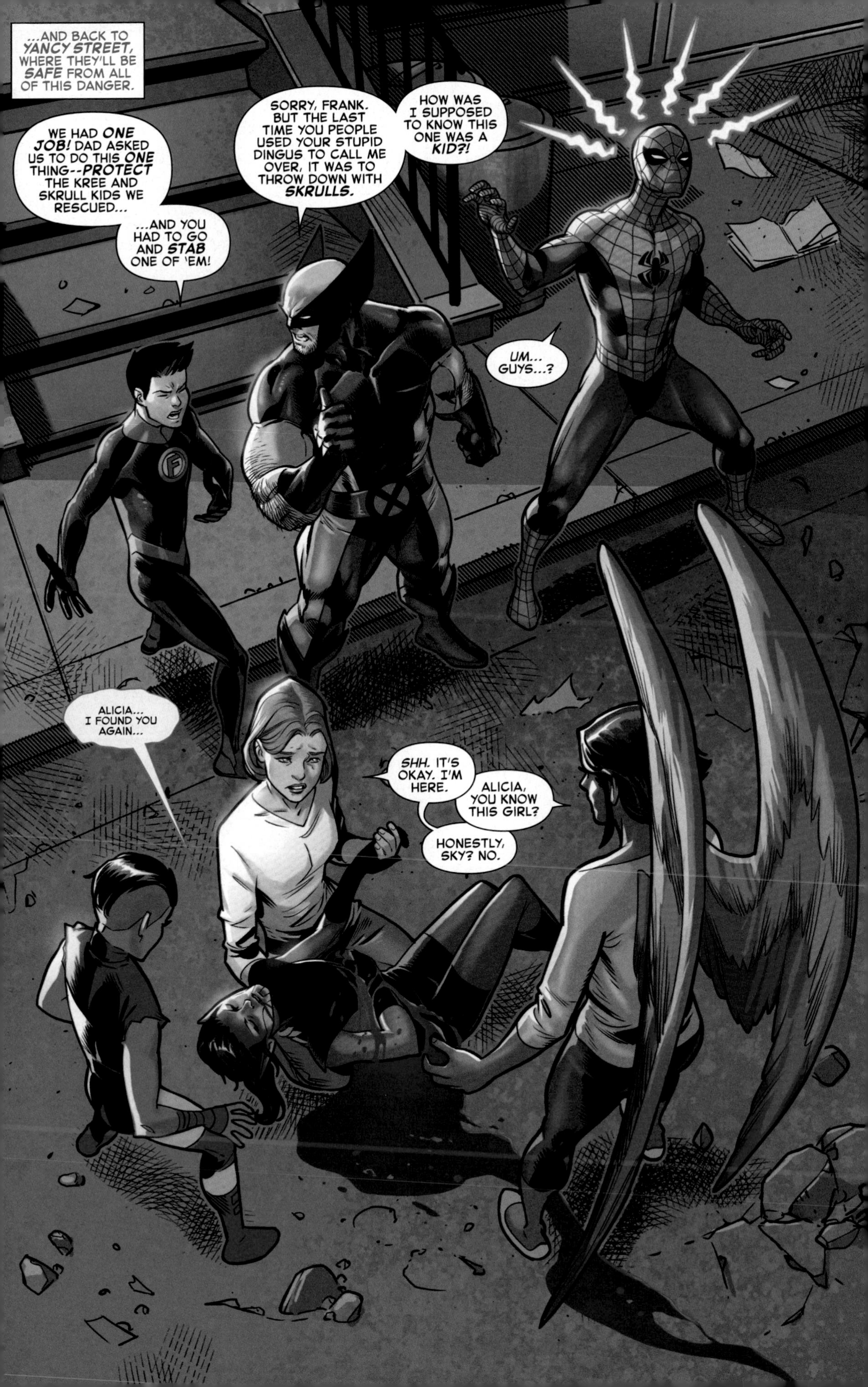
...AND BACK TO YANCY STREET, WHERE THEY'LL BE SAFE FROM ALL OF THIS DANGER.
WE HAD ONE JOB! DAD ASKED US TO DO THIS ONE THING--PROTECT THE KREE AND SKRULL KIDS WE RESCUED...
...AND YOU HAD TO GO AND STAB ONE OF 'EM!
SORRY, FRANK. BUT THE LAST TIME YOU PEOPLE USED YOUR STUPID DINGUS TO CALL ME OVER, IT WAS TO THROW DOWN WITH SKRULLS.
HOW WAS I SUPPOSED TO KNOW THIS ONE WAS A KID?!
UM... GUYS...?
ALICIA... I FOUND YOU AGAIN...
SHH. IT'S OKAY. I'M HERE.
ALICIA, YOU KNOW THIS GIRL?
HONESTLY, SKY? NO.

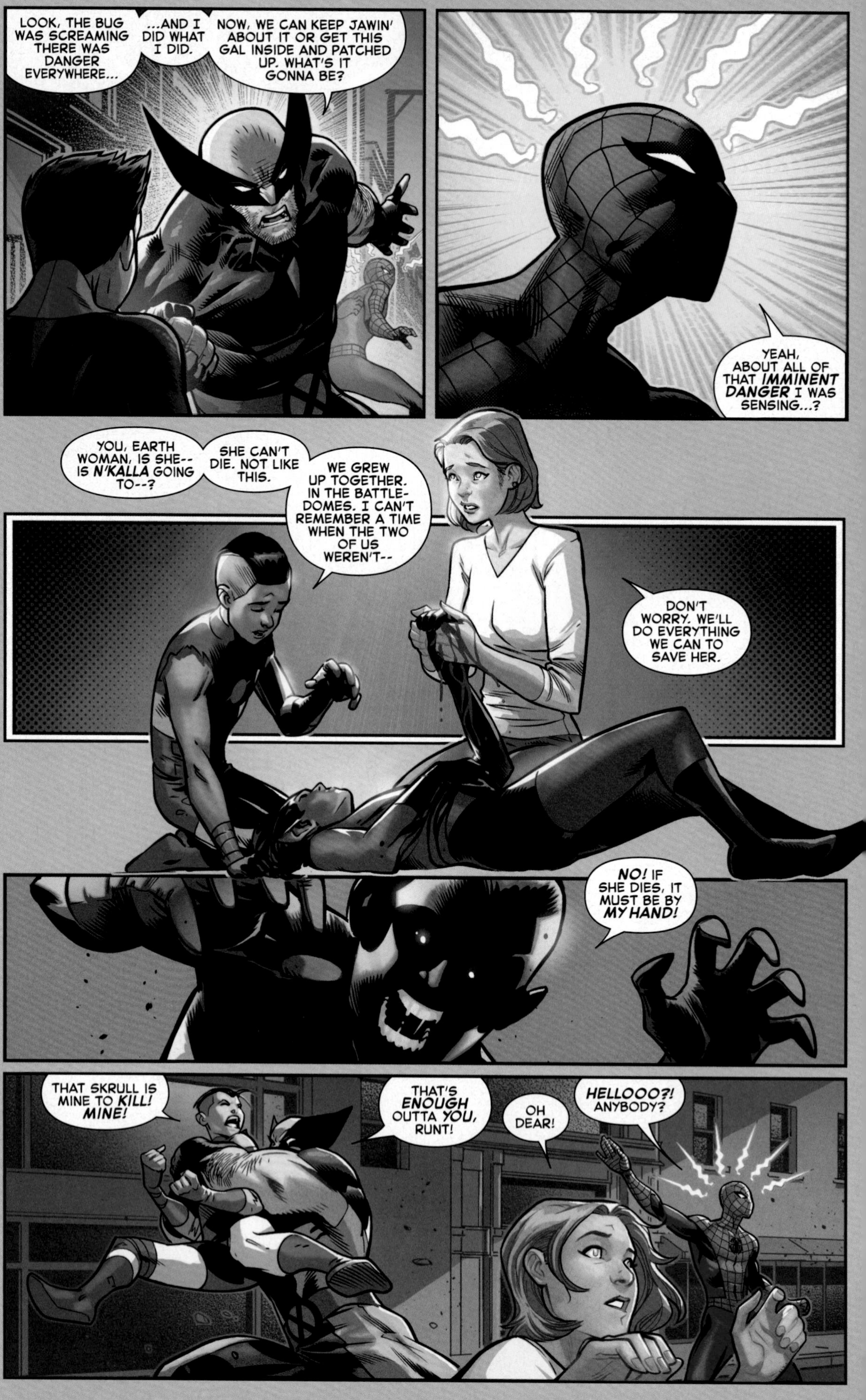
LOOK, THE BUG WAS SCREAMING THERE WAS DANGER EVERYWHERE...
...AND I DID WHAT I DID.
NOW, WE CAN KEEP JAWIN' ABOUT IT OR GET THIS GAL INSIDE AND PATCHED UP. WHAT'S IT GONNA BE?
YEAH, ABOUT ALL OF THAT IMMINENT DANGER I WAS SENSING...?
YOU, EARTH WOMAN, IS SHE-- IS N'KALLA GOING TO--?
SHE CAN'T DIE. NOT LIKE THIS.
WE GREW UP TOGETHER. IN THE BATTLE-DOMES. I CAN'T REMEMBER A TIME WHEN THE TWO OF US WEREN'T--
DON'T WORRY. WE'LL DO EVERYTHING WE CAN TO SAVE HER.
NO! IF SHE DIES, IT MUST BE BY MY HAND!
THAT SKRULL IS MINE TO KILL! MINE!
THAT'S ENOUGH OUTTA YOU, RUNT!
OH DEAR!
HELLOOO?! ANYBODY?

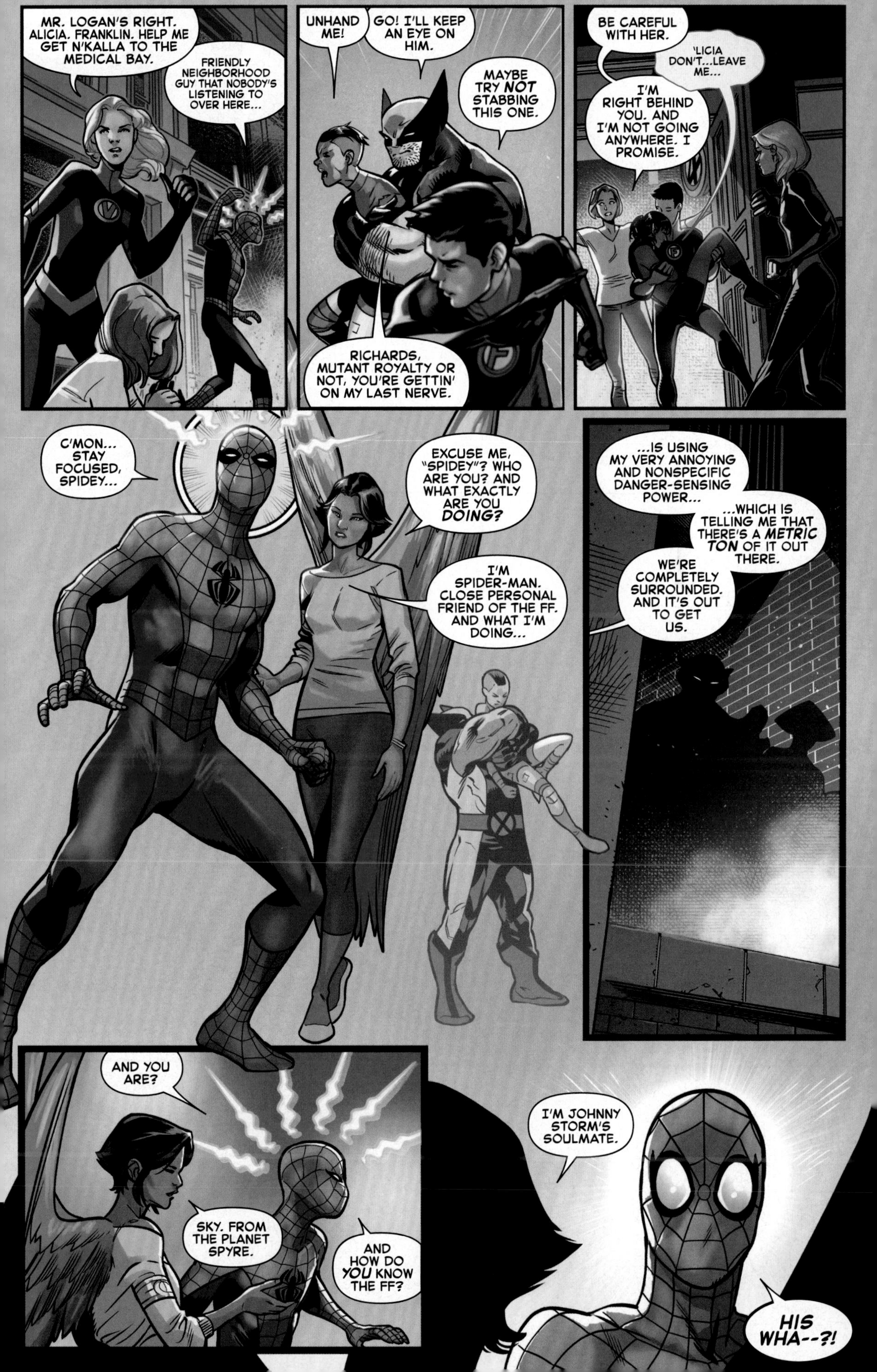
MR. LOGAN'S RIGHT. ALICIA. FRANKLIN. HELP ME GET N'KALLA TO THE MEDICAL BAY.
FRIENDLY NEIGHBORHOOD GUY THAT NOBODY'S LISTENING TO OVER HERE...
UNHAND ME!
GO! I'LL KEEP AN EYE ON HIM.
MAYBE TRY NOT STABBING THIS ONE.
RICHARDS, MUTANT ROYALTY OR NOT, YOU'RE GETTIN' ON MY LAST NERVE.
BE CAREFUL WITH HER.
'LICIA DON'T...LEAVE ME...
I'M RIGHT BEHIND YOU. AND I'M NOT GOING ANYWHERE. I PROMISE.
C'MON... STAY FOCUSED, SPIDEY...
EXCUSE ME, "SPIDEY"? WHO ARE YOU? AND WHAT EXACTLY ARE YOU DOING?
I'M SPIDER-MAN. CLOSE PERSONAL FRIEND OF THE FF. AND WHAT I'M DOING...
...IS USING MY VERY ANNOYING AND NONSPECIFIC DANGER-SENSING POWER...
...WHICH IS TELLING ME THAT THERE'S A METRIC TON OF IT OUT THERE.
WE'RE COMPLETELY SURROUNDED. AND IT'S OUT TO GET US.
AND YOU ARE?
SKY. FROM THE PLANET SPYRE.
AND HOW DO YOU KNOW THE FF?
I'M JOHNNY STORM'S SOULMATE.
HIS WHA--?!

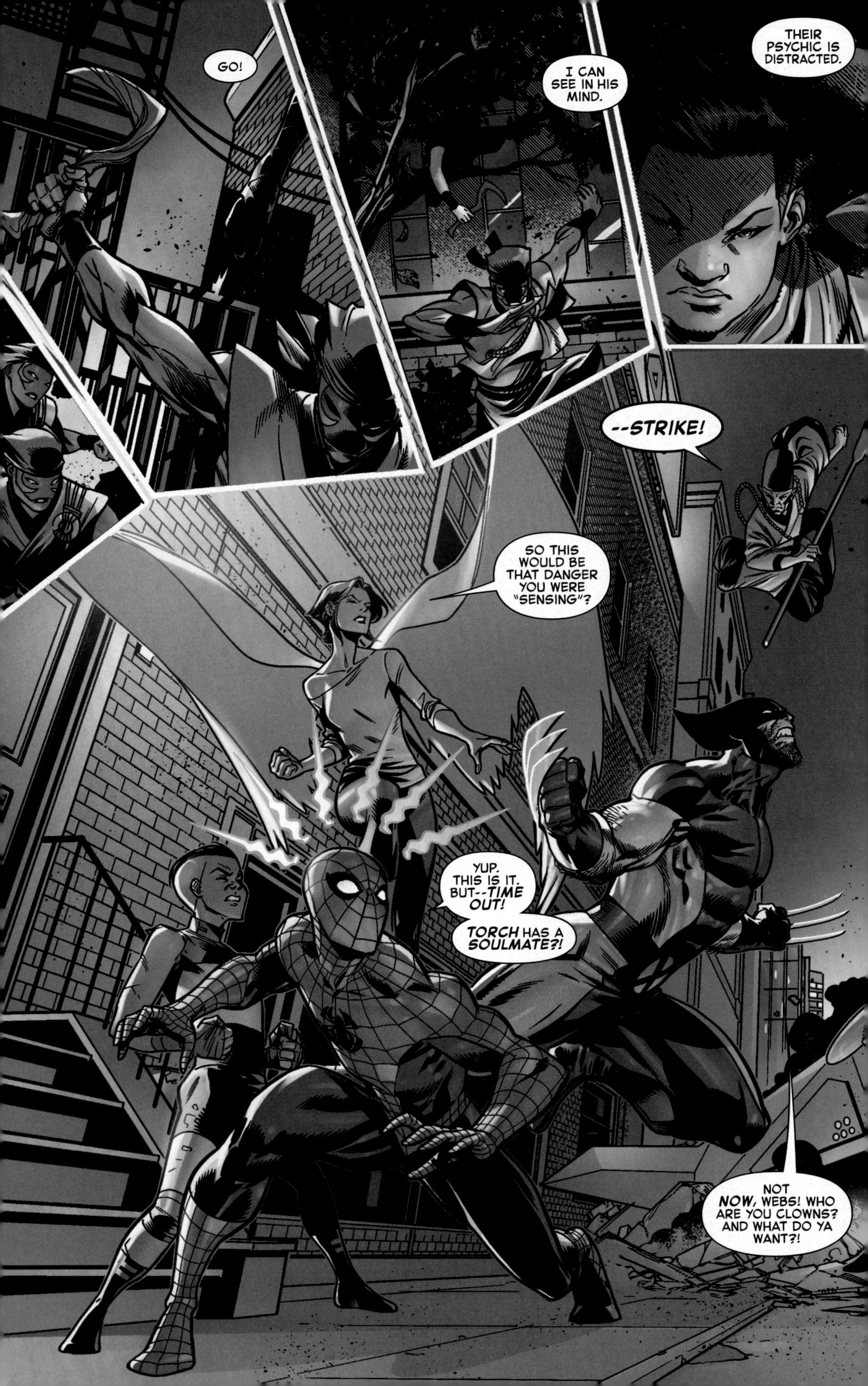
GO!
I CAN SEE IN HIS MIND.
THEIR PSYCHIC IS DISTRACTED.
--STRIKE!
SO THIS WOULD BE THAT DANGER YOU WERE "SENSING"?
YUP. THIS IS IT. BUT--TIME OUT!
TORCH HAS A SOULMATE?!
NOT NOW, WEBS! WHO ARE YOU CLOWNS? AND WHAT DO YA WANT?!

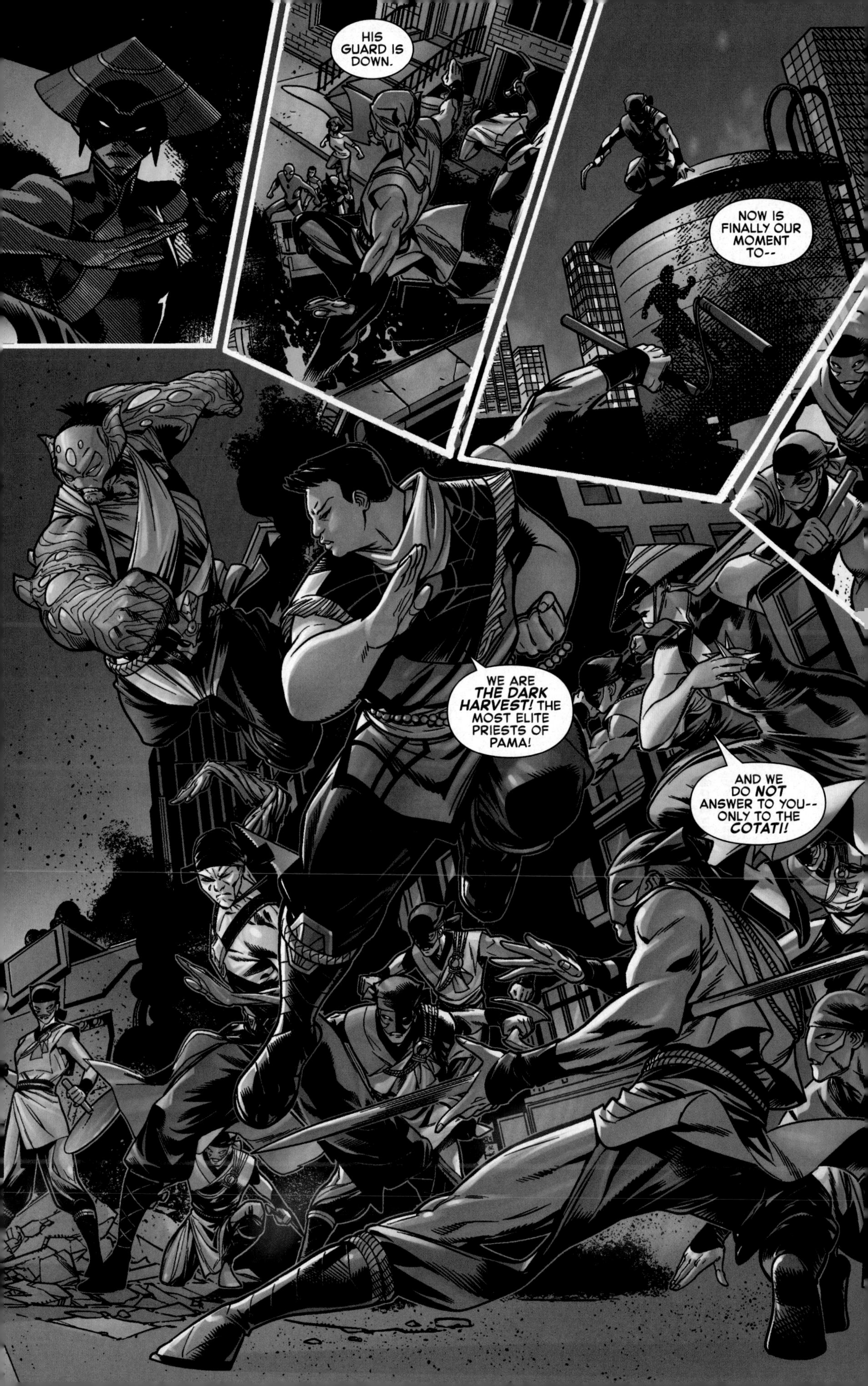
HIS GUARD IS DOWN.
NOW IS FINALLY OUR MOMENT TO--
WE ARE THE DARK HARVEST! THE MOST ELITE PRIESTS OF PAMA!
AND WE DO NOT ANSWER TO YOU-- ONLY TO THE COTATI!

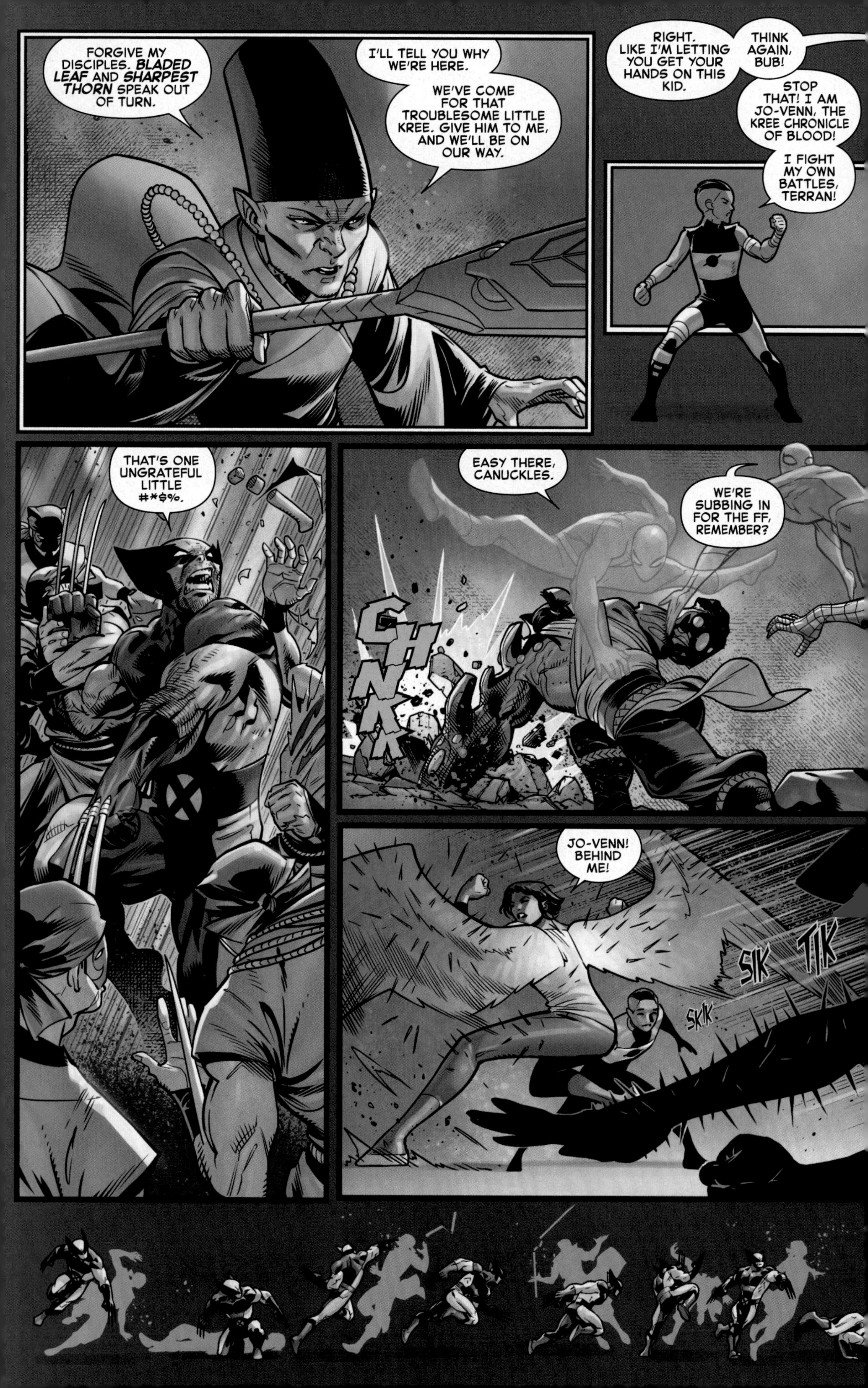
FORGIVE MY DISCIPLES. BLADED LEAF AND SHARPEST THORN SPEAK OUT OF TURN.
I'LL TELL YOU WHY WE'RE HERE.
WE'VE COME FOR THAT TROUBLESOME LITTLE KREE. GIVE HIM TO ME, AND WE'LL BE ON OUR WAY.
RIGHT. LIKE I'M LETTING YOU GET YOUR HANDS ON THIS KID.
THINK AGAIN, BUB!
STOP THAT! I AM JO-VENN, THE KREE CHRONICLE OF BLOOD!
I FIGHT MY OWN BATTLES, TERRAN!
THAT'S ONE UNGRATEFUL LITTLE #*$%.
EASY THERE, CANUCKLES.
WE'RE SUBBING IN FOR THE FF, REMEMBER?
CHNK
JO-VENN! BEHIND ME!
SIK
TIK
SK'IK

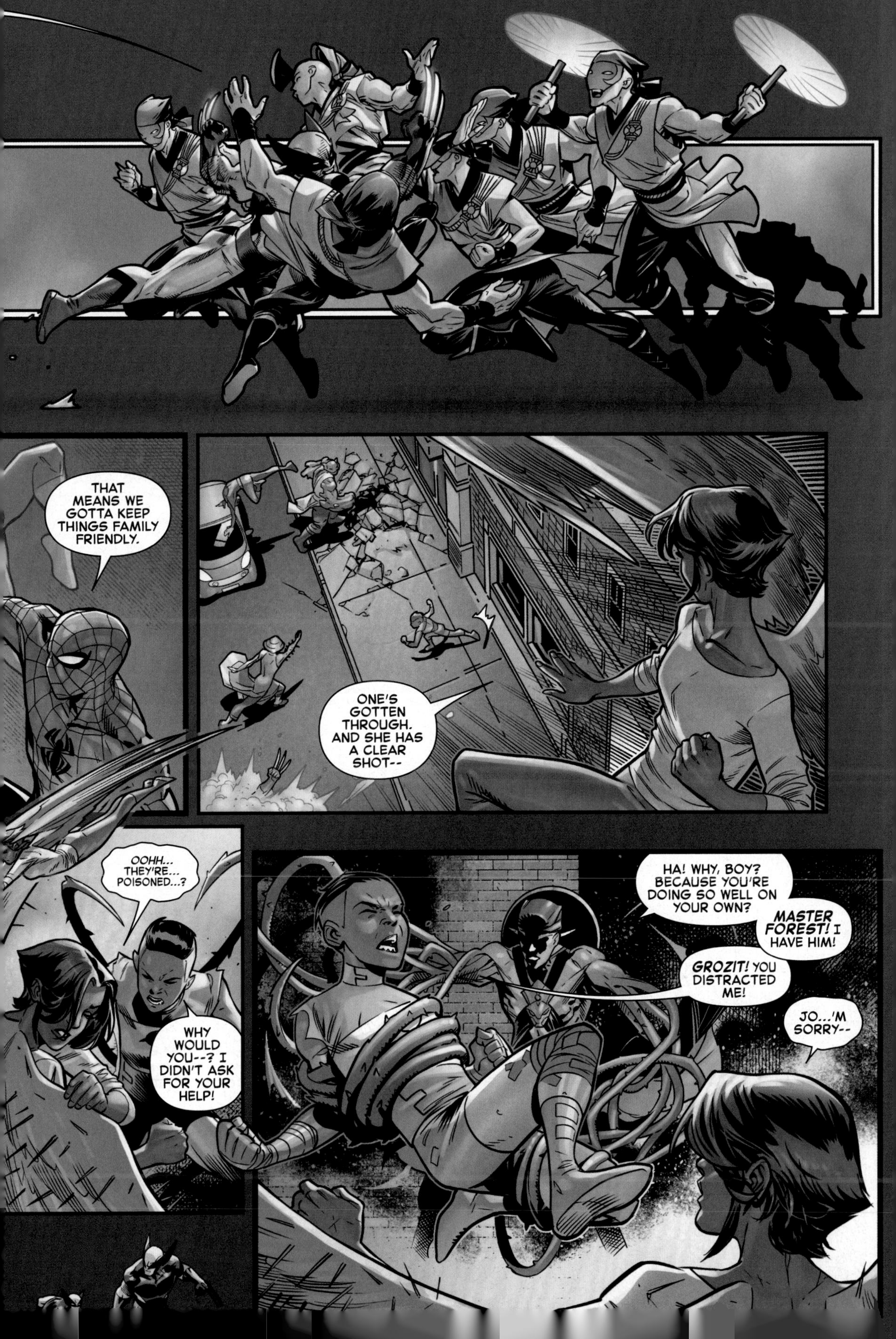
THAT MEANS WE GOTTA KEEP THINGS FAMILY FRIENDLY.
ONE'S GOTTEN THROUGH. AND SHE HAS A CLEAR SHOT--
OOHH... THEY'RE... POISONED...?
WHY WOULD YOU--? I DIDN'T ASK FOR YOUR HELP!
HA! WHY, BOY? BECAUSE YOU'RE DOING SO WELL ON YOUR OWN?
MASTER FOREST! I HAVE HIM!
GROZIT! YOU DISTRACTED ME!
JO...'M SORRY--

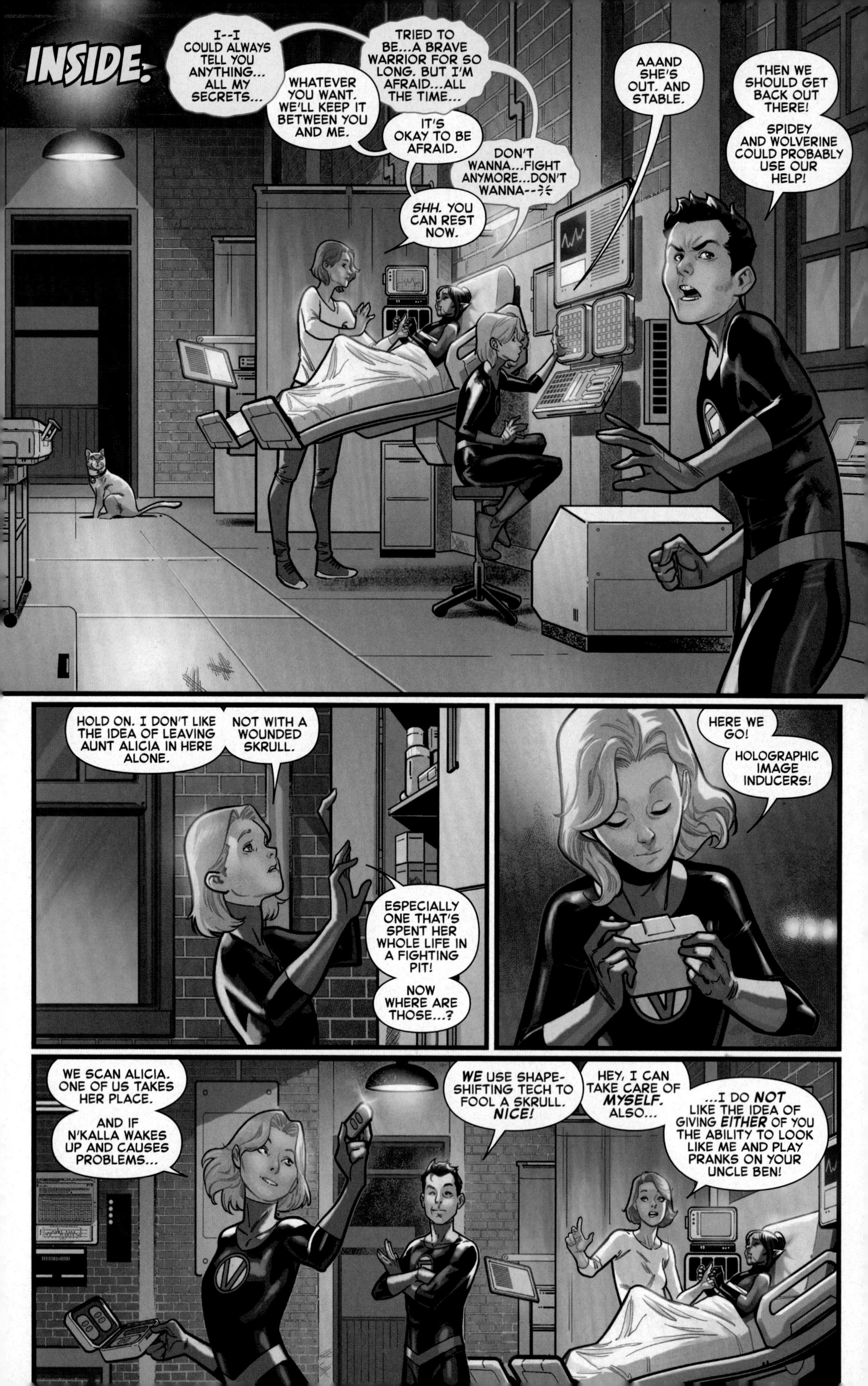
INSIDE.
I--I COULD ALWAYS TELL YOU ANYTHING... ALL MY SECRETS...
WHATEVER YOU WANT. WE'LL KEEP IT BETWEEN YOU AND ME.
TRIED TO BE...A BRAVE WARRIOR FOR SO LONG. BUT I'M AFRAID...ALL THE TIME...
IT'S OKAY TO BE AFRAID.
DON'T WANNA...FIGHT ANYMORE...DON'T WANNA--
SHH. YOU CAN REST NOW.
AAAND SHE'S OUT. AND STABLE.
THEN WE SHOULD GET BACK OUT THERE!
SPIDEY AND WOLVERINE COULD PROBABLY USE OUR HELP!
HOLD ON. I DON'T LIKE THE IDEA OF LEAVING AUNT ALICIA IN HERE ALONE.
NOT WITH A WOUNDED SKRULL.
ESPECIALLY ONE THAT'S SPENT HER WHOLE LIFE IN A FIGHTING PIT!
NOW WHERE ARE THOSE...?
HERE WE GO!
HOLOGRAPHIC IMAGE INDUCERS!
WE SCAN ALICIA. ONE OF US TAKES HER PLACE.
AND IF N'KALLA WAKES UP AND CAUSES PROBLEMS...
WE USE SHAPE-SHIFTING TECH TO FOOL A SKRULL. NICE!
HEY, I CAN TAKE CARE OF MYSELF. ALSO...
...I DO NOT LIKE THE IDEA OF GIVING EITHER OF YOU THE ABILITY TO LOOK LIKE ME AND PLAY PRANKS ON YOUR UNCLE BEN!

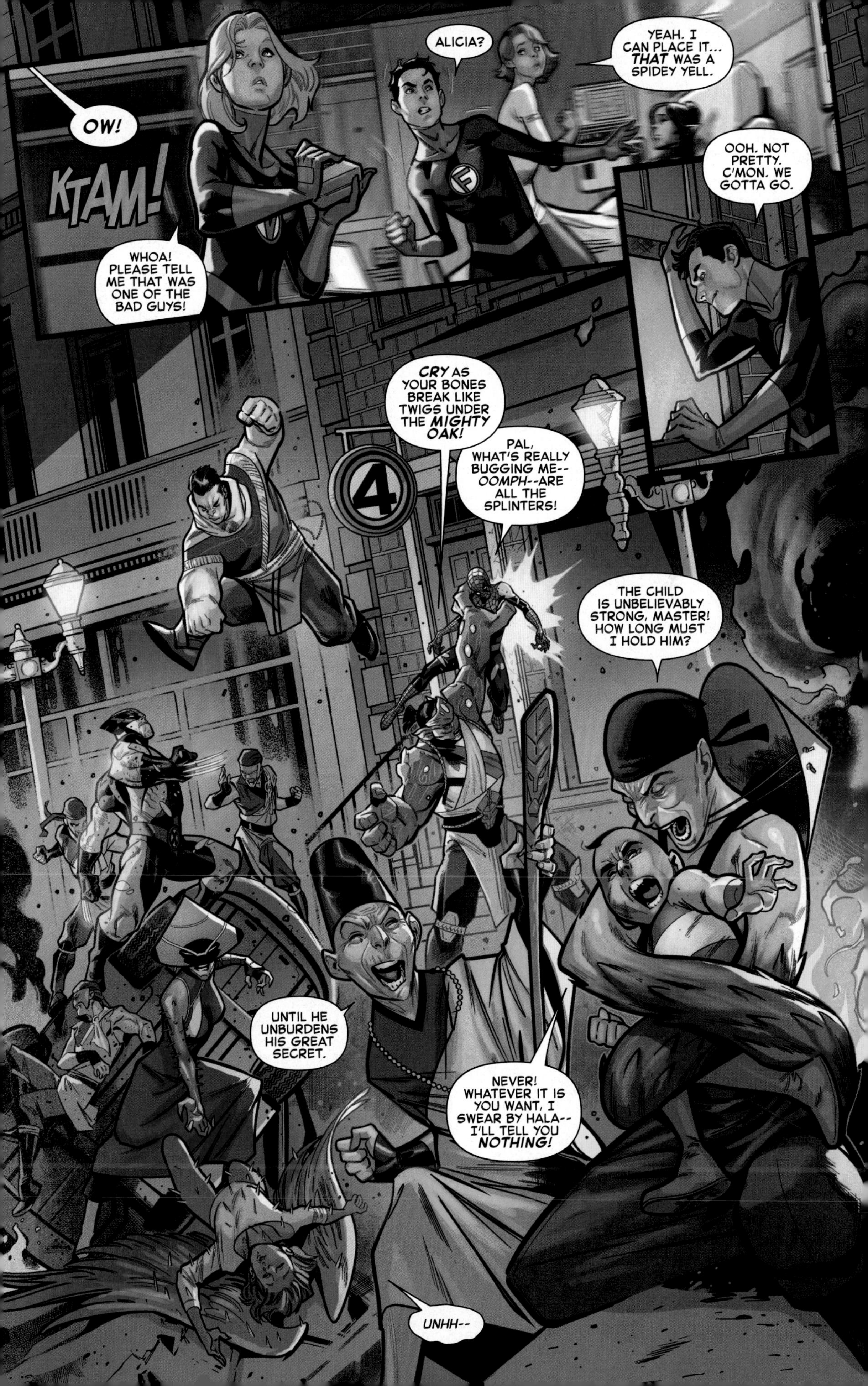
OW!
KTAM!
WHOA! PLEASE TELL ME THAT WAS ONE OF THE BAD GUYS!
ALICIA?
YEAH. I CAN PLACE IT... THAT WAS A SPIDEY YELL.
OOH. NOT PRETTY. C'MON. WE GOTTA GO.
CRY AS YOUR BONES BREAK LIKE TWIGS UNDER THE MIGHTY OAK!
PAL, WHAT'S REALLY BUGGING ME-- OOMPH--ARE ALL THE SPLINTERS!
THE CHILD IS UNBELIEVABLY STRONG, MASTER! HOW LONG MUST I HOLD HIM?
UNTIL HE UNBURDENS HIS GREAT SECRET.
NEVER! WHATEVER IT IS YOU WANT, I SWEAR BY HALA-- I'LL TELL YOU NOTHING!
UNHH--

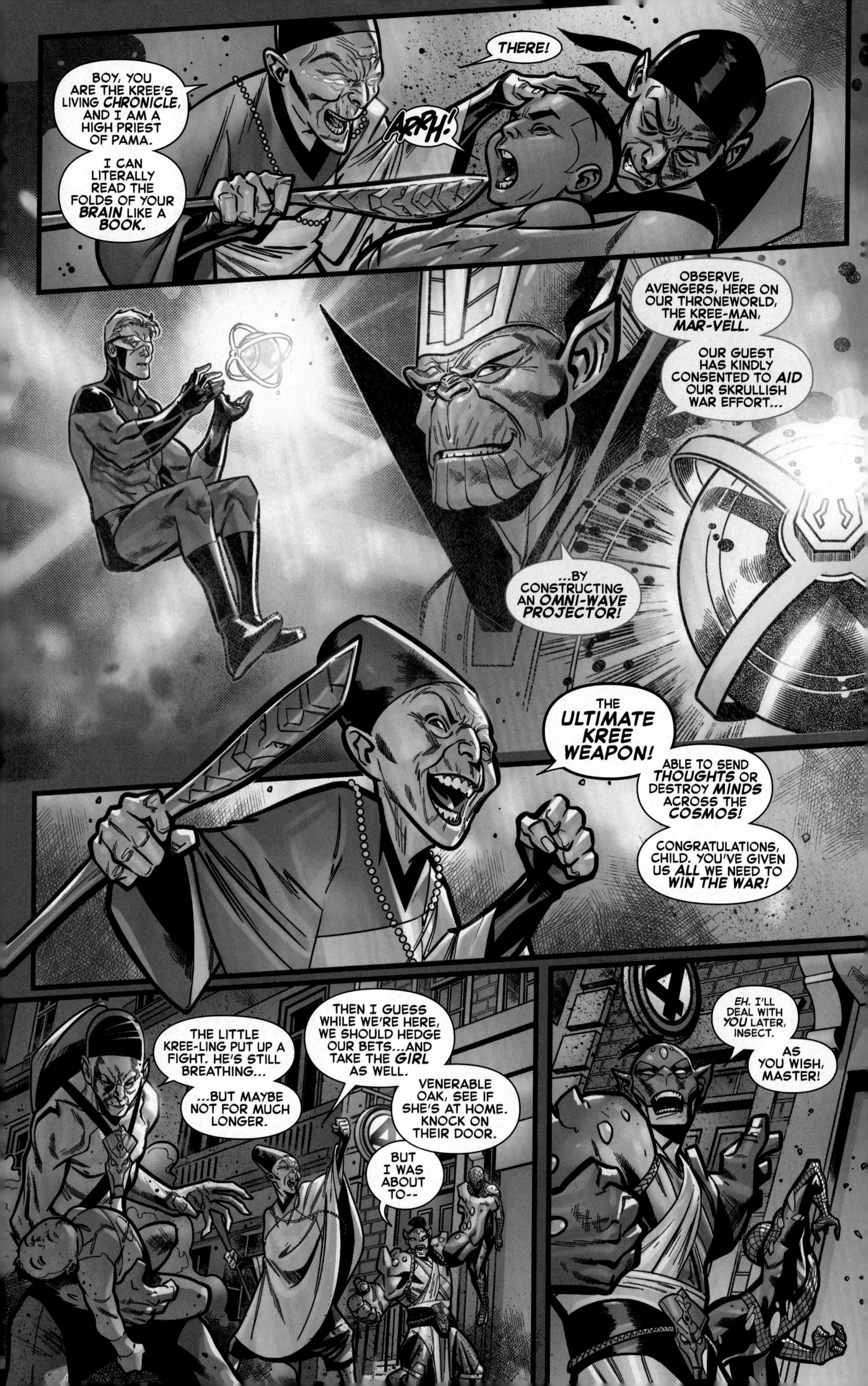
BOY, YOU ARE THE KREE'S LIVING CHRONICLE, AND I AM A HIGH PRIEST OF PAMA.
I CAN LITERALLY READ THE FOLDS OF YOUR BRAIN LIKE A BOOK.
THERE!
ARRH!
OBSERVE, AVENGERS, HERE ON OUR THRONEWORLD, THE KREE-MAN, MAR-VELL.
OUR GUEST HAS KINDLY CONSENTED TO AID OUR SKRULLISH WAR EFFORT...
...BY CONSTRUCTING AN OMNI-WAVE PROJECTOR!
THE ULTIMATE KREE WEAPON!
ABLE TO SEND THOUGHTS OR DESTROY MINDS ACROSS THE COSMOS!
CONGRATULATIONS, CHILD. YOU'VE GIVEN US ALL WE NEED TO WIN THE WAR!
THE LITTLE KREE-LING PUT UP A FIGHT. HE'S STILL BREATHING...
...BUT MAYBE NOT FOR MUCH LONGER.
THEN I GUESS WHILE WE'RE HERE, WE SHOULD HEDGE OUR BETS...AND TAKE THE GIRL AS WELL.
VENERABLE OAK, SEE IF SHE'S AT HOME. KNOCK ON THEIR DOOR.
BUT I WAS ABOUT TO--
EH. I'LL DEAL WITH YOU LATER, INSECT.
AS YOU WISH, MASTER!

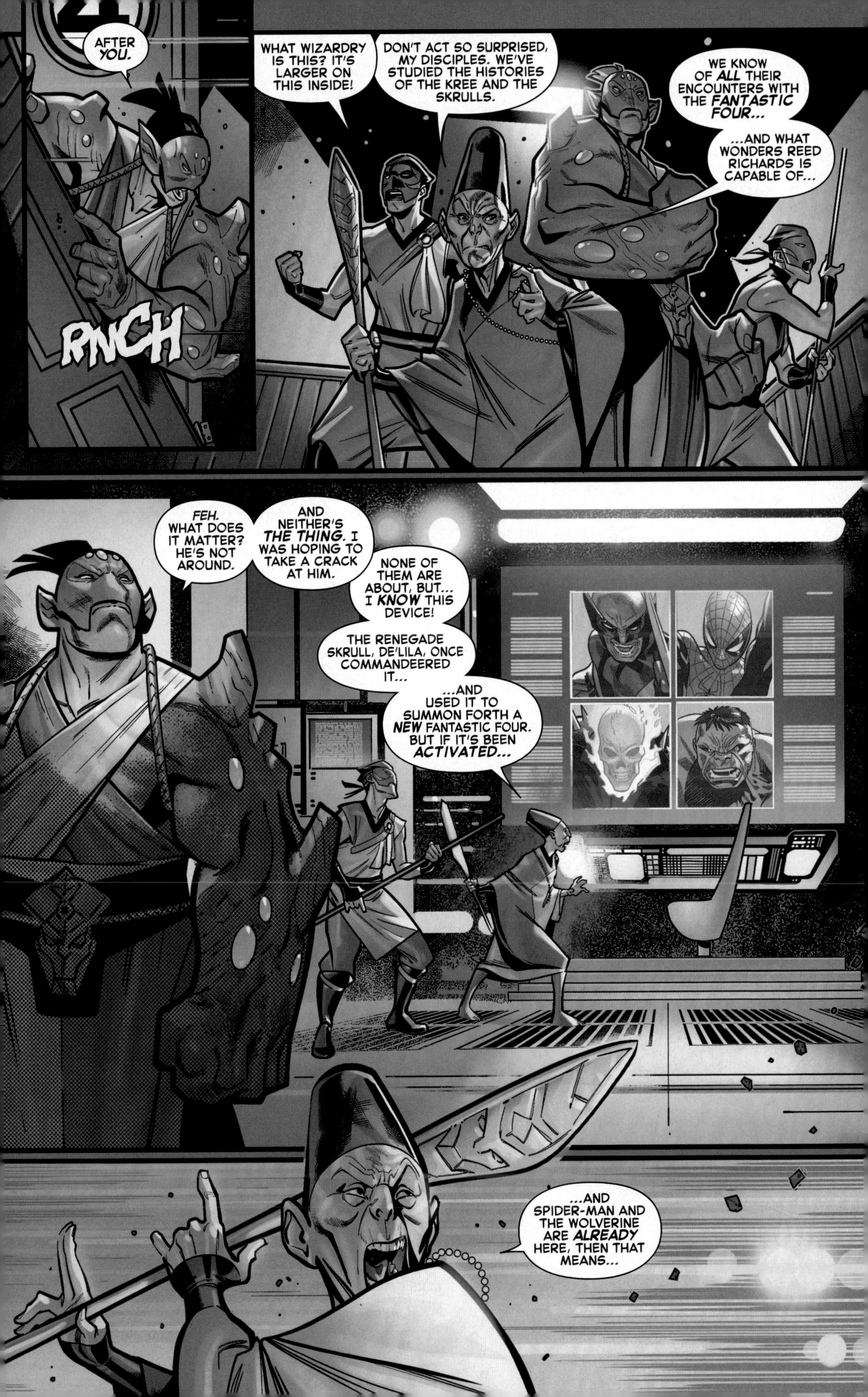
AFTER YOU.
RNCH
WHAT WIZARDRY IS THIS? IT'S LARGER ON THIS INSIDE!
DON'T ACT SO SURPRISED, MY DISCIPLES. WE'VE STUDIED THE HISTORIES OF THE KREE AND THE SKRULLS.
WE KNOW OF ALL THEIR ENCOUNTERS WITH THE FANTASTIC FOUR...
...AND WHAT WONDERS REED RICHARDS IS CAPABLE OF...
FEH. WHAT DOES IT MATTER? HE'S NOT AROUND.
AND NEITHER'S THE THING. I WAS HOPING TO TAKE A CRACK AT HIM.
NONE OF THEM ARE ABOUT, BUT... I KNOW THIS DEVICE!
THE RENEGADE SKRULL, DE'LILA, ONCE COMMANDEERED IT...
...AND USED IT TO SUMMON FORTH A NEW FANTASTIC FOUR. BUT IF IT'S BEEN ACTIVATED...
...AND SPIDER-MAN AND THE WOLVERINE ARE ALREADY HERE, THEN THAT MEANS...

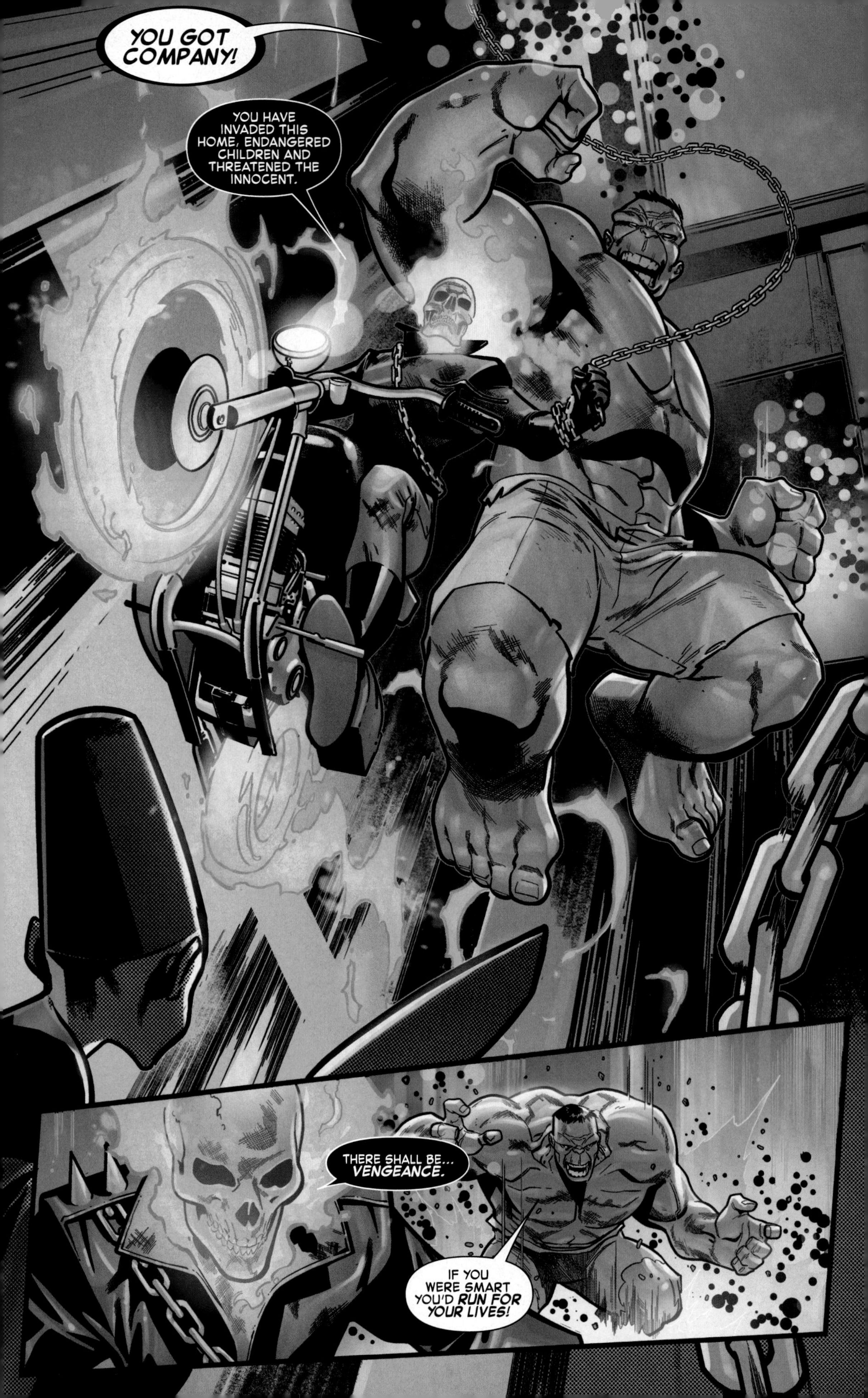
YOU GOT COMPANY!
YOU HAVE INVADED THIS HOME, ENDANGERED CHILDREN AND THREATENED THE INNOCENT.
THERE SHALL BE... VENGEANCE.
IF YOU WERE SMART YOU'D RUN FOR YOUR LIVES!

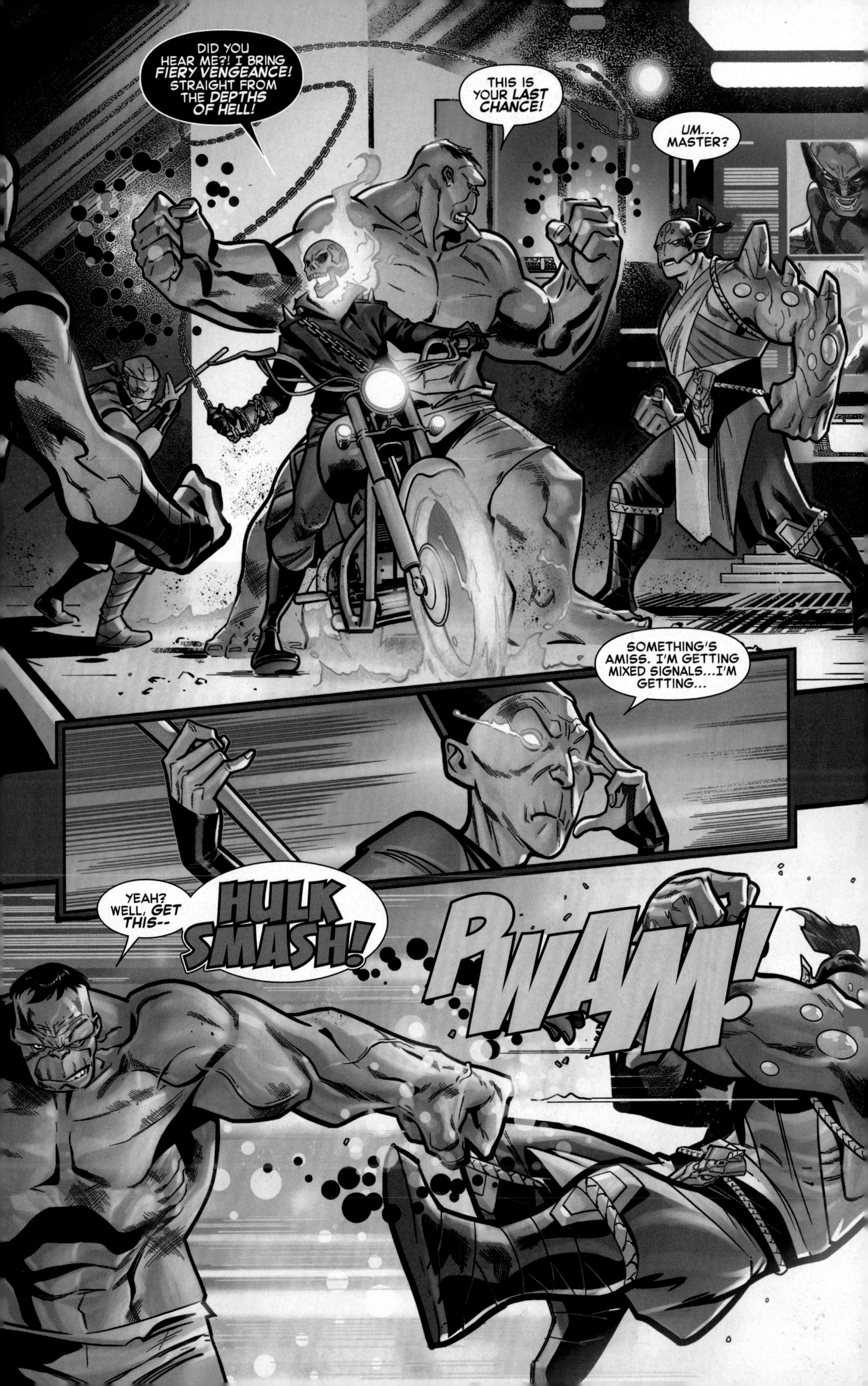
DID YOU HEAR ME?! I BRING FIERY VENGEANCE! STRAIGHT FROM THE DEPTHS OF HELL!
THIS IS YOUR LAST CHANCE!
UM... MASTER?
SOMETHING'S AMISS. I'M GETTING MIXED SIGNALS...I'M GETTING...
YEAH? WELL, GET THIS--
HULK SMASH!
PWAM!

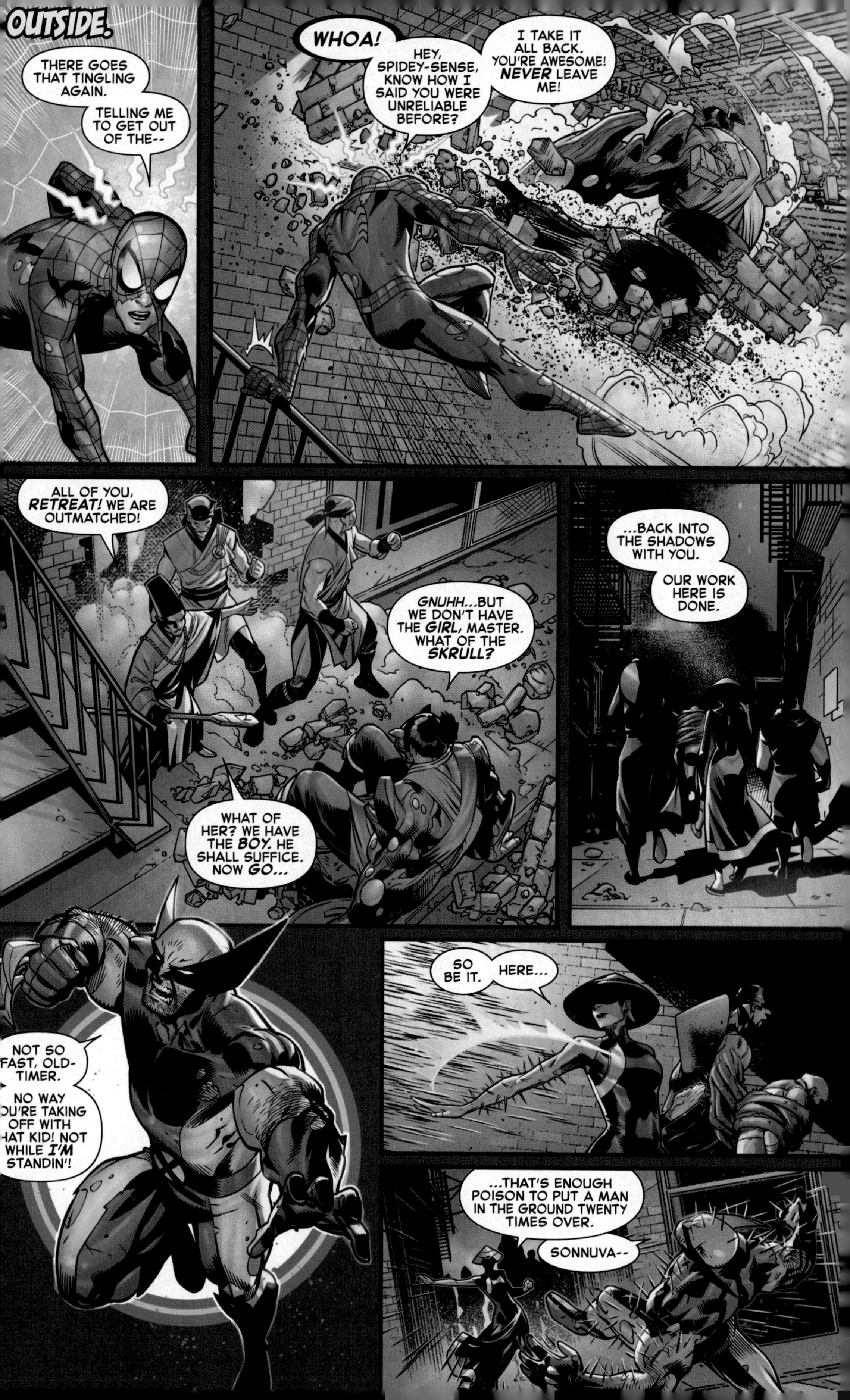
OUTSIDE.
THERE GOES THAT TINGLING AGAIN.
TELLING ME TO GET OUT OF THE--
WHOA!
HEY, SPIDEY-SENSE, KNOW HOW I SAID YOU WERE UNRELIABLE BEFORE?
I TAKE IT ALL BACK. YOU'RE AWESOME! NEVER LEAVE ME!
ALL OF YOU, RETREAT! WE ARE OUTMATCHED!
GNUHH...BUT WE DON'T HAVE THE GIRL, MASTER. WHAT OF THE SKRULL?
WHAT OF HER? WE HAVE THE BOY. HE SHALL SUFFICE. NOW GO...
...BACK INTO THE SHADOWS WITH YOU.
OUR WORK HERE IS DONE.
NOT SO FAST, OLD-TIMER.
NO WAY YOU'RE TAKING OFF WITH THAT KID! NOT WHILE I'M STANDIN'!
SO BE IT.
HERE...
...THAT'S ENOUGH POISON TO PUT A MAN IN THE GROUND TWENTY TIMES OVER.
SONNUVA--

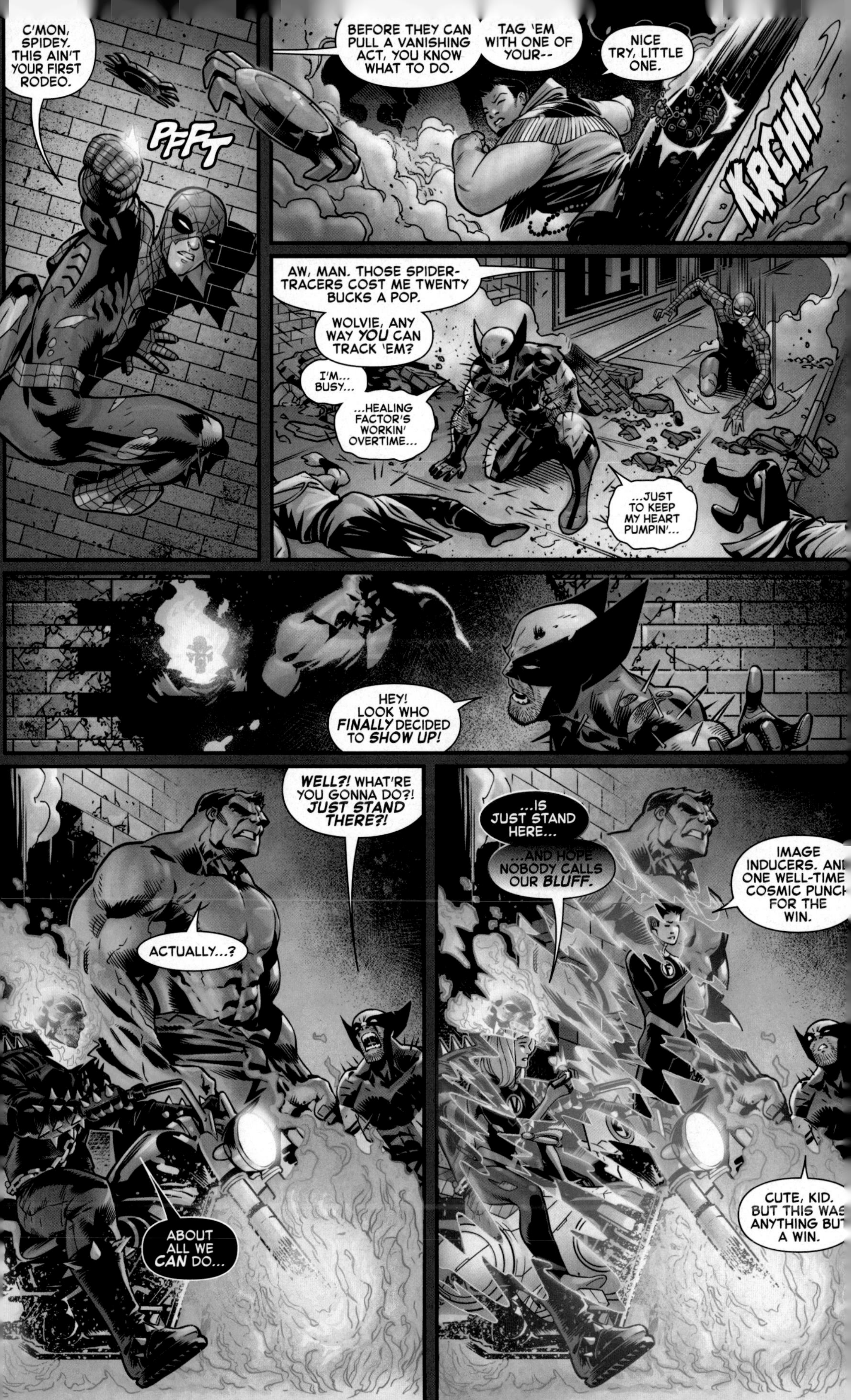
C'MON, SPIDEY. THIS AIN'T YOUR FIRST RODEO.
PFFT
BEFORE THEY CAN PULL A VANISHING ACT, YOU KNOW WHAT TO DO.
TAG 'EM WITH ONE OF YOUR--
NICE TRY, LITTLE ONE.
KRCHH
AW, MAN. THOSE SPIDER-TRACERS COST ME TWENTY BUCKS A POP.
WOLVIE, ANY WAY YOU CAN TRACK 'EM?
I'M... BUSY...
...HEALING FACTOR'S WORKIN' OVERTIME...
...JUST TO KEEP MY HEART PUMPIN'...
HEY! LOOK WHO FINALLY DECIDED TO SHOW UP!
WELL?! WHAT'RE YOU GONNA DO?! JUST STAND THERE?!
ACTUALLY...?
ABOUT ALL WE CAN DO...
...IS JUST STAND HERE...
...AND HOPE NOBODY CALLS OUR BLUFF.
IMAGE INDUCERS. AND ONE WELL-TIME COSMIC PUNCH FOR THE WIN.
CUTE, KID. BUT THIS WAS ANYTHING BUT A WIN.

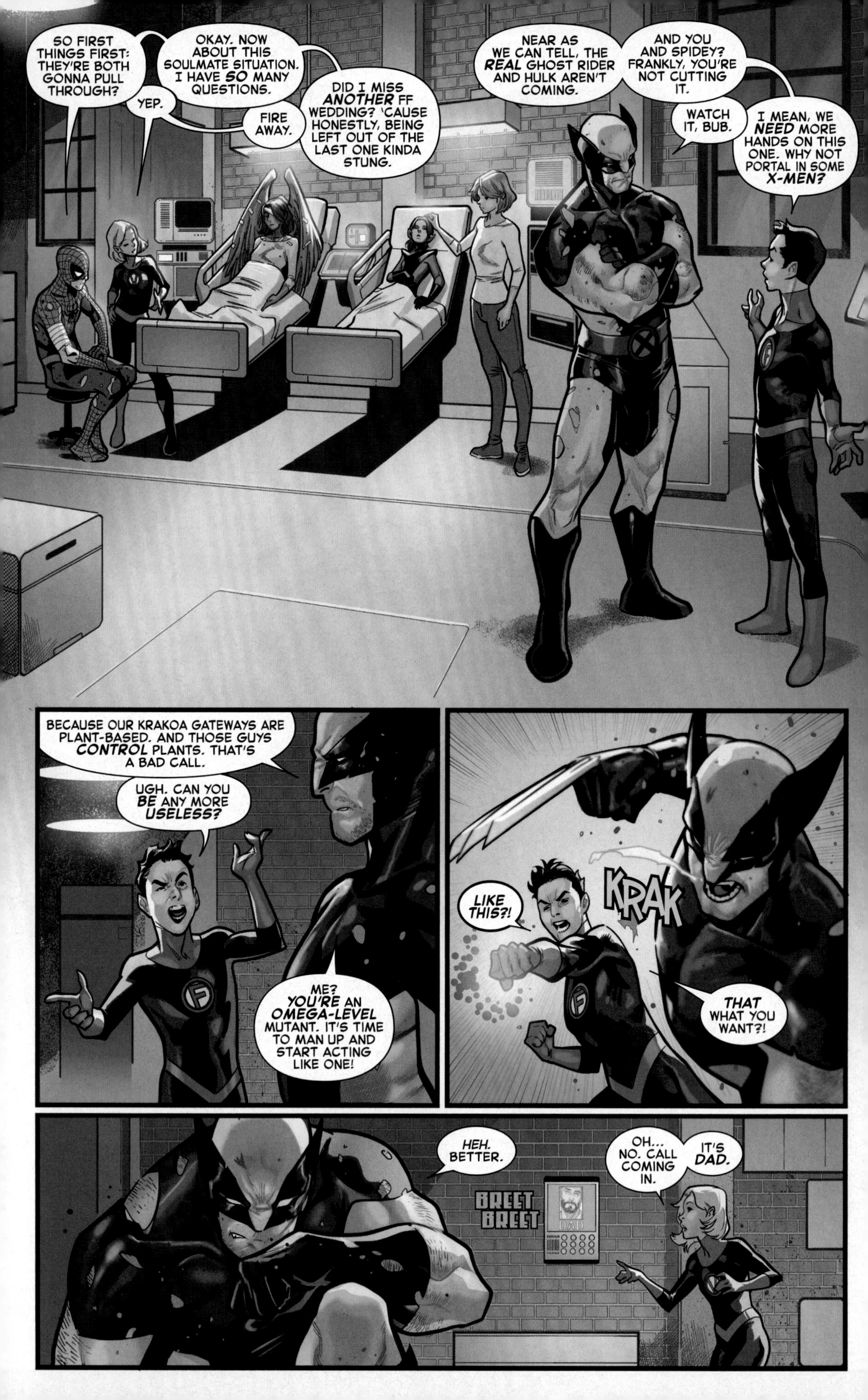
SO FIRST THINGS FIRST: THEY'RE BOTH GONNA PULL THROUGH?
YEP.
OKAY. NOW ABOUT THIS SOULMATE SITUATION. I HAVE SO MANY QUESTIONS.
FIRE AWAY.
DID I MISS ANOTHER FF WEDDING? 'CAUSE HONESTLY, BEING LEFT OUT OF THE LAST ONE KINDA STUNG.
NEAR AS WE CAN TELL, THE REAL GHOST RIDER AND HULK AREN'T COMING.
AND YOU AND SPIDEY? FRANKLY, YOU'RE NOT CUTTING IT.
WATCH IT, BUB.
I MEAN, WE NEED MORE HANDS ON THIS ONE. WHY NOT PORTAL IN SOME X-MEN?
BECAUSE OUR KRAKOA GATEWAYS ARE PLANT-BASED. AND THOSE GUYS CONTROL PLANTS. THAT'S A BAD CALL.
UGH. CAN YOU BE ANY MORE USELESS?
ME? YOU'RE AN OMEGA-LEVEL MUTANT. IT'S TIME TO MAN UP AND START ACTING LIKE ONE!
LIKE THIS?!
KRAK
THAT WHAT YOU WANT?!
HEH. BETTER.
BREET BREET
DAD
OH... NO. CALL COMING IN.
IT'S DAD.

GREAT! "HEY, DAD. GUESS WHAT? WE COULDN'T EVEN PULL OFF BABYSITTING."

IT'S NOT LIKE THAT.

HE TRUSTED US WITH TWO KIDS, VAL! WE LOST ONE AND ALMOST GOT THE OTHER ONE KILLED.

WE WERE IN OVER OUR HEADS AND WE ASKED FOR HELP. THAT'S WHAT WE TELL HIM.

THE TRUTH.

HEY, DAD.

HI. JUST CHECKING IN. HOW ARE--

WOLVERINE? SPIDER-MAN? WHAT BRINGS YOU TWO OVER? IS EVERYTHING ALL RIGHT?

NOT REALLY, FATHER. IT'S LIKE THIS...

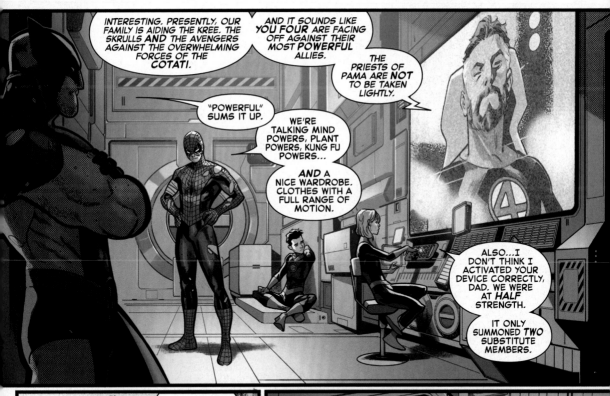

INTERESTING. PRESENTLY, OUR FAMILY IS AIDING THE KREE. THE SKRULLS AND THE AVENGERS AGAINST THE OVERWHELMING FORCES OF THE COTATI.

AND IT SOUNDS LIKE YOU FOUR ARE FACING OFF AGAINST THEIR MOST POWERFUL ALLIES.

THE PRIESTS OF PAMA ARE NOT TO BE TAKEN LIGHTLY.

"POWERFUL" SUMS IT UP.

WE'RE TALKING MIND POWERS, PLANT POWERS, KUNG FU POWERS...

AND A NICE WARDROBE. CLOTHES WITH A FULL RANGE OF MOTION.

ALSO...I DON'T THINK I ACTIVATED YOUR DEVICE CORRECTLY, DAD. WE WERE AT HALF STRENGTH.

IT ONLY SUMMONED TWO SUBSTITUTE MEMBERS.

YOU'RE RIGHT, DEAR. IT NEEDS SOME FINE-TUNING.

LET ME SEE WHAT I CAN DO REMOTELY FROM MY END.

DING

THERE. I THINK YOU'LL FIND EVERYTHING YOU NEED IN THE FABRICATOR.

AND, VALERIA, THERE'S SOMETHING YOU SHOULD KNOW...

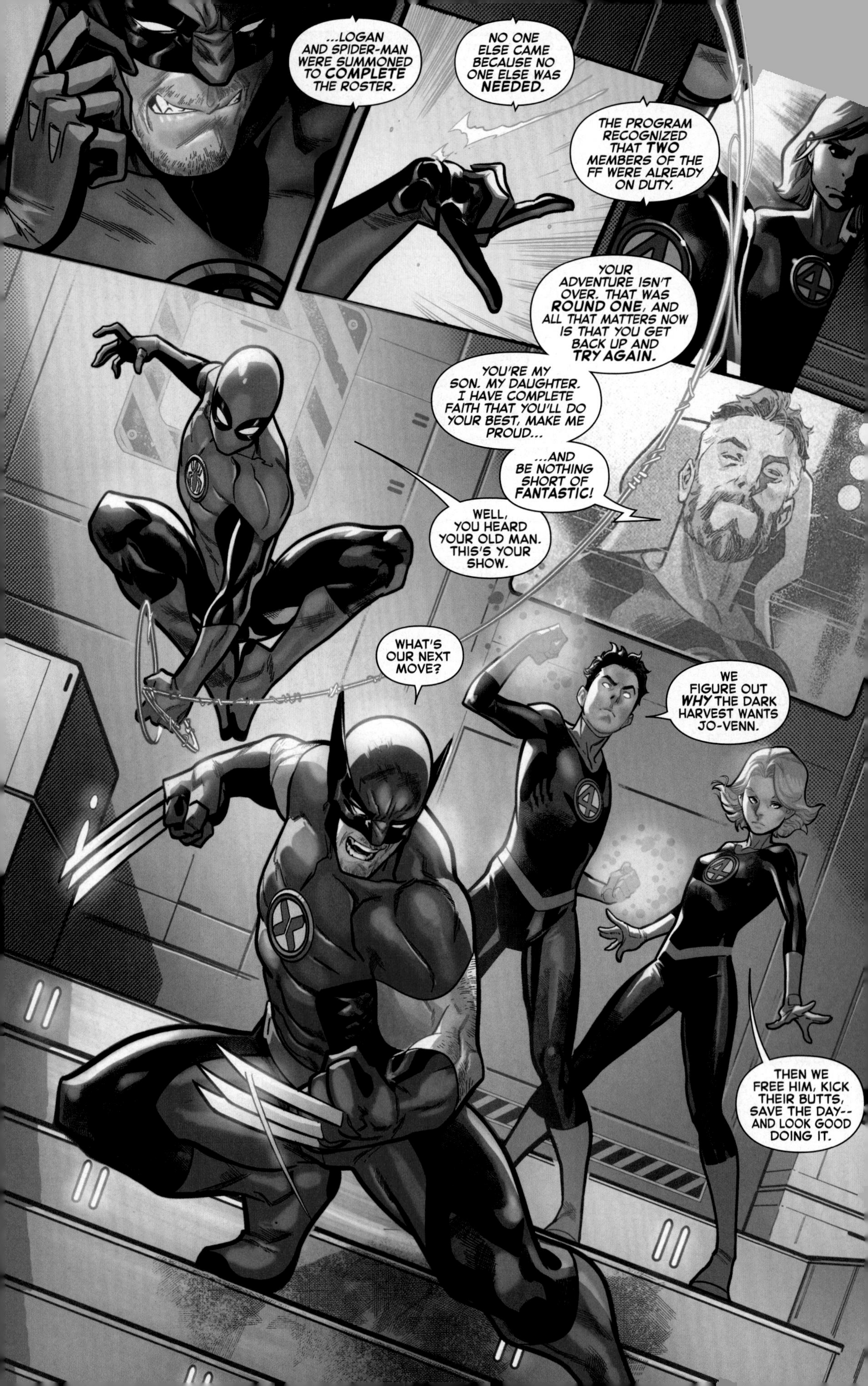
...LOGAN AND SPIDER-MAN WERE SUMMONED TO COMPLETE THE ROSTER.
NO ONE ELSE CAME BECAUSE NO ONE ELSE WAS NEEDED.
THE PROGRAM RECOGNIZED THAT TWO MEMBERS OF THE FF WERE ALREADY ON DUTY.
YOUR ADVENTURE ISN'T OVER. THAT WAS ROUND ONE, AND ALL THAT MATTERS NOW IS THAT YOU GET BACK UP AND TRY AGAIN.
YOU'RE MY SON. MY DAUGHTER. I HAVE COMPLETE FAITH THAT YOU'LL DO YOUR BEST, MAKE ME PROUD...
...AND BE NOTHING SHORT OF FANTASTIC!
WELL, YOU HEARD YOUR OLD MAN. THIS'S YOUR SHOW.
WHAT'S OUR NEXT MOVE?
WE FIGURE OUT WHY THE DARK HARVEST WANTS JO-VENN.
THEN WE FREE HIM, KICK THEIR BUTTS, SAVE THE DAY-- AND LOOK GOOD DOING IT.

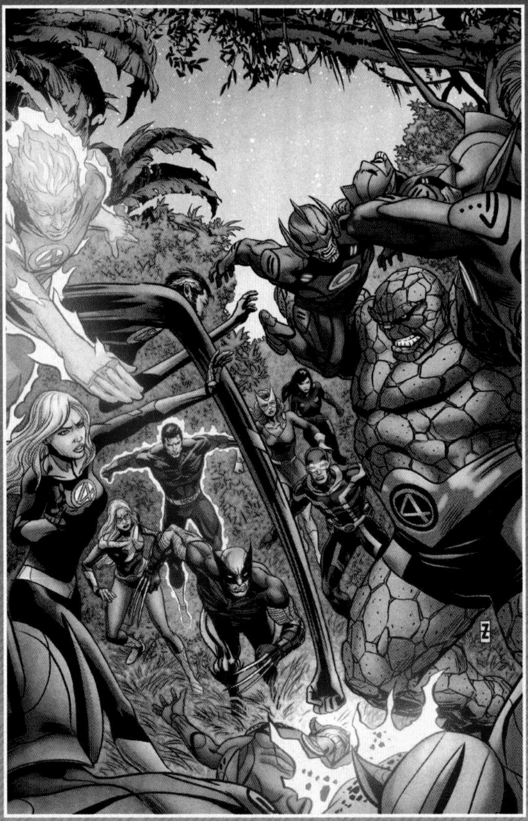

#21 Action Figure variant by
Patch Zircher & **Morry Hollowell**

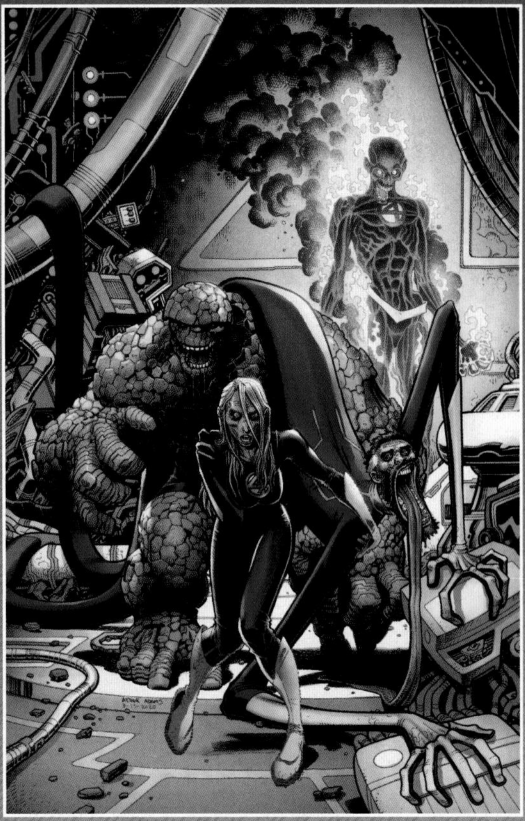

#21 Zombies variant by
Arthur Adams & **Jason Keith**

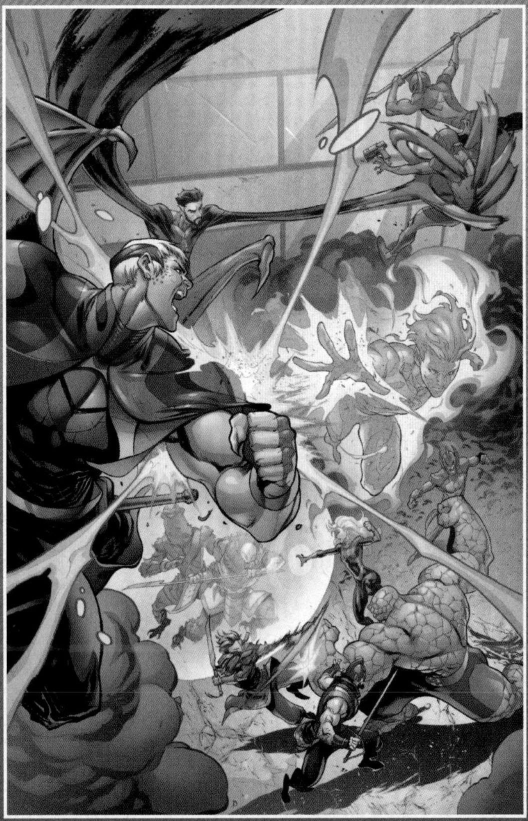

#22 variant by
Iban Coello & **Espen Grundetjern**

23

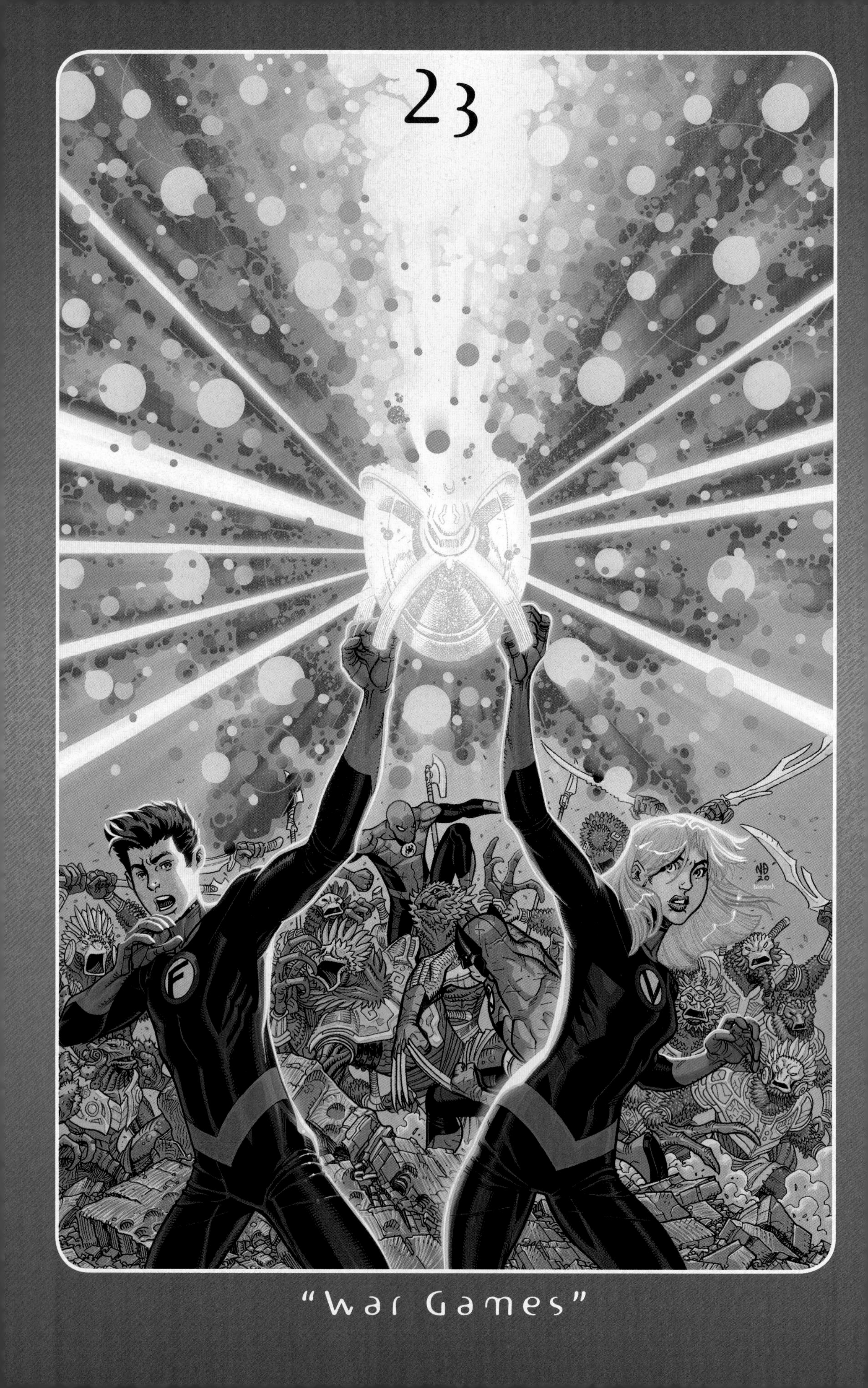

"War Games"

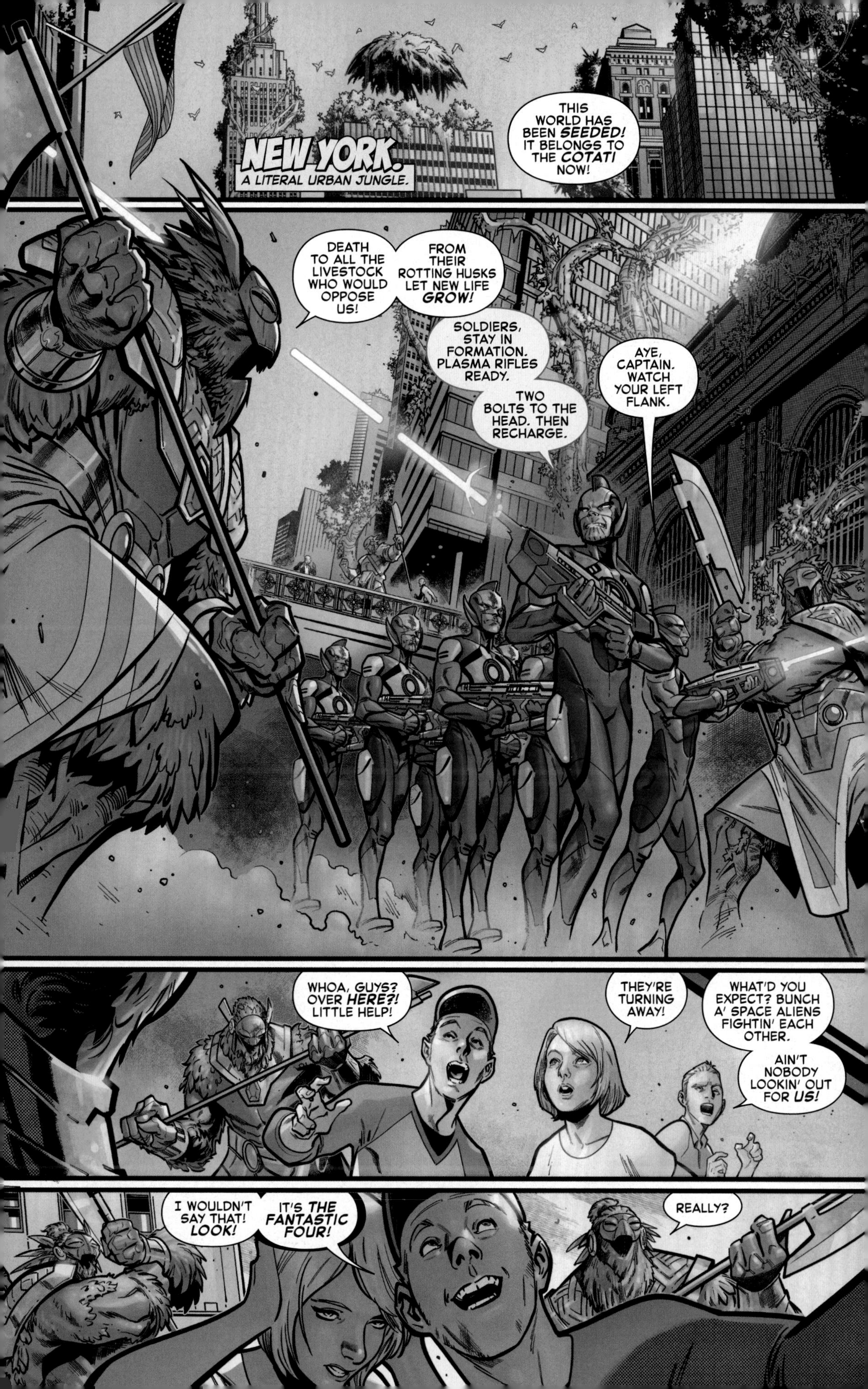
NEW YORK.
A LITERAL URBAN JUNGLE.
THIS WORLD HAS BEEN SEEDED! IT BELONGS TO THE COTATI NOW!
DEATH TO ALL THE LIVESTOCK WHO WOULD OPPOSE US!
FROM THEIR ROTTING HUSKS LET NEW LIFE GROW!
SOLDIERS, STAY IN FORMATION. PLASMA RIFLES READY.
TWO BOLTS TO THE HEAD. THEN RECHARGE.
AYE, CAPTAIN. WATCH YOUR LEFT FLANK.
WHOA, GUYS? OVER HERE?! LITTLE HELP!
THEY'RE TURNING AWAY!
WHAT'D YOU EXPECT? BUNCH A' SPACE ALIENS FIGHTIN' EACH OTHER.
AIN'T NOBODY LOOKIN' OUT FOR US!
I WOULDN'T SAY THAT! LOOK!
IT'S THE FANTASTIC FOUR!
REALLY?

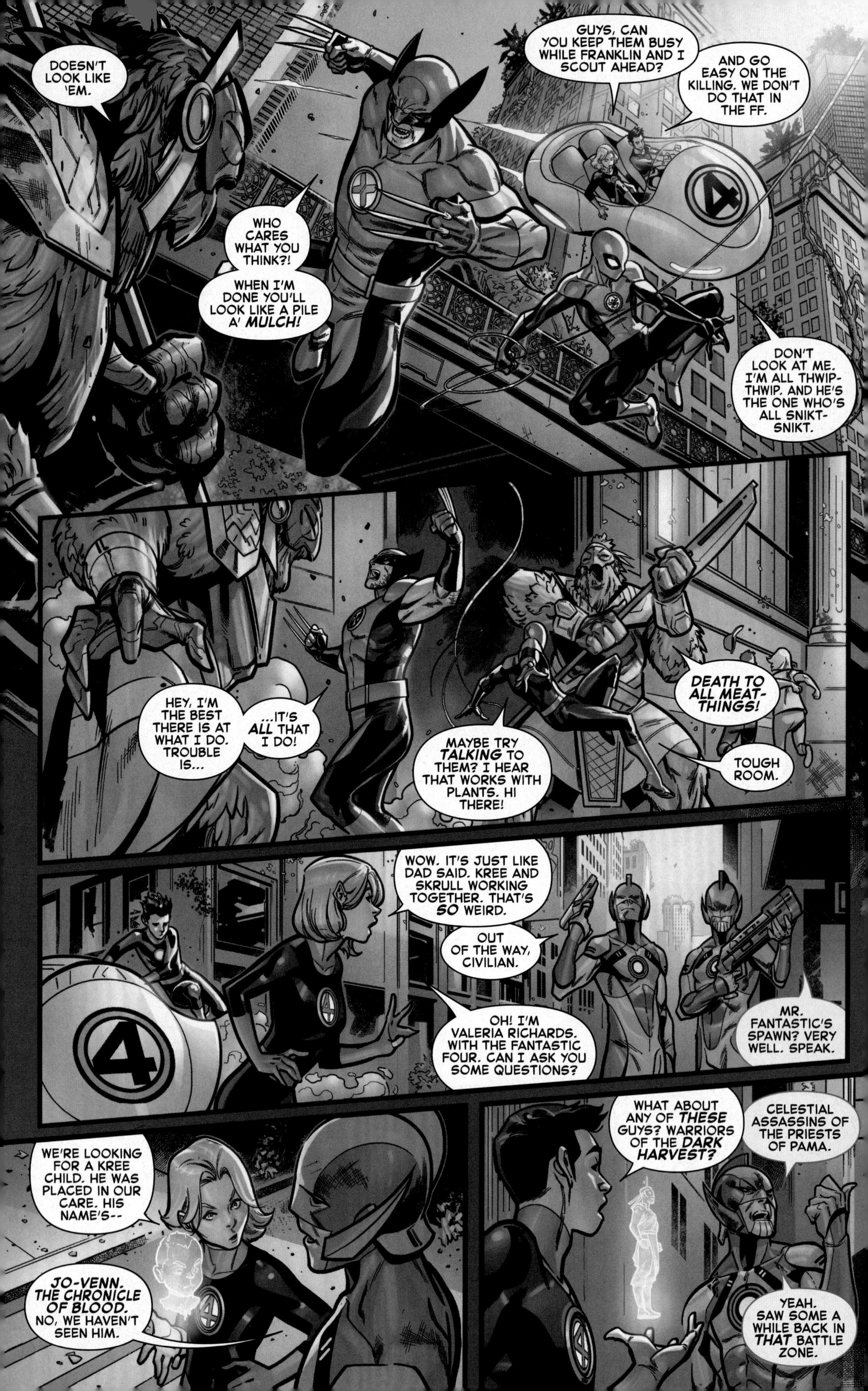
DOESN'T LOOK LIKE 'EM.
WHO CARES WHAT YOU THINK?!
WHEN I'M DONE YOU'LL LOOK LIKE A PILE A' *MULCH!*
GUYS, CAN YOU KEEP THEM BUSY WHILE FRANKLIN AND I SCOUT AHEAD?
AND GO EASY ON THE KILLING. WE DON'T DO THAT IN THE FF.
DON'T LOOK AT ME. I'M ALL THWIP-THWIP. AND HE'S THE ONE WHO'S ALL SNIKT-SNIKT.
HEY, I'M THE BEST THERE IS AT WHAT I DO. TROUBLE IS...
...IT'S *ALL* THAT I DO!
MAYBE TRY *TALKING* TO THEM? I HEAR THAT WORKS WITH PLANTS. HI THERE!
DEATH TO ALL MEAT-THINGS!
TOUGH ROOM.
WOW. IT'S JUST LIKE DAD SAID. KREE AND SKRULL WORKING TOGETHER. THAT'S *SO* WEIRD.
OUT OF THE WAY, CIVILIAN.
OH! I'M VALERIA RICHARDS. WITH THE FANTASTIC FOUR. CAN I ASK YOU SOME QUESTIONS?
MR. FANTASTIC'S SPAWN? VERY WELL. SPEAK.
WE'RE LOOKING FOR A KREE CHILD. HE WAS PLACED IN OUR CARE. HIS NAME'S--
JO-VENN. THE CHRONICLE OF BLOOD. NO, WE HAVEN'T SEEN HIM.
WHAT ABOUT ANY OF *THESE* GUYS? WARRIORS OF THE *DARK HARVEST?*
CELESTIAL ASSASSINS OF THE PRIESTS OF PAMA.
YEAH. SAW SOME A WHILE BACK IN *THAT* BATTLE ZONE.

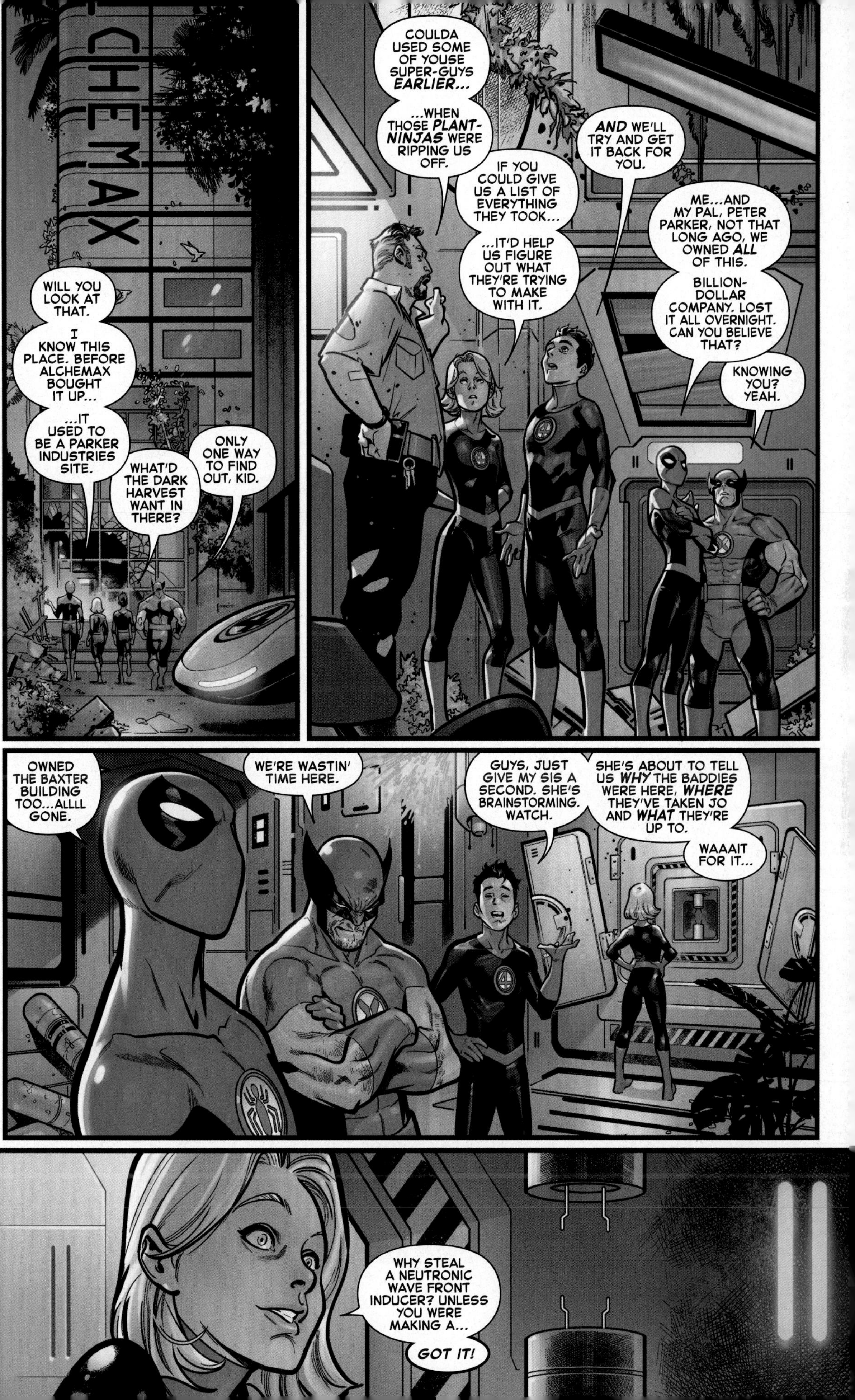
ALCHEMAX
WILL YOU LOOK AT THAT.
I KNOW THIS PLACE. BEFORE ALCHEMAX BOUGHT IT UP...
...IT USED TO BE A PARKER INDUSTRIES SITE.
WHAT'D THE DARK HARVEST WANT IN THERE?
ONLY ONE WAY TO FIND OUT, KID.
COULDA USED SOME OF YOUSE SUPER-GUYS EARLIER...
...WHEN THOSE PLANT-NINJAS WERE RIPPING US OFF.
IF YOU COULD GIVE US A LIST OF EVERYTHING THEY TOOK...
...IT'D HELP US FIGURE OUT WHAT THEY'RE TRYING TO MAKE WITH IT.
AND WE'LL TRY AND GET IT BACK FOR YOU.
ME...AND MY PAL, PETER PARKER, NOT THAT LONG AGO, WE OWNED ALL OF THIS.
BILLION-DOLLAR COMPANY. LOST IT ALL OVERNIGHT. CAN YOU BELIEVE THAT?
KNOWING YOU? YEAH.
OWNED THE BAXTER BUILDING TOO...ALLLL GONE.
WE'RE WASTIN' TIME HERE.
GUYS, JUST GIVE MY SIS A SECOND. SHE'S BRAINSTORMING. WATCH.
SHE'S ABOUT TO TELL US WHY THE BADDIES WERE HERE, WHERE THEY'VE TAKEN JO AND WHAT THEY'RE UP TO.
WAAAIT FOR IT...
WHY STEAL A NEUTRONIC WAVE FRONT INDUCER? UNLESS YOU WERE MAKING A...
GOT IT!

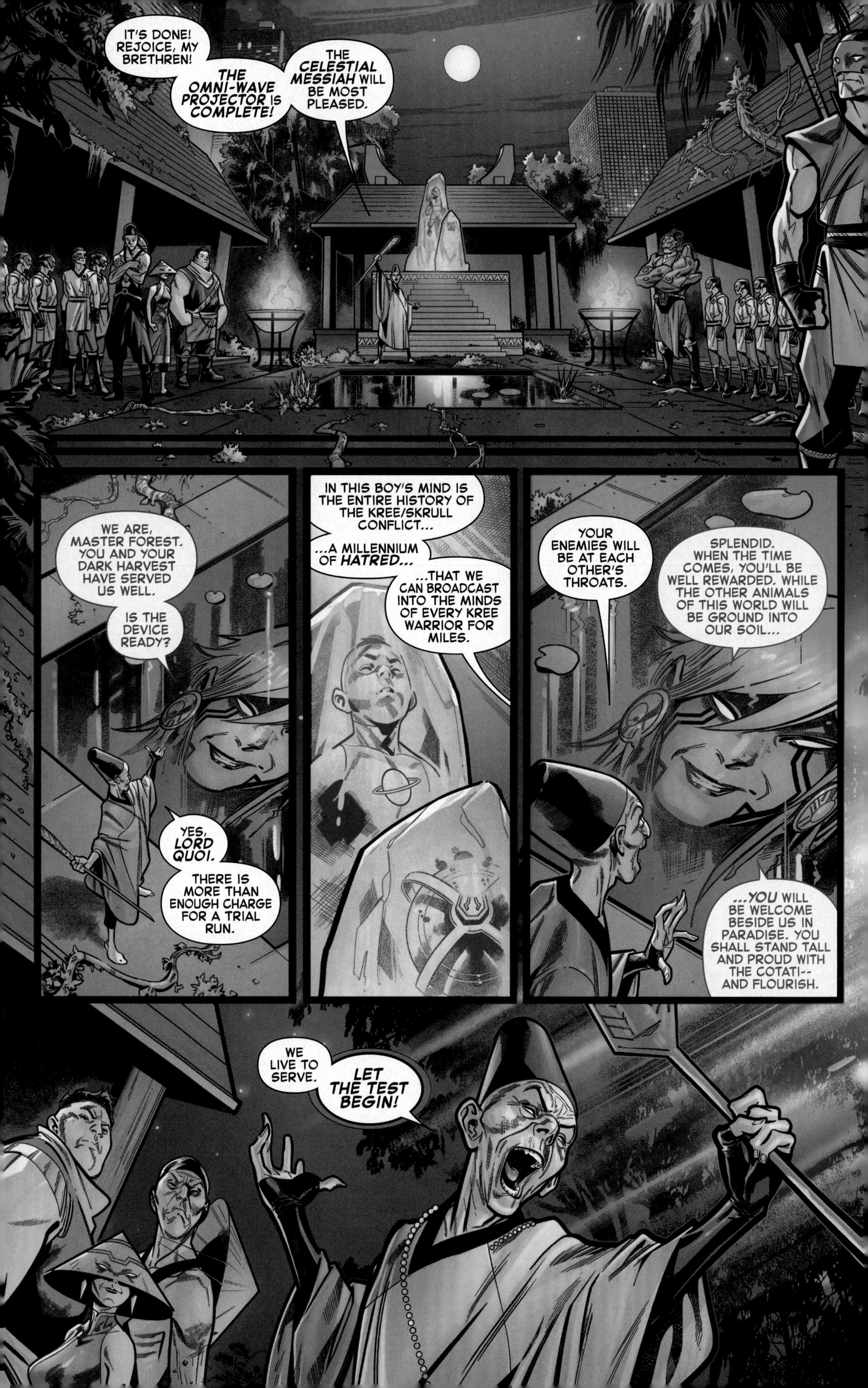
IT'S DONE! REJOICE, MY BRETHREN!
THE OMNI-WAVE PROJECTOR IS COMPLETE!
THE CELESTIAL MESSIAH WILL BE MOST PLEASED.
WE ARE, MASTER FOREST. YOU AND YOUR DARK HARVEST HAVE SERVED US WELL.
IS THE DEVICE READY?
YES, LORD QUOI.
THERE IS MORE THAN ENOUGH CHARGE FOR A TRIAL RUN.
IN THIS BOY'S MIND IS THE ENTIRE HISTORY OF THE KREE/SKRULL CONFLICT...
...A MILLENNIUM OF HATRED...
...THAT WE CAN BROADCAST INTO THE MINDS OF EVERY KREE WARRIOR FOR MILES.
YOUR ENEMIES WILL BE AT EACH OTHER'S THROATS.
SPLENDID. WHEN THE TIME COMES, YOU'LL BE WELL REWARDED. WHILE THE OTHER ANIMALS OF THIS WORLD WILL BE GROUND INTO OUR SOIL...
...YOU WILL BE WELCOME BESIDE US IN PARADISE. YOU SHALL STAND TALL AND PROUD WITH THE COTATI-- AND FLOURISH.
WE LIVE TO SERVE.
LET THE TEST BEGIN!

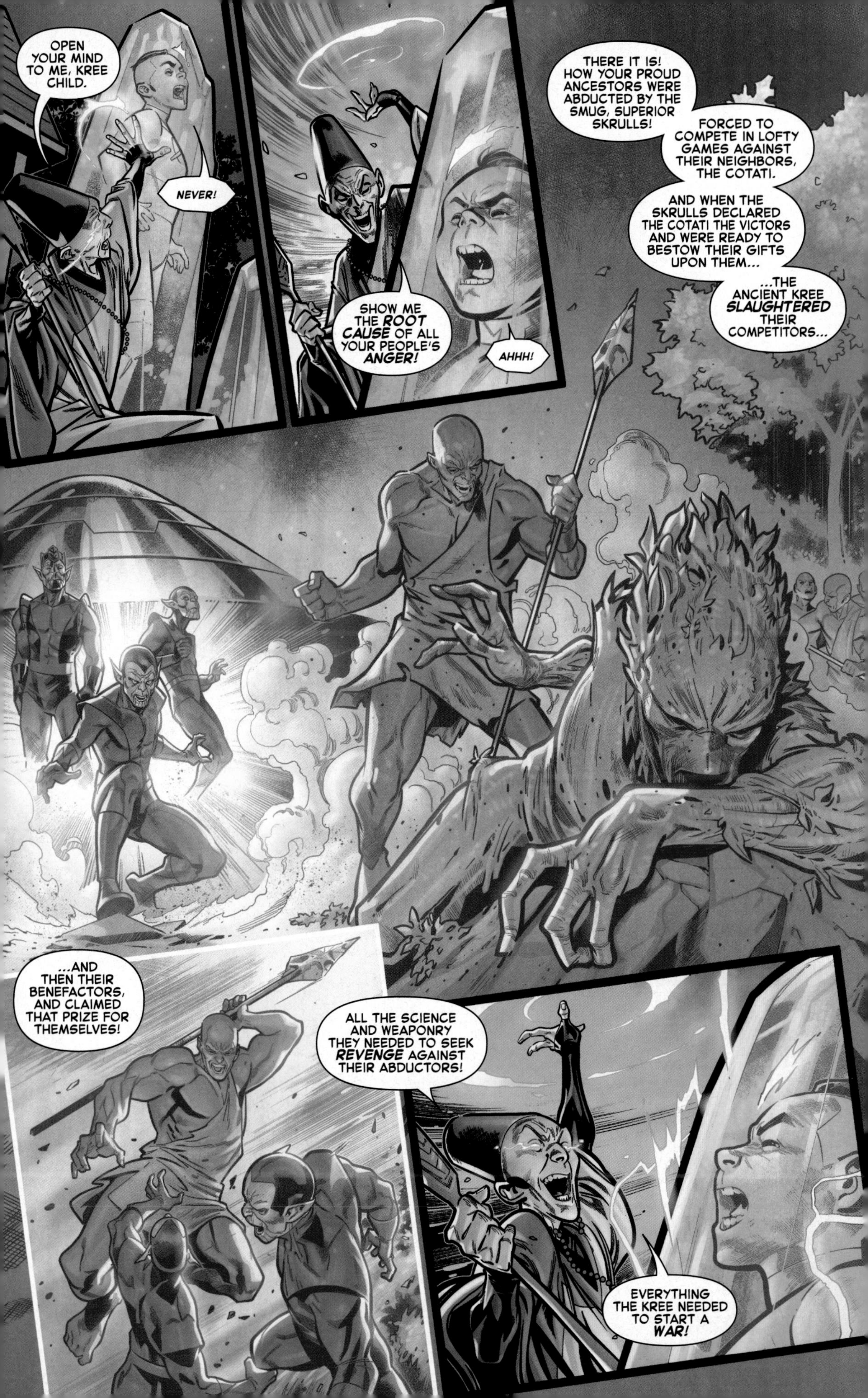
OPEN YOUR MIND TO ME, KREE CHILD.
NEVER!
SHOW ME THE ROOT CAUSE OF ALL YOUR PEOPLE'S ANGER!
AHHH!
THERE IT IS! HOW YOUR PROUD ANCESTORS WERE ABDUCTED BY THE SMUG, SUPERIOR SKRULLS!
FORCED TO COMPETE IN LOFTY GAMES AGAINST THEIR NEIGHBORS, THE COTATI.
AND WHEN THE SKRULLS DECLARED THE COTATI THE VICTORS AND WERE READY TO BESTOW THEIR GIFTS UPON THEM...
...THE ANCIENT KREE SLAUGHTERED THEIR COMPETITORS...
...AND THEN THEIR BENEFACTORS, AND CLAIMED THAT PRIZE FOR THEMSELVES!
ALL THE SCIENCE AND WEAPONRY THEY NEEDED TO SEEK REVENGE AGAINST THEIR ABDUCTORS!
EVERYTHING THE KREE NEEDED TO START A WAR!

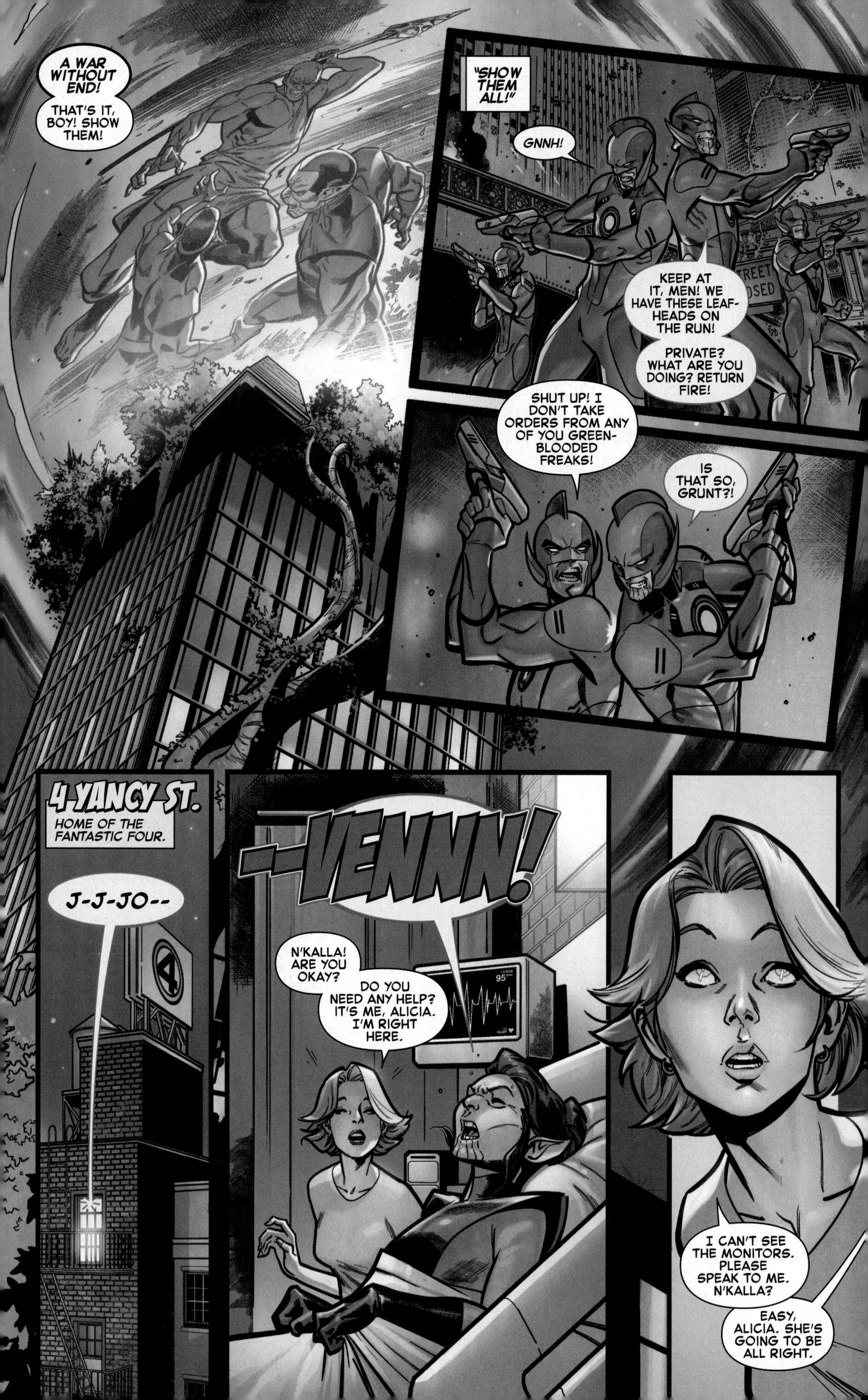
A WAR WITHOUT END!
THAT'S IT, BOY! SHOW THEM!
"SHOW THEM ALL!"
GNNH!
KEEP AT IT, MEN! WE HAVE THESE LEAF-HEADS ON THE RUN!
PRIVATE? WHAT ARE YOU DOING? RETURN FIRE!
SHUT UP! I DON'T TAKE ORDERS FROM ANY OF YOU GREEN-BLOODED FREAKS!
IS THAT SO, GRUNT?!
4 YANCY ST.
HOME OF THE FANTASTIC FOUR.
J-J-JO--
--VENNN!
N'KALLA! ARE YOU OKAY?
DO YOU NEED ANY HELP? IT'S ME, ALICIA. I'M RIGHT HERE.
I CAN'T SEE THE MONITORS. PLEASE SPEAK TO ME. N'KALLA?
EASY, ALICIA. SHE'S GOING TO BE ALL RIGHT.

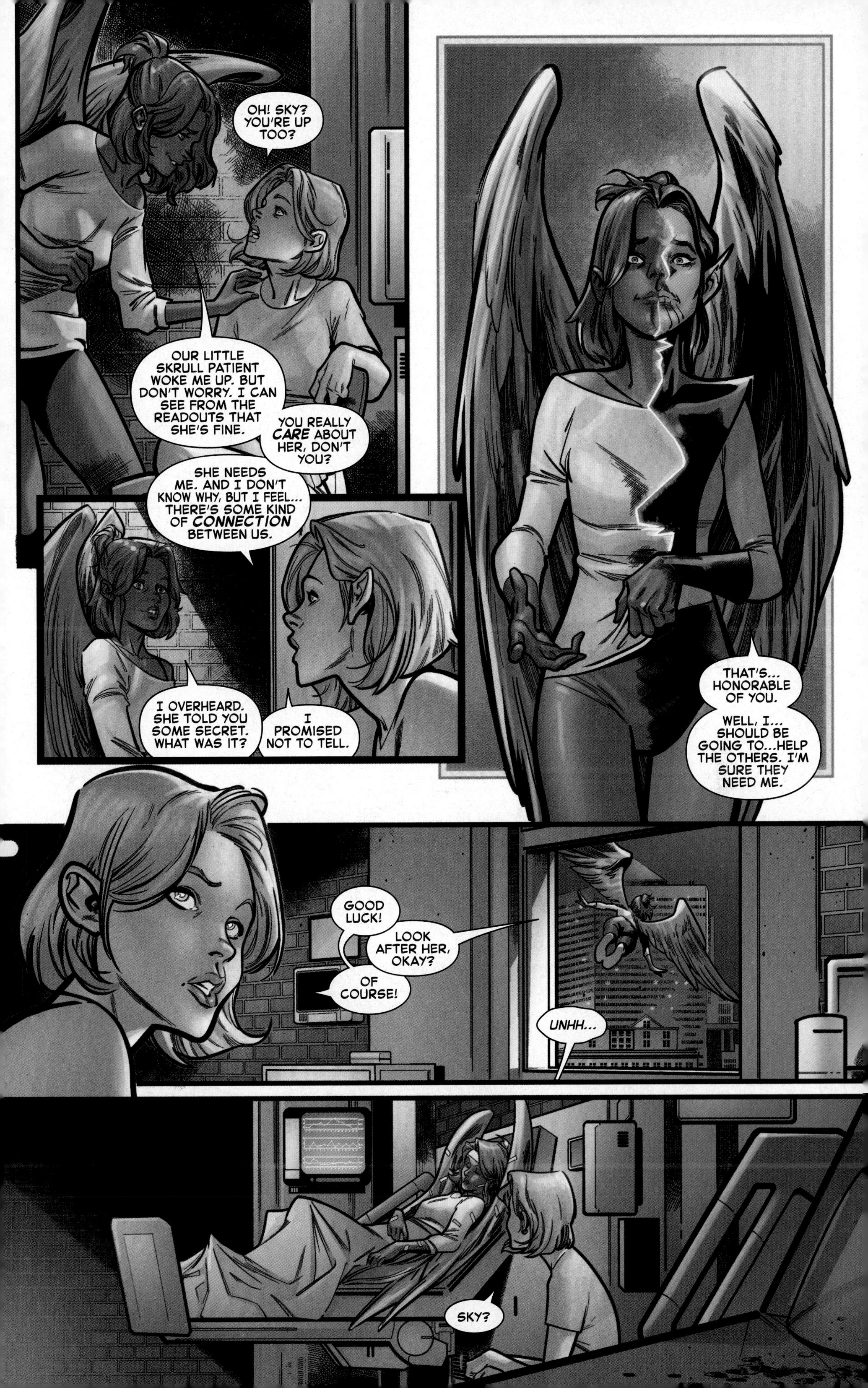
OH! SKY? YOU'RE UP TOO?
OUR LITTLE SKRULL PATIENT WOKE ME UP. BUT DON'T WORRY. I CAN SEE FROM THE READOUTS THAT SHE'S FINE.
YOU REALLY CARE ABOUT HER, DON'T YOU?
SHE NEEDS ME. AND I DON'T KNOW WHY, BUT I FEEL... THERE'S SOME KIND OF CONNECTION BETWEEN US.
I OVERHEARD. SHE TOLD YOU SOME SECRET. WHAT WAS IT?
I PROMISED NOT TO TELL.
THAT'S... HONORABLE OF YOU.
WELL, I... SHOULD BE GOING TO...HELP THE OTHERS. I'M SURE THEY NEED ME.
GOOD LUCK!
LOOK AFTER HER, OKAY?
OF COURSE!
UNHH...
SKY?

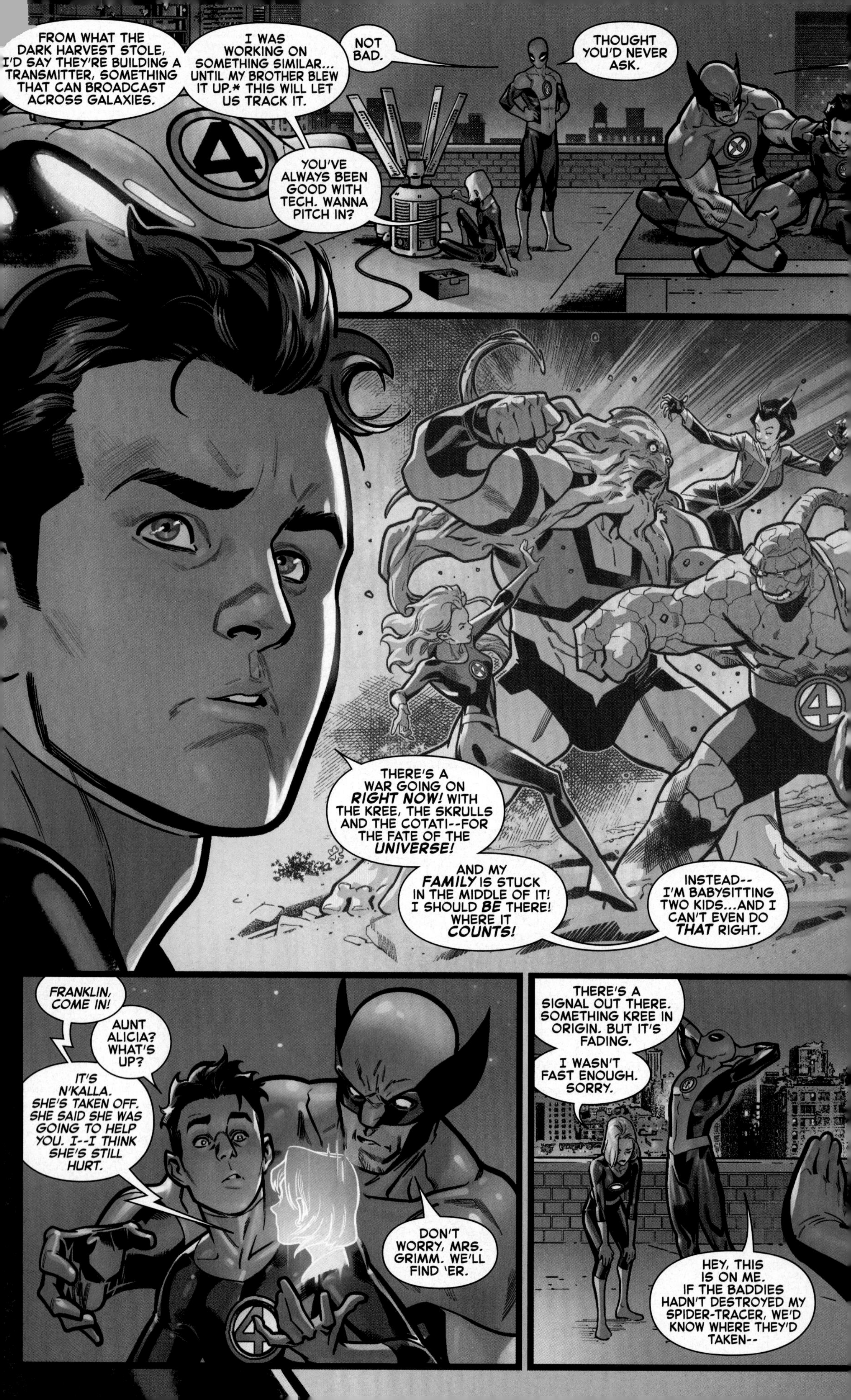
FROM WHAT THE DARK HARVEST STOLE, I'D SAY THEY'RE BUILDING A TRANSMITTER, SOMETHING THAT CAN BROADCAST ACROSS GALAXIES.
I WAS WORKING ON SOMETHING SIMILAR... UNTIL MY BROTHER BLEW IT UP.* THIS WILL LET US TRACK IT.
NOT BAD.
YOU'VE ALWAYS BEEN GOOD WITH TECH. WANNA PITCH IN?
THOUGHT YOU'D NEVER ASK.
THERE'S A WAR GOING ON RIGHT NOW! WITH THE KREE, THE SKRULLS AND THE COTATI--FOR THE FATE OF THE UNIVERSE!
AND MY FAMILY IS STUCK IN THE MIDDLE OF IT! I SHOULD BE THERE! WHERE IT COUNTS!
INSTEAD-- I'M BABYSITTING TWO KIDS...AND I CAN'T EVEN DO THAT RIGHT.
FRANKLIN, COME IN!
AUNT ALICIA? WHAT'S UP?
IT'S N'KALLA. SHE'S TAKEN OFF. SHE SAID SHE WAS GOING TO HELP YOU. I--I THINK SHE'S STILL HURT.
DON'T WORRY, MRS. GRIMM. WE'LL FIND 'ER.
THERE'S A SIGNAL OUT THERE. SOMETHING KREE IN ORIGIN. BUT IT'S FADING.
I WASN'T FAST ENOUGH. SORRY.
HEY, THIS IS ON ME. IF THE BADDIES HADN'T DESTROYED MY SPIDER-TRACER, WE'D KNOW WHERE THEY'D TAKEN--

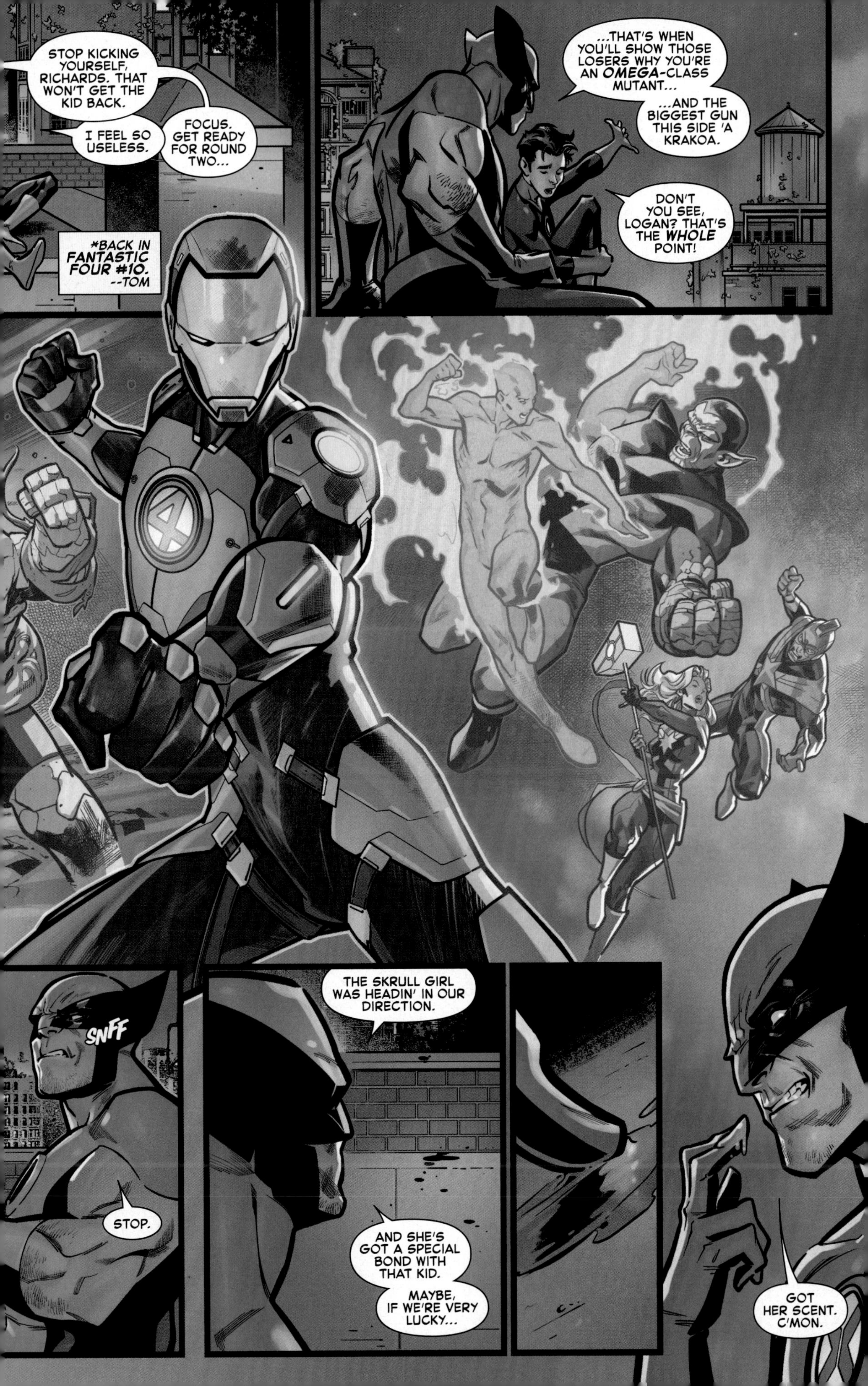
STOP KICKING YOURSELF, RICHARDS. THAT WON'T GET THE KID BACK.
I FEEL SO USELESS.
FOCUS. GET READY FOR ROUND TWO...
*BACK IN FANTASTIC FOUR #10. --TOM
...THAT'S WHEN YOU'LL SHOW THOSE LOSERS WHY YOU'RE AN OMEGA-CLASS MUTANT...
...AND THE BIGGEST GUN THIS SIDE 'A KRAKOA.
DON'T YOU SEE, LOGAN? THAT'S THE WHOLE POINT!
SNFF
STOP.
THE SKRULL GIRL WAS HEADIN' IN OUR DIRECTION.
AND SHE'S GOT A SPECIAL BOND WITH THAT KID.
MAYBE, IF WE'RE VERY LUCKY...
GOT HER SCENT. C'MON.

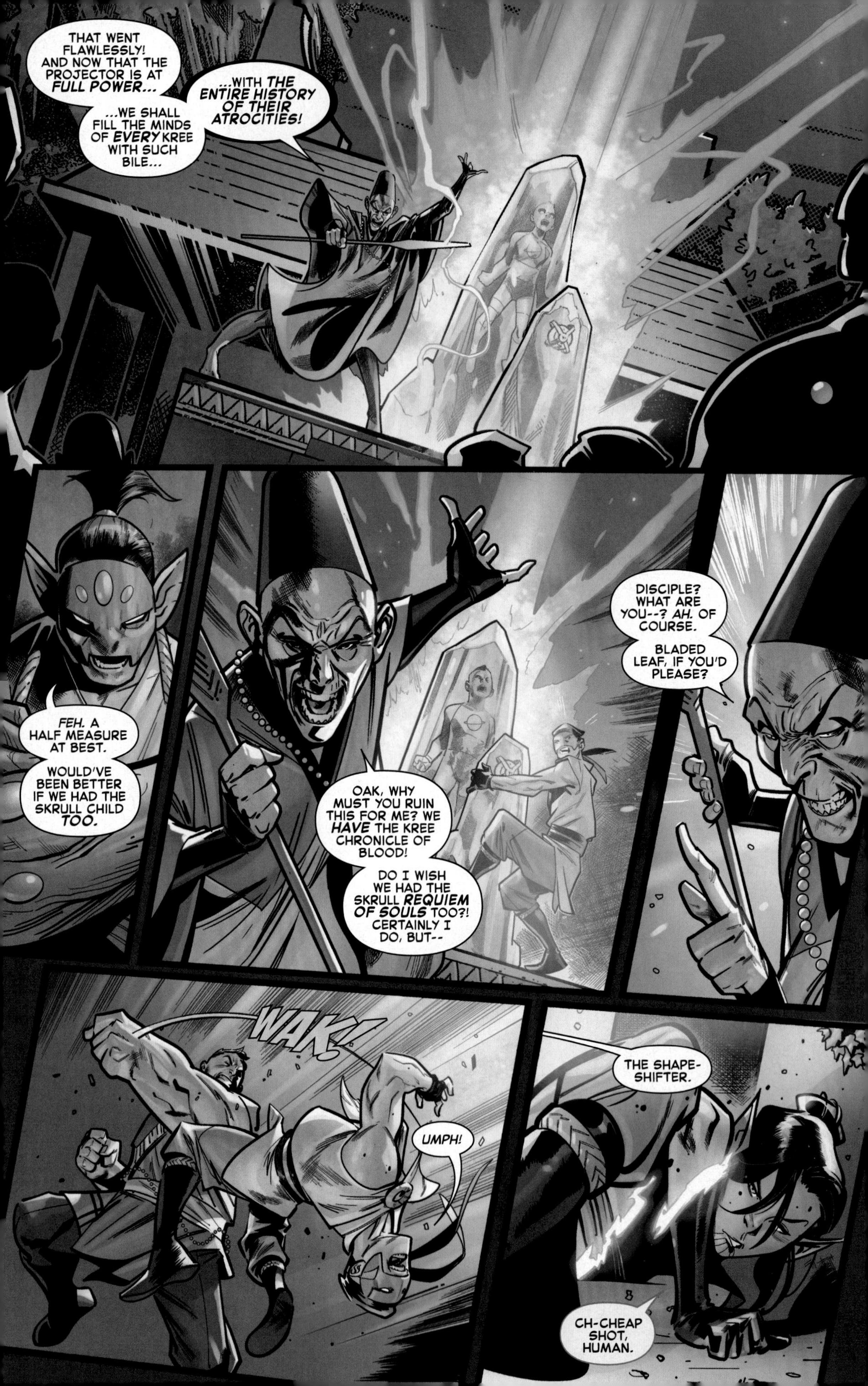
THAT WENT FLAWLESSLY! AND NOW THAT THE PROJECTOR IS AT FULL POWER...
...WE SHALL FILL THE MINDS OF EVERY KREE WITH SUCH BILE...
...WITH THE ENTIRE HISTORY OF THEIR ATROCITIES!
FEH. A HALF MEASURE AT BEST.
WOULD'VE BEEN BETTER IF WE HAD THE SKRULL CHILD TOO.
OAK, WHY MUST YOU RUIN THIS FOR ME? WE HAVE THE KREE CHRONICLE OF BLOOD!
DO I WISH WE HAD THE SKRULL REQUIEM OF SOULS TOO?! CERTAINLY I DO, BUT--
DISCIPLE? WHAT ARE YOU--? AH. OF COURSE.
BLADED LEAF, IF YOU'D PLEASE?
WAK!!
UMPH!
THE SHAPE-SHIFTER.
CH-CHEAP SHOT, HUMAN.

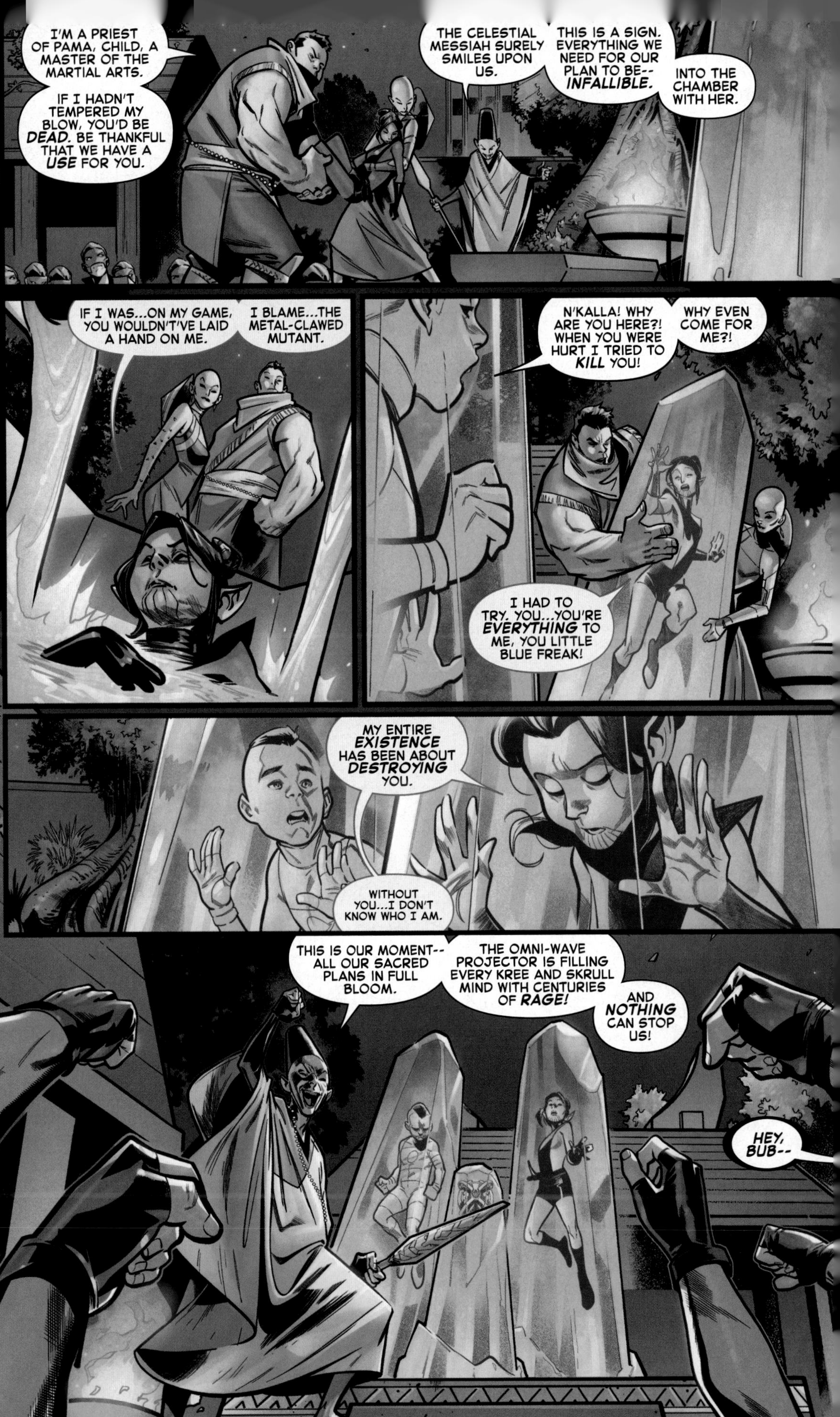
I'M A PRIEST OF PAMA, CHILD, A MASTER OF THE MARTIAL ARTS.
IF I HADN'T TEMPERED MY BLOW, YOU'D BE DEAD. BE THANKFUL THAT WE HAVE A USE FOR YOU.
THE CELESTIAL MESSIAH SURELY SMILES UPON US.
THIS IS A SIGN. EVERYTHING WE NEED FOR OUR PLAN TO BE-- INFALLIBLE.
INTO THE CHAMBER WITH HER.
IF I WAS...ON MY GAME, YOU WOULDN'T'VE LAID A HAND ON ME.
I BLAME...THE METAL-CLAWED MUTANT.
N'KALLA! WHY ARE YOU HERE?! WHEN YOU WERE HURT I TRIED TO KILL YOU!
WHY EVEN COME FOR ME?!
I HAD TO TRY. YOU...YOU'RE EVERYTHING TO ME, YOU LITTLE BLUE FREAK!
MY ENTIRE EXISTENCE HAS BEEN ABOUT DESTROYING YOU.
WITHOUT YOU...I DON'T KNOW WHO I AM.
THIS IS OUR MOMENT-- ALL OUR SACRED PLANS IN FULL BLOOM.
THE OMNI-WAVE PROJECTOR IS FILLING EVERY KREE AND SKRULL MIND WITH CENTURIES OF RAGE!
AND NOTHING CAN STOP US!
HEY, BUB--

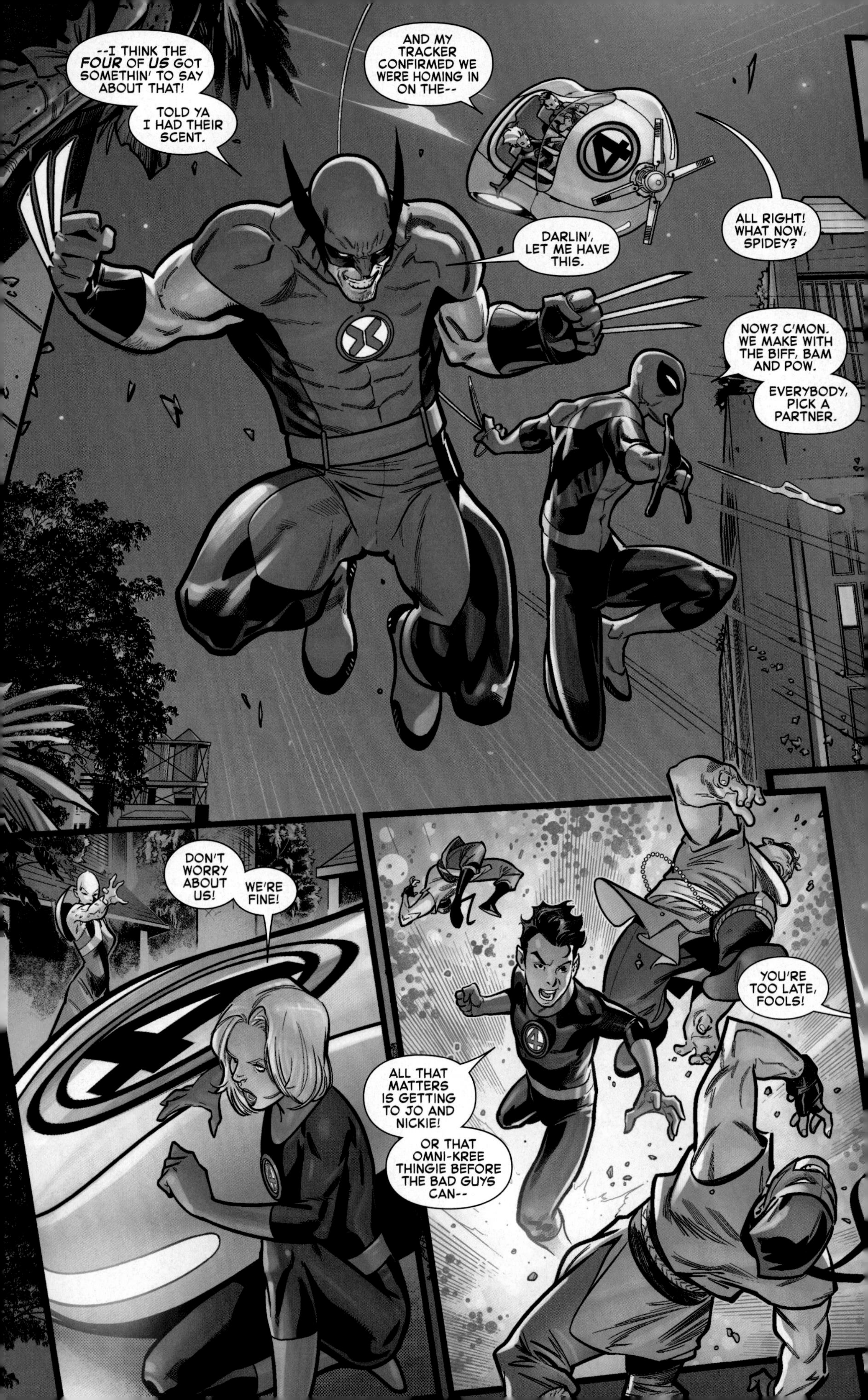
--I THINK THE FOUR OF US GOT SOMETHIN' TO SAY ABOUT THAT!
TOLD YA I HAD THEIR SCENT.
AND MY TRACKER CONFIRMED WE WERE HOMING IN ON THE--
DARLIN', LET ME HAVE THIS.
ALL RIGHT! WHAT NOW, SPIDEY?
NOW? C'MON. WE MAKE WITH THE BIFF, BAM AND POW.
EVERYBODY, PICK A PARTNER.
DON'T WORRY ABOUT US!
WE'RE FINE!
YOU'RE TOO LATE, FOOLS!
ALL THAT MATTERS IS GETTING TO JO AND NICKIE!
OR THAT OMNI-KREE THINGIE BEFORE THE BAD GUYS CAN--

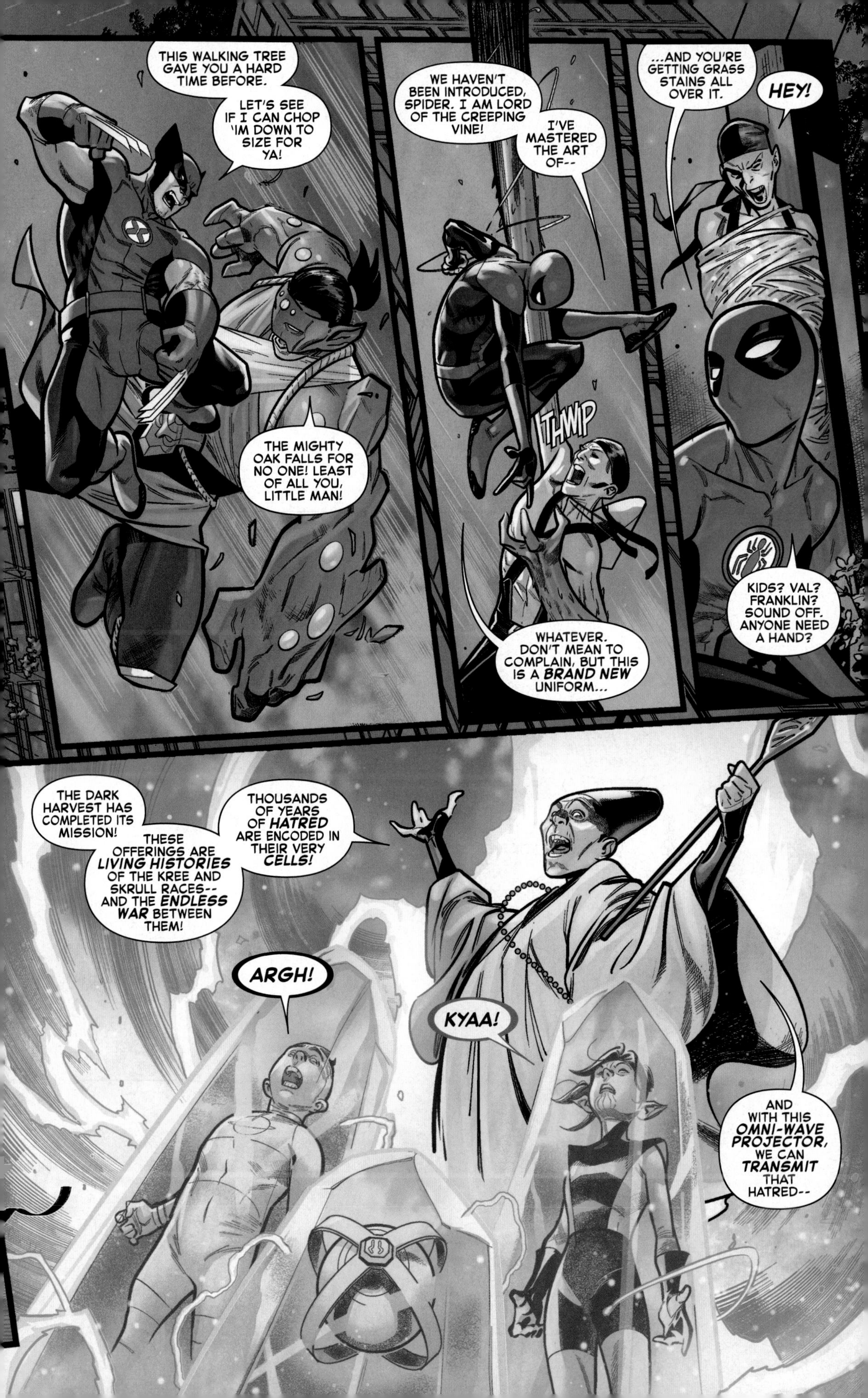
THIS WALKING TREE GAVE YOU A HARD TIME BEFORE.
LET'S SEE IF I CAN CHOP 'IM DOWN TO SIZE FOR YA!
THE MIGHTY OAK FALLS FOR NO ONE! LEAST OF ALL YOU, LITTLE MAN!
WE HAVEN'T BEEN INTRODUCED, SPIDER. I AM LORD OF THE CREEPING VINE!
I'VE MASTERED THE ART OF--
THWIP
WHATEVER. DON'T MEAN TO COMPLAIN, BUT THIS IS A BRAND NEW UNIFORM...
...AND YOU'RE GETTING GRASS STAINS ALL OVER IT.
HEY!
KIDS? VAL? FRANKLIN? SOUND OFF. ANYONE NEED A HAND?
THE DARK HARVEST HAS COMPLETED ITS MISSION!
THESE OFFERINGS ARE LIVING HISTORIES OF THE KREE AND SKRULL RACES-- AND THE ENDLESS WAR BETWEEN THEM!
THOUSANDS OF YEARS OF HATRED ARE ENCODED IN THEIR VERY CELLS!
ARGH!
KYAA!
AND WITH THIS OMNI-WAVE PROJECTOR, WE CAN TRANSMIT THAT HATRED--

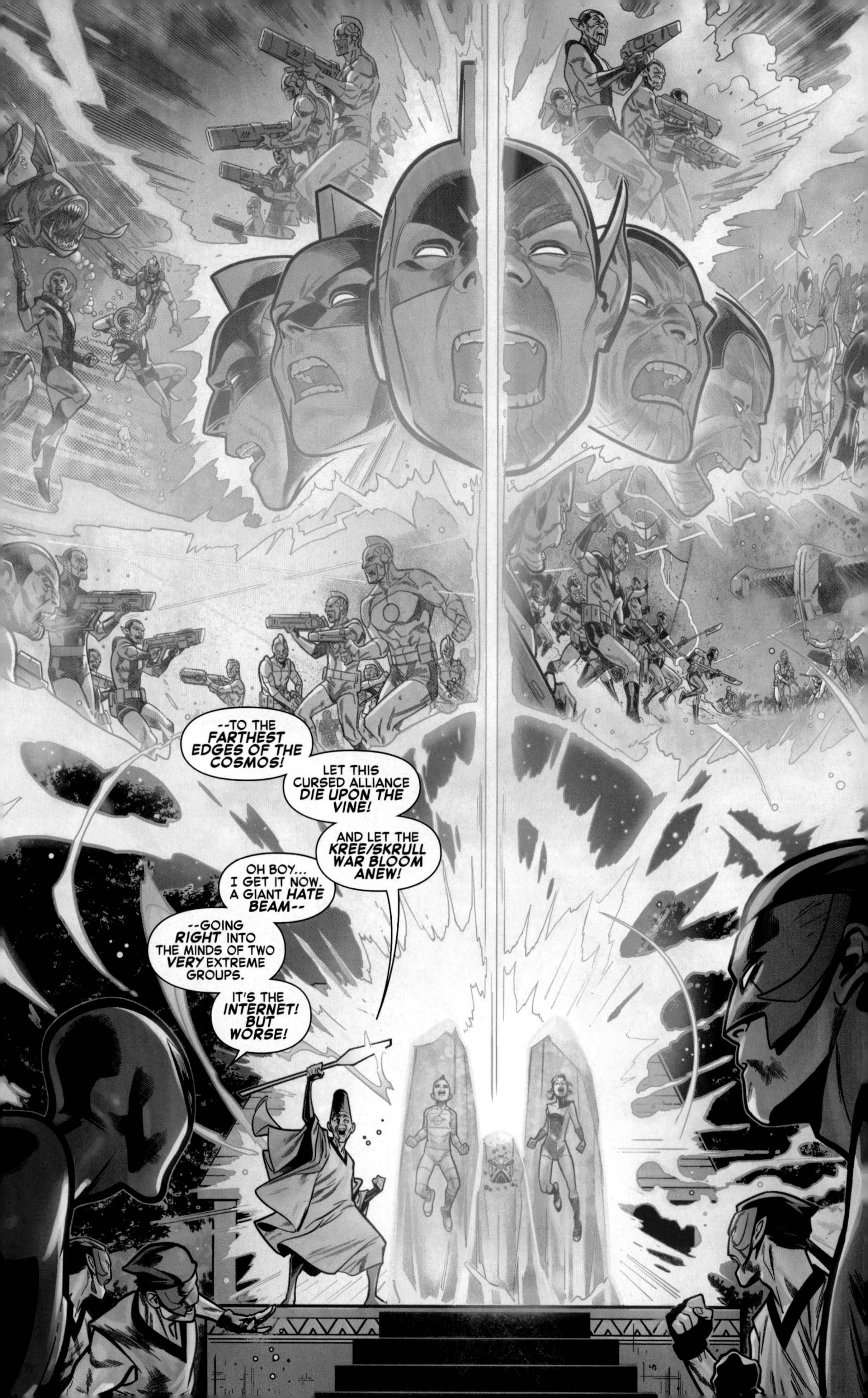
--TO THE FARTHEST EDGES OF THE COSMOS!
LET THIS CURSED ALLIANCE DIE UPON THE VINE!
AND LET THE KREE/SKRULL WAR BLOOM ANEW!
OH BOY... I GET IT NOW. A GIANT HATE BEAM--
--GOING RIGHT INTO THE MINDS OF TWO VERY EXTREME GROUPS.
IT'S THE INTERNET! BUT WORSE!

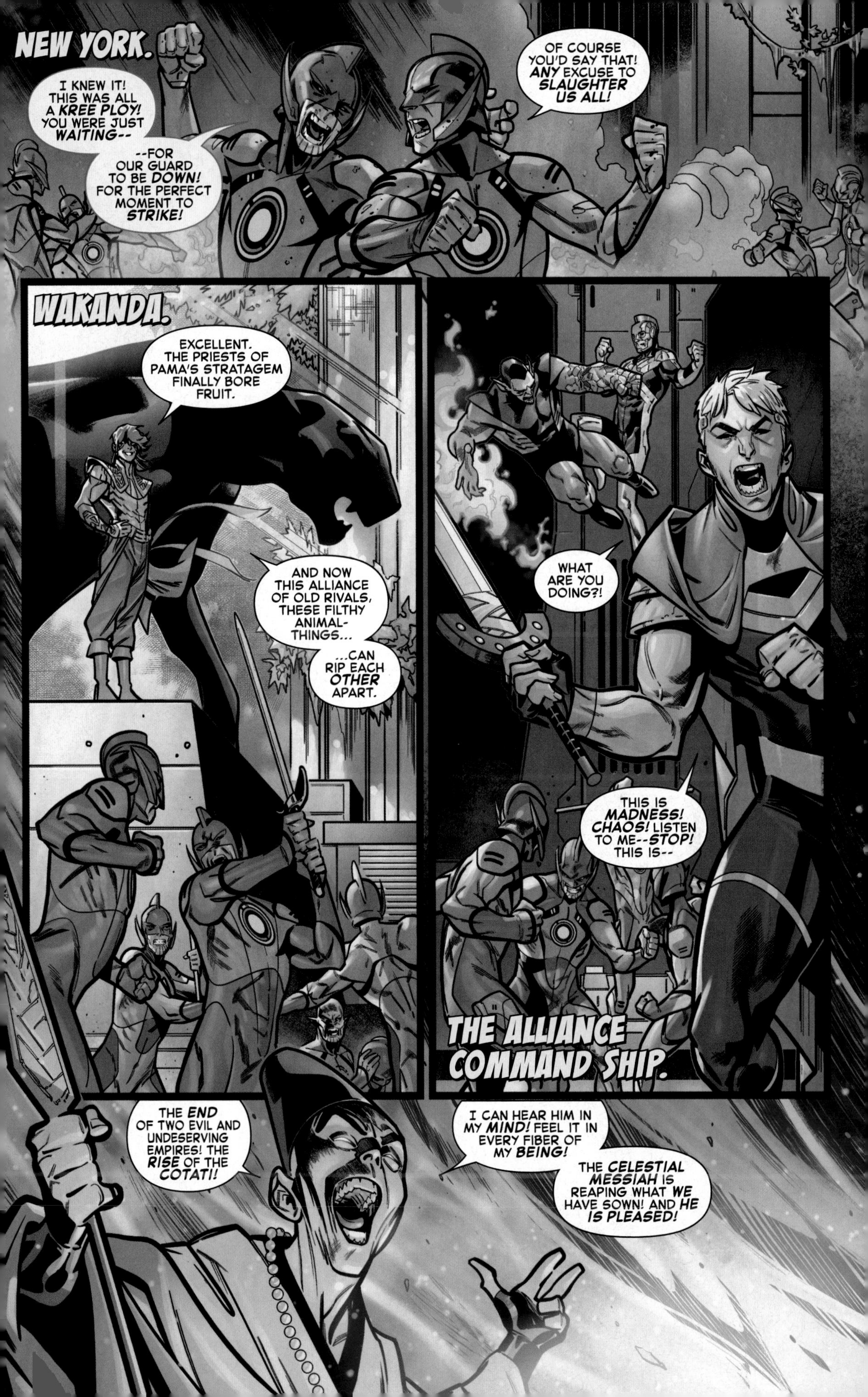
NEW YORK.
I KNEW IT! THIS WAS ALL A KREE PLOY! YOU WERE JUST WAITING--
--FOR OUR GUARD TO BE DOWN! FOR THE PERFECT MOMENT TO STRIKE!
OF COURSE YOU'D SAY THAT! ANY EXCUSE TO SLAUGHTER US ALL!
WAKANDA.
EXCELLENT. THE PRIESTS OF PAMA'S STRATAGEM FINALLY BORE FRUIT.
AND NOW THIS ALLIANCE OF OLD RIVALS, THESE FILTHY ANIMAL-THINGS...
...CAN RIP EACH OTHER APART.
WHAT ARE YOU DOING?!
THIS IS MADNESS! CHAOS! LISTEN TO ME--STOP! THIS IS--
THE ALLIANCE COMMAND SHIP.
THE END OF TWO EVIL AND UNDESERVING EMPIRES! THE RISE OF THE COTATI!
I CAN HEAR HIM IN MY MIND! FEEL IT IN EVERY FIBER OF MY BEING!
THE CELESTIAL MESSIAH IS REAPING WHAT WE HAVE SOWN! AND HE IS PLEASED!

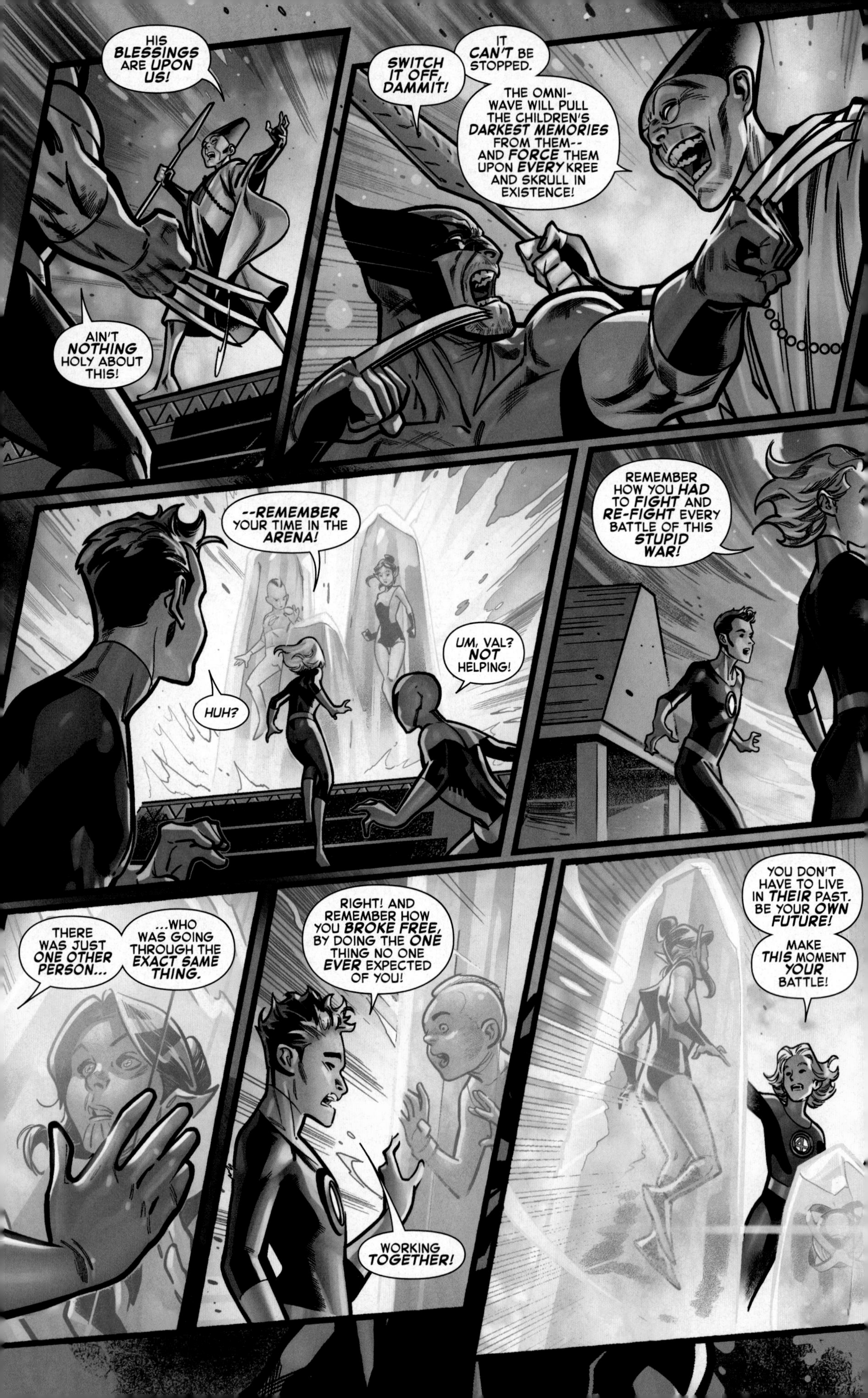
HIS BLESSINGS ARE UPON US!
AIN'T NOTHING HOLY ABOUT THIS!
SWITCH IT OFF, DAMMIT!
IT CAN'T BE STOPPED.
THE OMNI-WAVE WILL PULL THE CHILDREN'S DARKEST MEMORIES FROM THEM--
AND FORCE THEM UPON EVERY KREE AND SKRULL IN EXISTENCE!
--REMEMBER YOUR TIME IN THE ARENA!
HUH?
UM, VAL? NOT HELPING!
REMEMBER HOW YOU HAD TO FIGHT AND RE-FIGHT EVERY BATTLE OF THIS STUPID WAR!
THERE WAS JUST ONE OTHER PERSON...
...WHO WAS GOING THROUGH THE EXACT SAME THING.
RIGHT! AND REMEMBER HOW YOU BROKE FREE, BY DOING THE ONE THING NO ONE EVER EXPECTED OF YOU!
WORKING TOGETHER!
YOU DON'T HAVE TO LIVE IN THEIR PAST. BE YOUR OWN FUTURE!
MAKE THIS MOMENT YOUR BATTLE!

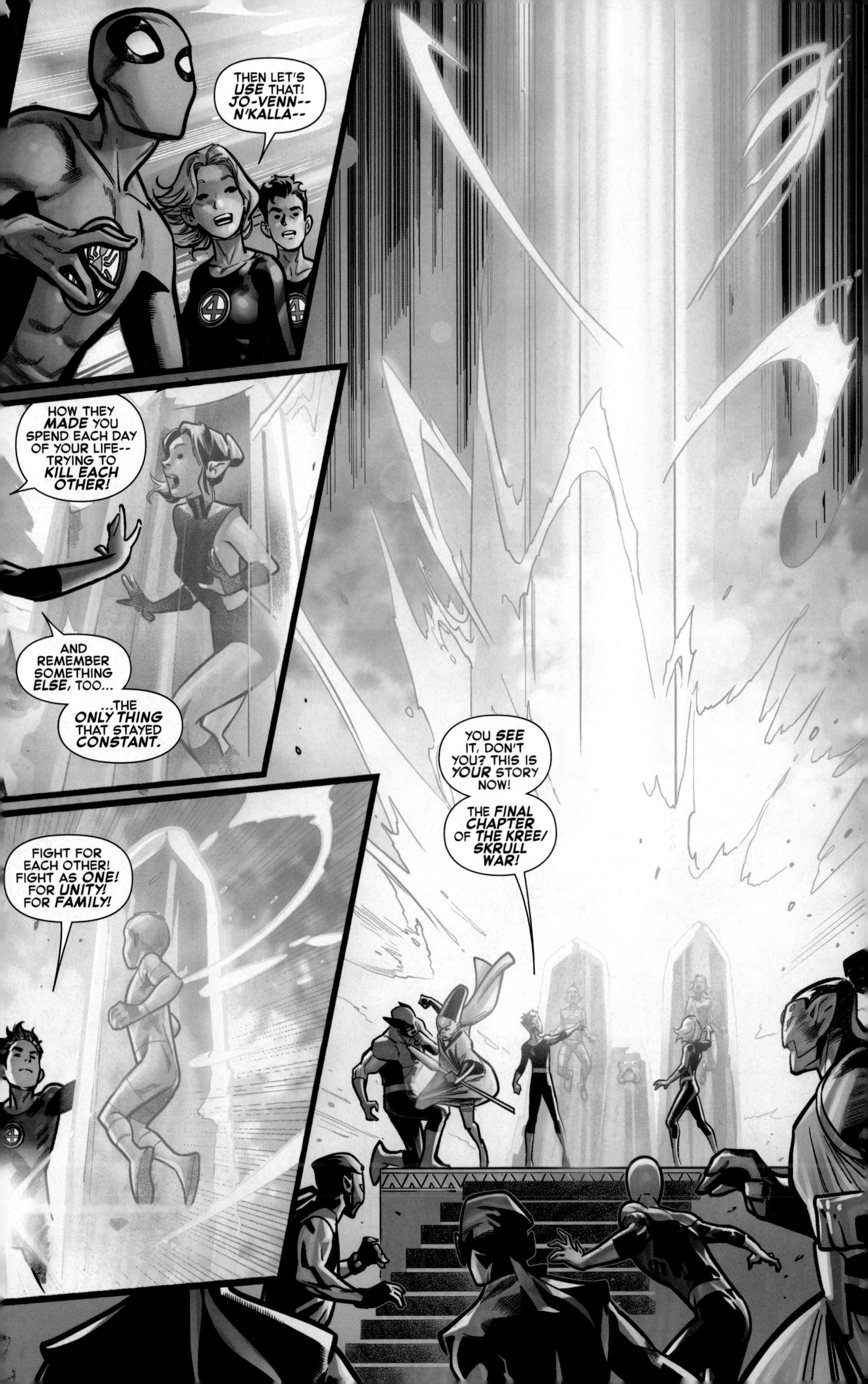
THEN LET'S USE THAT! JO-VENN-- N'KALLA--
HOW THEY MADE YOU SPEND EACH DAY OF YOUR LIFE-- TRYING TO KILL EACH OTHER!
AND REMEMBER SOMETHING ELSE, TOO...
...THE ONLY THING THAT STAYED CONSTANT.
FIGHT FOR EACH OTHER! FIGHT AS ONE! FOR UNITY! FOR FAMILY!
YOU SEE IT, DON'T YOU? THIS IS YOUR STORY NOW!
THE FINAL CHAPTER OF THE KREE/ SKRULL WAR!

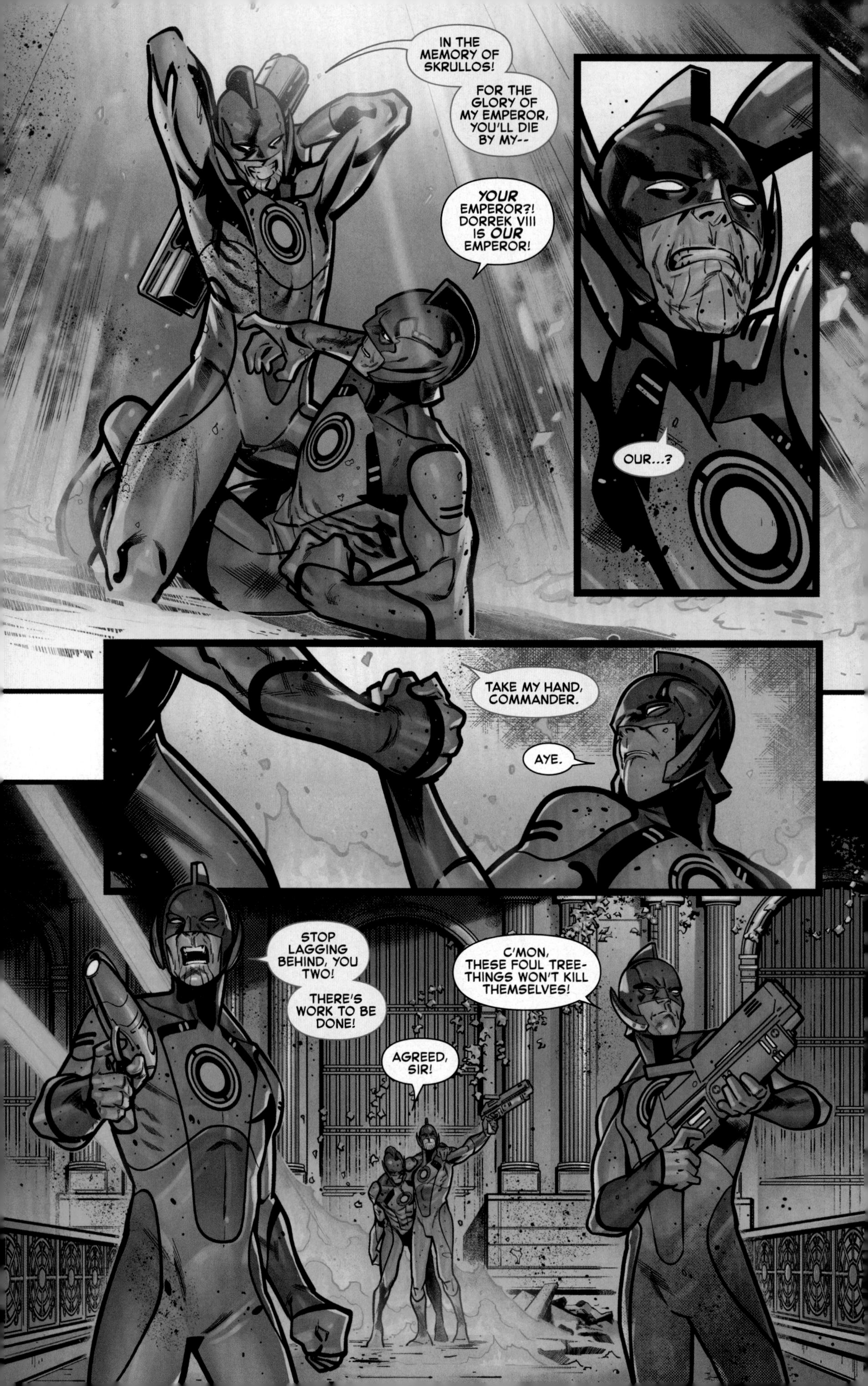
IN THE MEMORY OF SKRULLOS!
FOR THE GLORY OF MY EMPEROR, YOU'LL DIE BY MY--
YOUR EMPEROR?! DORREK VIII IS OUR EMPEROR!
OUR...?
TAKE MY HAND, COMMANDER.
AYE.
STOP LAGGING BEHIND, YOU TWO!
THERE'S WORK TO BE DONE!
AGREED, SIR!
C'MON, THESE FOUL TREE-THINGS WON'T KILL THEMSELVES!

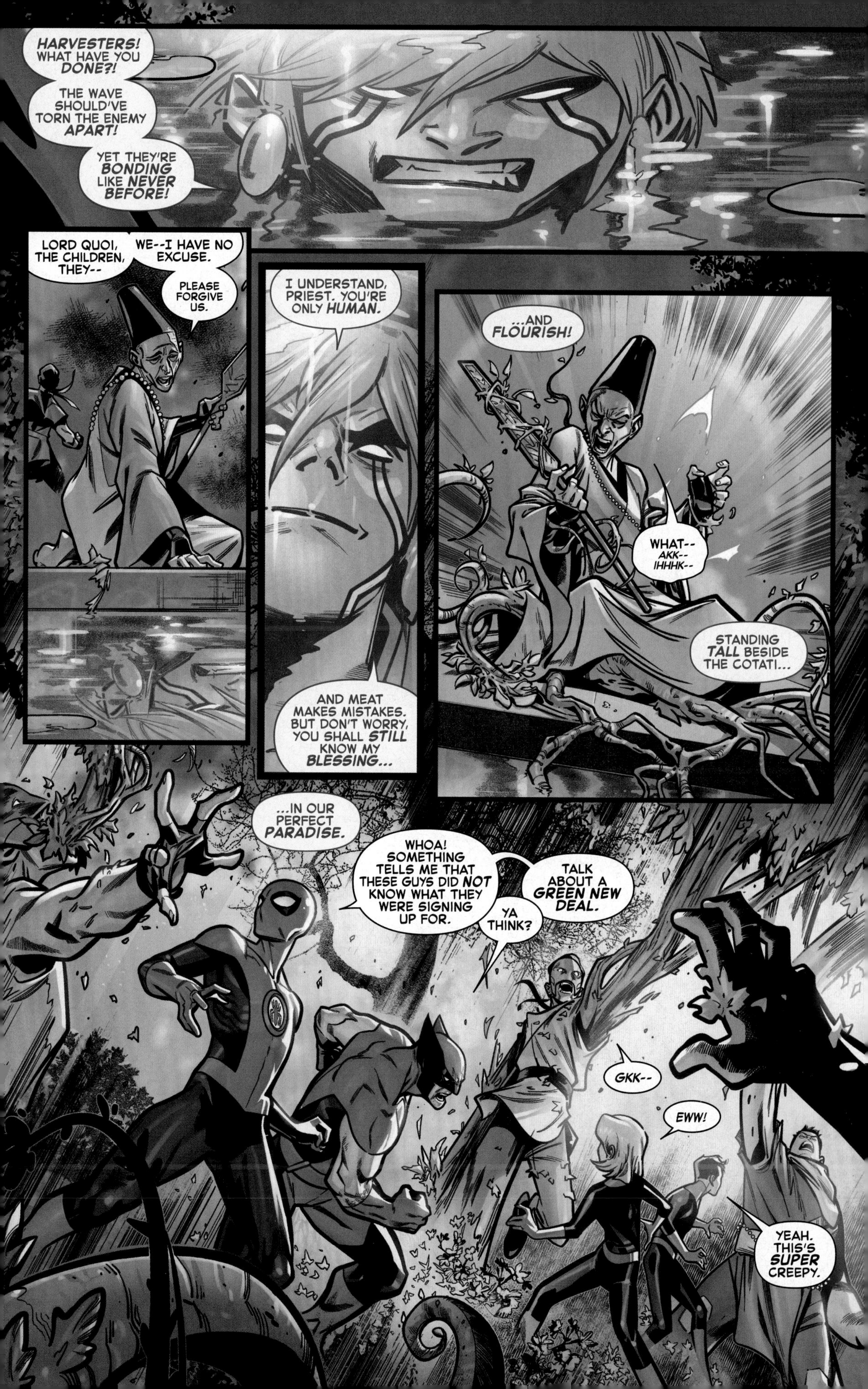
HARVESTERS! WHAT HAVE YOU DONE?!
THE WAVE SHOULD'VE TORN THE ENEMY APART!
YET THEY'RE BONDING LIKE NEVER BEFORE!
LORD QUOI, THE CHILDREN, THEY--
WE--I HAVE NO EXCUSE.
PLEASE FORGIVE US.
I UNDERSTAND, PRIEST. YOU'RE ONLY HUMAN.
AND MEAT MAKES MISTAKES. BUT DON'T WORRY, YOU SHALL STILL KNOW MY BLESSING...
...AND FLOURISH!
WHAT-- AKK-- IHHHK--
STANDING TALL BESIDE THE COTATI...
...IN OUR PERFECT PARADISE.
WHOA! SOMETHING TELLS ME THAT THESE GUYS DID NOT KNOW WHAT THEY WERE SIGNING UP FOR.
TALK ABOUT A GREEN NEW DEAL.
YA THINK?
GKK--
EWW!
YEAH. THIS'S SUPER CREEPY.

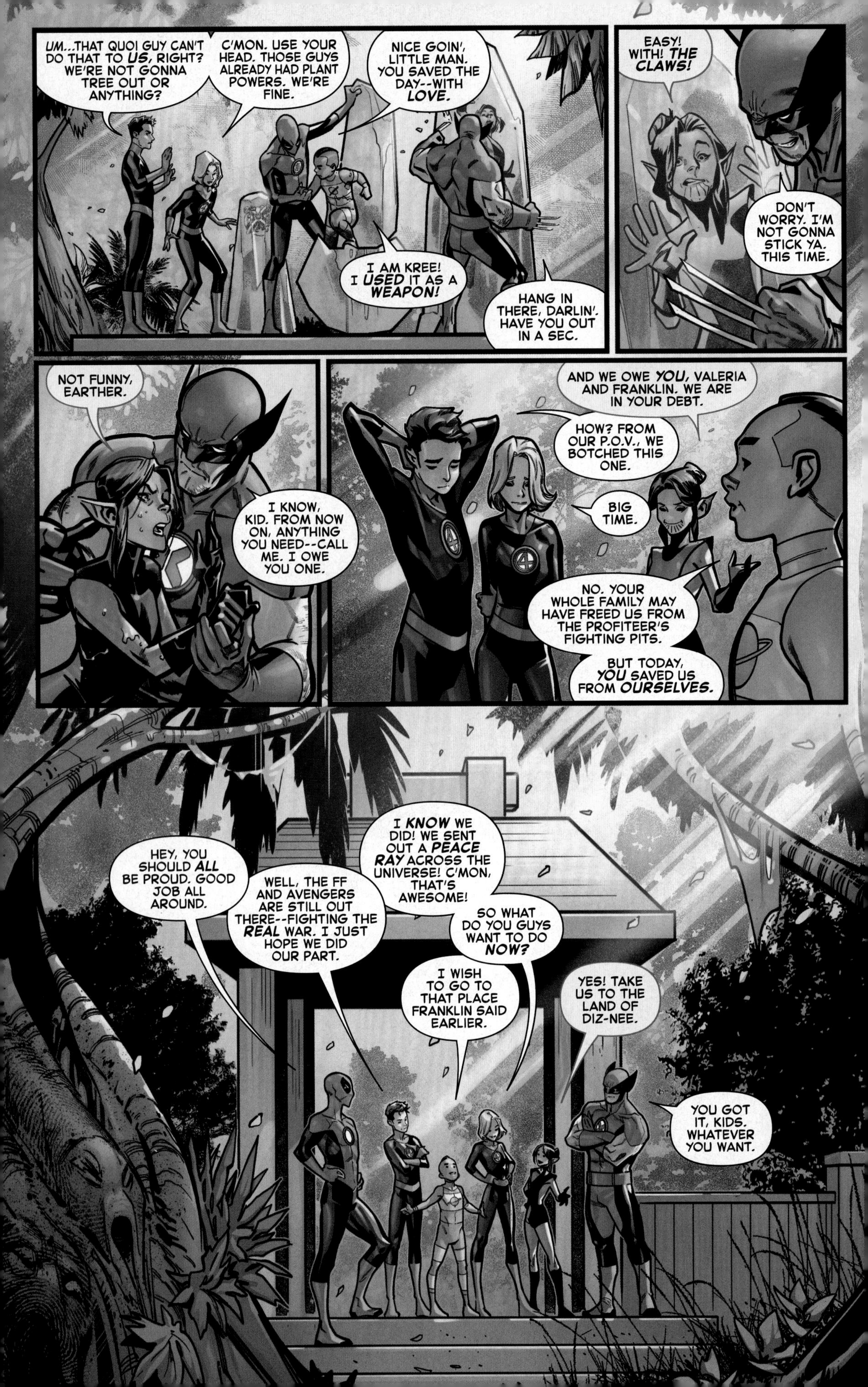
UM...THAT QUOI GUY CAN'T DO THAT TO US, RIGHT? WE'RE NOT GONNA TREE OUT OR ANYTHING?
C'MON. USE YOUR HEAD. THOSE GUYS ALREADY HAD PLANT POWERS. WE'RE FINE.
NICE GOIN', LITTLE MAN. YOU SAVED THE DAY--WITH LOVE.
I AM KREE! I USED IT AS A WEAPON!
HANG IN THERE, DARLIN'. HAVE YOU OUT IN A SEC.
EASY! WITH! THE CLAWS!
DON'T WORRY. I'M NOT GONNA STICK YA. THIS TIME.
NOT FUNNY, EARTHER.
I KNOW, KID. FROM NOW ON, ANYTHING YOU NEED--CALL ME. I OWE YOU ONE.
AND WE OWE YOU, VALERIA AND FRANKLIN. WE ARE IN YOUR DEBT.
HOW? FROM OUR P.O.V., WE BOTCHED THIS ONE.
BIG TIME.
NO. YOUR WHOLE FAMILY MAY HAVE FREED US FROM THE PROFITEER'S FIGHTING PITS.
BUT TODAY, YOU SAVED US FROM OURSELVES.
HEY, YOU SHOULD ALL BE PROUD. GOOD JOB ALL AROUND.
WELL, THE FF AND AVENGERS ARE STILL OUT THERE--FIGHTING THE REAL WAR. I JUST HOPE WE DID OUR PART.
I KNOW WE DID! WE SENT OUT A PEACE RAY ACROSS THE UNIVERSE! C'MON, THAT'S AWESOME!
SO WHAT DO YOU GUYS WANT TO DO NOW?
I WISH TO GO TO THAT PLACE FRANKLIN SAID EARLIER.
YES! TAKE US TO THE LAND OF DIZ-NEE.
YOU GOT IT, KIDS. WHATEVER YOU WANT.

#23 variant by
Khoi Pham & **Morry Hollowell**

Empyre: Fallout – Fantastic Four variant by
Carmen Carnero & **Rachelle Rosenberg**

Empyre: Fallout – Fantastic Four variant by
Alan Davis & **Morry Hollowell**

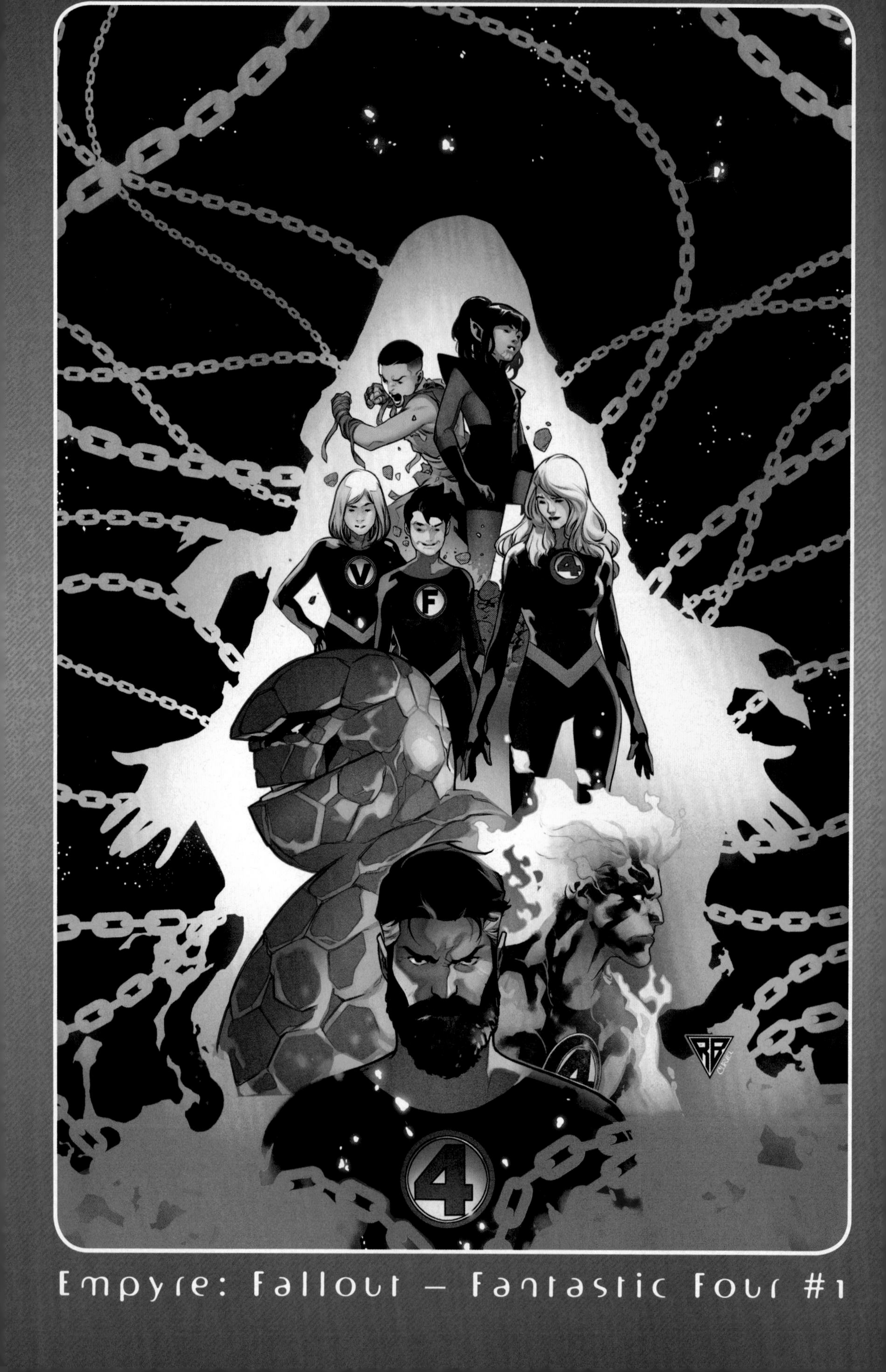

Empyre: Fallout – Fantastic Four #1

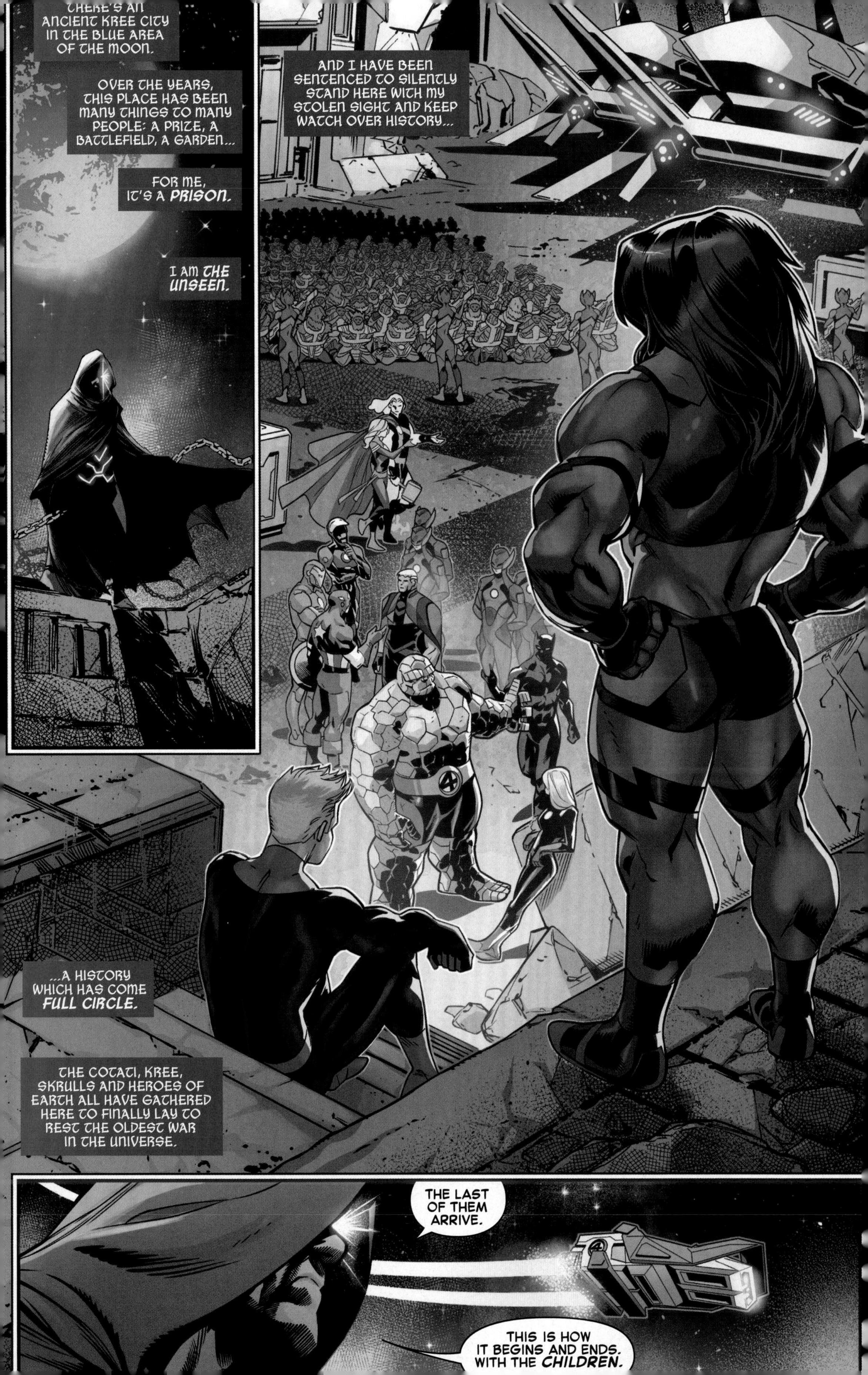
THERE'S AN ANCIENT KREE CITY IN THE BLUE AREA OF THE MOON.
OVER THE YEARS, THIS PLACE HAS BEEN MANY THINGS TO MANY PEOPLE: A PRIZE, A BATTLEFIELD, A GARDEN...
FOR ME, IT'S A PRISON.
I AM THE UNSEEN.
AND I HAVE BEEN SENTENCED TO SILENTLY STAND HERE WITH MY STOLEN SIGHT AND KEEP WATCH OVER HISTORY...
...A HISTORY WHICH HAS COME FULL CIRCLE.
THE COTATI, KREE, SKRULLS AND HEROES OF EARTH ALL HAVE GATHERED HERE TO FINALLY LAY TO REST THE OLDEST WAR IN THE UNIVERSE.
THE LAST OF THEM ARRIVE.
THIS IS HOW IT BEGINS AND ENDS. WITH THE CHILDREN.

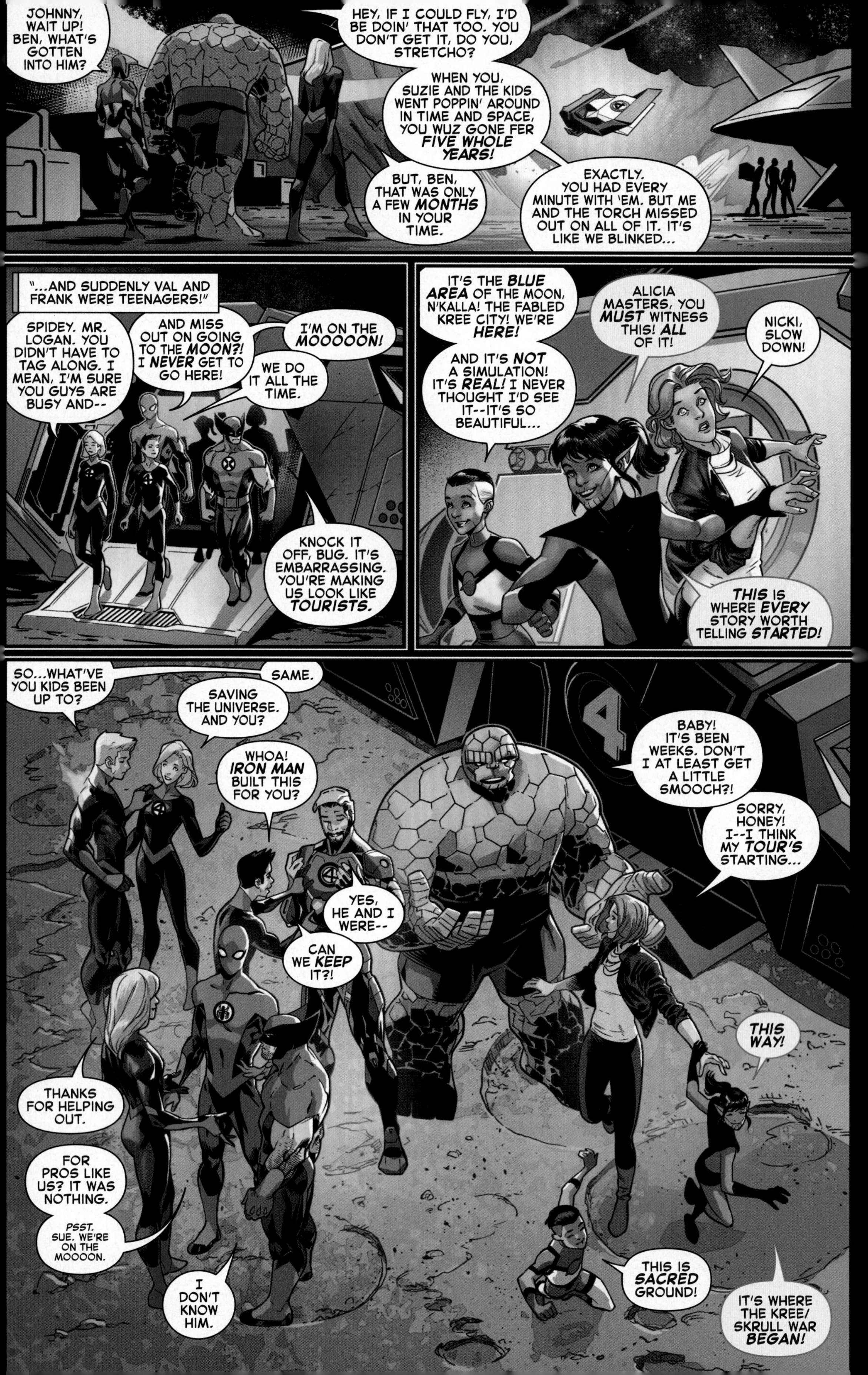
JOHNNY, WAIT UP! BEN, WHAT'S GOTTEN INTO HIM?
HEY, IF I COULD FLY, I'D BE DOIN' THAT TOO. YOU DON'T GET IT, DO YOU, STRETCHO?
WHEN YOU, SUZIE AND THE KIDS WENT POPPIN' AROUND IN TIME AND SPACE, YOU WUZ GONE FER FIVE WHOLE YEARS!
BUT, BEN, THAT WAS ONLY A FEW MONTHS IN YOUR TIME.
EXACTLY. YOU HAD EVERY MINUTE WITH 'EM. BUT ME AND THE TORCH MISSED OUT ON ALL OF IT. IT'S LIKE WE BLINKED...
"...AND SUDDENLY VAL AND FRANK WERE TEENAGERS!"
SPIDEY. MR. LOGAN. YOU DIDN'T HAVE TO TAG ALONG. I MEAN, I'M SURE YOU GUYS ARE BUSY AND--
AND MISS OUT ON GOING TO THE MOON?! I NEVER GET TO GO HERE!
I'M ON THE MOOOOON!
WE DO IT ALL THE TIME.
KNOCK IT OFF, BUG. IT'S EMBARRASSING. YOU'RE MAKING US LOOK LIKE TOURISTS.
IT'S THE BLUE AREA OF THE MOON, N'KALLA! THE FABLED KREE CITY! WE'RE HERE!
AND IT'S NOT A SIMULATION! IT'S REAL! I NEVER THOUGHT I'D SEE IT--IT'S SO BEAUTIFUL...
ALICIA MASTERS, YOU MUST WITNESS THIS! ALL OF IT!
NICKI, SLOW DOWN!
THIS IS WHERE EVERY STORY WORTH TELLING STARTED!
SO...WHAT'VE YOU KIDS BEEN UP TO?
SAVING THE UNIVERSE. AND YOU?
SAME.
WHOA! IRON MAN BUILT THIS FOR YOU?
YES, HE AND I WERE--
CAN WE KEEP IT?!
BABY! IT'S BEEN WEEKS. DON'T I AT LEAST GET A LITTLE SMOOCH?!
SORRY, HONEY! I--I THINK MY TOUR'S STARTING...
THIS WAY!
THANKS FOR HELPING OUT.
FOR PROS LIKE US? IT WAS NOTHING.
PSST. SUE. WE'RE ON THE MOOOON.
I DON'T KNOW HIM.
THIS IS SACRED GROUND!
IT'S WHERE THE KREE/ SKRULL WAR BEGAN!

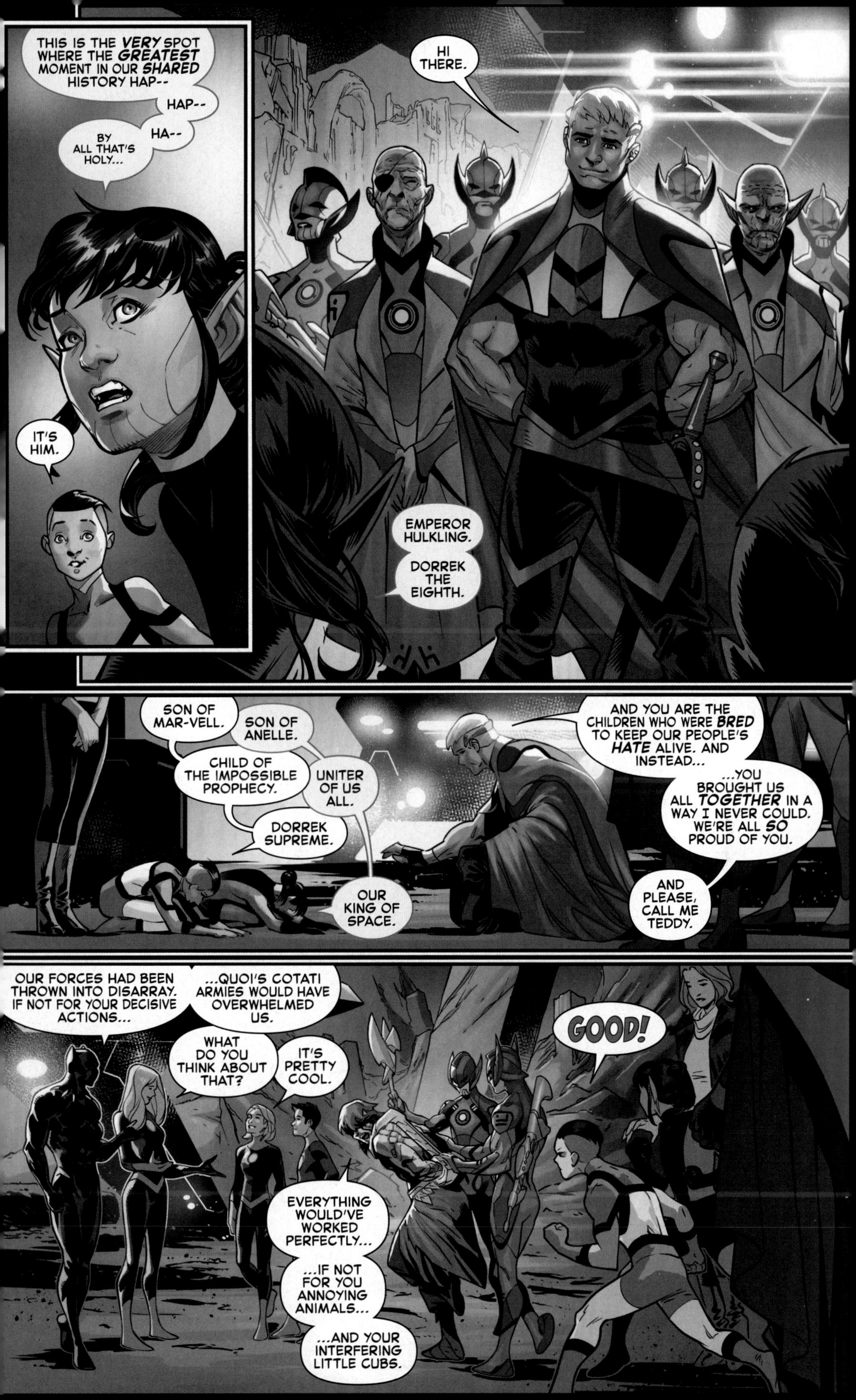
THIS IS THE VERY SPOT WHERE THE GREATEST MOMENT IN OUR SHARED HISTORY HAP--
HAP--
HA--
BY ALL THAT'S HOLY...
IT'S HIM.
HI THERE.
EMPEROR HULKLING.
DORREK THE EIGHTH.
SON OF MAR-VELL.
SON OF ANELLE.
CHILD OF THE IMPOSSIBLE PROPHECY.
UNITER OF US ALL.
DORREK SUPREME.
OUR KING OF SPACE.
AND YOU ARE THE CHILDREN WHO WERE BRED TO KEEP OUR PEOPLE'S HATE ALIVE. AND INSTEAD...
...YOU BROUGHT US ALL TOGETHER IN A WAY I NEVER COULD. WE'RE ALL SO PROUD OF YOU.
AND PLEASE, CALL ME TEDDY.
OUR FORCES HAD BEEN THROWN INTO DISARRAY. IF NOT FOR YOUR DECISIVE ACTIONS...
...QUOI'S COTATI ARMIES WOULD HAVE OVERWHELMED US.
WHAT DO YOU THINK ABOUT THAT?
IT'S PRETTY COOL.
GOOD!
EVERYTHING WOULD'VE WORKED PERFECTLY...
...IF NOT FOR YOU ANNOYING ANIMALS...
...AND YOUR INTERFERING LITTLE CUBS.

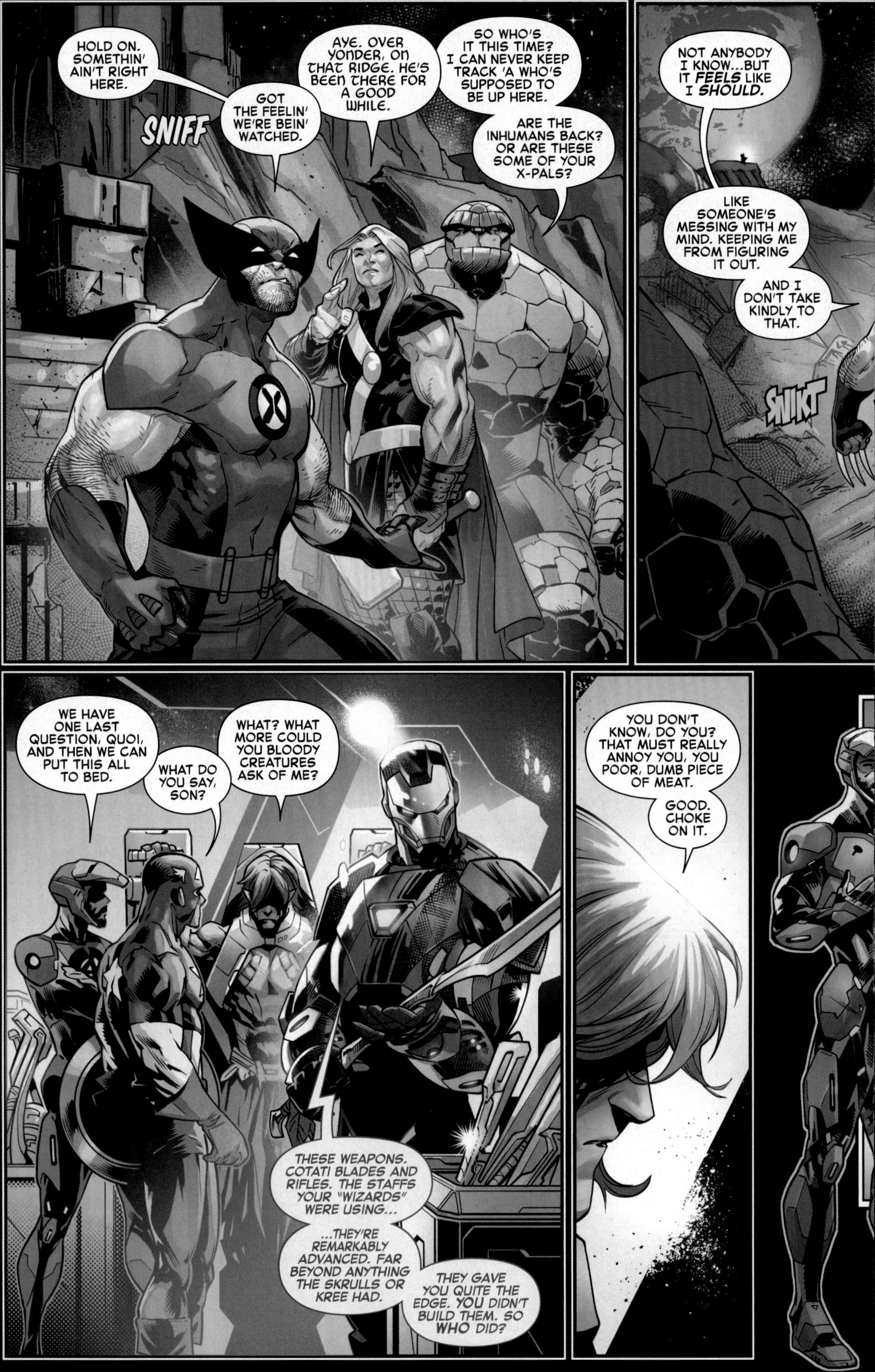
HOLD ON. SOMETHIN' AIN'T RIGHT HERE.
SNIFF
GOT THE FEELIN' WE'RE BEIN' WATCHED.
AYE. OVER YONDER, ON THAT RIDGE. HE'S BEEN THERE FOR A GOOD WHILE.
SO WHO'S IT THIS TIME? I CAN NEVER KEEP TRACK 'A WHO'S SUPPOSED TO BE UP HERE.
ARE THE INHUMANS BACK? OR ARE THESE SOME OF YOUR X-PALS?
NOT ANYBODY I KNOW...BUT IT FEELS LIKE I SHOULD.
LIKE SOMEONE'S MESSING WITH MY MIND. KEEPING ME FROM FIGURING IT OUT.
AND I DON'T TAKE KINDLY TO THAT.
SNIKT
WE HAVE ONE LAST QUESTION, QUOI, AND THEN WE CAN PUT THIS ALL TO BED.
WHAT DO YOU SAY, SON?
WHAT? WHAT MORE COULD YOU BLOODY CREATURES ASK OF ME?
THESE WEAPONS. COTATI BLADES AND RIFLES. THE STAFFS YOUR "WIZARDS" WERE USING...
...THEY'RE REMARKABLY ADVANCED. FAR BEYOND ANYTHING THE SKRULLS OR KREE HAD.
THEY GAVE YOU QUITE THE EDGE. YOU DIDN'T BUILD THEM. SO WHO DID?
YOU DON'T KNOW, DO YOU? THAT MUST REALLY ANNOY YOU, YOU POOR, DUMB PIECE OF MEAT.
GOOD. CHOKE ON IT.

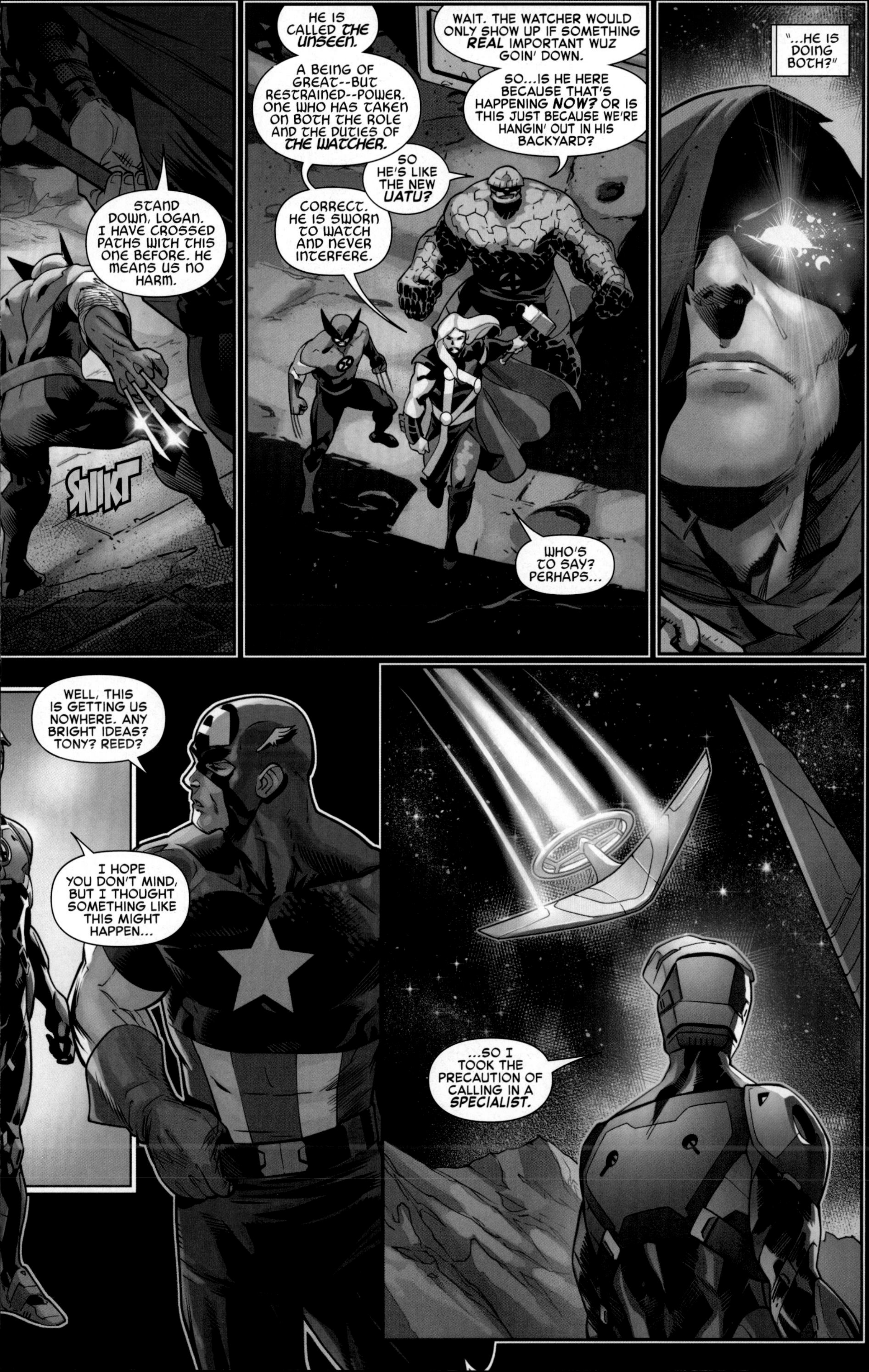
STAND DOWN, LOGAN. I HAVE CROSSED PATHS WITH THIS ONE BEFORE. HE MEANS US NO HARM.
SNIKT
HE IS CALLED THE UNSEEN.
A BEING OF GREAT--BUT RESTRAINED--POWER. ONE WHO HAS TAKEN ON BOTH THE ROLE AND THE DUTIES OF THE WATCHER.
SO HE'S LIKE THE NEW UATU?
CORRECT. HE IS SWORN TO WATCH AND NEVER INTERFERE.
WAIT. THE WATCHER WOULD ONLY SHOW UP IF SOMETHING REAL IMPORTANT WUZ GOIN' DOWN.
SO...IS HE HERE BECAUSE THAT'S HAPPENING NOW? OR IS THIS JUST BECAUSE WE'RE HANGIN' OUT IN HIS BACKYARD?
WHO'S TO SAY? PERHAPS...
"...HE IS DOING BOTH?"
WELL, THIS IS GETTING US NOWHERE. ANY BRIGHT IDEAS? TONY? REED?
I HOPE YOU DON'T MIND, BUT I THOUGHT SOMETHING LIKE THIS MIGHT HAPPEN...
...SO I TOOK THE PRECAUTION OF CALLING IN A SPECIALIST.

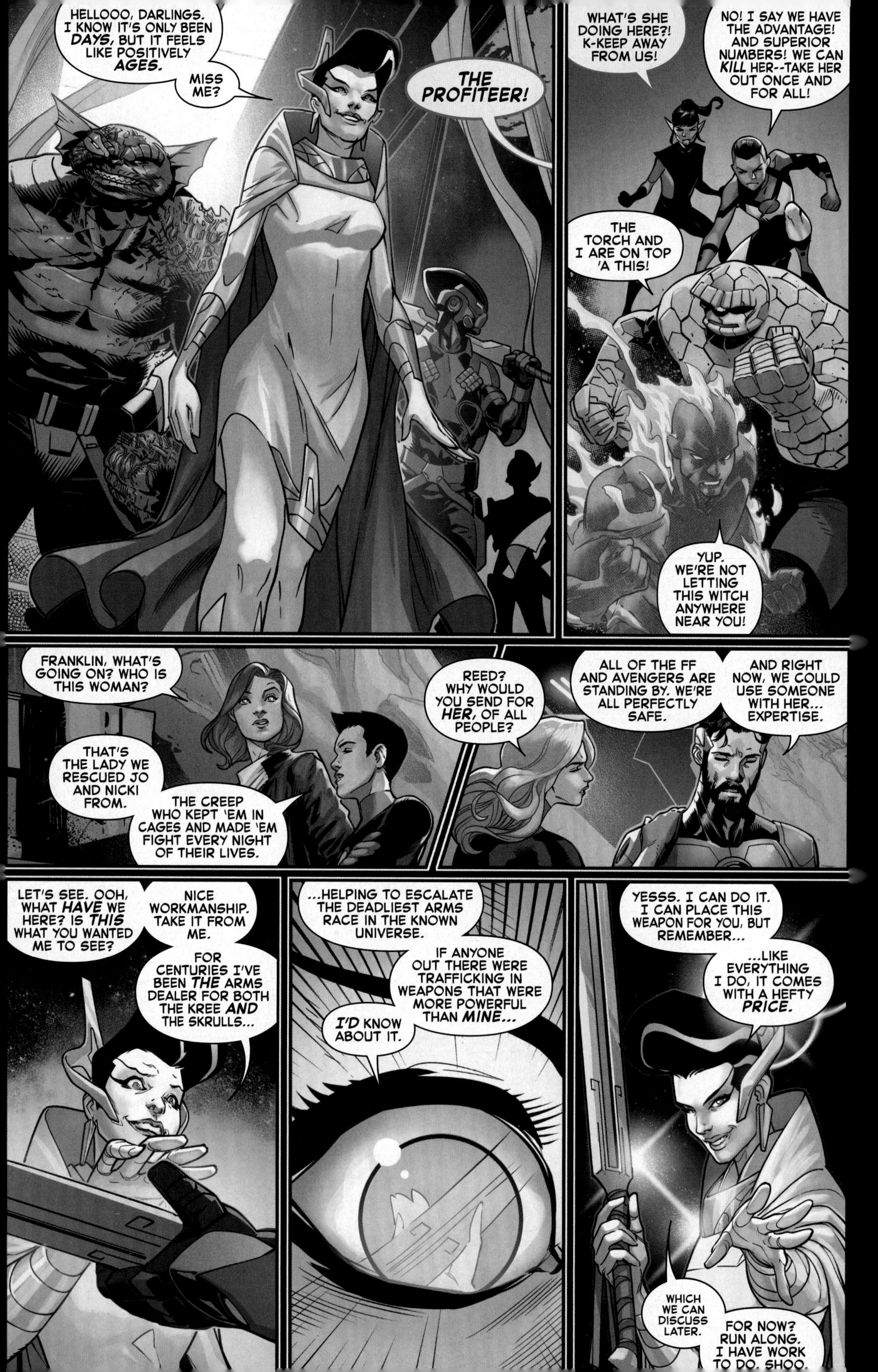
HELLOOO, DARLINGS. I KNOW IT'S ONLY BEEN DAYS, BUT IT FEELS LIKE POSITIVELY AGES.
MISS ME?
THE PROFITEER!
WHAT'S SHE DOING HERE?! K-KEEP AWAY FROM US!
NO! I SAY WE HAVE THE ADVANTAGE! AND SUPERIOR NUMBERS! WE CAN KILL HER--TAKE HER OUT ONCE AND FOR ALL!
THE TORCH AND I ARE ON TOP 'A THIS!
YUP. WE'RE NOT LETTING THIS WITCH ANYWHERE NEAR YOU!
FRANKLIN, WHAT'S GOING ON? WHO IS THIS WOMAN?
THAT'S THE LADY WE RESCUED JO AND NICKI FROM.
THE CREEP WHO KEPT 'EM IN CAGES AND MADE 'EM FIGHT EVERY NIGHT OF THEIR LIVES.
REED? WHY WOULD YOU SEND FOR HER, OF ALL PEOPLE?
ALL OF THE FF AND AVENGERS ARE STANDING BY. WE'RE ALL PERFECTLY SAFE.
AND RIGHT NOW, WE COULD USE SOMEONE WITH HER... EXPERTISE.
LET'S SEE. OOH, WHAT HAVE WE HERE? IS THIS WHAT YOU WANTED ME TO SEE?
NICE WORKMANSHIP. TAKE IT FROM ME.
FOR CENTURIES I'VE BEEN THE ARMS DEALER FOR BOTH THE KREE AND THE SKRULLS...
...HELPING TO ESCALATE THE DEADLIEST ARMS RACE IN THE KNOWN UNIVERSE.
IF ANYONE OUT THERE WERE TRAFFICKING IN WEAPONS THAT WERE MORE POWERFUL THAN MINE...
I'D KNOW ABOUT IT.
YESSS. I CAN DO IT. I CAN PLACE THIS WEAPON FOR YOU, BUT REMEMBER...
...LIKE EVERYTHING I DO, IT COMES WITH A HEFTY PRICE.
WHICH WE CAN DISCUSS LATER.
FOR NOW? RUN ALONG. I HAVE WORK TO DO. SHOO.

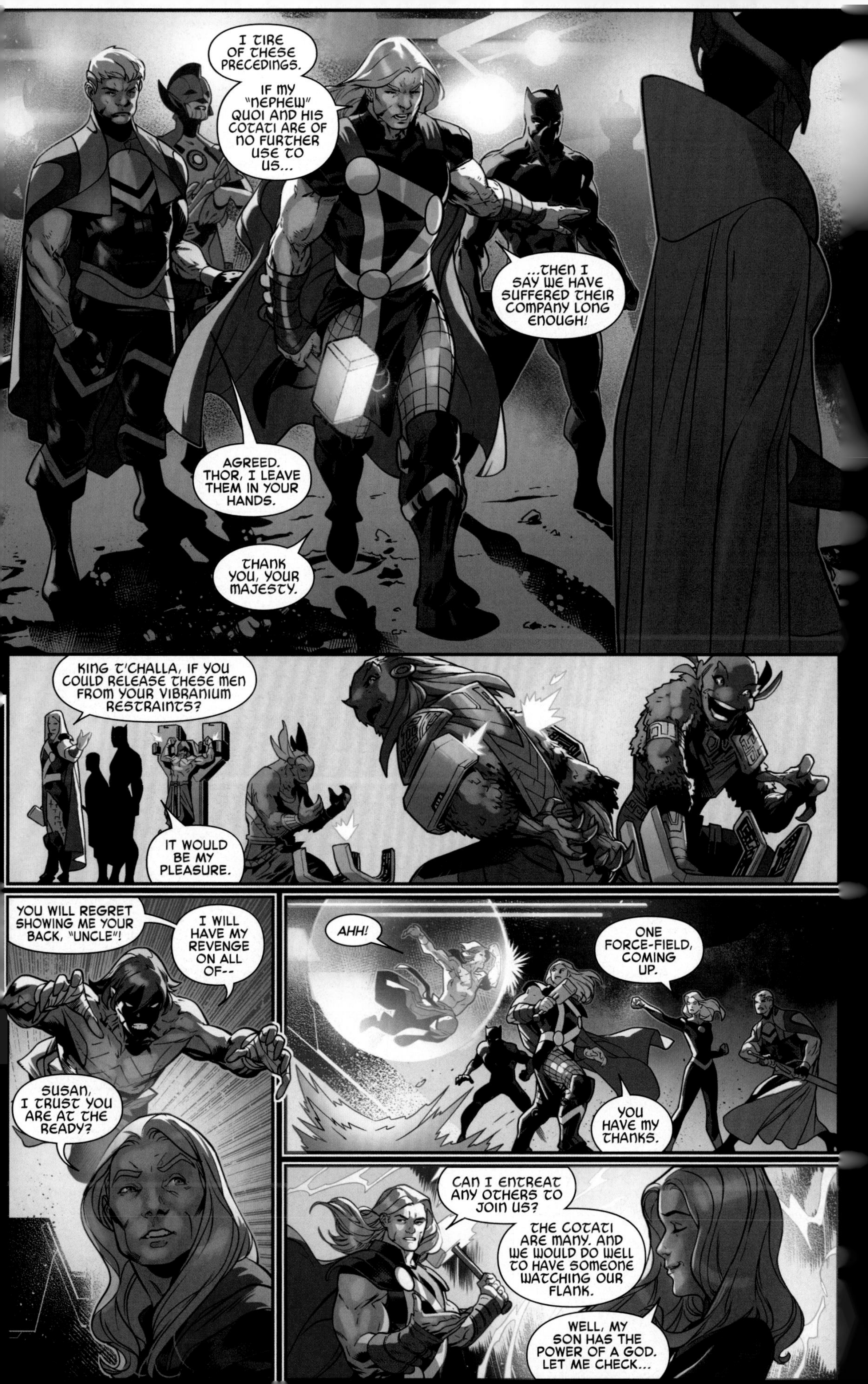
I TIRE OF THESE PRECEDINGS.
IF MY "NEPHEW" QUOI AND HIS COTATI ARE OF NO FURTHER USE TO US...
...THEN I SAY WE HAVE SUFFERED THEIR COMPANY LONG ENOUGH!
AGREED. THOR, I LEAVE THEM IN YOUR HANDS.
THANK YOU, YOUR MAJESTY.
KING T'CHALLA, IF YOU COULD RELEASE THESE MEN FROM YOUR VIBRANIUM RESTRAINTS?
IT WOULD BE MY PLEASURE.
YOU WILL REGRET SHOWING ME YOUR BACK, "UNCLE"!
I WILL HAVE MY REVENGE ON ALL OF--
SUSAN, I TRUST YOU ARE AT THE READY?
AHH!
ONE FORCE-FIELD, COMING UP.
YOU HAVE MY THANKS.
CAN I ENTREAT ANY OTHERS TO JOIN US?
THE COTATI ARE MANY. AND WE WOULD DO WELL TO HAVE SOMEONE WATCHING OUR FLANK.
WELL, MY SON HAS THE POWER OF A GOD. LET ME CHECK...

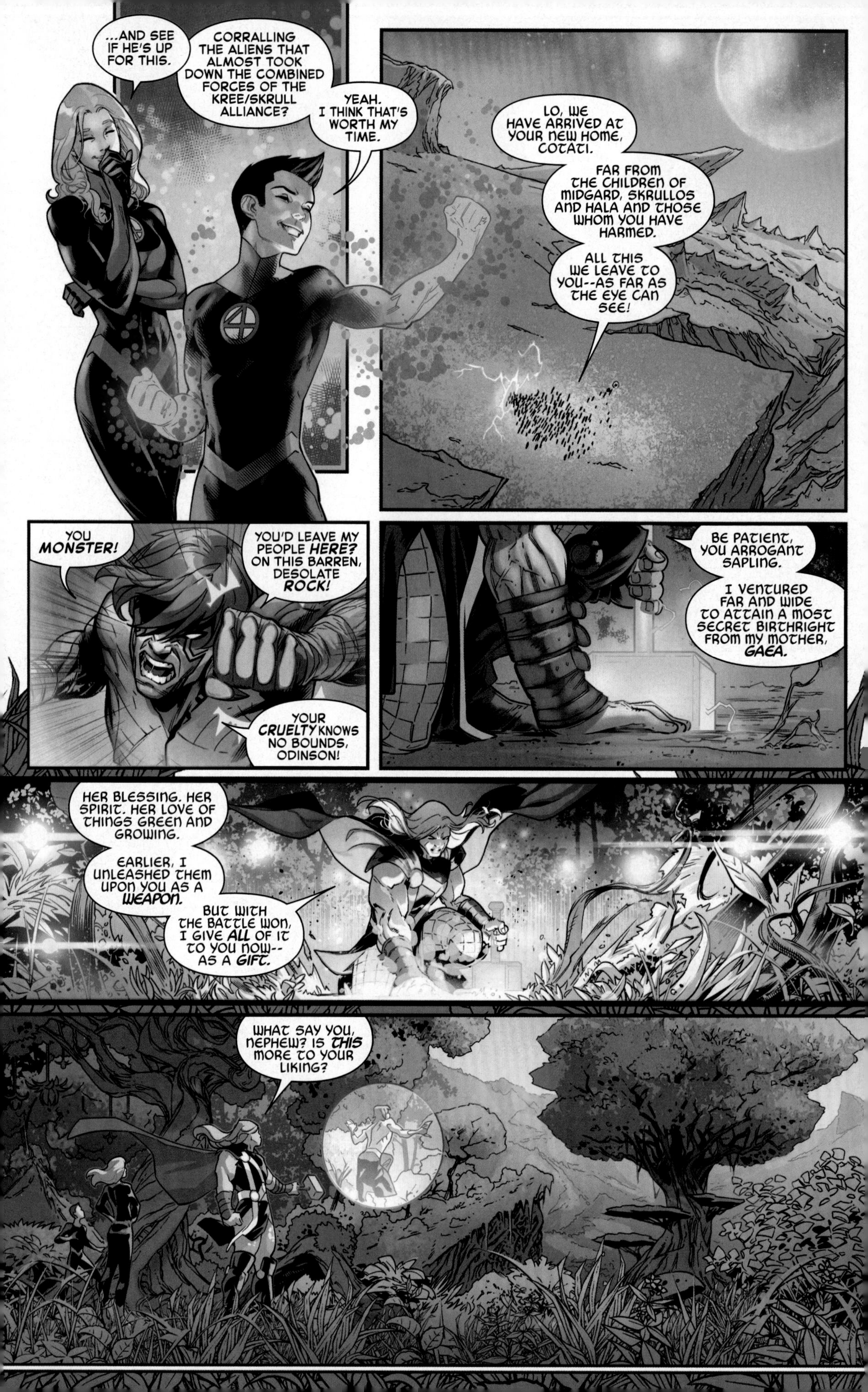

...AND SEE IF HE'S UP FOR THIS.
CORRALLING THE ALIENS THAT ALMOST TOOK DOWN THE COMBINED FORCES OF THE KREE/SKRULL ALLIANCE?
YEAH. I THINK THAT'S WORTH MY TIME.
LO, WE HAVE ARRIVED AT YOUR NEW HOME, COTATI.
FAR FROM THE CHILDREN OF MIDGARD, SKRULLOS AND HALA AND THOSE WHOM YOU HAVE HARMED.
ALL THIS WE LEAVE TO YOU--AS FAR AS THE EYE CAN SEE!
YOU MONSTER!
YOU'D LEAVE MY PEOPLE HERE? ON THIS BARREN, DESOLATE ROCK!
YOUR CRUELTY KNOWS NO BOUNDS, ODINSON!
BE PATIENT, YOU ARROGANT SAPLING.
I VENTURED FAR AND WIDE TO ATTAIN A MOST SECRET BIRTHRIGHT FROM MY MOTHER, GAEA.
HER BLESSING. HER SPIRIT. HER LOVE OF THINGS GREEN AND GROWING.
EARLIER, I UNLEASHED THEM UPON YOU AS A WEAPON.
BUT WITH THE BATTLE WON, I GIVE ALL OF IT TO YOU NOW--AS A GIFT.
WHAT SAY YOU, NEPHEW? IS THIS MORE TO YOUR LIKING?

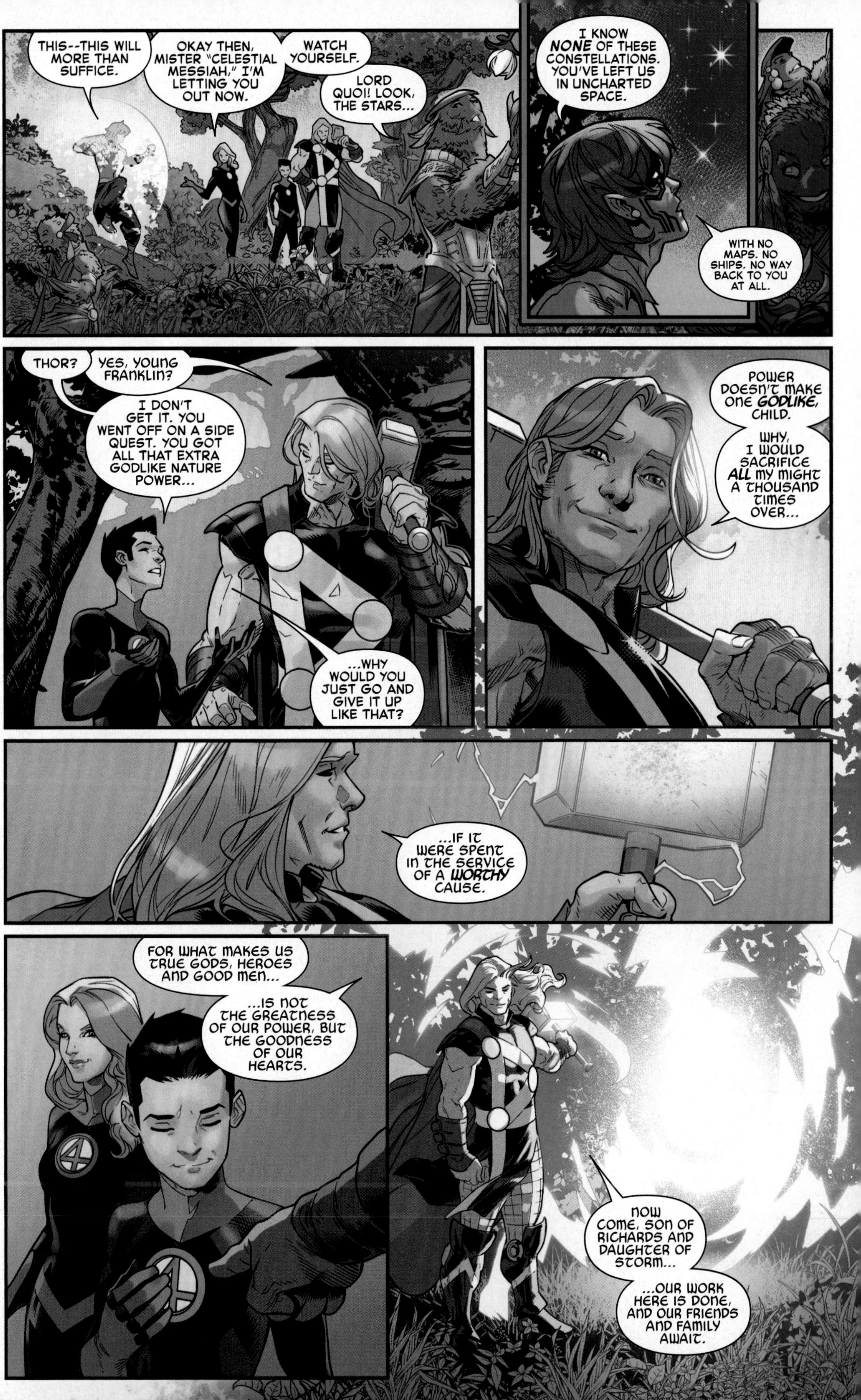
THIS--THIS WILL MORE THAN SUFFICE.
OKAY THEN, MISTER "CELESTIAL MESSIAH," I'M LETTING YOU OUT NOW.
WATCH YOURSELF.
LORD QUOI! LOOK, THE STARS...
I KNOW NONE OF THESE CONSTELLATIONS. YOU'VE LEFT US IN UNCHARTED SPACE.
WITH NO MAPS. NO SHIPS. NO WAY BACK TO YOU AT ALL.
THOR?
YES, YOUNG FRANKLIN?
I DON'T GET IT. YOU WENT OFF ON A SIDE QUEST. YOU GOT ALL THAT EXTRA GODLIKE NATURE POWER...
...WHY WOULD YOU JUST GO AND GIVE IT UP LIKE THAT?
POWER DOESN'T MAKE ONE GODLIKE, CHILD.
WHY, I WOULD SACRIFICE ALL MY MIGHT A THOUSAND TIMES OVER...
...IF IT WERE SPENT IN THE SERVICE OF A WORTHY CAUSE.
FOR WHAT MAKES US TRUE GODS, HEROES AND GOOD MEN...
...IS NOT THE GREATNESS OF OUR POWER, BUT THE GOODNESS OF OUR HEARTS.
NOW COME, SON OF RICHARDS AND DAUGHTER OF STORM...
...OUR WORK HERE IS DONE, AND OUR FRIENDS AND FAMILY AWAIT.

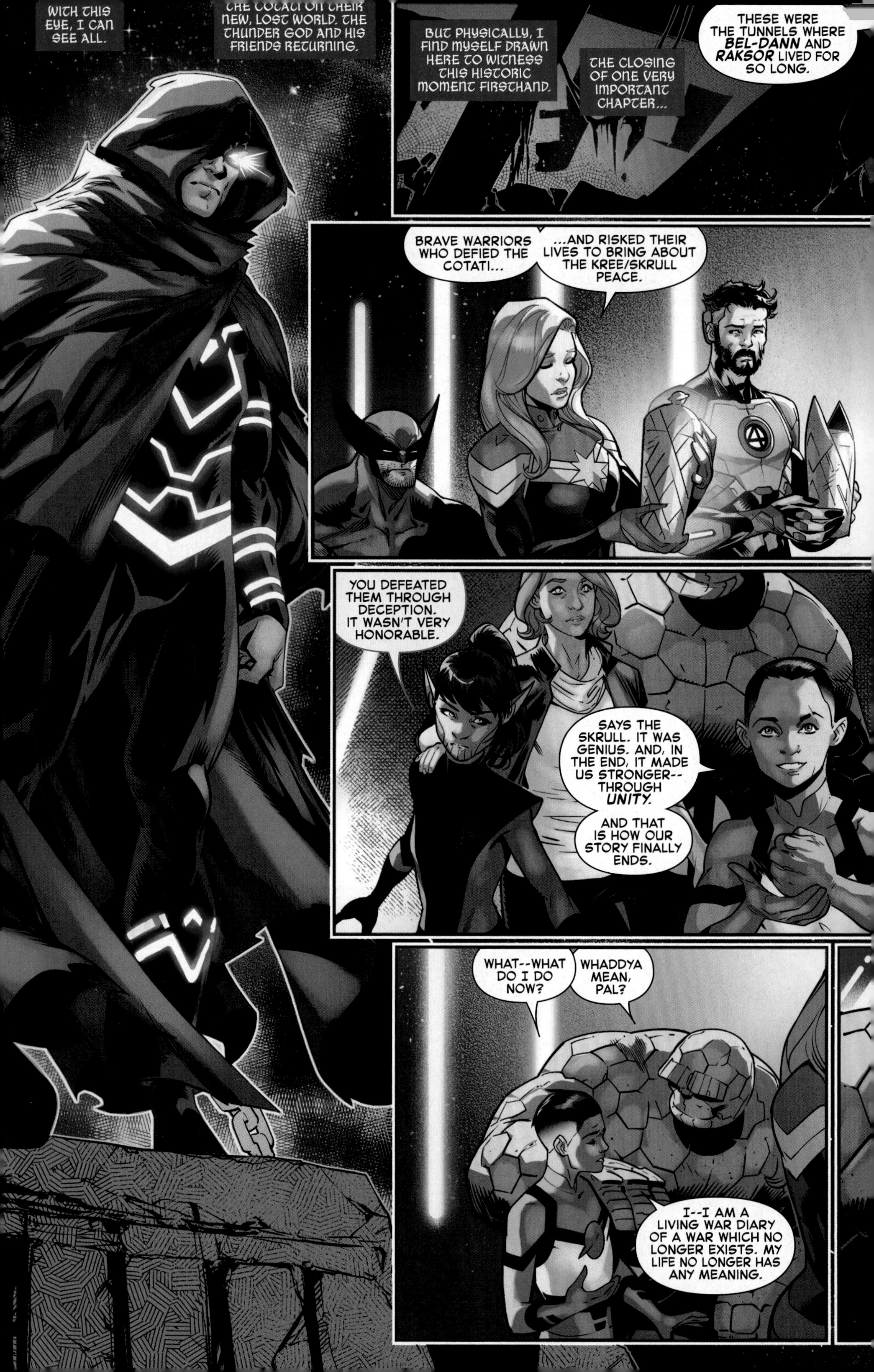
WITH THIS EYE, I CAN SEE ALL.
THE COTATI ON THEIR NEW, LOST WORLD. THE THUNDER GOD AND HIS FRIENDS RETURNING.
BUT PHYSICALLY, I FIND MYSELF DRAWN HERE TO WITNESS THIS HISTORIC MOMENT FIRSTHAND.
THE CLOSING OF ONE VERY IMPORTANT CHAPTER...
THESE WERE THE TUNNELS WHERE BEL-DANN AND RAKSOR LIVED FOR SO LONG.
BRAVE WARRIORS WHO DEFIED THE COTATI...
...AND RISKED THEIR LIVES TO BRING ABOUT THE KREE/SKRULL PEACE.
YOU DEFEATED THEM THROUGH DECEPTION. IT WASN'T VERY HONORABLE.
SAYS THE SKRULL. IT WAS GENIUS. AND, IN THE END, IT MADE US STRONGER--THROUGH UNITY.
AND THAT IS HOW OUR STORY FINALLY ENDS.
WHAT--WHAT DO I DO NOW?
WHADDYA MEAN, PAL?
I--I AM A LIVING WAR DIARY OF A WAR WHICH NO LONGER EXISTS. MY LIFE NO LONGER HAS ANY MEANING.

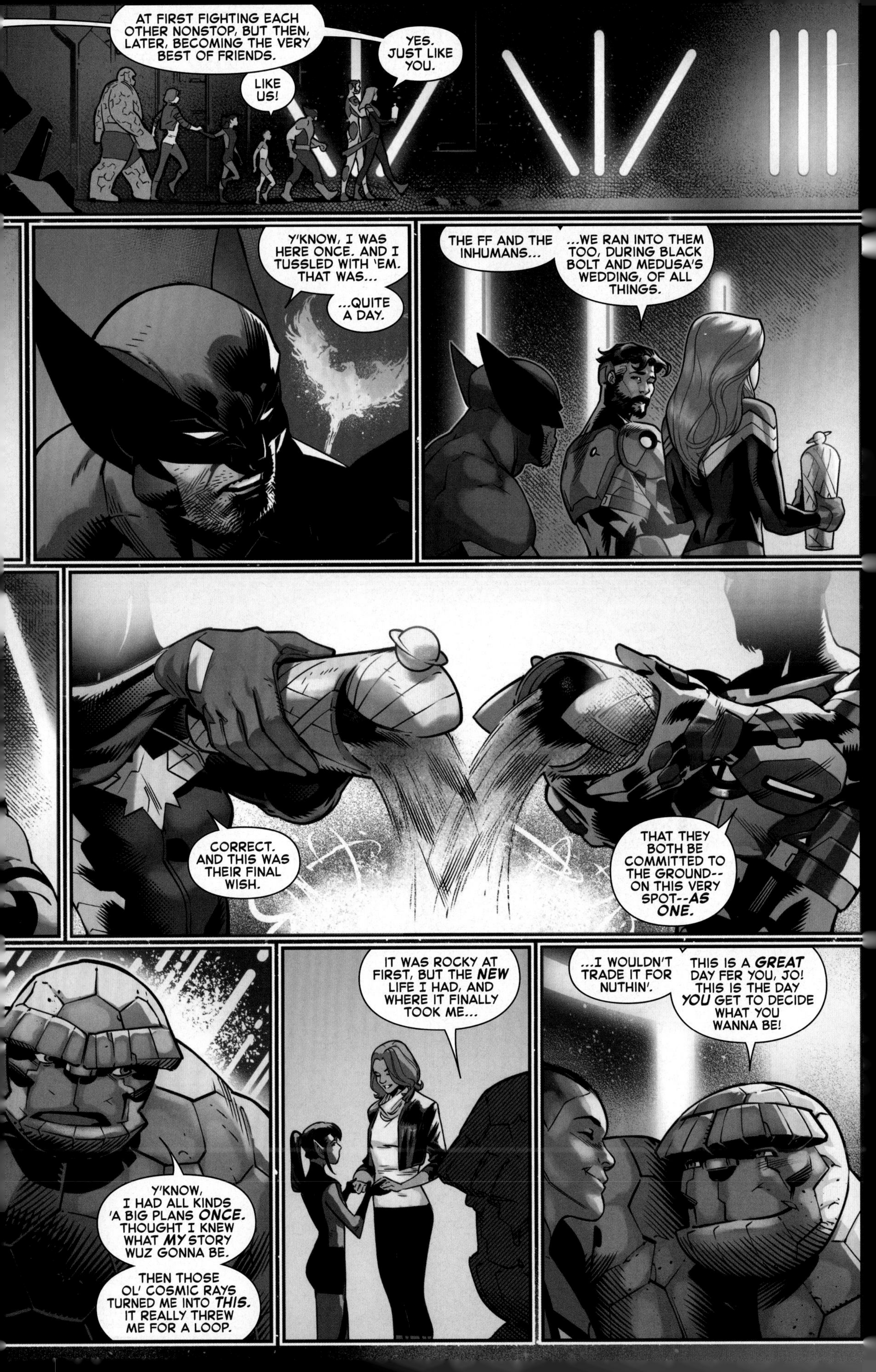
AT FIRST FIGHTING EACH OTHER NONSTOP, BUT THEN, LATER, BECOMING THE VERY BEST OF FRIENDS.
YES. JUST LIKE YOU.
LIKE US!
Y'KNOW, I WAS HERE ONCE. AND I TUSSLED WITH 'EM. THAT WAS...
...QUITE A DAY.
THE FF AND THE INHUMANS...
...WE RAN INTO THEM TOO, DURING BLACK BOLT AND MEDUSA'S WEDDING, OF ALL THINGS.
CORRECT. AND THIS WAS THEIR FINAL WISH.
THAT THEY BOTH BE COMMITTED TO THE GROUND-- ON THIS VERY SPOT--AS ONE.
Y'KNOW, I HAD ALL KINDS 'A BIG PLANS ONCE. THOUGHT I KNEW WHAT MY STORY WUZ GONNA BE.
THEN THOSE OL' COSMIC RAYS TURNED ME INTO THIS. IT REALLY THREW ME FOR A LOOP.
IT WAS ROCKY AT FIRST, BUT THE NEW LIFE I HAD, AND WHERE IT FINALLY TOOK ME...
...I WOULDN'T TRADE IT FOR NUTHIN'.
THIS IS A GREAT DAY FER YOU, JO! THIS IS THE DAY YOU GET TO DECIDE WHAT YOU WANNA BE!

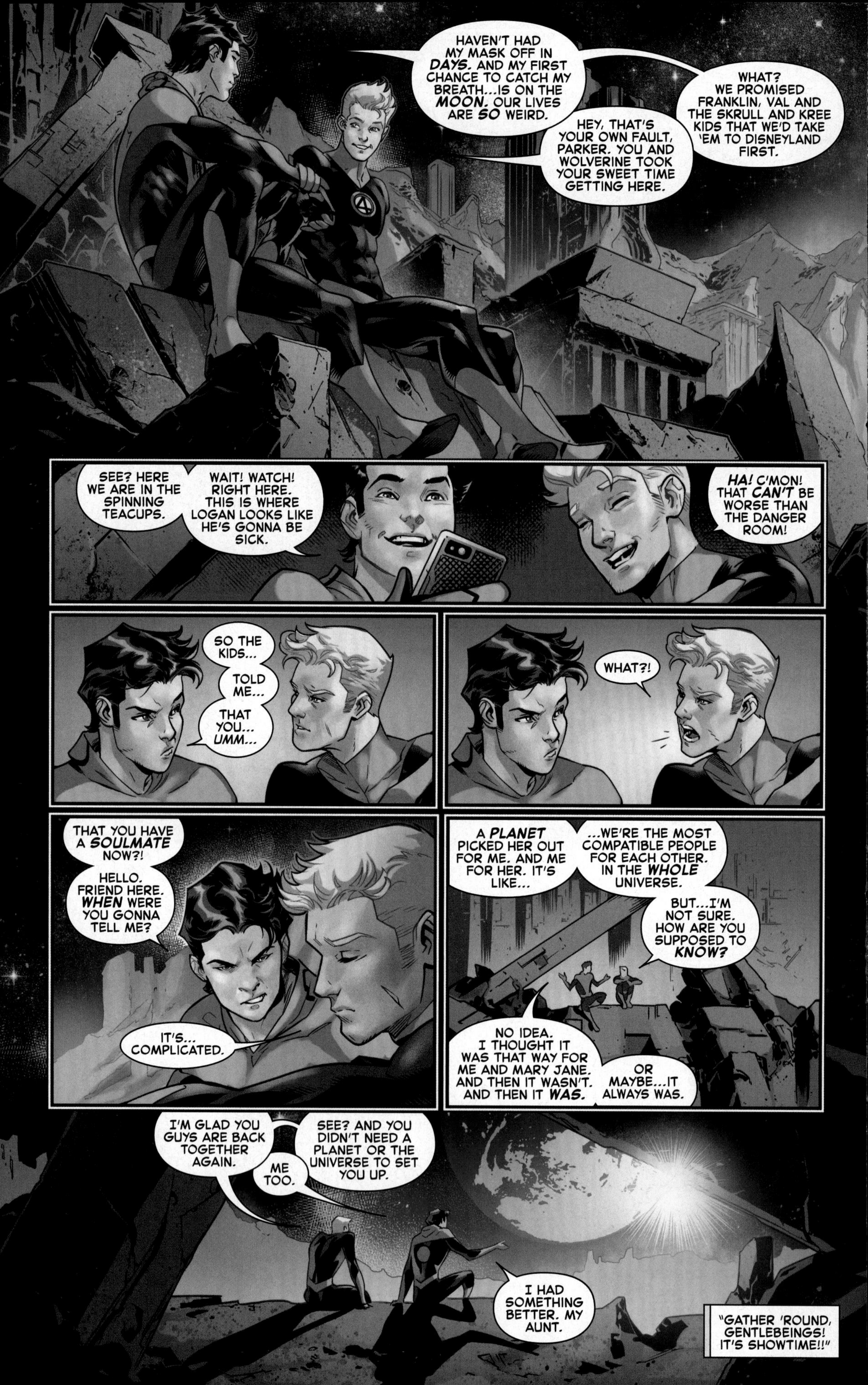
HAVEN'T HAD MY MASK OFF IN DAYS. AND MY FIRST CHANCE TO CATCH MY BREATH...IS ON THE MOON. OUR LIVES ARE SO WEIRD.
HEY, THAT'S YOUR OWN FAULT, PARKER. YOU AND WOLVERINE TOOK YOUR SWEET TIME GETTING HERE.
WHAT? WE PROMISED FRANKLIN, VAL AND THE SKRULL AND KREE KIDS THAT WE'D TAKE 'EM TO DISNEYLAND FIRST.
SEE? HERE WE ARE IN THE SPINNING TEACUPS.
WAIT! WATCH! RIGHT HERE. THIS IS WHERE LOGAN LOOKS LIKE HE'S GONNA BE SICK.
HA! C'MON! THAT CAN'T BE WORSE THAN THE DANGER ROOM!
SO THE KIDS...
TOLD ME...
THAT YOU... UMM...
WHAT?!
THAT YOU HAVE A SOULMATE NOW?!
HELLO. FRIEND HERE. WHEN WERE YOU GONNA TELL ME?
IT'S... COMPLICATED.
A PLANET PICKED HER OUT FOR ME. AND ME FOR HER. IT'S LIKE...
...WE'RE THE MOST COMPATIBLE PEOPLE FOR EACH OTHER. IN THE WHOLE UNIVERSE.
BUT...I'M NOT SURE. HOW ARE YOU SUPPOSED TO KNOW?
NO IDEA. I THOUGHT IT WAS THAT WAY FOR ME AND MARY JANE. AND THEN IT WASN'T. AND THEN IT WAS.
OR MAYBE...IT ALWAYS WAS.
I'M GLAD YOU GUYS ARE BACK TOGETHER AGAIN.
ME TOO.
SEE? AND YOU DIDN'T NEED A PLANET OR THE UNIVERSE TO SET YOU UP.
I HAD SOMETHING BETTER. MY AUNT.
"GATHER 'ROUND, GENTLEBEINGS! IT'S SHOWTIME!!"

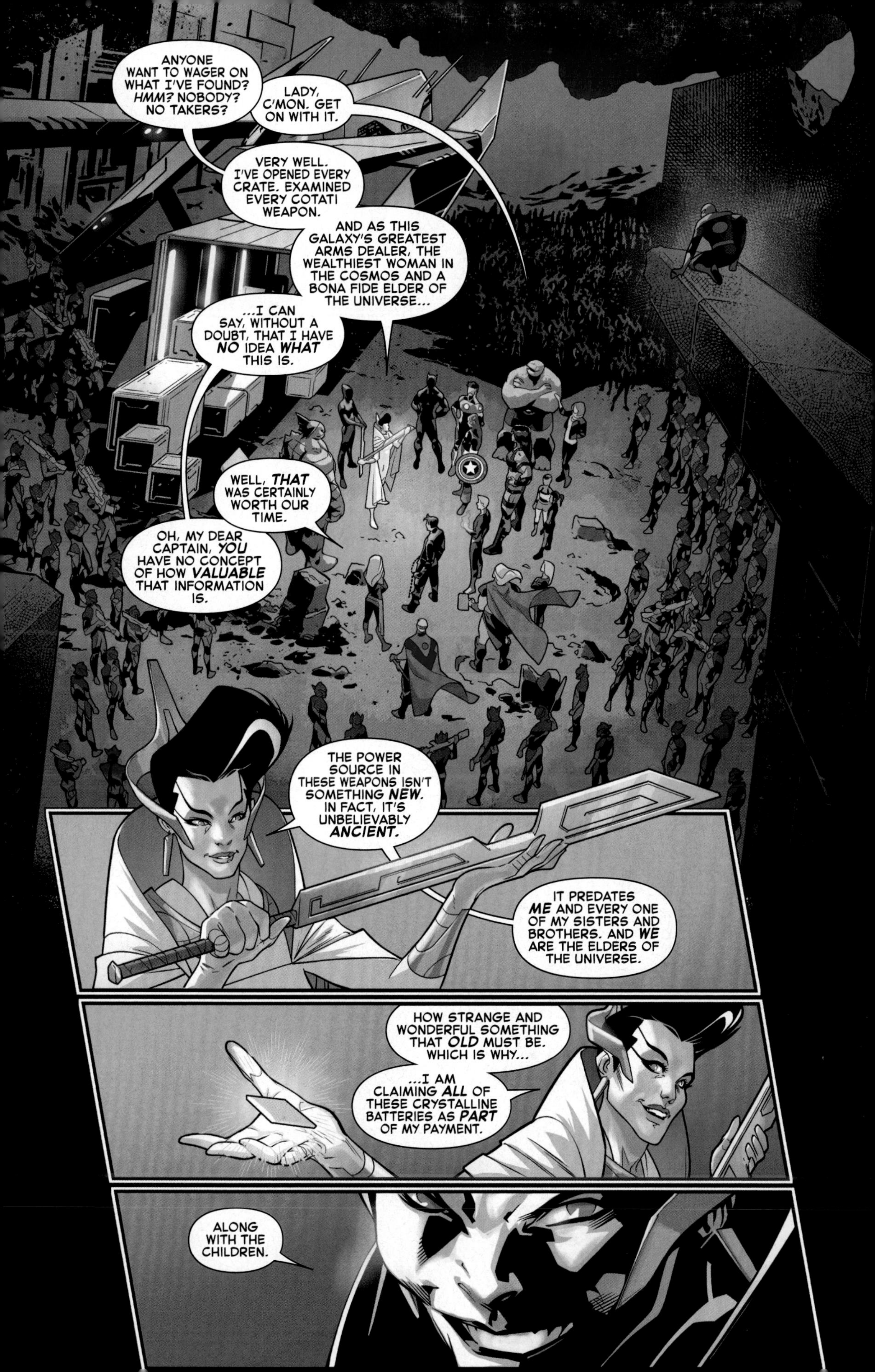
ANYONE WANT TO WAGER ON WHAT I'VE FOUND? HMM? NOBODY? NO TAKERS?
LADY, C'MON. GET ON WITH IT.
VERY WELL. I'VE OPENED EVERY CRATE. EXAMINED EVERY COTATI WEAPON.
AND AS THIS GALAXY'S GREATEST ARMS DEALER, THE WEALTHIEST WOMAN IN THE COSMOS AND A BONA FIDE ELDER OF THE UNIVERSE...
...I CAN SAY, WITHOUT A DOUBT, THAT I HAVE NO IDEA WHAT THIS IS.
WELL, THAT WAS CERTAINLY WORTH OUR TIME.
OH, MY DEAR CAPTAIN, YOU HAVE NO CONCEPT OF HOW VALUABLE THAT INFORMATION IS.
THE POWER SOURCE IN THESE WEAPONS ISN'T SOMETHING NEW. IN FACT, IT'S UNBELIEVABLY ANCIENT.
IT PREDATES ME AND EVERY ONE OF MY SISTERS AND BROTHERS. AND WE ARE THE ELDERS OF THE UNIVERSE.
HOW STRANGE AND WONDERFUL SOMETHING THAT OLD MUST BE. WHICH IS WHY...
...I AM CLAIMING ALL OF THESE CRYSTALLINE BATTERIES AS PART OF MY PAYMENT.
ALONG WITH THE CHILDREN.

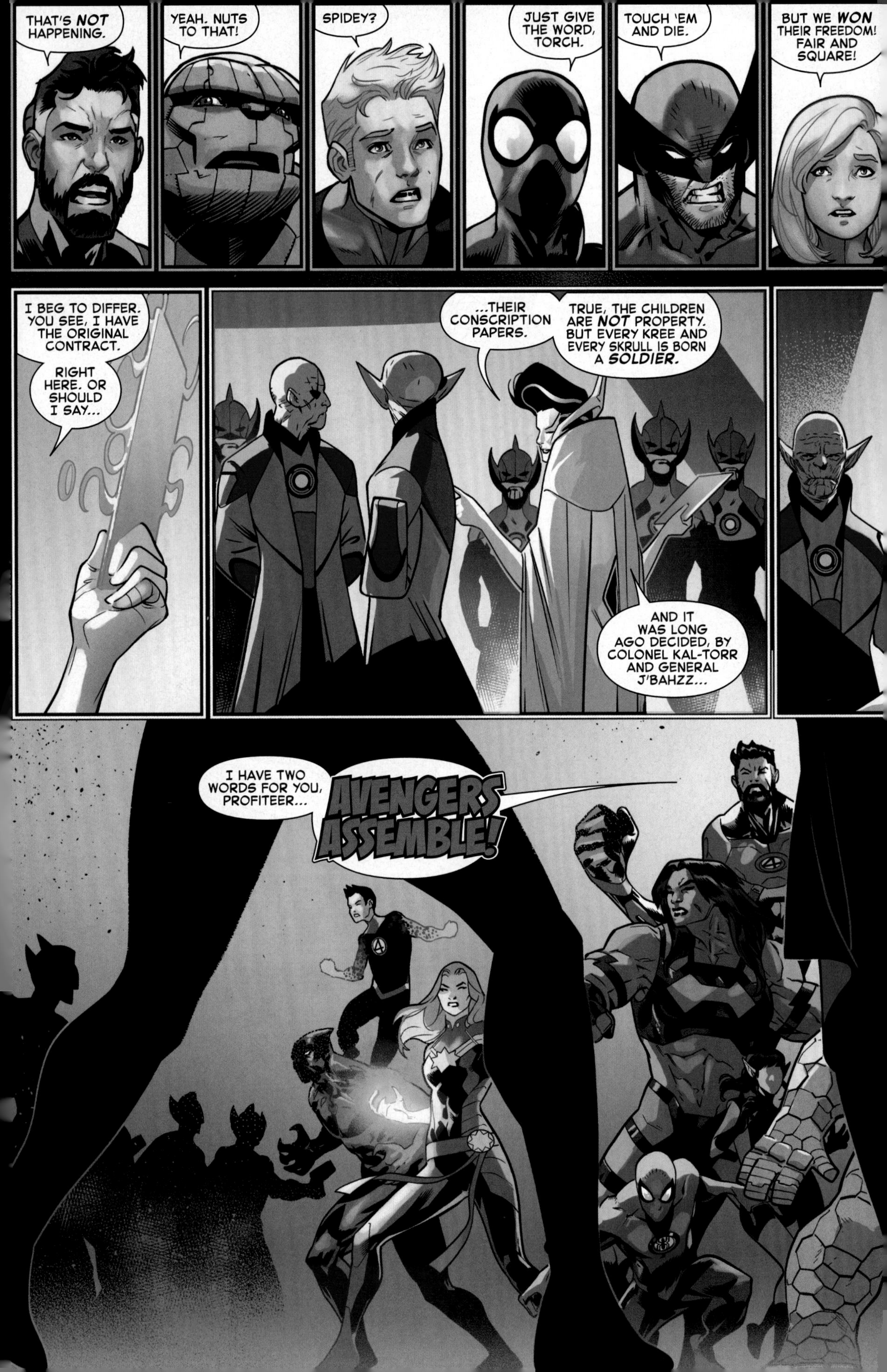
THAT'S NOT HAPPENING.
YEAH. NUTS TO THAT!
SPIDEY?
JUST GIVE THE WORD, TORCH.
TOUCH 'EM AND DIE.
BUT WE WON THEIR FREEDOM! FAIR AND SQUARE!
I BEG TO DIFFER. YOU SEE, I HAVE THE ORIGINAL CONTRACT.
RIGHT HERE. OR SHOULD I SAY...
...THEIR CONSCRIPTION PAPERS.
TRUE, THE CHILDREN ARE NOT PROPERTY. BUT EVERY KREE AND EVERY SKRULL IS BORN A SOLDIER.
AND IT WAS LONG AGO DECIDED, BY COLONEL KAL-TORR AND GENERAL J'BAHZZ...
I HAVE TWO WORDS FOR YOU, PROFITEER...
AVENGERS ASSEMBLE!

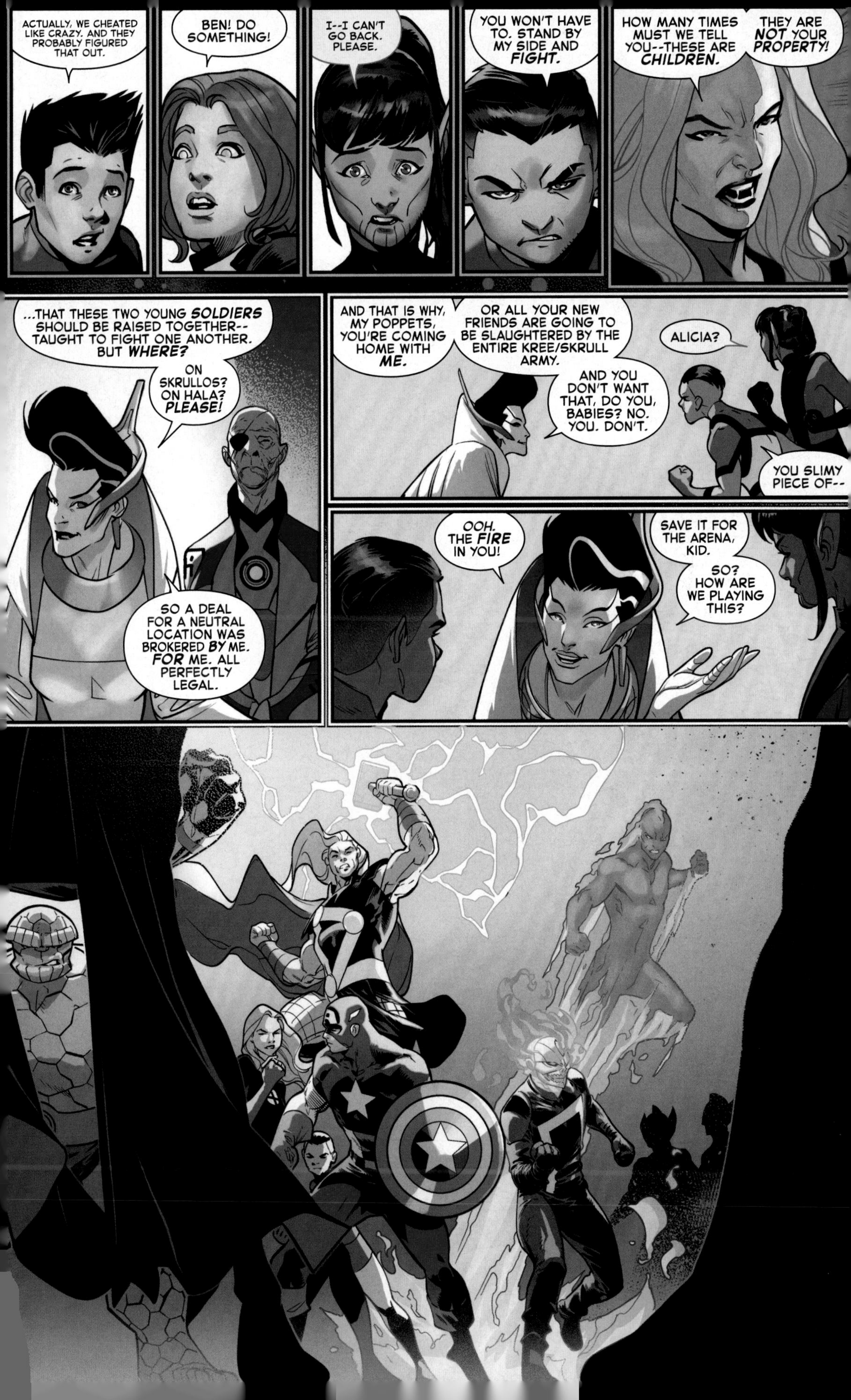

ACTUALLY, WE CHEATED LIKE CRAZY. AND THEY PROBABLY FIGURED THAT OUT.
BEN! DO SOMETHING!
I--I CAN'T GO BACK. PLEASE.
YOU WON'T HAVE TO. STAND BY MY SIDE AND FIGHT.
HOW MANY TIMES MUST WE TELL YOU--THESE ARE CHILDREN.
THEY ARE NOT YOUR PROPERTY!
...THAT THESE TWO YOUNG SOLDIERS SHOULD BE RAISED TOGETHER-- TAUGHT TO FIGHT ONE ANOTHER. BUT WHERE?
ON SKRULLOS? ON HALA? PLEASE!
SO A DEAL FOR A NEUTRAL LOCATION WAS BROKERED BY ME. FOR ME. ALL PERFECTLY LEGAL.
AND THAT IS WHY, MY POPPETS, YOU'RE COMING HOME WITH ME.
OR ALL YOUR NEW FRIENDS ARE GOING TO BE SLAUGHTERED BY THE ENTIRE KREE/SKRULL ARMY.
AND YOU DON'T WANT THAT, DO YOU, BABIES? NO. YOU. DON'T.
ALICIA?
YOU SLIMY PIECE OF--
OOH. THE FIRE IN YOU!
SAVE IT FOR THE ARENA, KID.
SO? HOW ARE WE PLAYING THIS?

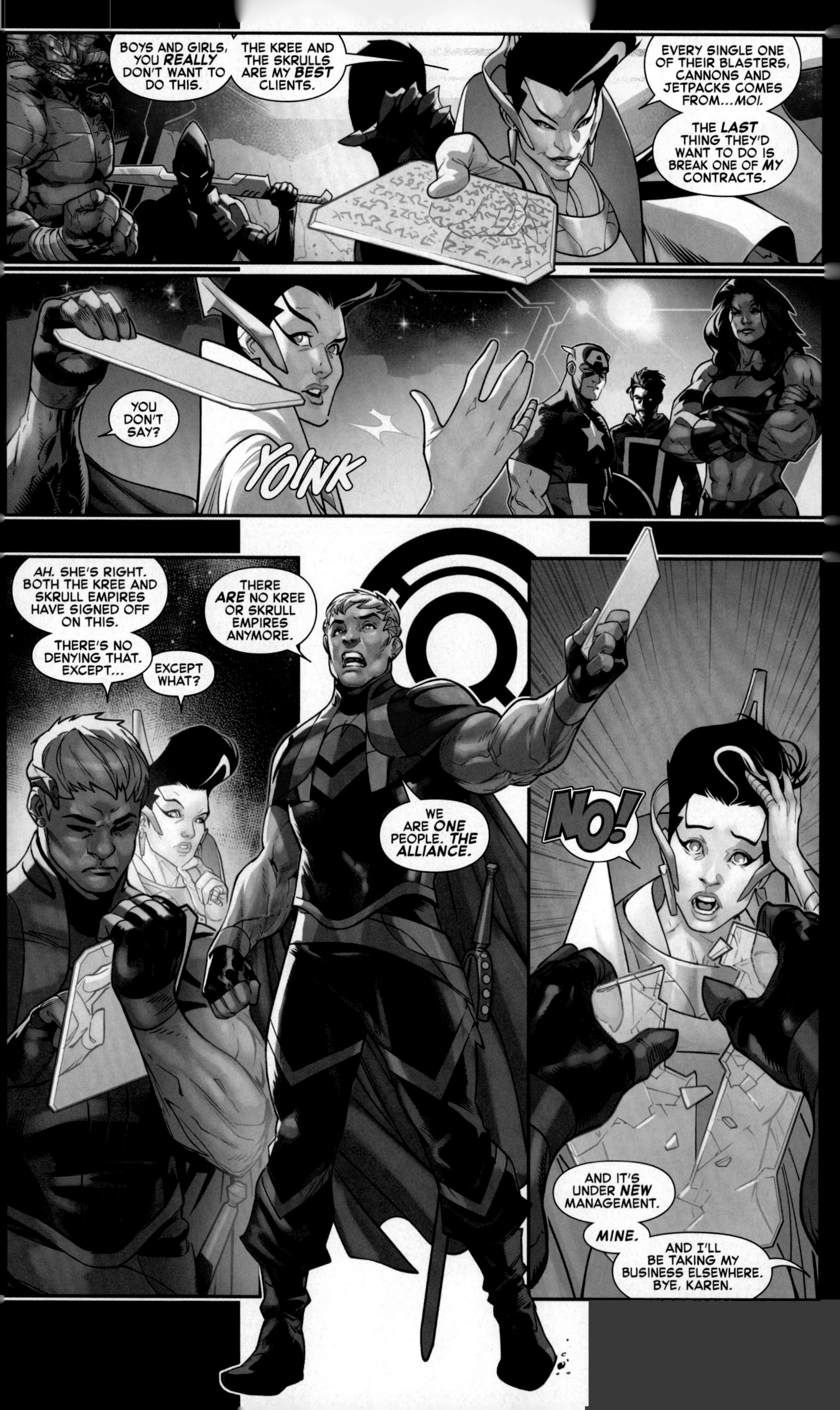

BOYS AND GIRLS, YOU REALLY DON'T WANT TO DO THIS.
THE KREE AND THE SKRULLS ARE MY BEST CLIENTS.
EVERY SINGLE ONE OF THEIR BLASTERS, CANNONS AND JETPACKS COMES FROM...MOI.
THE LAST THING THEY'D WANT TO DO IS BREAK ONE OF MY CONTRACTS.
YOU DON'T SAY?
YOINK
AH. SHE'S RIGHT. BOTH THE KREE AND SKRULL EMPIRES HAVE SIGNED OFF ON THIS.
THERE'S NO DENYING THAT. EXCEPT...
EXCEPT WHAT?
THERE ARE NO KREE OR SKRULL EMPIRES ANYMORE.
WE ARE ONE PEOPLE. THE ALLIANCE.
NO!
AND IT'S UNDER NEW MANAGEMENT.
MINE.
AND I'LL BE TAKING MY BUSINESS ELSEWHERE. BYE, KAREN.

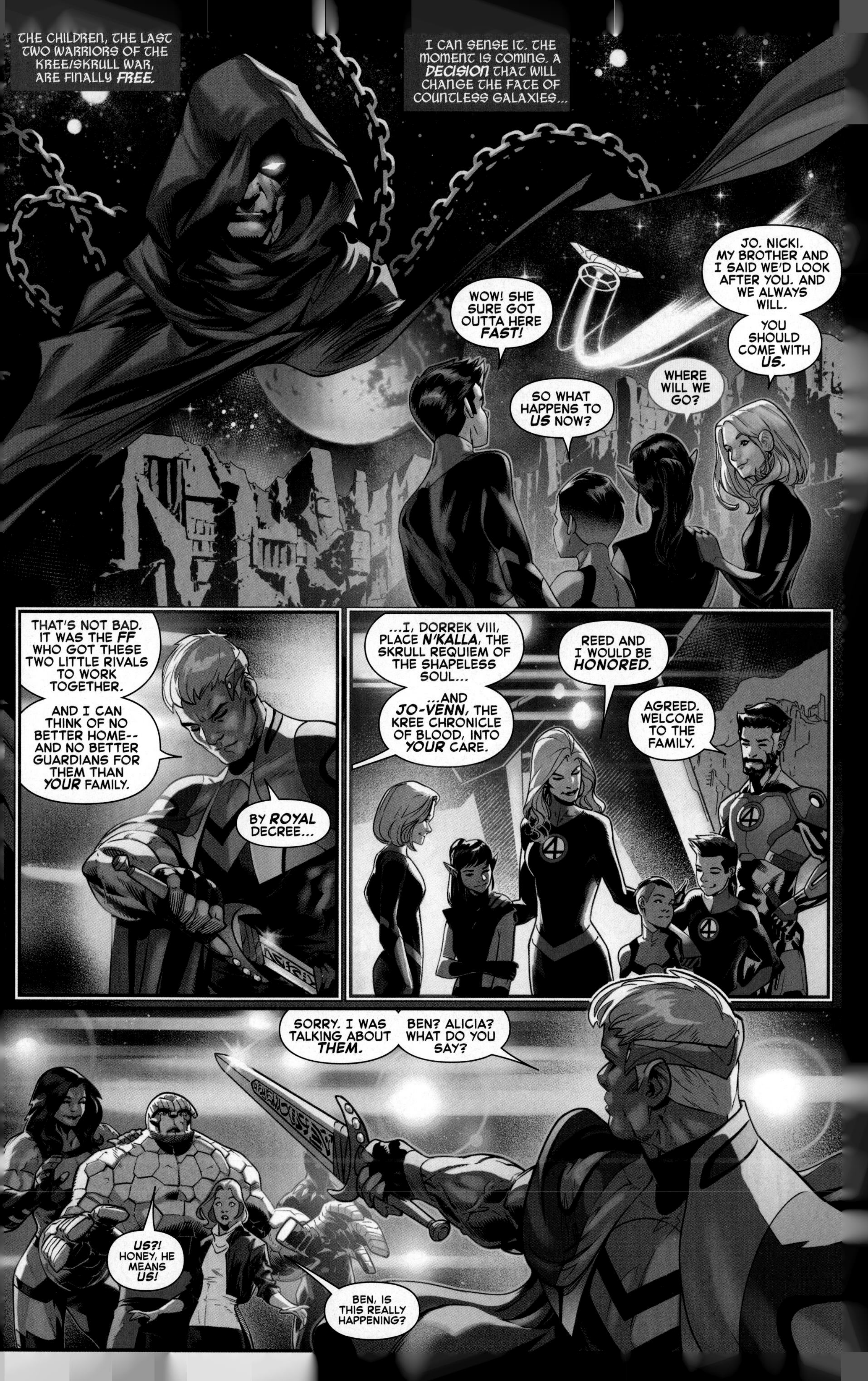
THE CHILDREN, THE LAST TWO WARRIORS OF THE KREE/SKRULL WAR, ARE FINALLY FREE.
I CAN SENSE IT. THE MOMENT IS COMING. A DECISION THAT WILL CHANGE THE FATE OF COUNTLESS GALAXIES...
WOW! SHE SURE GOT OUTTA HERE FAST!
JO. NICKI. MY BROTHER AND I SAID WE'D LOOK AFTER YOU. AND WE ALWAYS WILL.
YOU SHOULD COME WITH US.
WHERE WILL WE GO?
SO WHAT HAPPENS TO US NOW?
THAT'S NOT BAD. IT WAS THE FF WHO GOT THESE TWO LITTLE RIVALS TO WORK TOGETHER.
AND I CAN THINK OF NO BETTER HOME-- AND NO BETTER GUARDIANS FOR THEM THAN YOUR FAMILY.
BY ROYAL DECREE...
...I, DORREK VIII, PLACE N'KALLA, THE SKRULL REQUIEM OF THE SHAPELESS SOUL...
...AND JO-VENN, THE KREE CHRONICLE OF BLOOD, INTO YOUR CARE.
REED AND I WOULD BE HONORED.
AGREED. WELCOME TO THE FAMILY.
SORRY. I WAS TALKING ABOUT THEM.
BEN? ALICIA? WHAT DO YOU SAY?
US?! HONEY, HE MEANS US!
BEN, IS THIS REALLY HAPPENING?

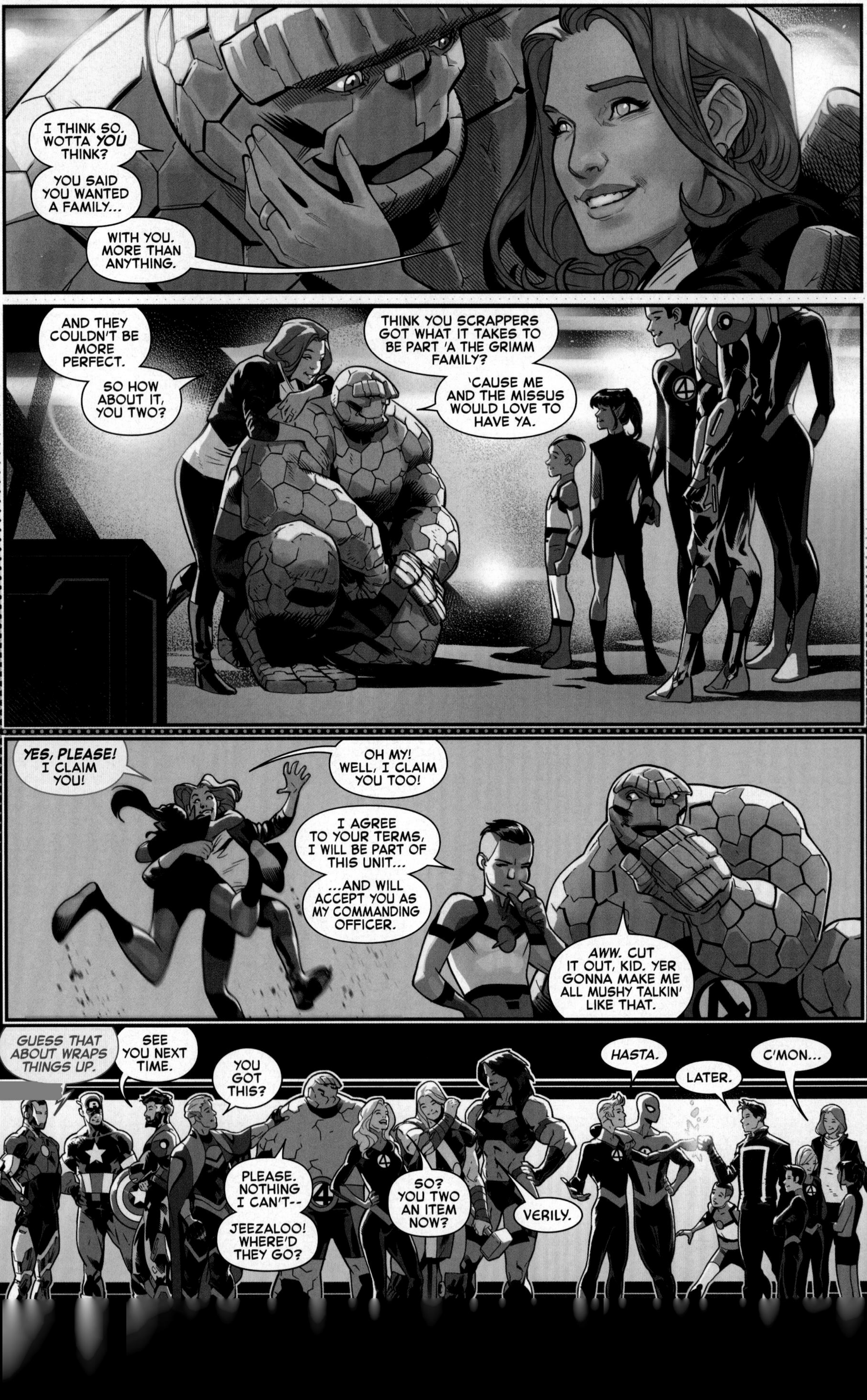
I THINK SO. WOTTA YOU THINK?
YOU SAID YOU WANTED A FAMILY...
WITH YOU. MORE THAN ANYTHING.
AND THEY COULDN'T BE MORE PERFECT.
SO HOW ABOUT IT, YOU TWO?
THINK YOU SCRAPPERS GOT WHAT IT TAKES TO BE PART 'A THE GRIMM FAMILY?
'CAUSE ME AND THE MISSUS WOULD LOVE TO HAVE YA.
YES, PLEASE! I CLAIM YOU!
OH MY! WELL, I CLAIM YOU TOO!
I AGREE TO YOUR TERMS, I WILL BE PART OF THIS UNIT...
...AND WILL ACCEPT YOU AS MY COMMANDING OFFICER.
AWW. CUT IT OUT, KID. YER GONNA MAKE ME ALL MUSHY TALKIN' LIKE THAT.
GUESS THAT ABOUT WRAPS THINGS UP.
SEE YOU NEXT TIME.
YOU GOT THIS?
PLEASE. NOTHING I CAN'T--
JEEZALOO! WHERE'D THEY GO?
SO? YOU TWO AN ITEM NOW?
VERILY.
HASTA.
LATER.
C'MON...

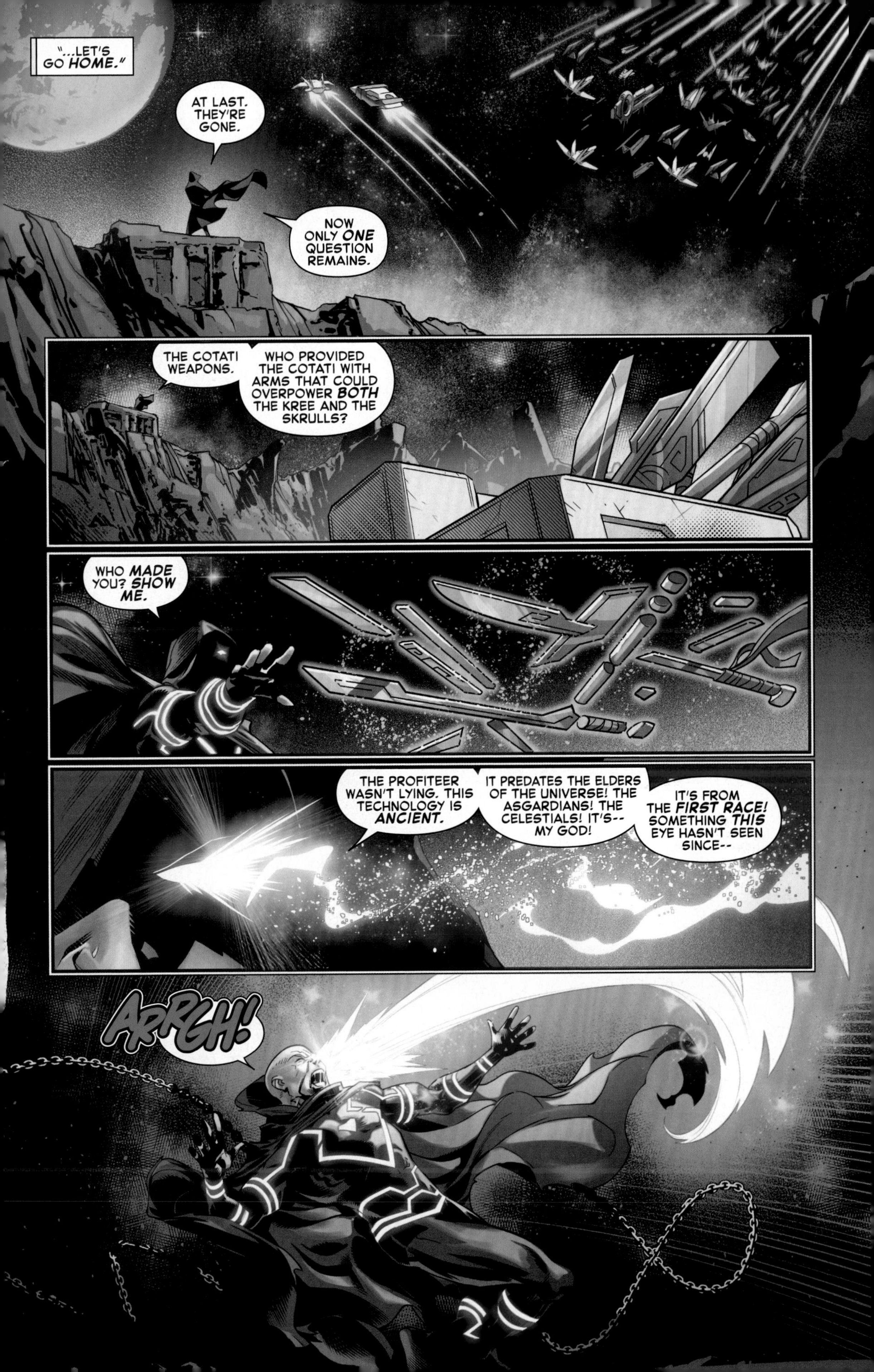
"...LET'S GO HOME."
AT LAST. THEY'RE GONE.
NOW ONLY ONE QUESTION REMAINS.
THE COTATI WEAPONS.
WHO PROVIDED THE COTATI WITH ARMS THAT COULD OVERPOWER BOTH THE KREE AND THE SKRULLS?
WHO MADE YOU? SHOW ME.
THE PROFITEER WASN'T LYING. THIS TECHNOLOGY IS ANCIENT.
IT PREDATES THE ELDERS OF THE UNIVERSE! THE ASGARDIANS! THE CELESTIALS! IT'S-- MY GOD!
IT'S FROM THE FIRST RACE! SOMETHING THIS EYE HASN'T SEEN SINCE--
ARRGH!

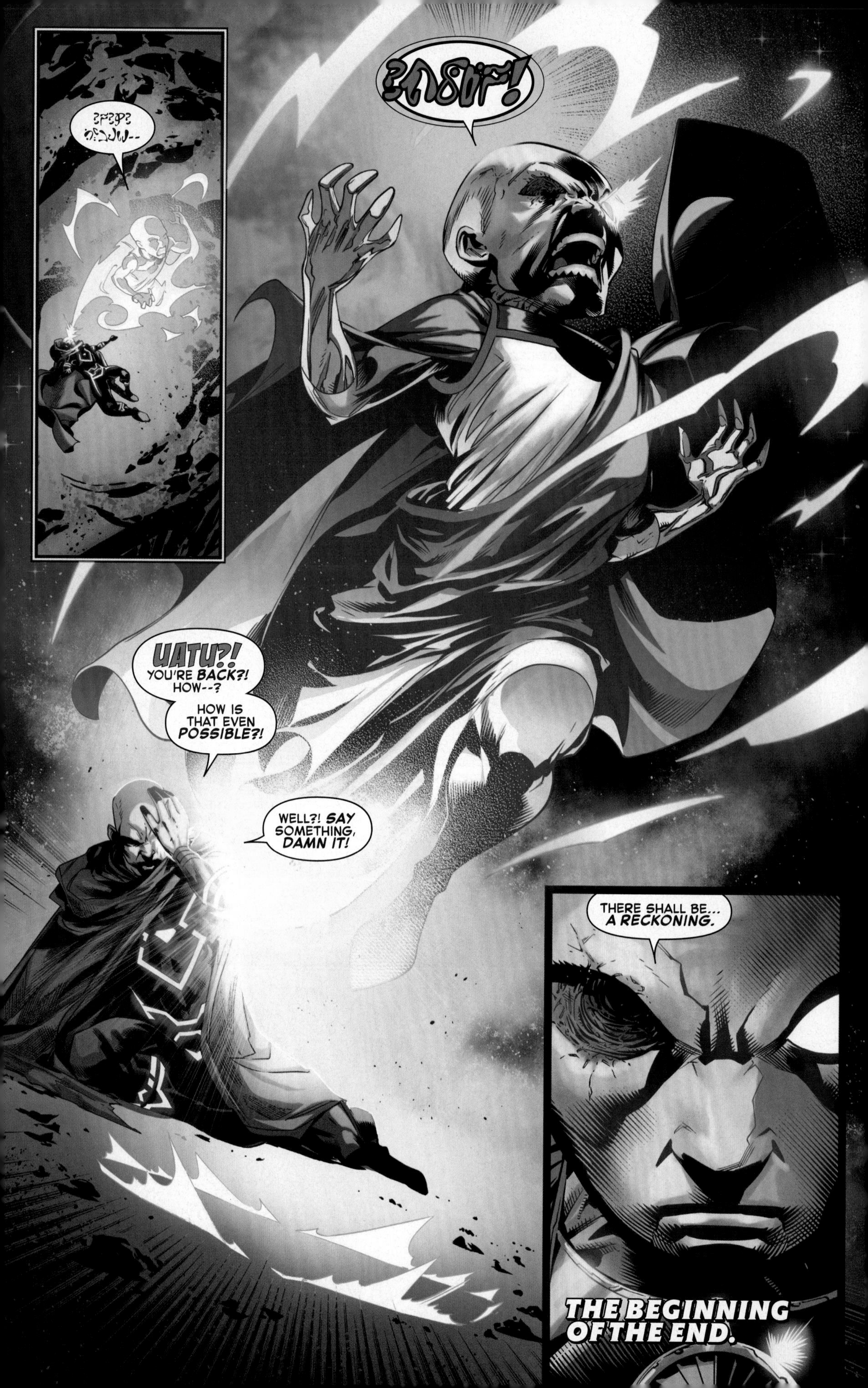
UATU?! YOU'RE BACK?! HOW--?
HOW IS THAT EVEN POSSIBLE?!
WELL?! SAY SOMETHING, DAMN IT!
THERE SHALL BE... A RECKONING.
THE BEGINNING OF THE END.

24

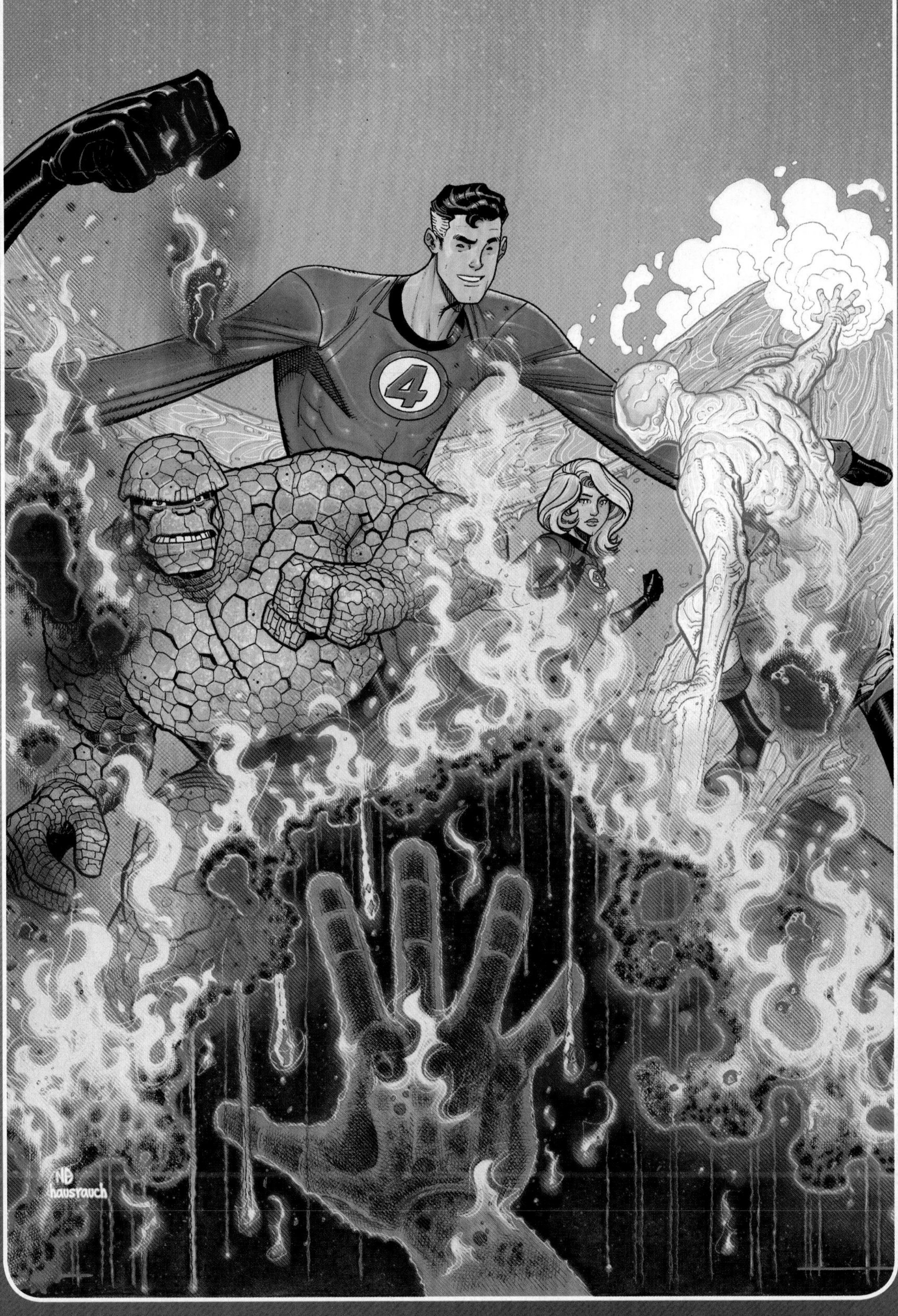
hausrauch

"Cold Snap"

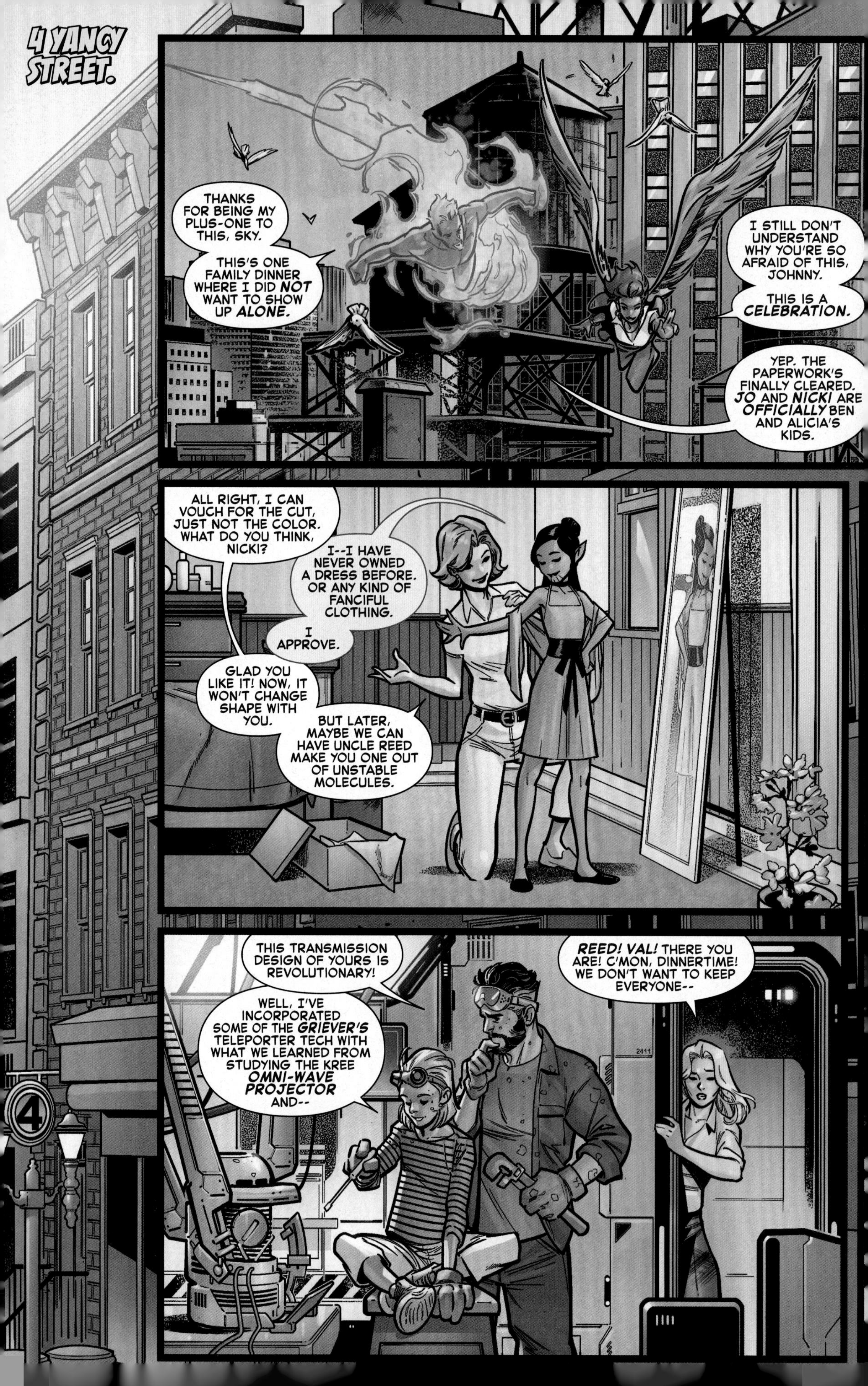
4 YANCY STREET.
THANKS FOR BEING MY PLUS-ONE TO THIS, SKY.
THIS'S ONE FAMILY DINNER WHERE I DID NOT WANT TO SHOW UP ALONE.
I STILL DON'T UNDERSTAND WHY YOU'RE SO AFRAID OF THIS, JOHNNY.
THIS IS A CELEBRATION.
YEP. THE PAPERWORK'S FINALLY CLEARED. JO AND NICKI ARE OFFICIALLY BEN AND ALICIA'S KIDS.
ALL RIGHT, I CAN VOUCH FOR THE CUT, JUST NOT THE COLOR. WHAT DO YOU THINK, NICKI?
I--I HAVE NEVER OWNED A DRESS BEFORE. OR ANY KIND OF FANCIFUL CLOTHING.
I APPROVE.
GLAD YOU LIKE IT! NOW, IT WON'T CHANGE SHAPE WITH YOU.
BUT LATER, MAYBE WE CAN HAVE UNCLE REED MAKE YOU ONE OUT OF UNSTABLE MOLECULES.
THIS TRANSMISSION DESIGN OF YOURS IS REVOLUTIONARY!
WELL, I'VE INCORPORATED SOME OF THE GRIEVER'S TELEPORTER TECH WITH WHAT WE LEARNED FROM STUDYING THE KREE OMNI-WAVE PROJECTOR AND--
REED! VAL! THERE YOU ARE! C'MON, DINNERTIME! WE DON'T WANT TO KEEP EVERYONE--

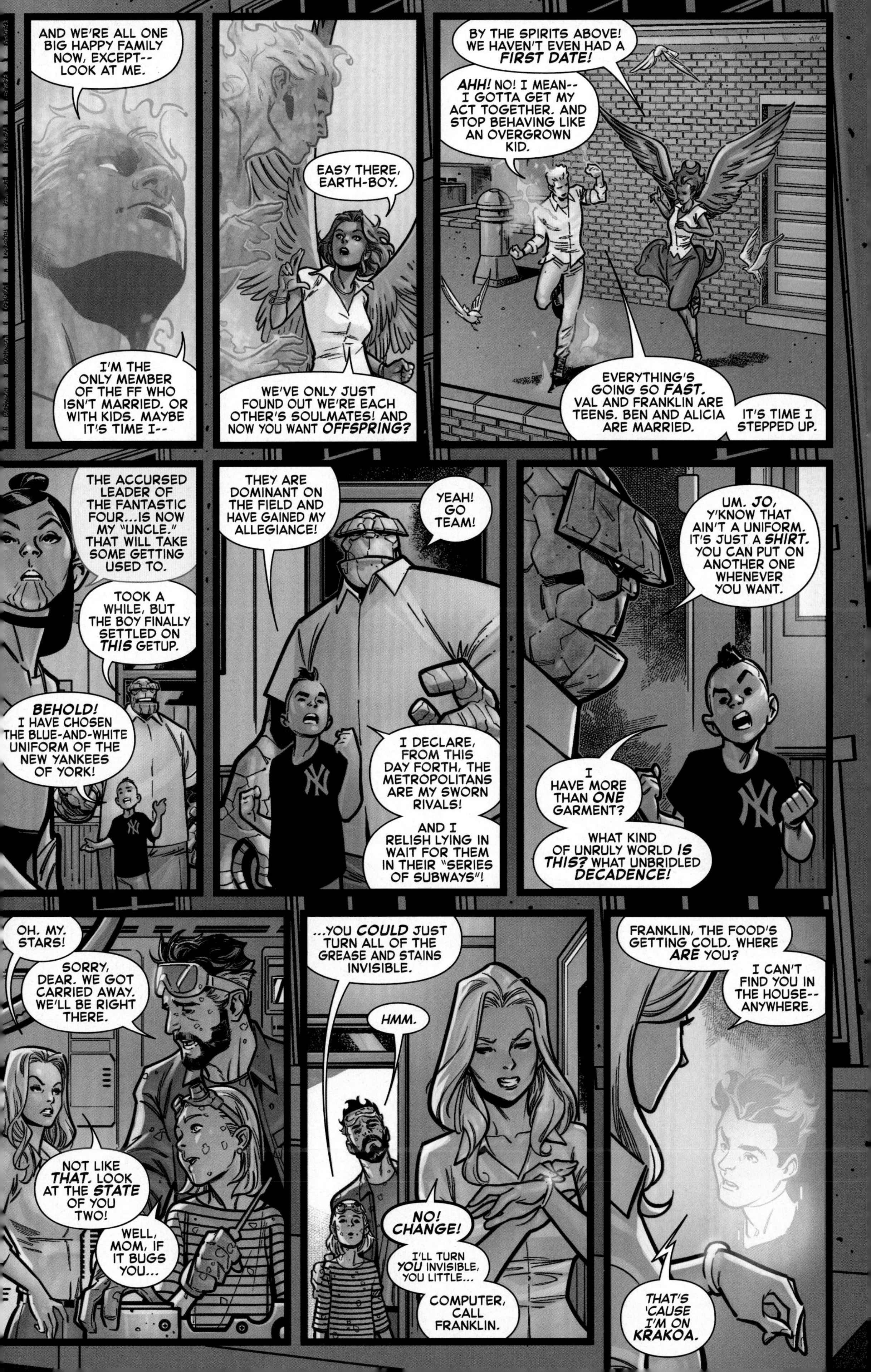
AND WE'RE ALL ONE BIG HAPPY FAMILY NOW, EXCEPT-- LOOK AT ME.
I'M THE ONLY MEMBER OF THE FF WHO ISN'T MARRIED. OR WITH KIDS. MAYBE IT'S TIME I--
EASY THERE, EARTH-BOY.
WE'VE ONLY JUST FOUND OUT WE'RE EACH OTHER'S SOULMATES! AND NOW YOU WANT OFFSPRING?
BY THE SPIRITS ABOVE! WE HAVEN'T EVEN HAD A FIRST DATE!
AHH! NO! I MEAN-- I GOTTA GET MY ACT TOGETHER. AND STOP BEHAVING LIKE AN OVERGROWN KID.
EVERYTHING'S GOING SO FAST. VAL AND FRANKLIN ARE TEENS. BEN AND ALICIA ARE MARRIED.
IT'S TIME I STEPPED UP.
THE ACCURSED LEADER OF THE FANTASTIC FOUR...IS NOW MY "UNCLE." THAT WILL TAKE SOME GETTING USED TO.
TOOK A WHILE, BUT THE BOY FINALLY SETTLED ON THIS GETUP.
BEHOLD! I HAVE CHOSEN THE BLUE-AND-WHITE UNIFORM OF THE NEW YANKEES OF YORK!
THEY ARE DOMINANT ON THE FIELD AND HAVE GAINED MY ALLEGIANCE!
YEAH! GO TEAM!
I DECLARE, FROM THIS DAY FORTH, THE METROPOLITANS ARE MY SWORN RIVALS!
AND I RELISH LYING IN WAIT FOR THEM IN THEIR "SERIES OF SUBWAYS"!
UM. JO, Y'KNOW THAT AIN'T A UNIFORM. IT'S JUST A SHIRT. YOU CAN PUT ON ANOTHER ONE WHENEVER YOU WANT.
I HAVE MORE THAN ONE GARMENT?
WHAT KIND OF UNRULY WORLD IS THIS? WHAT UNBRIDLED DECADENCE!
OH. MY. STARS!
SORRY, DEAR. WE GOT CARRIED AWAY. WE'LL BE RIGHT THERE.
NOT LIKE THAT. LOOK AT THE STATE OF YOU TWO!
WELL, MOM, IF IT BUGS YOU...
...YOU COULD JUST TURN ALL OF THE GREASE AND STAINS INVISIBLE.
HMM.
NO! CHANGE!
I'LL TURN YOU INVISIBLE, YOU LITTLE...
COMPUTER, CALL FRANKLIN.
FRANKLIN, THE FOOD'S GETTING COLD. WHERE ARE YOU?
I CAN'T FIND YOU IN THE HOUSE-- ANYWHERE.
THAT'S 'CAUSE I'M ON KRAKOA.

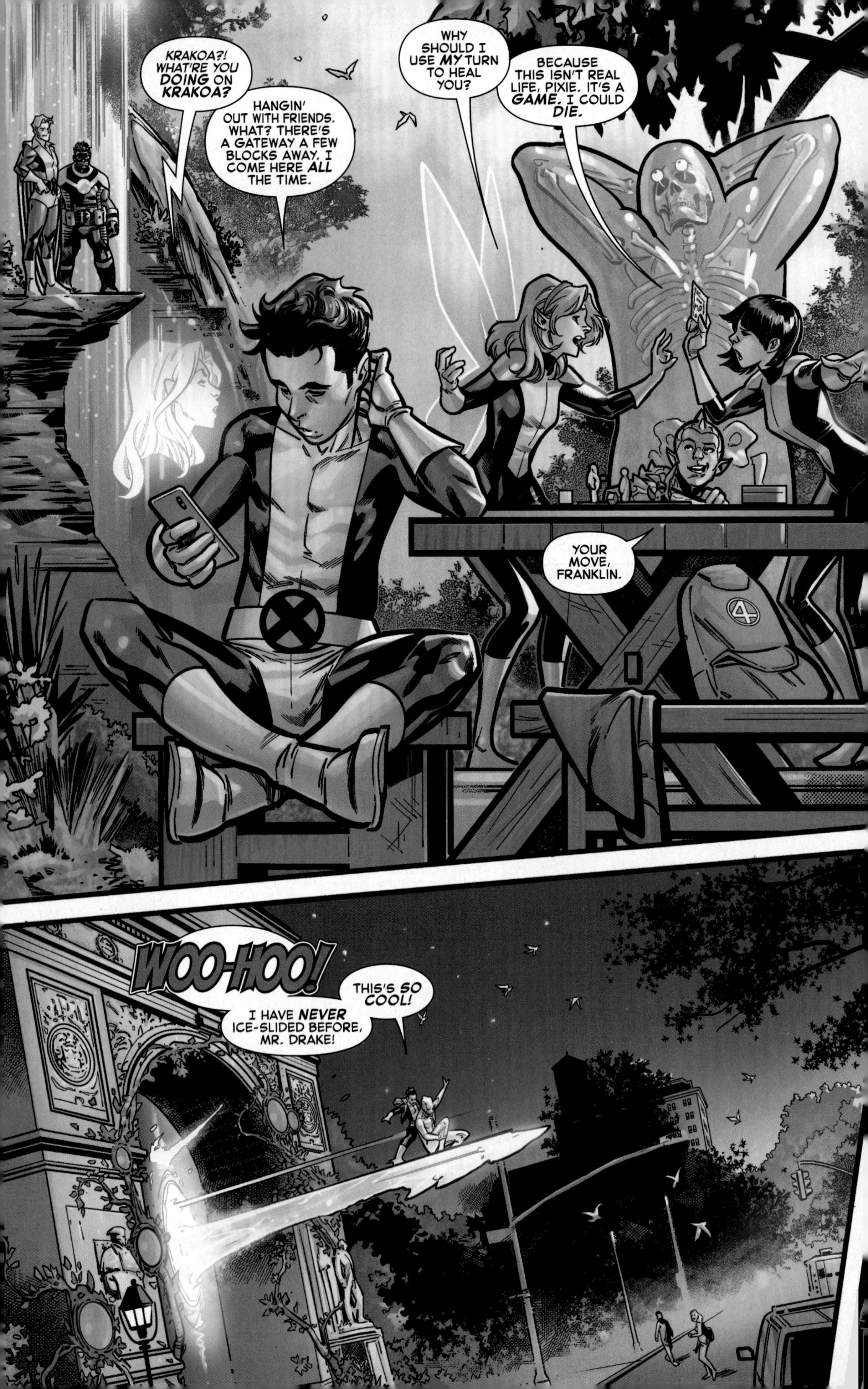

KRAKOA?! WHAT'RE YOU DOING ON KRAKOA?
HANGIN' OUT WITH FRIENDS. WHAT? THERE'S A GATEWAY A FEW BLOCKS AWAY. I COME HERE ALL THE TIME.
WHY SHOULD I USE MY TURN TO HEAL YOU?
BECAUSE THIS ISN'T REAL LIFE, PIXIE. IT'S A GAME. I COULD DIE.
YOUR MOVE, FRANKLIN.
WOO-HOO!
THIS'S SO COOL!
I HAVE NEVER ICE-SLIDED BEFORE, MR. DRAKE!

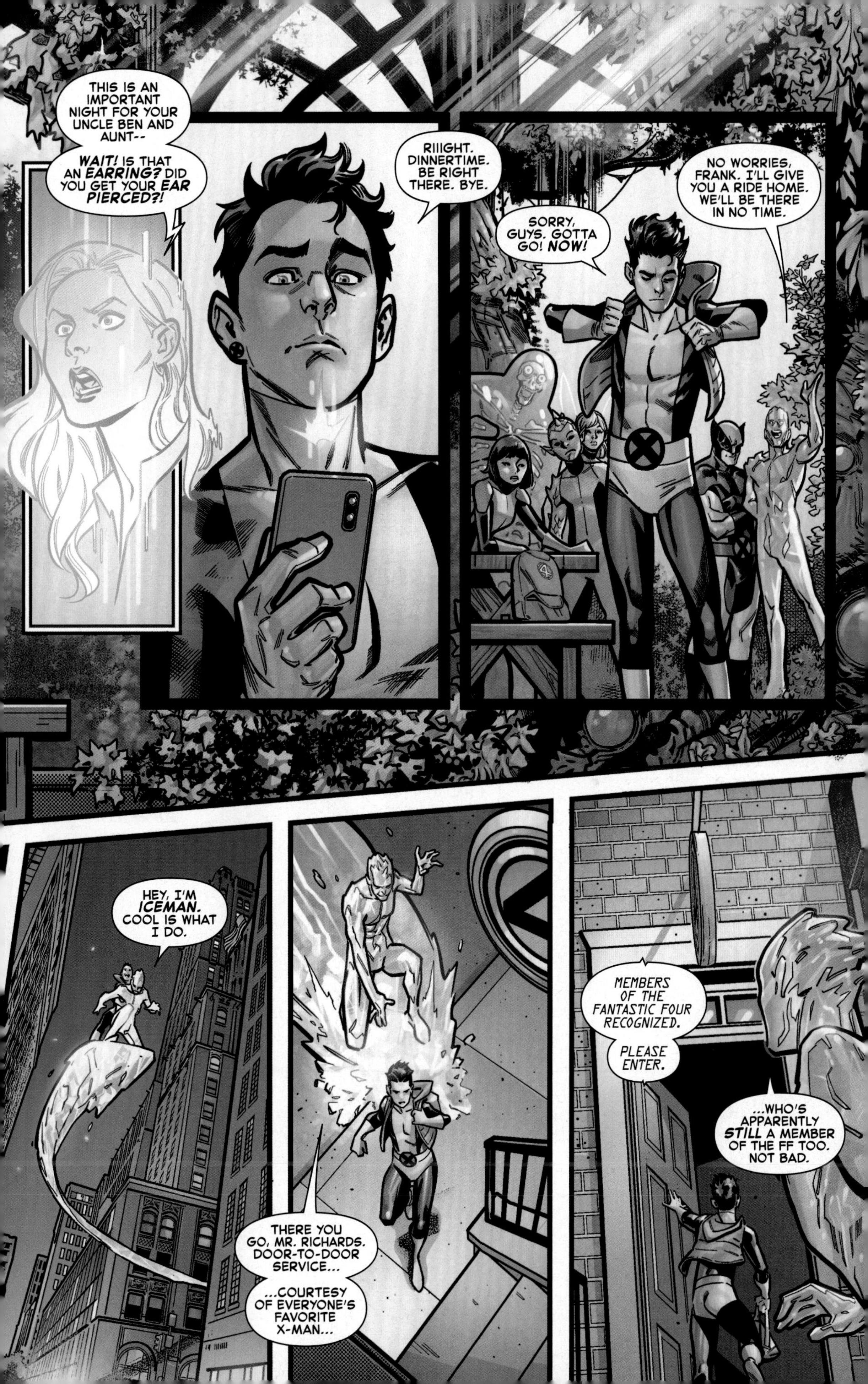
THIS IS AN IMPORTANT NIGHT FOR YOUR UNCLE BEN AND AUNT--
WAIT! IS THAT AN EARRING? DID YOU GET YOUR EAR PIERCED?!
RIIIGHT. DINNERTIME. BE RIGHT THERE. BYE.
SORRY, GUYS. GOTTA GO! NOW!
NO WORRIES, FRANK. I'LL GIVE YOU A RIDE HOME. WE'LL BE THERE IN NO TIME.
HEY, I'M ICEMAN. COOL IS WHAT I DO.
THERE YOU GO, MR. RICHARDS. DOOR-TO-DOOR SERVICE...
...COURTESY OF EVERYONE'S FAVORITE X-MAN...
MEMBERS OF THE FANTASTIC FOUR RECOGNIZED.
PLEASE ENTER.
...WHO'S APPARENTLY STILL A MEMBER OF THE FF TOO. NOT BAD.

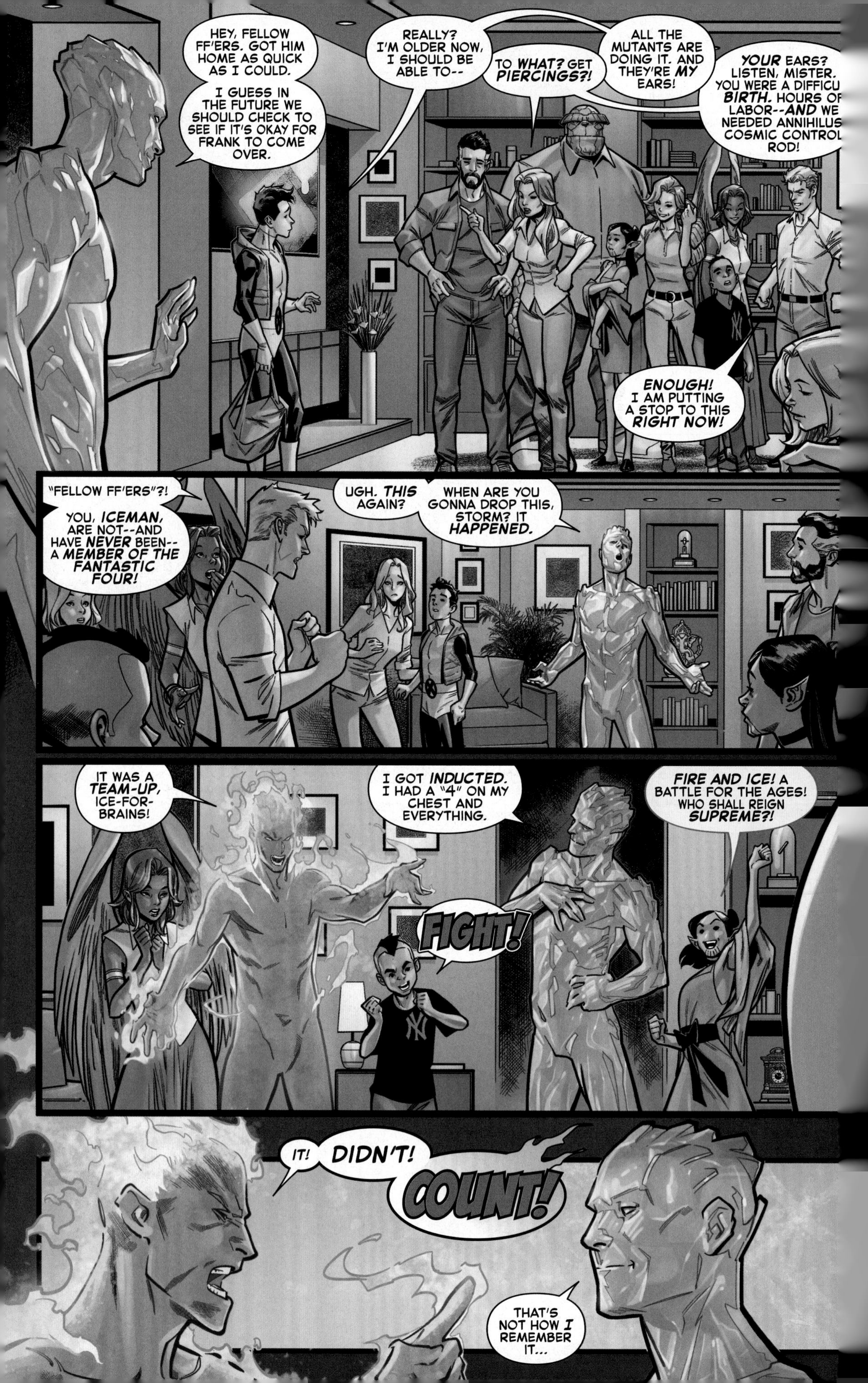
HEY, FELLOW FF'ERS. GOT HIM HOME AS QUICK AS I COULD.
I GUESS IN THE FUTURE WE SHOULD CHECK TO SEE IF IT'S OKAY FOR FRANK TO COME OVER.
REALLY? I'M OLDER NOW, I SHOULD BE ABLE TO--
TO WHAT? GET PIERCINGS?!
ALL THE MUTANTS ARE DOING IT. AND THEY'RE MY EARS!
YOUR EARS? LISTEN, MISTER. YOU WERE A DIFFICU BIRTH. HOURS OF LABOR--AND WE NEEDED ANNIHILUS COSMIC CONTROL ROD!
ENOUGH! I AM PUTTING A STOP TO THIS RIGHT NOW!
"FELLOW FF'ERS"?!
YOU, ICEMAN, ARE NOT--AND HAVE NEVER BEEN--A MEMBER OF THE FANTASTIC FOUR!
UGH. THIS AGAIN?
WHEN ARE YOU GONNA DROP THIS, STORM? IT HAPPENED.
IT WAS A TEAM-UP, ICE-FOR-BRAINS!
I GOT INDUCTED. I HAD A "4" ON MY CHEST AND EVERYTHING.
FIRE AND ICE! A BATTLE FOR THE AGES! WHO SHALL REIGN SUPREME?!
FIGHT!
IT! DIDN'T! COUNT!
THAT'S NOT HOW I REMEMBER IT...

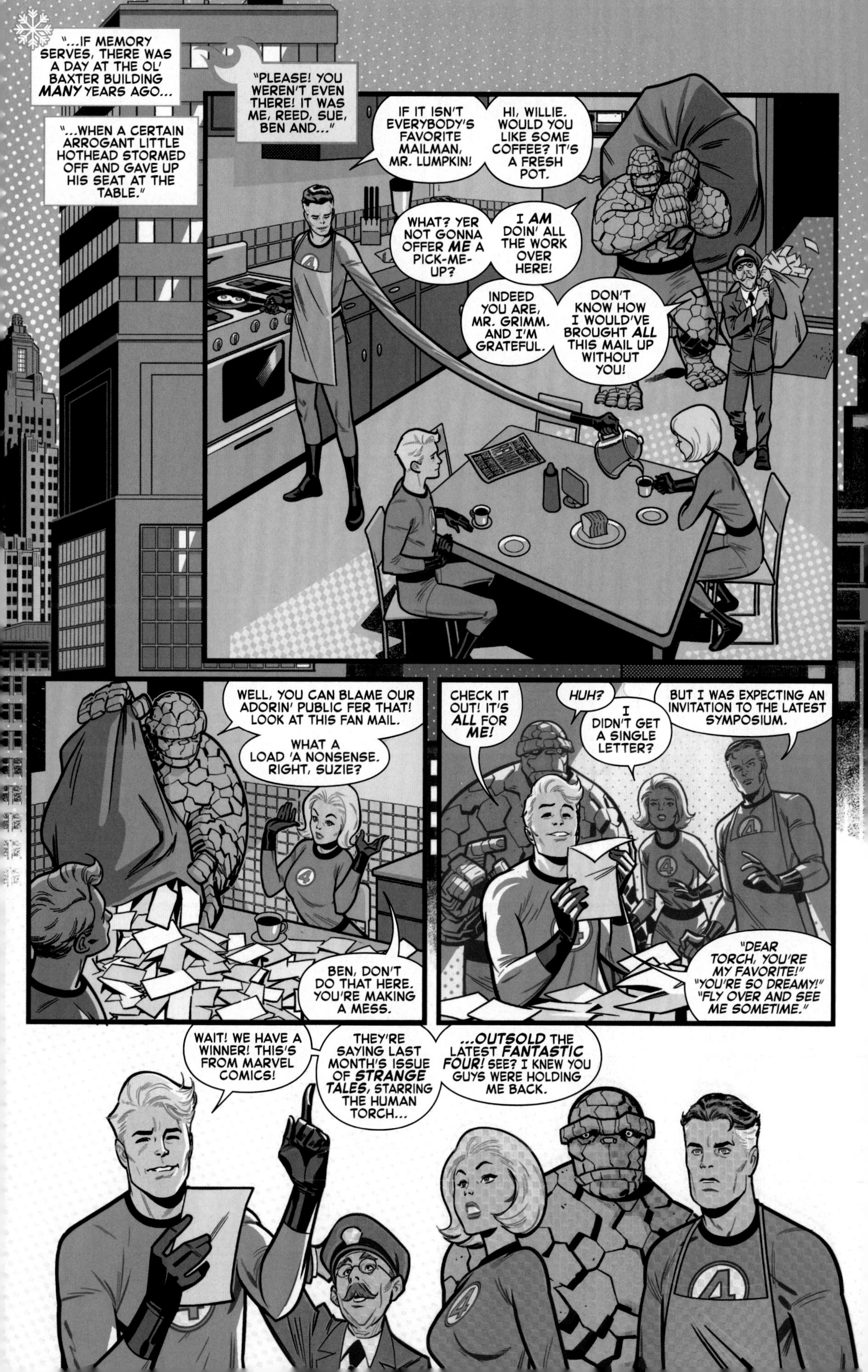
"...IF MEMORY SERVES, THERE WAS A DAY AT THE OL' BAXTER BUILDING MANY YEARS AGO...
"...WHEN A CERTAIN ARROGANT LITTLE HOTHEAD STORMED OFF AND GAVE UP HIS SEAT AT THE TABLE."
"PLEASE! YOU WEREN'T EVEN THERE! IT WAS ME, REED, SUE, BEN AND..."
IF IT ISN'T EVERYBODY'S FAVORITE MAILMAN, MR. LUMPKIN!
HI, WILLIE. WOULD YOU LIKE SOME COFFEE? IT'S A FRESH POT.
WHAT? YER NOT GONNA OFFER ME A PICK-ME-UP?
I AM DOIN' ALL THE WORK OVER HERE!
INDEED YOU ARE, MR. GRIMM. AND I'M GRATEFUL.
DON'T KNOW HOW I WOULD'VE BROUGHT ALL THIS MAIL UP WITHOUT YOU!
WELL, YOU CAN BLAME OUR ADORIN' PUBLIC FER THAT! LOOK AT THIS FAN MAIL.
WHAT A LOAD 'A NONSENSE. RIGHT, SUZIE?
BEN, DON'T DO THAT HERE. YOU'RE MAKING A MESS.
CHECK IT OUT! IT'S ALL FOR ME!
HUH?
I DIDN'T GET A SINGLE LETTER?
BUT I WAS EXPECTING AN INVITATION TO THE LATEST SYMPOSIUM.
"DEAR TORCH, YOU'RE MY FAVORITE!" "YOU'RE SO DREAMY!" "FLY OVER AND SEE ME SOMETIME."
WAIT! WE HAVE A WINNER! THIS'S FROM MARVEL COMICS!
THEY'RE SAYING LAST MONTH'S ISSUE OF STRANGE TALES, STARRING THE HUMAN TORCH...
...OUTSOLD THE LATEST FANTASTIC FOUR! SEE? I KNEW YOU GUYS WERE HOLDING ME BACK.

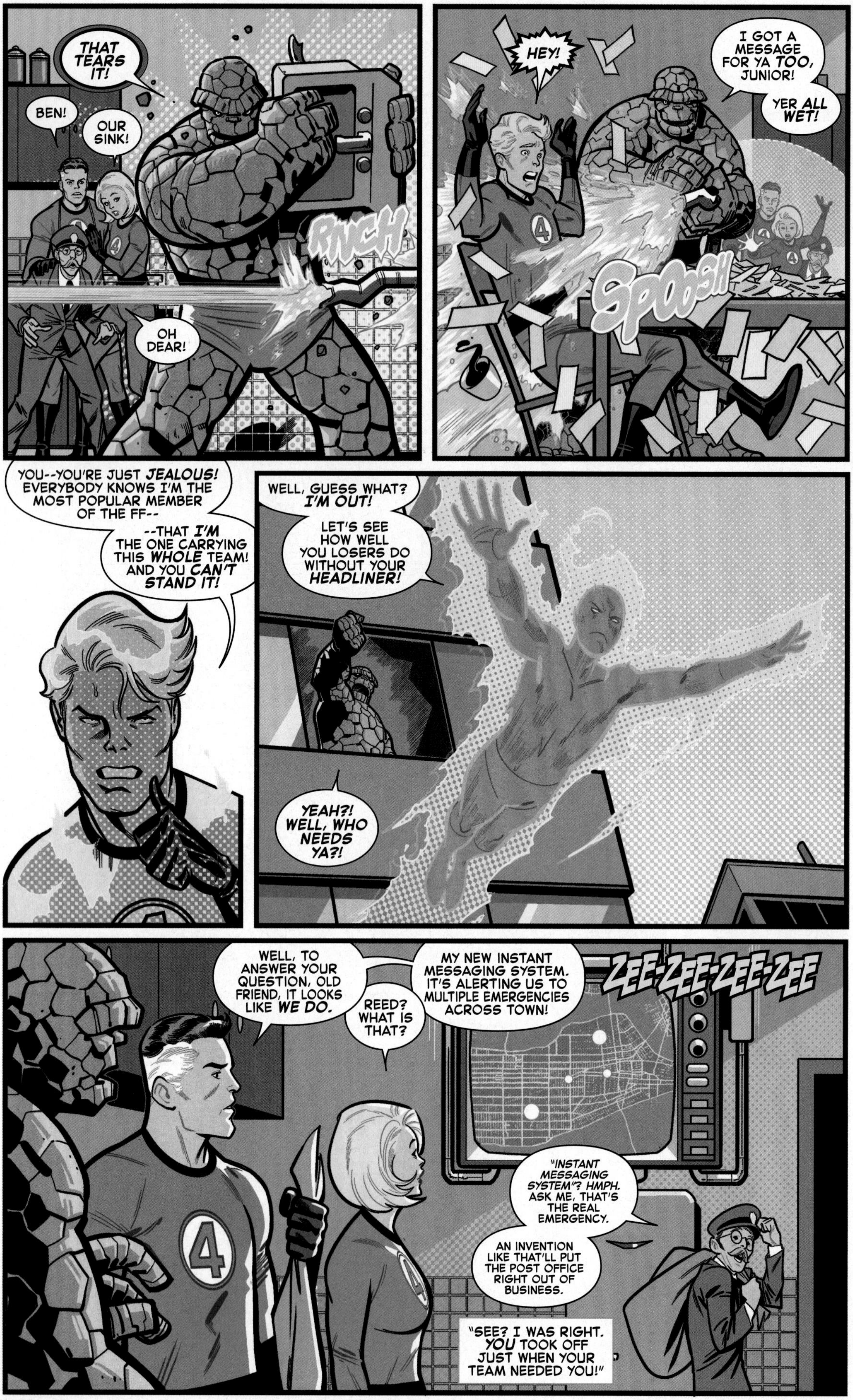
THAT TEARS IT!
BEN!
OUR SINK!
RNCH
OH DEAR!
HEY!
I GOT A MESSAGE FOR YA TOO, JUNIOR!
YER ALL WET!
SPOOSH
YOU--YOU'RE JUST JEALOUS! EVERYBODY KNOWS I'M THE MOST POPULAR MEMBER OF THE FF--
--THAT I'M THE ONE CARRYING THIS WHOLE TEAM! AND YOU CAN'T STAND IT!
WELL, GUESS WHAT? I'M OUT!
LET'S SEE HOW WELL YOU LOSERS DO WITHOUT YOUR HEADLINER!
YEAH?! WELL, WHO NEEDS YA?!
WELL, TO ANSWER YOUR QUESTION, OLD FRIEND, IT LOOKS LIKE WE DO.
REED? WHAT IS THAT?
MY NEW INSTANT MESSAGING SYSTEM. IT'S ALERTING US TO MULTIPLE EMERGENCIES ACROSS TOWN!
ZEE-ZEE-ZEE-ZEE
"INSTANT MESSAGING SYSTEM"? HMPH. ASK ME, THAT'S THE REAL EMERGENCY.
AN INVENTION LIKE THAT'LL PUT THE POST OFFICE RIGHT OUT OF BUSINESS.
"SEE? I WAS RIGHT. YOU TOOK OFF JUST WHEN YOUR TEAM NEEDED YOU!"

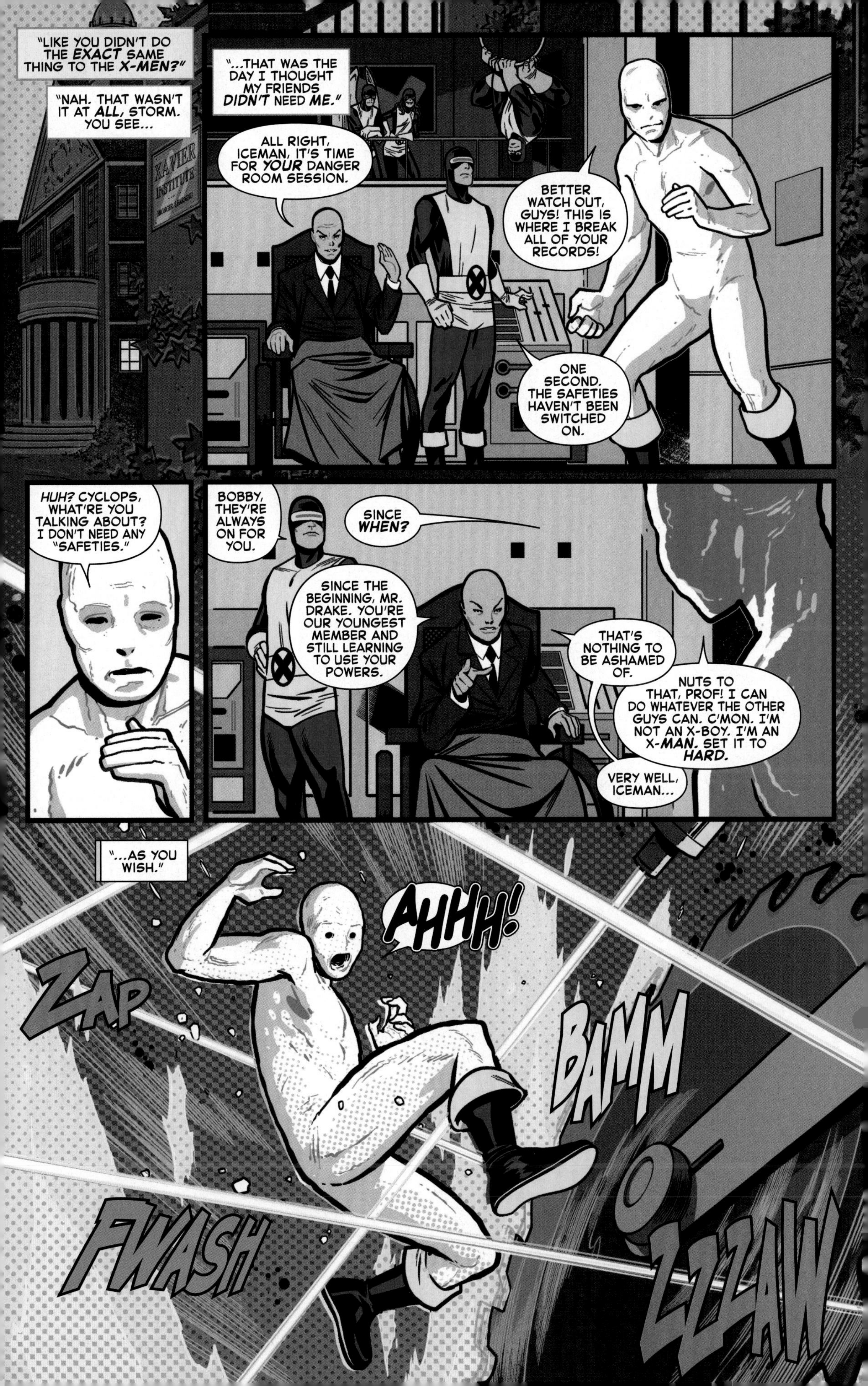
"LIKE YOU DIDN'T DO THE *EXACT* SAME THING TO THE *X-MEN?"*
"NAH. THAT WASN'T IT AT *ALL,* STORM. YOU SEE...
XAVIER INSTITUTE
"...THAT WAS THE DAY I THOUGHT MY FRIENDS *DIDN'T* NEED *ME."*
ALL RIGHT, ICEMAN, IT'S TIME FOR *YOUR* DANGER ROOM SESSION.
BETTER WATCH OUT, GUYS! THIS IS WHERE I BREAK ALL OF YOUR RECORDS!
ONE SECOND. THE SAFETIES HAVEN'T BEEN SWITCHED ON.
HUH? CYCLOPS, WHAT'RE YOU TALKING ABOUT? I DON'T NEED ANY "SAFETIES."
BOBBY, THEY'RE ALWAYS ON FOR YOU.
SINCE *WHEN?*
SINCE THE BEGINNING, MR. DRAKE. YOU'RE OUR YOUNGEST MEMBER AND STILL LEARNING TO USE YOUR POWERS.
THAT'S NOTHING TO BE ASHAMED OF.
NUTS TO THAT, PROF! I CAN DO WHATEVER THE OTHER GUYS CAN. C'MON. I'M NOT AN X-BOY. I'M AN X-*MAN.* SET IT TO *HARD.*
VERY WELL, ICEMAN...
"...AS YOU WISH."
AHHH!
ZAP
BAMM
FWASH
ZZZAW

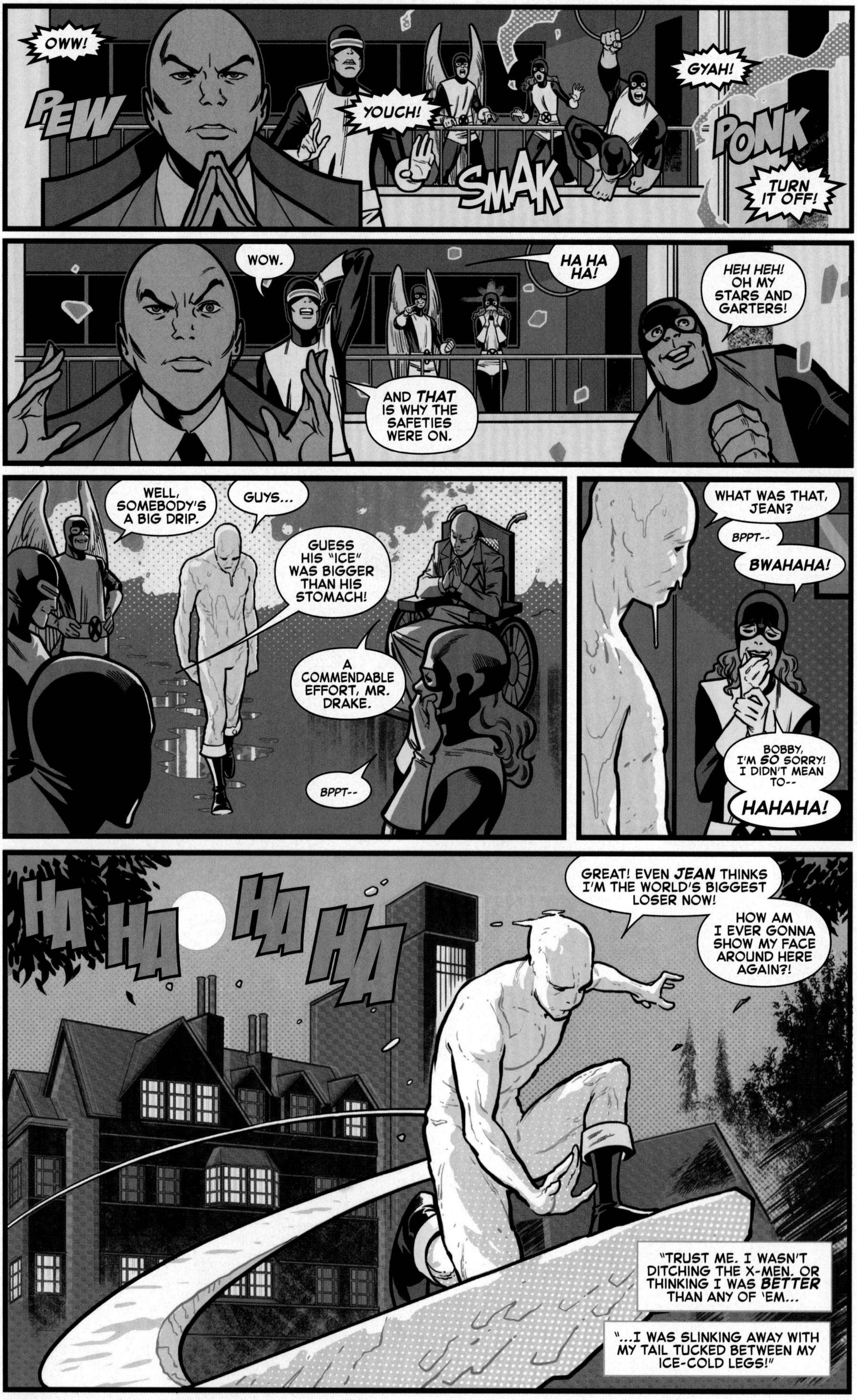
OWW!
PEW
YOUCH!
GYAH!
SMAK
PONK
TURN IT OFF!
WOW.
HA HA HA!
HEH HEH! OH MY STARS AND GARTERS!
AND THAT IS WHY THE SAFETIES WERE ON.
WELL, SOMEBODY'S A BIG DRIP.
GUYS...
GUESS HIS "ICE" WAS BIGGER THAN HIS STOMACH!
A COMMENDABLE EFFORT, MR. DRAKE.
BPPT--
WHAT WAS THAT, JEAN?
BPPT--
BWAHAHA!
BOBBY, I'M SO SORRY! I DIDN'T MEAN TO--
HAHAHA!
HA HA HA HA
GREAT! EVEN JEAN THINKS I'M THE WORLD'S BIGGEST LOSER NOW!
HOW AM I EVER GONNA SHOW MY FACE AROUND HERE AGAIN?!
"TRUST ME. I WASN'T DITCHING THE X-MEN. OR THINKING I WAS BETTER THAN ANY OF 'EM...
"...I WAS SLINKING AWAY WITH MY TAIL TUCKED BETWEEN MY ICE-COLD LEGS!"

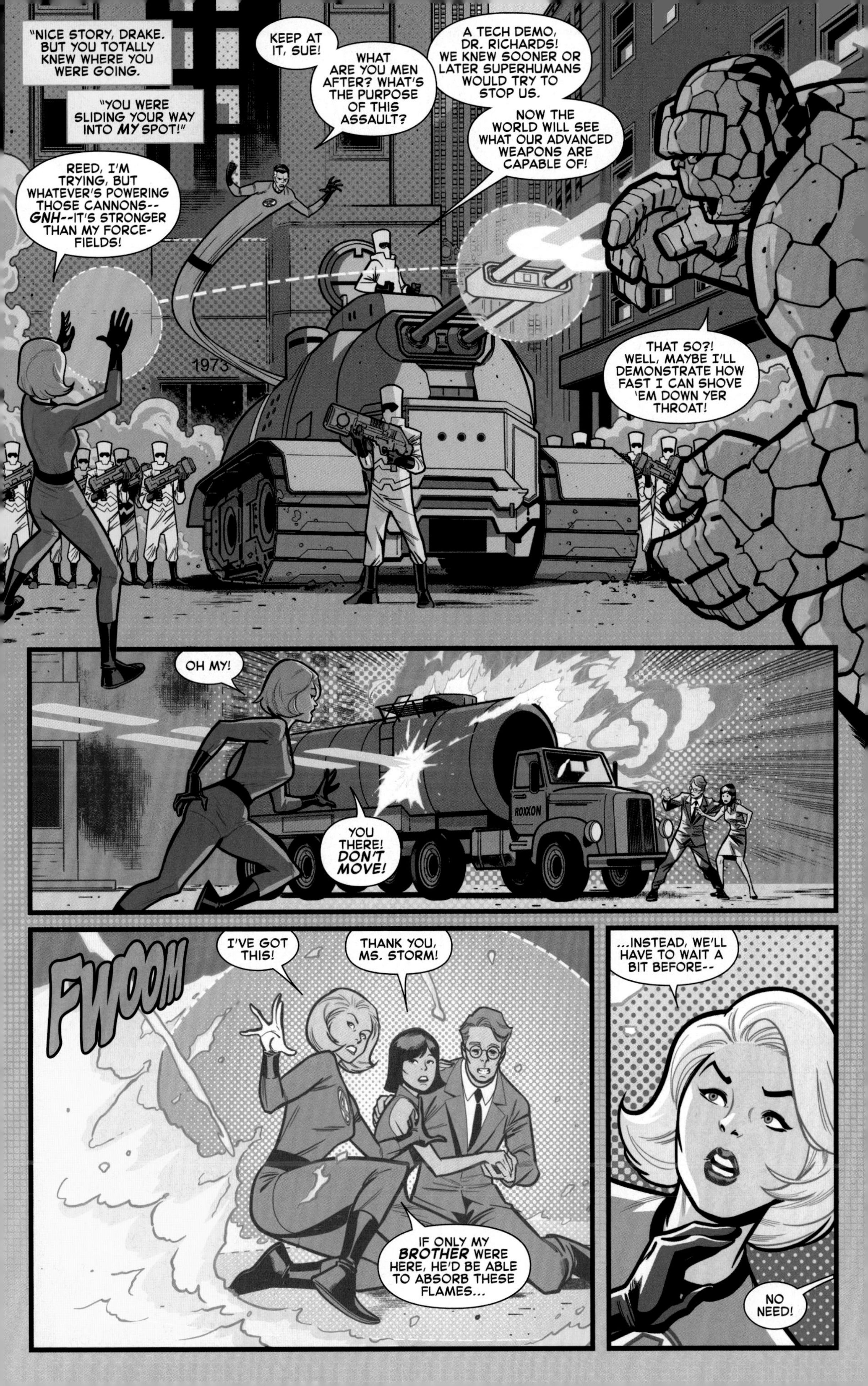
"NICE STORY, DRAKE. BUT YOU TOTALLY KNEW WHERE YOU WERE GOING.
"YOU WERE SLIDING YOUR WAY INTO MY SPOT!"
KEEP AT IT, SUE!
WHAT ARE YOU MEN AFTER? WHAT'S THE PURPOSE OF THIS ASSAULT?
A TECH DEMO, DR. RICHARDS! WE KNEW SOONER OR LATER SUPERHUMANS WOULD TRY TO STOP US.
NOW THE WORLD WILL SEE WHAT OUR ADVANCED WEAPONS ARE CAPABLE OF!
REED, I'M TRYING, BUT WHATEVER'S POWERING THOSE CANNONS-- GNH--IT'S STRONGER THAN MY FORCE-FIELDS!
1973
THAT SO?! WELL, MAYBE I'LL DEMONSTRATE HOW FAST I CAN SHOVE 'EM DOWN YER THROAT!
OH MY!
YOU THERE! DON'T MOVE!
ROXXON
FWOOM
I'VE GOT THIS!
THANK YOU, MS. STORM!
IF ONLY MY BROTHER WERE HERE, HE'D BE ABLE TO ABSORB THESE FLAMES...
...INSTEAD, WE'LL HAVE TO WAIT A BIT BEFORE--
NO NEED!

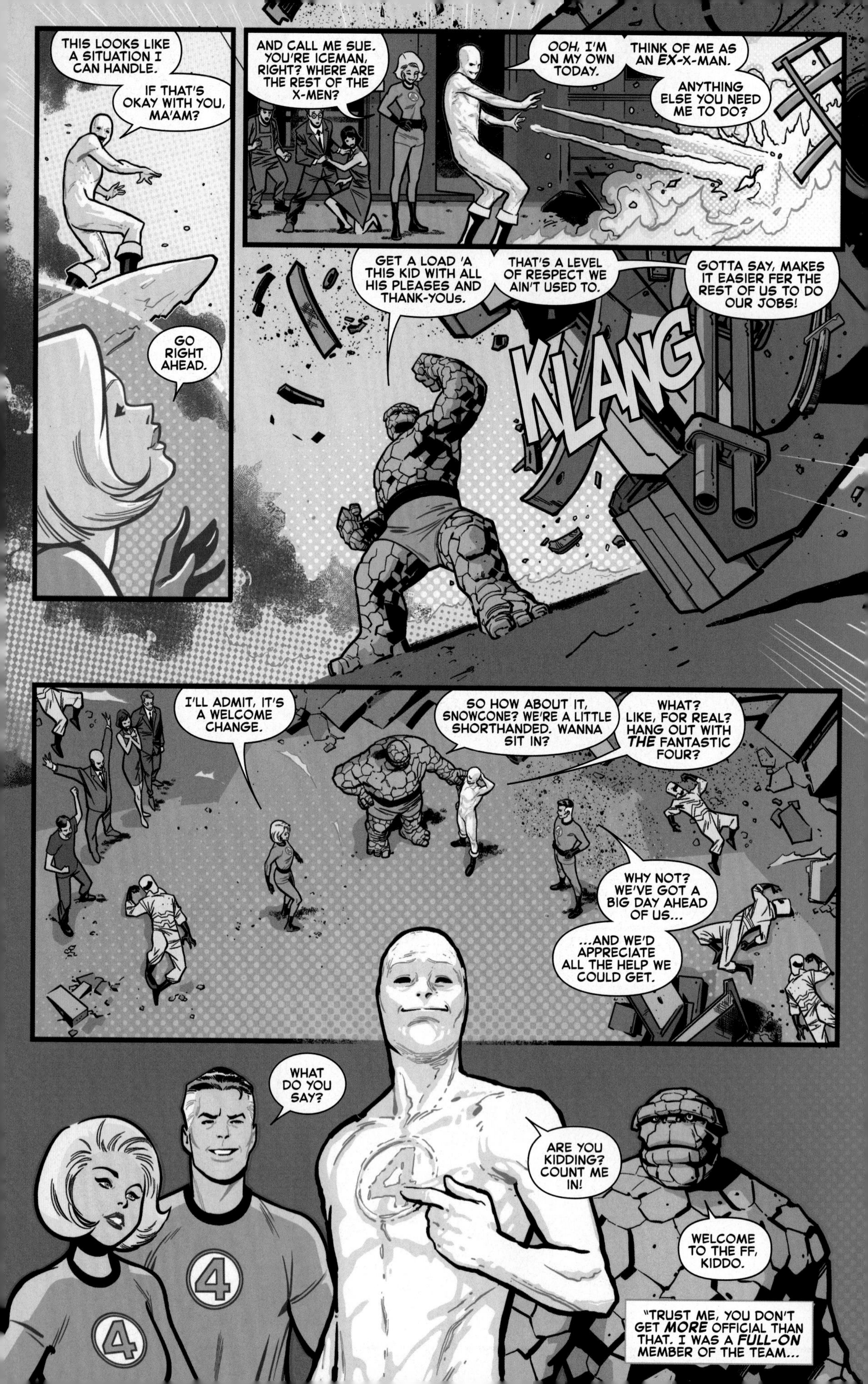
THIS LOOKS LIKE A SITUATION I CAN HANDLE.
IF THAT'S OKAY WITH YOU, MA'AM?
GO RIGHT AHEAD.
AND CALL ME SUE. YOU'RE ICEMAN, RIGHT? WHERE ARE THE REST OF THE X-MEN?
OOH, I'M ON MY OWN TODAY.
THINK OF ME AS AN EX-X-MAN.
ANYTHING ELSE YOU NEED ME TO DO?
GET A LOAD 'A THIS KID WITH ALL HIS PLEASES AND THANK-YOUS.
THAT'S A LEVEL OF RESPECT WE AIN'T USED TO.
GOTTA SAY, MAKES IT EASIER FER THE REST OF US TO DO OUR JOBS!
KLANG
I'LL ADMIT, IT'S A WELCOME CHANGE.
SO HOW ABOUT IT, SNOWCONE? WE'RE A LITTLE SHORTHANDED. WANNA SIT IN?
WHAT? LIKE, FOR REAL? HANG OUT WITH THE FANTASTIC FOUR?
WHY NOT? WE'VE GOT A BIG DAY AHEAD OF US...
...AND WE'D APPRECIATE ALL THE HELP WE COULD GET.
WHAT DO YOU SAY?
ARE YOU KIDDING? COUNT ME IN!
WELCOME TO THE FF, KIDDO.
"TRUST ME, YOU DON'T GET MORE OFFICIAL THAN THAT. I WAS A FULL-ON MEMBER OF THE TEAM...

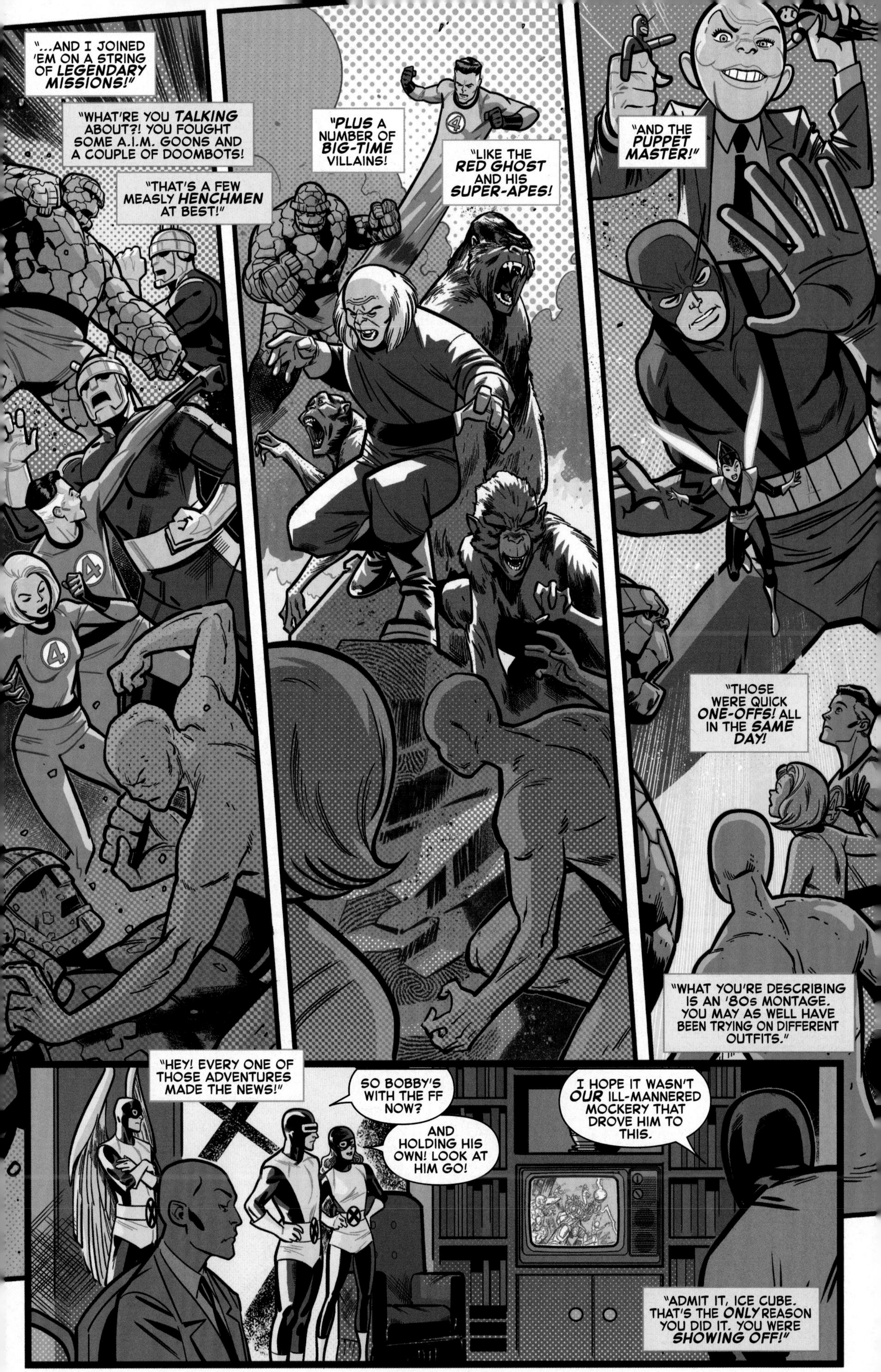
"...AND I JOINED 'EM ON A STRING OF LEGENDARY MISSIONS!"
"WHAT'RE YOU TALKING ABOUT?! YOU FOUGHT SOME A.I.M. GOONS AND A COUPLE OF DOOMBOTS!
"THAT'S A FEW MEASLY HENCHMEN AT BEST!"
"PLUS A NUMBER OF BIG-TIME VILLAINS!
"LIKE THE RED GHOST AND HIS SUPER-APES!
"AND THE PUPPET MASTER!"
"THOSE WERE QUICK ONE-OFFS! ALL IN THE SAME DAY!
"WHAT YOU'RE DESCRIBING IS AN '80s MONTAGE. YOU MAY AS WELL HAVE BEEN TRYING ON DIFFERENT OUTFITS."
"HEY! EVERY ONE OF THOSE ADVENTURES MADE THE NEWS!"
SO BOBBY'S WITH THE FF NOW?
AND HOLDING HIS OWN! LOOK AT HIM GO!
I HOPE IT WASN'T OUR ILL-MANNERED MOCKERY THAT DROVE HIM TO THIS.
"ADMIT IT, ICE CUBE. THAT'S THE ONLY REASON YOU DID IT. YOU WERE SHOWING OFF!"

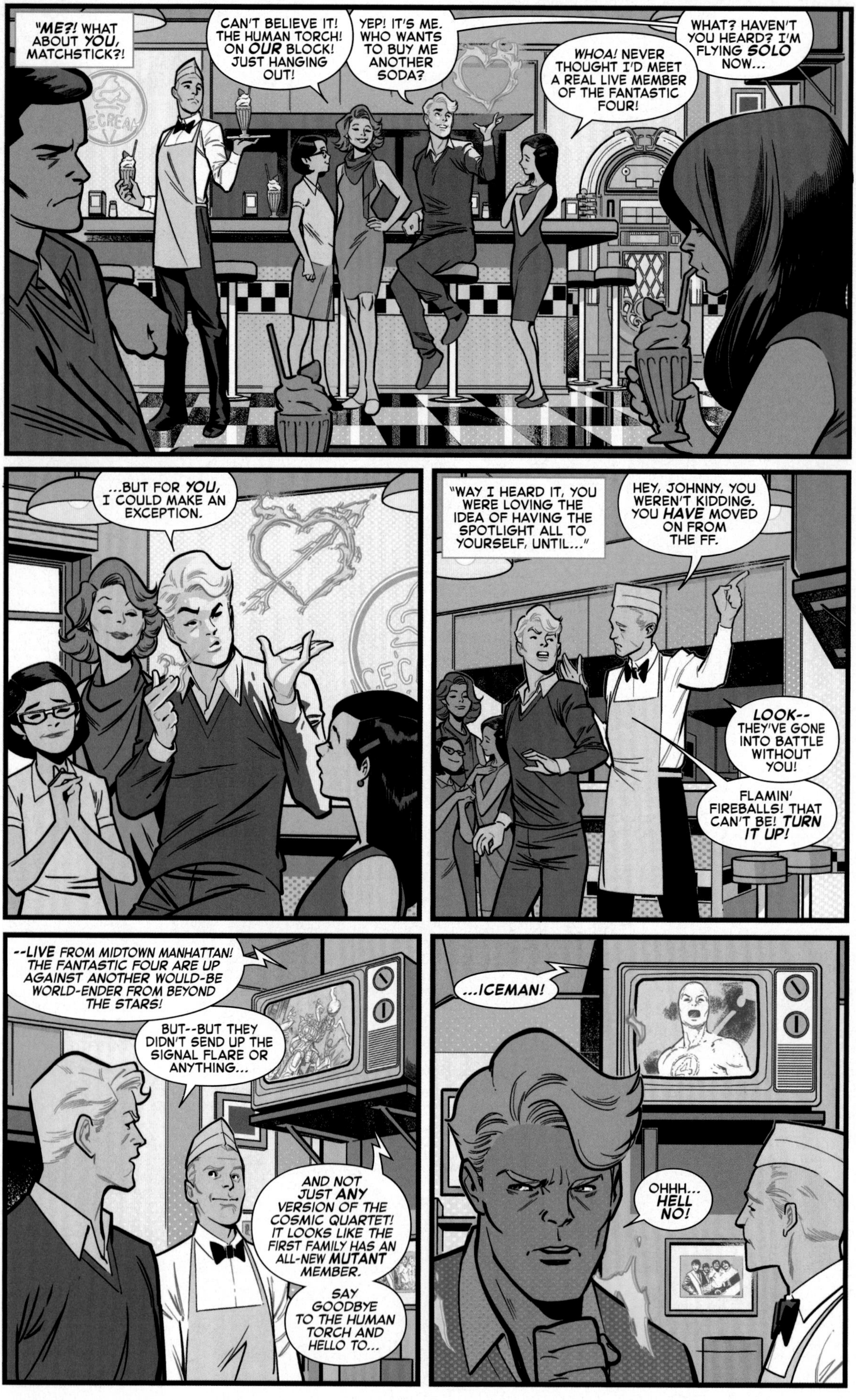
"ME?! WHAT ABOUT YOU, MATCHSTICK?!
CAN'T BELIEVE IT! THE HUMAN TORCH! ON OUR BLOCK! JUST HANGING OUT!
YEP! IT'S ME. WHO WANTS TO BUY ME ANOTHER SODA?
WHOA! NEVER THOUGHT I'D MEET A REAL LIVE MEMBER OF THE FANTASTIC FOUR!
WHAT? HAVEN'T YOU HEARD? I'M FLYING SOLO NOW...
...BUT FOR YOU, I COULD MAKE AN EXCEPTION.
"WAY I HEARD IT, YOU WERE LOVING THE IDEA OF HAVING THE SPOTLIGHT ALL TO YOURSELF, UNTIL..."
HEY, JOHNNY, YOU WEREN'T KIDDING. YOU HAVE MOVED ON FROM THE FF.
LOOK-- THEY'VE GONE INTO BATTLE WITHOUT YOU!
FLAMIN' FIREBALLS! THAT CAN'T BE! TURN IT UP!
--LIVE FROM MIDTOWN MANHATTAN! THE FANTASTIC FOUR ARE UP AGAINST ANOTHER WOULD-BE WORLD-ENDER FROM BEYOND THE STARS!
BUT--BUT THEY DIDN'T SEND UP THE SIGNAL FLARE OR ANYTHING...
AND NOT JUST ANY VERSION OF THE COSMIC QUARTET! IT LOOKS LIKE THE FIRST FAMILY HAS AN ALL-NEW MUTANT MEMBER.
SAY GOODBYE TO THE HUMAN TORCH AND HELLO TO...
...ICEMAN!
OHHH... HELL NO!

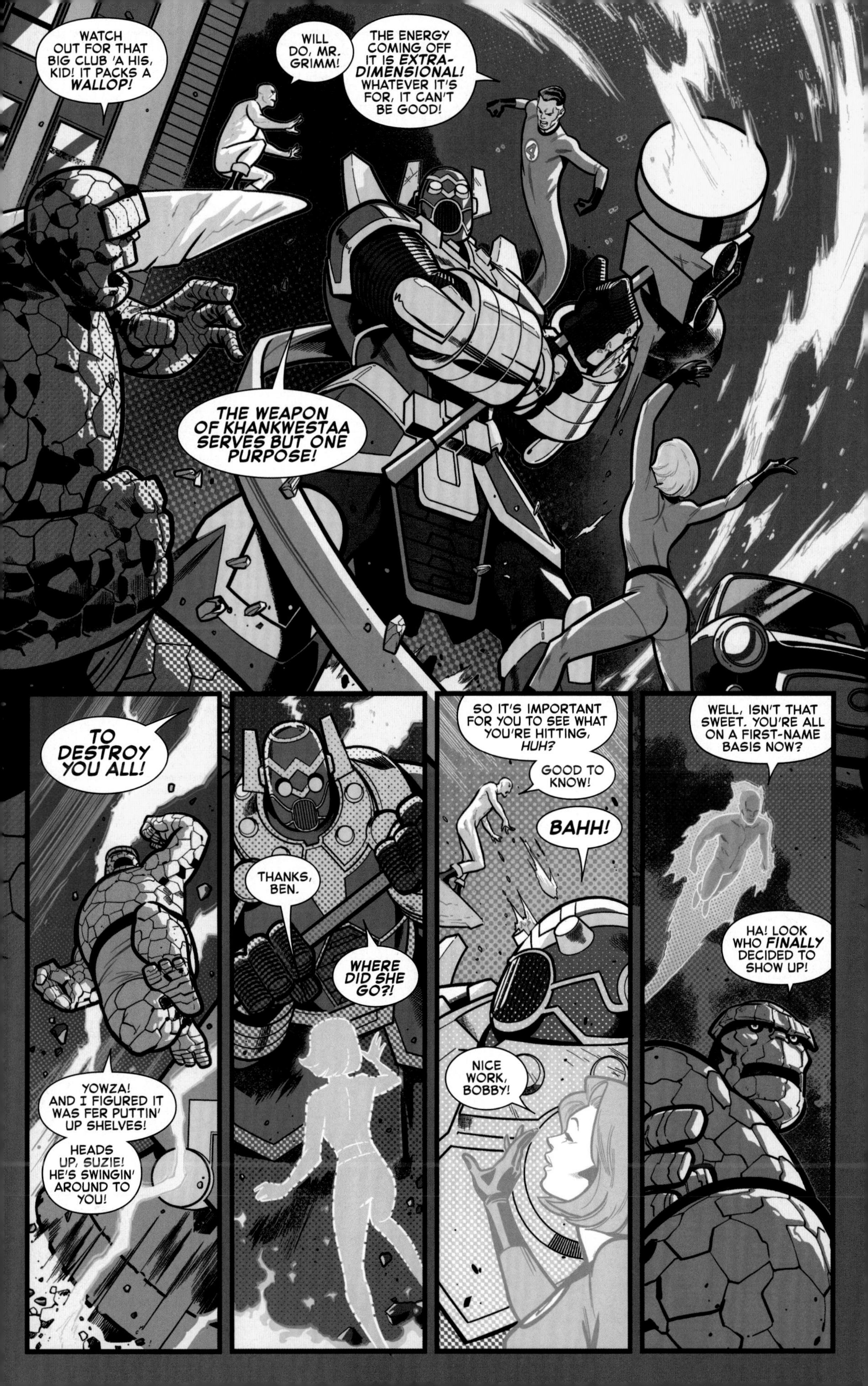
WATCH OUT FOR THAT BIG CLUB 'A HIS, KID! IT PACKS A WALLOP!
WILL DO, MR. GRIMM!
THE ENERGY COMING OFF IT IS EXTRA-DIMENSIONAL! WHATEVER IT'S FOR, IT CAN'T BE GOOD!
THE WEAPON OF KHANKWESTAA SERVES BUT ONE PURPOSE!
TO DESTROY YOU ALL!
YOWZA! AND I FIGURED IT WAS FER PUTTIN' UP SHELVES!
HEADS UP, SUZIE! HE'S SWINGIN' AROUND TO YOU!
THANKS, BEN.
WHERE DID SHE GO?!
SO IT'S IMPORTANT FOR YOU TO SEE WHAT YOU'RE HITTING, HUH?
GOOD TO KNOW!
BAHH!
NICE WORK, BOBBY!
WELL, ISN'T THAT SWEET. YOU'RE ALL ON A FIRST-NAME BASIS NOW?
HA! LOOK WHO FINALLY DECIDED TO SHOW UP!

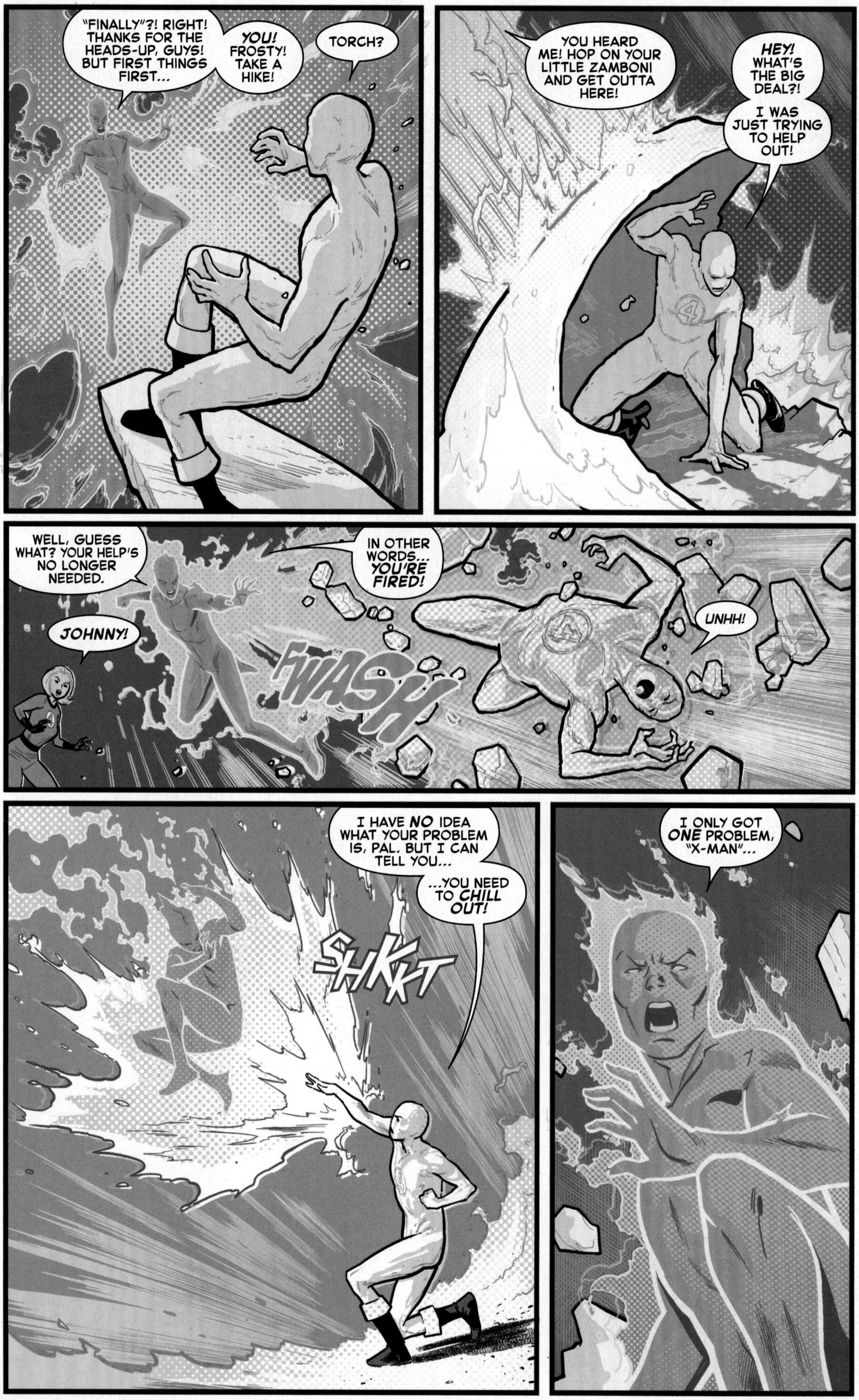
"FINALLY"?! RIGHT! THANKS FOR THE HEADS-UP, GUYS! BUT FIRST THINGS FIRST...
YOU! FROSTY! TAKE A HIKE!
TORCH?
YOU HEARD ME! HOP ON YOUR LITTLE ZAMBONI AND GET OUTTA HERE!
HEY! WHAT'S THE BIG DEAL?!
I WAS JUST TRYING TO HELP OUT!
WELL, GUESS WHAT? YOUR HELP'S NO LONGER NEEDED.
IN OTHER WORDS... YOU'RE FIRED!
JOHNNY!
FWASH
UNHH!
I HAVE NO IDEA WHAT YOUR PROBLEM IS, PAL. BUT I CAN TELL YOU...
...YOU NEED TO CHILL OUT!
SHKKKT
I ONLY GOT ONE PROBLEM, "X-MAN"...

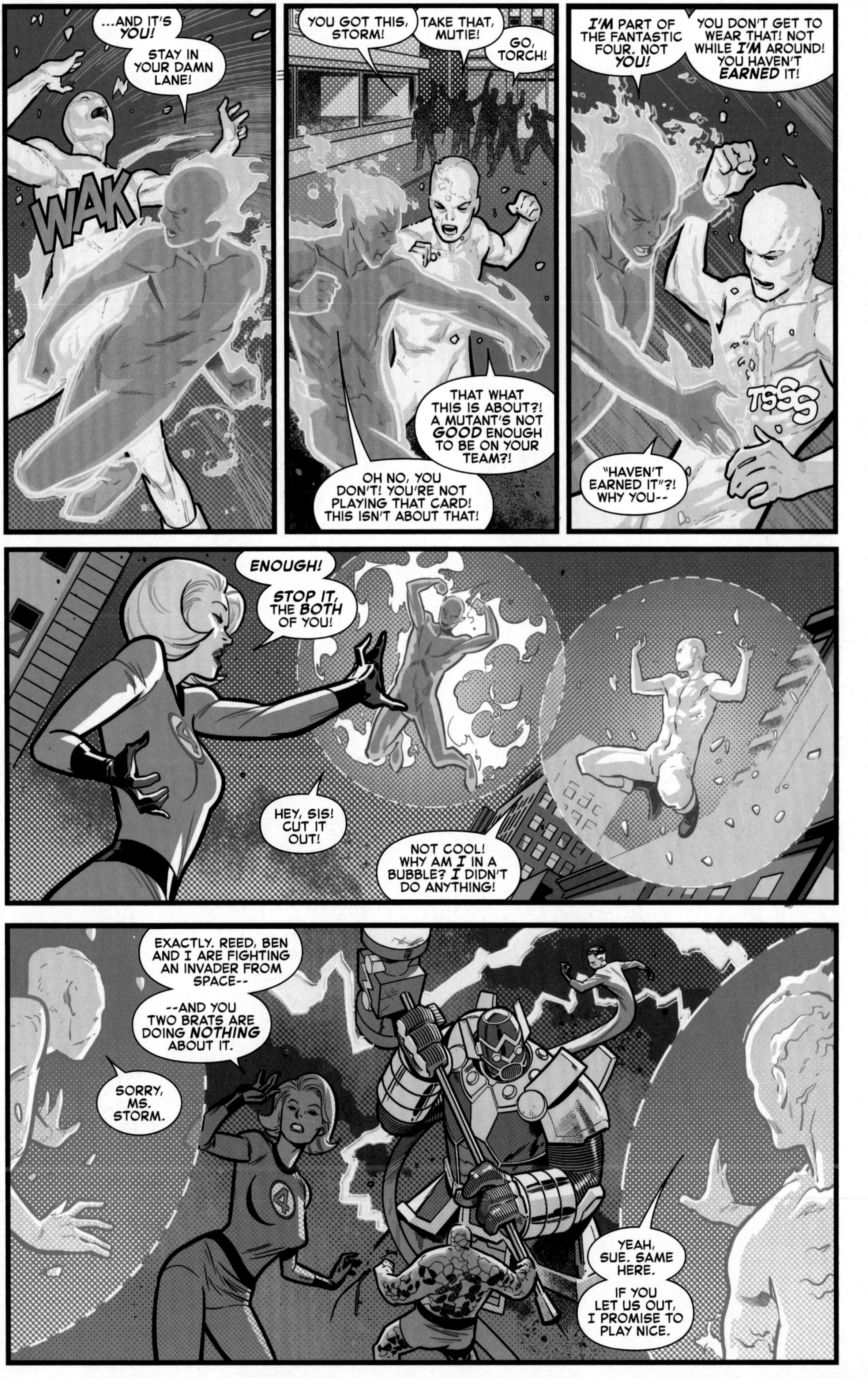
...AND IT'S YOU!
STAY IN YOUR DAMN LANE!
WAK
YOU GOT THIS, STORM!
TAKE THAT, MUTIE!
GO, TORCH!
THAT WHAT THIS IS ABOUT?! A MUTANT'S NOT GOOD ENOUGH TO BE ON YOUR TEAM?!
OH NO, YOU DON'T! YOU'RE NOT PLAYING THAT CARD! THIS ISN'T ABOUT THAT!
I'M PART OF THE FANTASTIC FOUR. NOT YOU!
YOU DON'T GET TO WEAR THAT! NOT WHILE I'M AROUND! YOU HAVEN'T EARNED IT!
TSSS
"HAVEN'T EARNED IT"?! WHY YOU--
ENOUGH!
STOP IT, THE BOTH OF YOU!
HEY, SIS! CUT IT OUT!
NOT COOL! WHY AM I IN A BUBBLE? I DIDN'T DO ANYTHING!
EXACTLY. REED, BEN AND I ARE FIGHTING AN INVADER FROM SPACE--
--AND YOU TWO BRATS ARE DOING NOTHING ABOUT IT.
SORRY, MS. STORM.
YEAH, SUE. SAME HERE.
IF YOU LET US OUT, I PROMISE TO PLAY NICE.

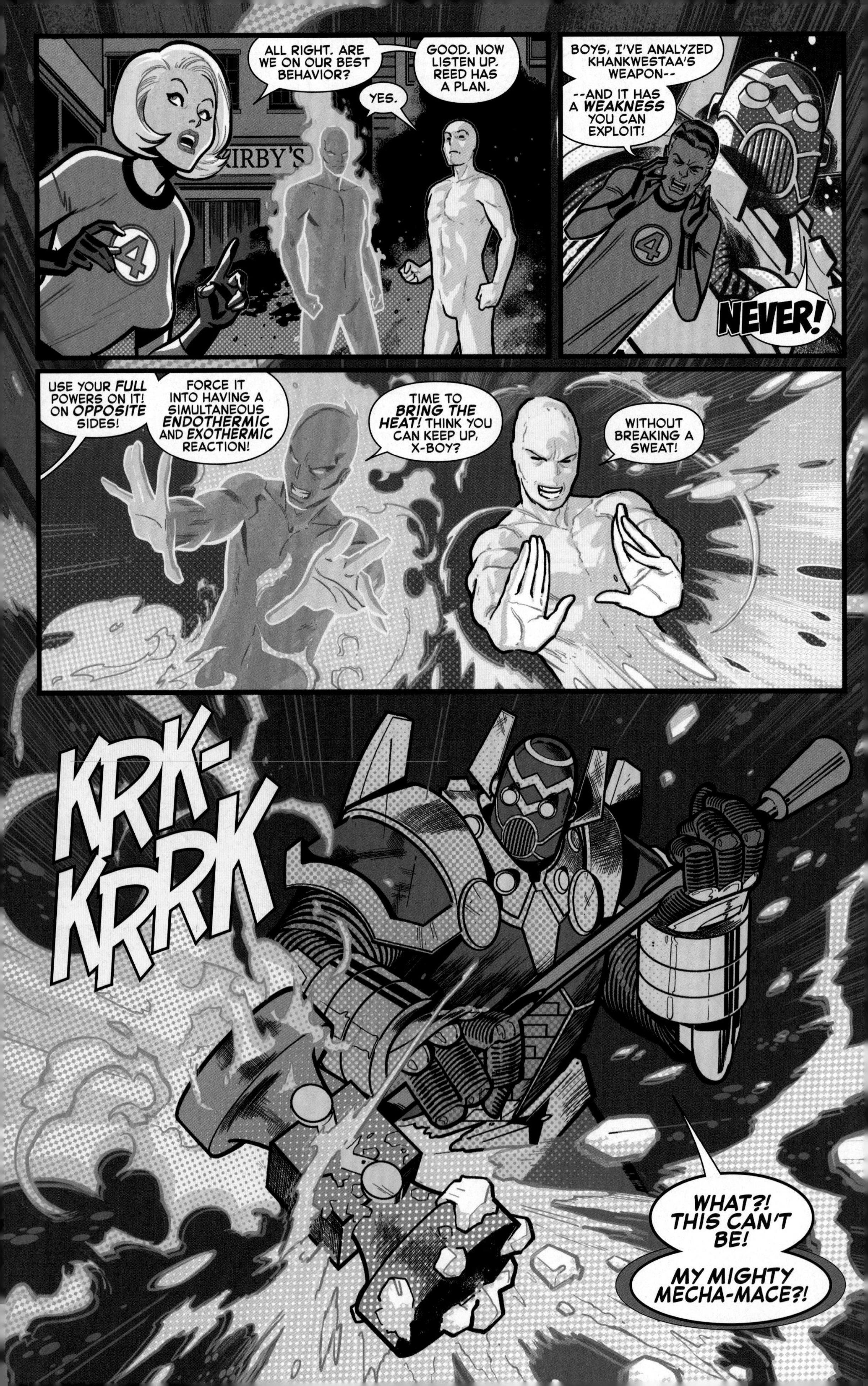

ALL RIGHT. ARE WE ON OUR BEST BEHAVIOR?
GOOD. NOW LISTEN UP. REED HAS A PLAN.
YES.
KIRBY'S
BOYS, I'VE ANALYZED KHANKWESTAA'S WEAPON--
--AND IT HAS A WEAKNESS YOU CAN EXPLOIT!
NEVER!
USE YOUR FULL POWERS ON IT! ON OPPOSITE SIDES!
FORCE IT INTO HAVING A SIMULTANEOUS ENDOTHERMIC AND EXOTHERMIC REACTION!
TIME TO BRING THE HEAT! THINK YOU CAN KEEP UP, X-BOY?
WITHOUT BREAKING A SWEAT!
KRK-KRRK
WHAT?! THIS CAN'T BE!
MY MIGHTY MECHA-MACE?!

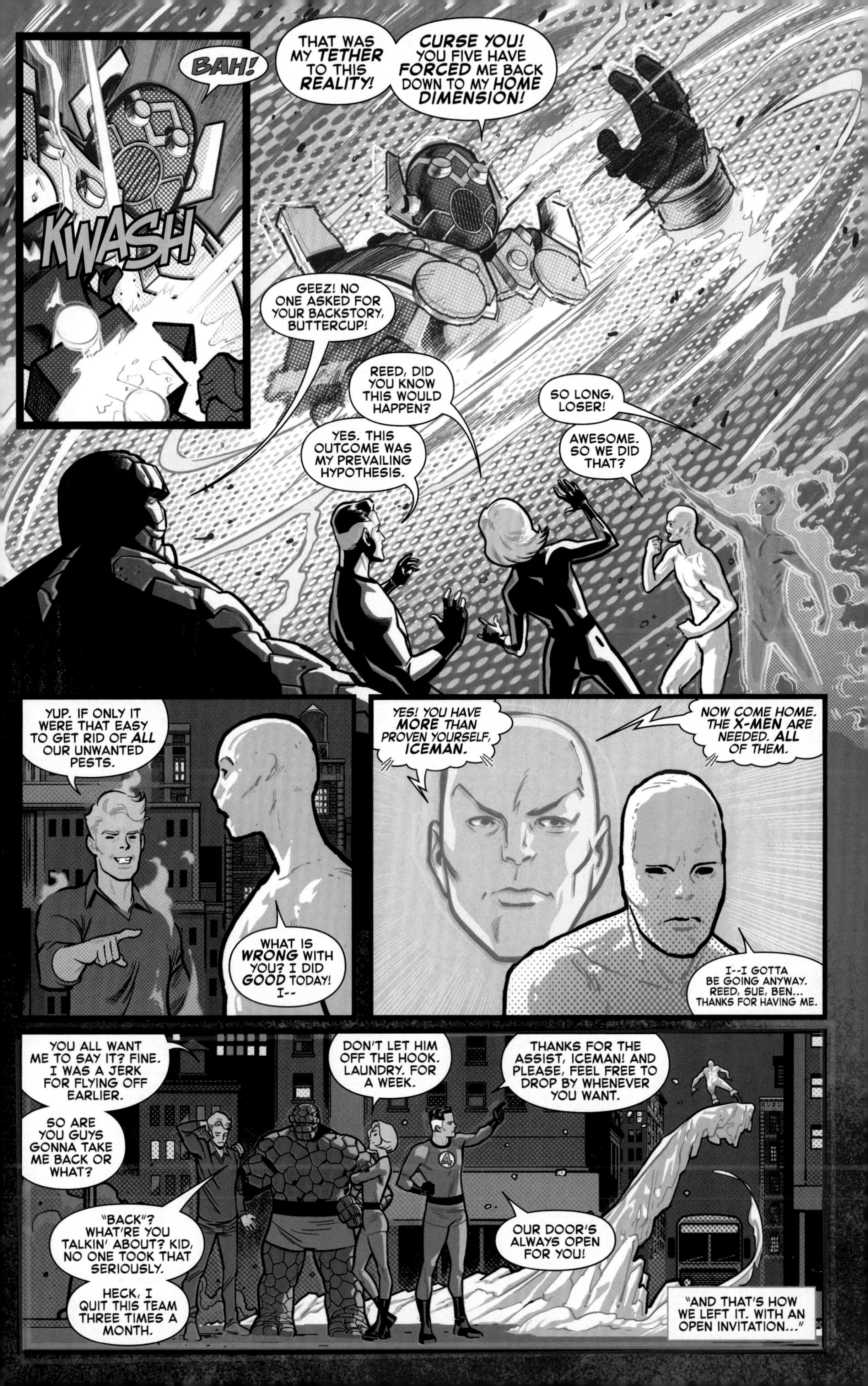
BAH!
KWASH
THAT WAS MY TETHER TO THIS REALITY!
CURSE YOU! YOU FIVE HAVE FORCED ME BACK DOWN TO MY HOME DIMENSION!
GEEZ! NO ONE ASKED FOR YOUR BACKSTORY, BUTTERCUP!
REED, DID YOU KNOW THIS WOULD HAPPEN?
YES. THIS OUTCOME WAS MY PREVAILING HYPOTHESIS.
SO LONG, LOSER!
AWESOME. SO WE DID THAT?
YUP. IF ONLY IT WERE THAT EASY TO GET RID OF ALL OUR UNWANTED PESTS.
WHAT IS WRONG WITH YOU? I DID GOOD TODAY! I--
YES! YOU HAVE MORE THAN PROVEN YOURSELF, ICEMAN.
NOW COME HOME. THE X-MEN ARE NEEDED. ALL OF THEM.
I--I GOTTA BE GOING ANYWAY. REED, SUE, BEN... THANKS FOR HAVING ME.
YOU ALL WANT ME TO SAY IT? FINE. I WAS A JERK FOR FLYING OFF EARLIER.
SO ARE YOU GUYS GONNA TAKE ME BACK OR WHAT?
"BACK"? WHAT'RE YOU TALKIN' ABOUT? KID, NO ONE TOOK THAT SERIOUSLY.
HECK, I QUIT THIS TEAM THREE TIMES A MONTH.
DON'T LET HIM OFF THE HOOK. LAUNDRY. FOR A WEEK.
THANKS FOR THE ASSIST, ICEMAN! AND PLEASE, FEEL FREE TO DROP BY WHENEVER YOU WANT.
OUR DOOR'S ALWAYS OPEN FOR YOU!
"AND THAT'S HOW WE LEFT IT. WITH AN OPEN INVITATION..."

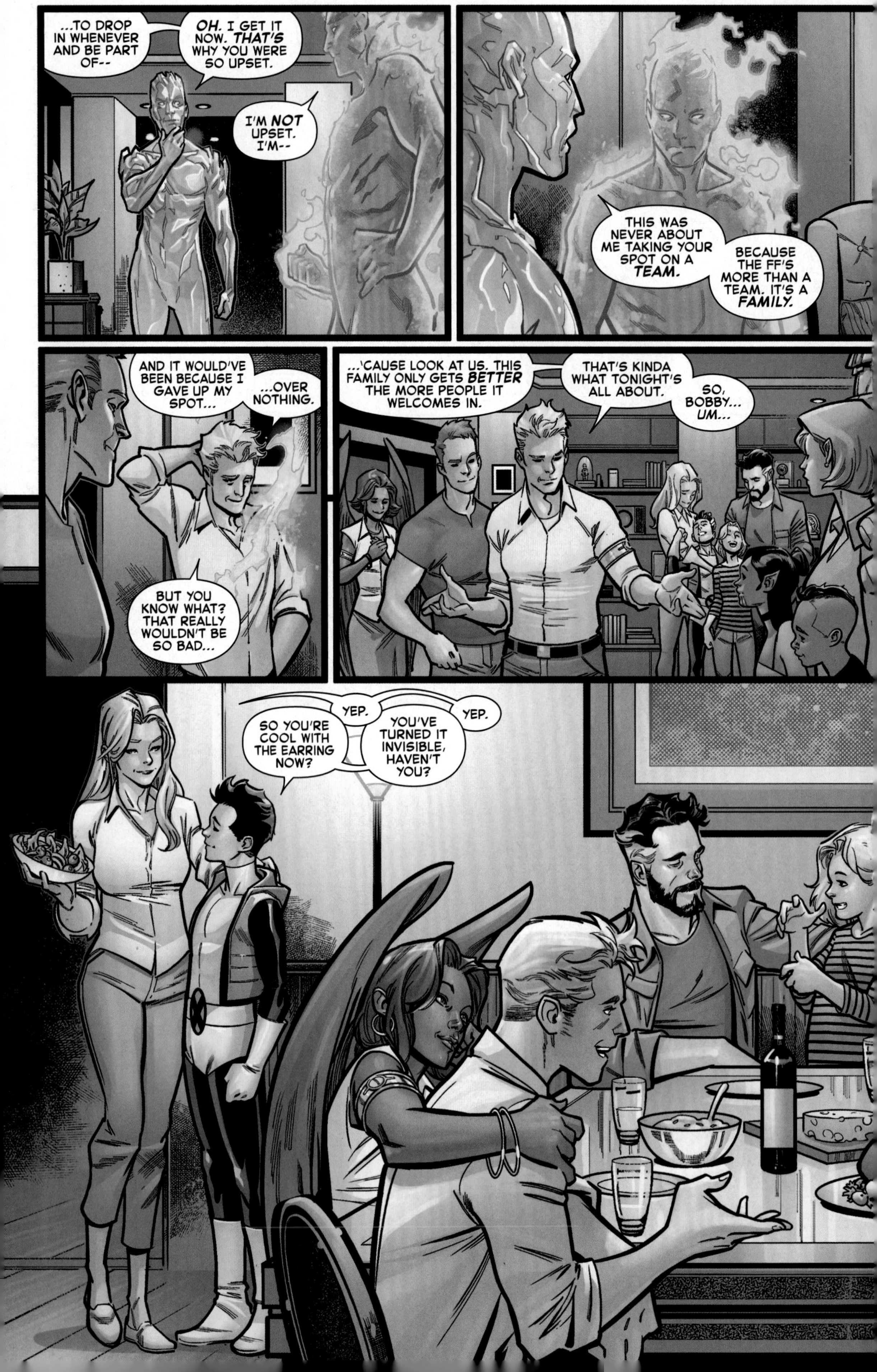
...TO DROP IN WHENEVER AND BE PART OF--
OH. I GET IT NOW. THAT'S WHY YOU WERE SO UPSET.
I'M NOT UPSET. I'M--
THIS WAS NEVER ABOUT ME TAKING YOUR SPOT ON A TEAM.
BECAUSE THE FF'S MORE THAN A TEAM. IT'S A FAMILY.
AND IT WOULD'VE BEEN BECAUSE I GAVE UP MY SPOT...
...OVER NOTHING.
BUT YOU KNOW WHAT? THAT REALLY WOULDN'T BE SO BAD...
...'CAUSE LOOK AT US. THIS FAMILY ONLY GETS BETTER THE MORE PEOPLE IT WELCOMES IN.
THAT'S KINDA WHAT TONIGHT'S ALL ABOUT.
SO, BOBBY... UM...
SO YOU'RE COOL WITH THE EARRING NOW?
YEP.
YOU'VE TURNED IT INVISIBLE, HAVEN'T YOU?
YEP.

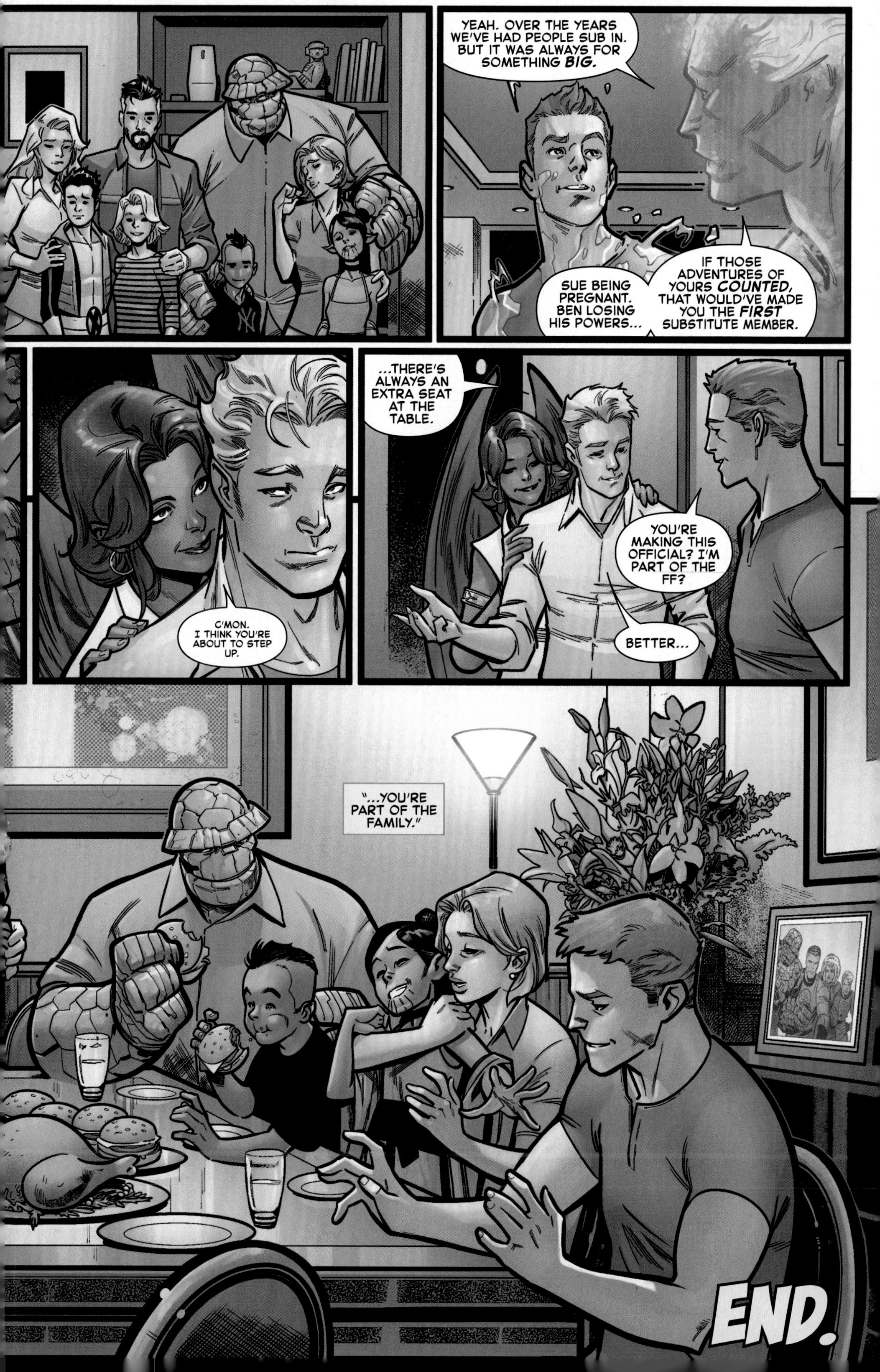
YEAH. OVER THE YEARS WE'VE HAD PEOPLE SUB IN. BUT IT WAS ALWAYS FOR SOMETHING BIG.
SUE BEING PREGNANT. BEN LOSING HIS POWERS...
IF THOSE ADVENTURES OF YOURS COUNTED, THAT WOULD'VE MADE YOU THE FIRST SUBSTITUTE MEMBER.
C'MON. I THINK YOU'RE ABOUT TO STEP UP.
YOU'RE MAKING THIS OFFICIAL? I'M PART OF THE FF?
BETTER...
...THERE'S ALWAYS AN EXTRA SEAT AT THE TABLE.
"...YOU'RE PART OF THE FAMILY."
END.

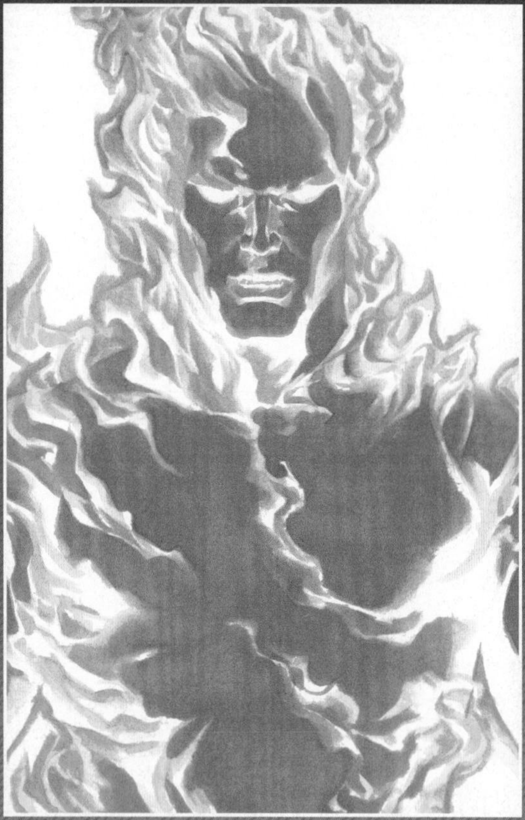

#24 Human Torch Timeless variant by
Alex Ross

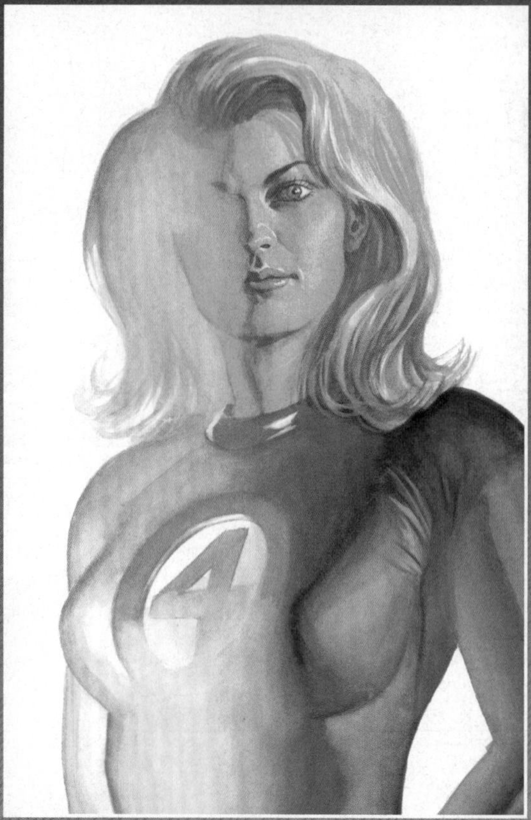

#24 Invisible Woman Timeless variant by
Alex Ross

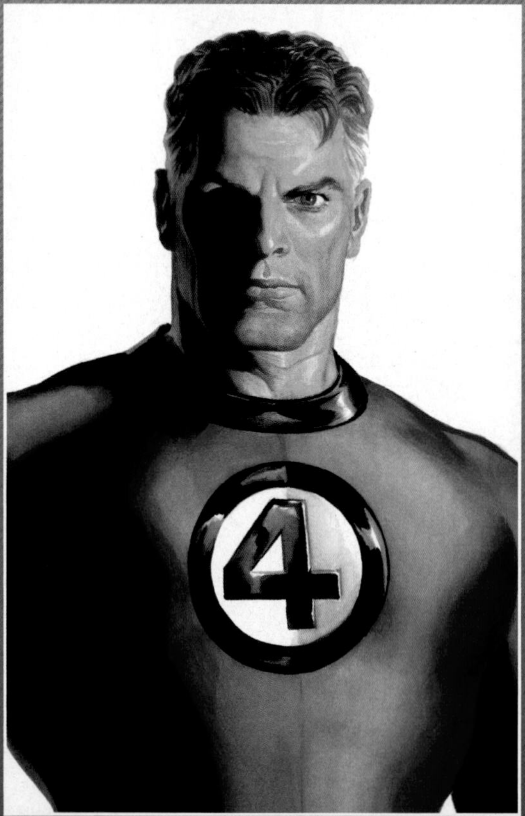

#24 Mr. Fantastic Timeless variant by
Alex Ross

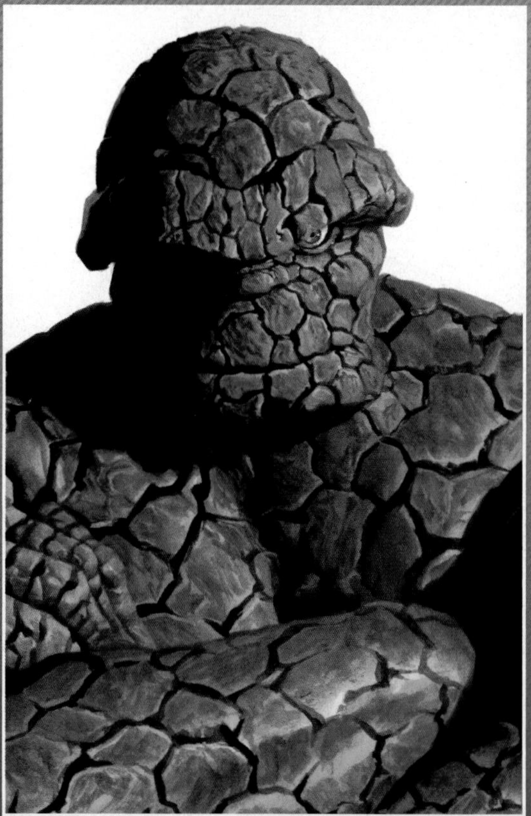

#24 Thing Timeless variant by
Alex Ross

END.

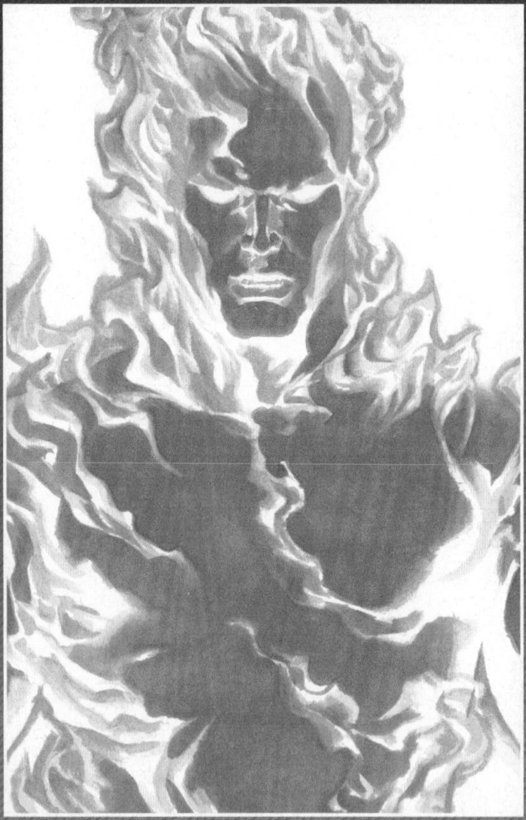

#24 Human Torch Timeless variant by
Alex Ross

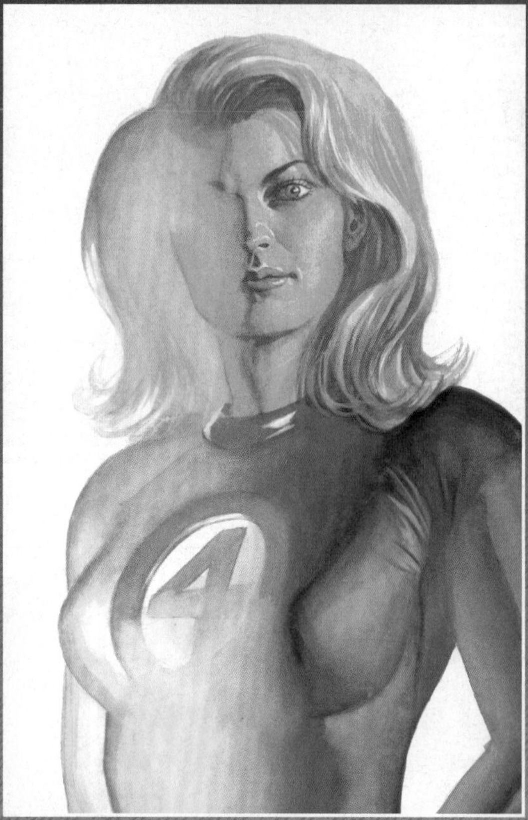

#24 Invisible Woman Timeless variant by
Alex Ross

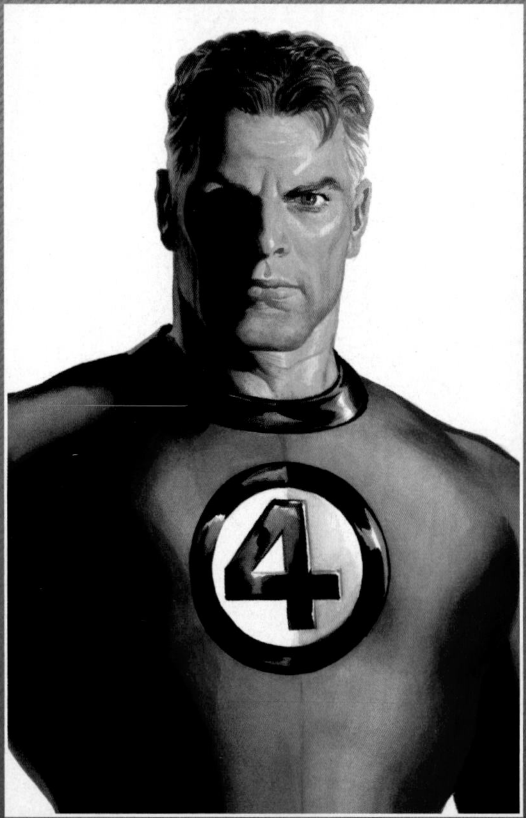

#24 Mr. Fantastic Timeless variant by
Alex Ross

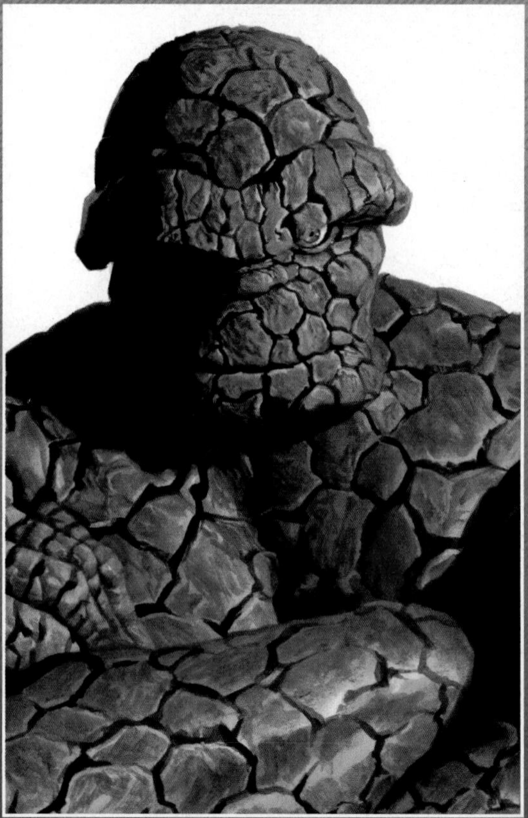

#24 Thing Timeless variant by
Alex Ross